Italian Opera in Global and Transnational Perspective

This volume of essays discusses the European and global expansion of Italian opera and the significance of this process for debates on opera at home in Italy. Covering different parts of Europe, the Americas and South East and East Asia, it investigates the impact of transnational musical exchanges on notions of national identity associated with the production and reception of Italian opera across the world. As a consequence of these exchanges between composers, impresarios, musicians and audiences, ideas of operatic Italianness (*italianità*) constantly changed and had to be reconfigured, reflecting the radically transformative experience of time and space that throughout the nineteenth century turned opera into a global aesthetic commodity. The book opens with a substantial introduction discussing key concepts in cross-disciplinary perspective and concludes with an epilogue relating its findings to different historiographical trends in transnational opera studies.

AXEL KÖRNER is Professor of Modern Cultural and Intellectual History at the University of Leipzig and Honorary Professor at University College London. He is author of *Politics of Culture in Liberal Italy* (2009) and *America in Italy* (2017), which won the American Historical Association's Marraro Prize.

PAULO M. KÜHL is Associate Professor at the University of Campinas, Brazil. He has published widely on Italian opera in Portugal and Brazil, with a focus on adaptations and translations of operas, censorship and libretto studies.

Italian Opera in Global and Transnational Perspective

Reimagining *Italianità* in the Long Nineteenth Century

Edited by
AXEL KÖRNER
University of Leipzig

PAULO M. KÜHL
University of Campinas, Brazil

Shaftesbury Road, Cambridge CB2 8EA, United Kingdom

One Liberty Plaza, 20th Floor, New York, NY 10006, USA

477 Williamstown Road, Port Melbourne, VIC 3207, Australia

314–321, 3rd Floor, Plot 3, Splendor Forum, Jasola District Centre, New Delhi – 110025, India

103 Penang Road, #05–06/07, Visioncrest Commercial, Singapore 238467

Cambridge University Press is part of Cambridge University Press & Assessment, a department of the University of Cambridge.

We share the University's mission to contribute to society through the pursuit of education, learning and research at the highest international levels of excellence.

www.cambridge.org
Information on this title: www.cambridge.org/9781108826884

DOI: 10.1017/9781108920636

© Cambridge University Press & Assessment 2022

This publication is in copyright. Subject to statutory exception and to the provisions of relevant collective licensing agreements, no reproduction of any part may take place without the written permission of Cambridge University Press & Assessment.

First published 2022
First paperback edition 2024

A catalogue record for this publication is available from the British Library

Library of Congress Cataloging-in-Publication data
Names: Köner, Axel, 1967– editor. | Kühl, Paulo M., editor.
Title: Italian opera in global and transnational perspective : reimagining italianità in the long nineteenth century / edited by Axel Körner, Paulo M. Kühl.
Description: [1.] | New York : Cambridge University Press, 2021. | Includes index. | Contents: Opera and *Italianità* in Transnational and Global Perspective : An Introduction / Axel Körner and Paulo Kühl – Giving Singers a Voice : The Italian Opera Company and the Press in Rio de Janeiro, 1820–1831 / Fernando Santos Berçot – Nina d'Aubigny's "Italian Voice" : A Musical Projection Screen in German National Discourse / Carolin Krahn – Italian Opera and Creole Identities : Manuel García in Independent Mexico (1826–1829) / Francesco Milella – Italian Opera in Vormärz Vienna : Gaetano Donizetti, Bartolomeo Merelli, and Habsburg Cultural Policies in the Mid-1830s / Claudio Vellutini – Southern Exchanges : Italian Opera in New Orleans, 1836–42 / Charlotte Bentley – 'For a moment, I felt like I was back in Italy' : Early South American Experiences of Italian Opera Singers (1840–1860) / José Manuel Izquierdo König – Reimagining Rossini : Obituaries as Transnational Narratives of Italian Opera / Arnold Jacobshagen – From Heaven and Hell to the Grail Hall via Sant'Andrea della Valle : Religious Identity and the Internationalisation of Operatic Styles in Liberal Italy / Andrew Holden – Arcadia Undone : Teresa Carreño's 1887 Italian Opera Company in Caracas / Ditlev Rindom – Italian Impresarios, American Minstrels and Parsi Theatre : Sonic Networks and the Negotiation of Opera in Colonial South and Southeast Asia / Rashna Darius Nicholson – German National Identity and Operatic *Italianità* : Franchetti's and Leoncavallo's Operas on German Myths / Richard Erkens – (Opera) Fever in Belle Époque Manaus : *Italianità* at the Teatro Amazonas, 1897–1907 / Rosie McMahon – Between 'Sung Theatre' and Asakusa Opera: In Search of *Italianità* in Early Japanese Opera History / Michael Facius – Epilogue / Benjamin Walton.
Identifiers: LCCN 2021039839 (print) | LCCN 2021039840 (ebook) | ISBN 9781108843867 (hardback) | ISBN 9781108920636 (ebook)
Subjects: LCSH: Opera – Italy – 19th century. | Opera – 19th century. | Opera and transnationalism.
Classification: LCC ML1733.4 .I73 2021 (print) | LCC ML1733.4 (ebook) | DDC 782.10945/09034–dc23
LC record available at https://lccn.loc.gov/2021039839
LC ebook record available at https://lccn.loc.gov/2021039840

ISBN   978-1-108-84386-7   Hardback
ISBN   978-1-108-82688-4   Paperback

Cambridge University Press & Assessment has no responsibility for the persistence or accuracy of URLs for external or third-party internet websites referred to in this publication and does not guarantee that any content on such websites is, or will remain, accurate or appropriate.

Contents

List of Figures   [*page* vii]
List of Tables   [ix]
List of Examples   [x]
Notes on Contributors   [xi]
Preface and Acknowledgements   [xv]

1   Opera and *Italianità* in Transnational and Global Perspective: An Introduction
    AXEL KÖRNER AND PAULO M. KÜHL   [1]

2   Giving Singers a Voice: The Italian Opera Company and the Press in Rio de Janeiro, 1820–1831
    FERNANDO SANTOS BERÇOT   [41]

3   Nina d'Aubigny's 'Italian Voice': A Musical Projection Screen in German National Discourse
    CAROLIN KRAHN   [59]

4   Italian Opera and Creole Identities: Manuel García in Independent Mexico (1826–1829)
    FRANCESCO MILELLA   [77]

5   Italian Opera in *Vormärz* Vienna: Gaetano Donizetti, Bartolomeo Merelli and Habsburg Cultural Policies in the Mid-1830s
    CLAUDIO VELLUTINI   [96]

6   Southern Exchanges: Italian Opera in New Orleans, 1836–1842
    CHARLOTTE BENTLEY   [113]

7   'For a Moment, I Felt Like I Was Back in Italy': Early South American Experiences of Italian Opera Singers (1840–1860)
    JOSÉ MANUEL IZQUIERDO KÖNIG   [133]

8 Reimagining Rossini: Obituaries as Transnational Narratives of Italian Opera
ARNOLD JACOBSHAGEN [147]

9 From Heaven and Hell to the Grail Hall via Sant'Andrea della Valle: Religious Identity and the Internationalisation of Operatic Styles in Liberal Italy
ANDREW HOLDEN [167]

10 Arcadia Undone: Teresa Carreño's 1887 Italian Opera Company in Caracas
DITLEV RINDOM [192]

11 Italian Impresarios, American Minstrels and Parsi Theatre: Sonic Networks and the Negotiation of Opera in Colonial South and South East Asia
RASHNA DARIUS NICHOLSON [214]

12 German National Identity and Operatic *Italianità*: Franchetti's and Leoncavallo's Operas on German Myths
RICHARD ERKENS [239]

13 (Opera) Fever in Belle Époque Manaus: *Italianità* at the Teatro Amazonas, 1897–1907
ROSIE MCMAHON [261]

14 Between 'Sung Theatre' and Asakusa Opera: In Search of *Italianità* in Early Japanese Opera History
MICHAEL FACIUS [278]

15 Epilogue
BENJAMIN WALTON [298]

Index [304]

Figures

1.1 J. Arago, *Vue de la salle de spectacle sur la place do Rocio, à Rio de Janeiro* (engraved by Lerouge and Bénard). Banco Itaú – Edouard Fraipont/Itaú Cultural, São Paulo [*page* 2]

1.2 Jacques Arago (sketch), *Châtiment des esclaves (Brésil)*. Bibliothèque nationale de France [3]

1.3 Utagawa Sadahide, *Female Foreigner with Western Instruments* (woodcut). Utagawa Sadahide 歌川 貞秀, 1807–c. 1878/1879) was a Japanese artist best known for his *Yokohama-e* pictures of foreigners [10]

2.1 'Acceptation provisoire de la constitution de Lisbonne à Rio de Janeiro, en 1821', from Jean-Baptiste Debret, *Voyage pittoresque et historique au Brésil* [42]

3.1 Nina d'Aubigny von Engelbrunner, *Briefe an Natalie über den Gesang* (Leipzig: Voß, 1803), unpaginated [63]

3.2 Pietro [Peter] Lichtenthal, *Dizionario e bibliografia della musica*, vol. 4 (Milan: Antonio Fontana, 1836), 151 [71]

4.1 First page of one of the new *recitativi* in Spanish (Scene V, Act II) composed by García to replace the previous spoken dialogue in Italian of the first version of *Un'ora di matrimonio* [92]

4.2 First page of the 'Ariettina D. Marco', the opening scene of Act II of the new version of *Un'ora di matrimonio* [93]

8.1 Benjamin Roubaud, *Rossini* (Paris: Imprimérie d'Aubert & Cie, 1839) [162]

8.2 Étienne Cajart, *Rossini* (Paris: Imprimérie Bertauts, c. 1855) [163]

9.1 *Asrael* (1888), costume sketch (figurino), Act I/iii (Alfredo Edel) ICON010178 [180]

9.2 *Asrael* (1888), costume sketch, Act IV (Alfredo Edel) ICON010181 [181]

9.3 *Cristoforo Colombo*, Act II, Scene VI. 'Salve Regina' [184]

9.4 *Salve Regina* plainsong chant. *Liber Usualis* (Rome: Tornaci, 1903), 92 [185]

9.5 Ettore Roseler Franz, *Ai Prati di Castello – S. Carlo al fondo* (1889) [188]

9.6 Recreation of Hohenstein's original set and costumes of *Tosca* (Act III, prelude) at the Teatro dell'Opera di Roma, directed by Alessandro Talevi (2015)   [189]
10.1 An advertisement for Carreño's opera company, as published in *La Opinion Nacional*, 16 February 1887   [203]
10.2 Typical patio (inner open court) of the house of a wealthy family, four persons, Caracas (1910)   [212]
11.1 Portrait of Augusto Cagli c. 1864, Hibling & Fields, Accession Number (H29438)   [224]
11.2 The Italian Opera Company, 1871, Hibling & Fields, Accession Number (H96.160/1642, H96.160/1643)   [229]
11.3 Bālīvālā, a famous singer-actor, and his Victoria Theatrical Company, which extensively toured South and South East Asia at the turn of the century   [233]
12.1 *Leoncavallo and the Rolandsbrunnen*, newspaper picture by Emilio Rendich   [244]

Tables

2.1 Members of the Italian Company of the Imperial Theatro São Pedro de Alcântara (1827–1828) [*page* 47]
6.1 Italian troupes' visits to New Orleans, 1836–42 [118]

Examples

12.1 Leoncavallo, *Der Roland von Berlin*, vocal score, appendix, 515 [*page* 250]
12.2 Franchetti, *Germania*, beginning of the Prologue, full score, rehearsal number 2 ('canzone popolare dell'epoca') [252]
12.3 Leoncavallo, *Der Roland von Berlin*, Act I, vocal score, rehearsal number 36, 69f [255]

Notes on Contributors

CHARLOTTE BENTLEY is a lecturer in music at the International Centre for Music Studies, Newcastle University, having previously held a Research Fellowship at Emmanuel College, Cambridge and a Teaching Fellowship in Musical Analysis, History and Philosophy at the University of Edinburgh. She has had articles published in *Cambridge Opera Journal* and the *Journal of the Royal Musical Association*, as well as chapters in a number of edited collections. Her monograph, *New Orleans and the Creation of Transatlantic Opera, 1819–1859*, will be published by the University of Chicago Press in 2022.

FERNANDO SANTOS BERÇOT completed his MA in Social History at Federal University of Rio de Janeiro. His research approaches the intersection between theatre and politics in Imperial Brazil, with a focus on Italian opera and French ballet in Rio de Janeiro. He works for the National Library of Brazil. As a member of the International Musicological Society's Group on Italo-Ibero-American Relationships, he contributed a chapter on opera in Southern Brazil to the volume *I fiumi che cantano: L'opera italiana nel bacino del Rio de La Plata*, edited by A. Cetrangolo and M. Paoletti (University of Bologna Digital Library, 2021).

RICHARD ERKENS teaches music history at Franz Liszt University of Music in Weimar. Previously, he was a Research Fellow in musicology at the German Historical Institute in Rome and at Humboldt University in Berlin. His *Puccini Handbuch* (Metzler/Bärenreiter, 2017) was awarded the title of Music Book of the Year by *Opernwelt* in 2018. Other publications include *Alberto Franchetti – Werkstudien zur italienischen Oper der langen Jahrhundertwende* (Peter Lang, 2011). His main research areas are the history of opera and music theatre in Italy, music dramaturgy, libretto studies, music criticism and eighteenth-century productions of opera.

MICHAEL FACIUS is Associate Professor at Tokyo College, the University of Tokyo. He studies Japan from the angles of global history, the history of knowledge and the history of translation. He is the author of *China übersetzen: Globalisierung und chinesisches Wissen in Japan im 19.*

Jahrhundert (Campus, 2017, in German, shortlisted for the ICAS book prize 2019). He held a British Academy Newton International Fellowship at University College London and was the coordinator of the Graduate School Global Intellectual History at Freie Universität Berlin.

ANDREW HOLDEN is Visiting Researcher in the School of Arts at Oxford Brookes University, where he completed a PhD on 'Opera Avanti a Dio: Religion and Opera in Liberal Italy'. His research spans the music and culture of nineteenth- and twentieth-century Italy, censorship, the structures of the contemporary opera industry and British cultural politics. Publications include 'A Slice of Operatic Life in London's East End 1880–1940', in Nicolò Palazzetti, Massimo Zicari and Andrew Holden (eds.) *Italian Musical Migrations* (Special issue *Journal of Modern Italian Studies*, February 2019); *Makers and Manners: Politics and Morality in Post-War Britain* (Politico's Publishing, 2004).

JOSÉ MANUEL IZQUIERDO KÖNIG (PhD in Music, University of Cambridge) is Associate Professor and Director of Research and Postgraduate Studies at the Faculty of Arts, Pontificia Universidad Católica de Chile. He has published widely in Spanish and English on nineteenth-century music in Latin America, as well as on opera and cultural heritage. He has received the Otto Mayer Serra award for Latin American musicology, as well as the tosc@ award for his research in the field of transnational opera studies. His PhD dissertation was awarded the Tesi Rossiniane Prize of the Fondazione Rossini in Pesaro.

ARNOLD JACOBSHAGEN is Professor of Musicology at the University of Music and Dance Cologne. After completing his PhD at the Freie Universität Berlin, he taught at the universities of Bayreuth and Vienna. He is a member of the Academia Europaea, president of the Joseph Haydn Institute and vice president of the German Musicological Society. His principal publications include *Gioachino Rossini und seine Zeit* (Laaber, 2015) and *Opera semiseria: Gattungskonvergenz und Kulturtransfer im Musiktheater* (Franz Steiner, 2005).

AXEL KÖRNER is Professor of Modern Cultural and Intellectual History at the University of Leipzig and Honorary Professor at University College London. He has held visiting positions at the Institute of Advanced Study, Princeton, at the École Normale Supérieure in Paris and at New York University. In addition to modern Italian and Habsburg history, he has published widely on the history of opera and music in transnational perspective. His *America in Italy: The United States in the Political Thought and Imagination of the Risorgimento, 1763–1865* (Princeton University

Press, 2017) won the Helen & Howard Marraro Prize of the American Historical Association.

CAROLIN KRAHN is Research Fellow in Musicology at the German Historical Institute in Rome. Previously, she held positions as Assistant Professor at the University of Vienna, as European Recovery Program PhD scholar at Stanford and as DAAD Visiting Fellow at Harvard. Her research centres on German and Italian music history and historiography. In addition to her monograph *Topographie der Imaginationen: Johann Friedrich Rochlitz' musikalisches Italien* (Hollitzer 2021), she co-edited the volume *Staunen: Perspektiven eines Phänomens zwischen Natur und Kultur* (Fink, 2019). She won the Chair's Award for Excellence in Teaching at Stanford and was the recipient of an international as well as a doctoral dissertation award at the University of Vienna.

PAULO M. KÜHL is Associate Professor of Art History and History of Opera at the University of Campinas, Brazil, where he is Dean of Graduate Studies in Music. He was a visiting scholar at New York University and has carried out research in several institutions in Italy, Portugal and France. He has published widely on Italian opera in Portugal and Brazil, with a focus on adaptations and translations of operas, censorship and libretto studies. His recent publications include 'The Prince of Harmony, His Favorite Disciple and Other Geniuses: The Diffusion of a "Classical" Repertory in Early Nineteenth-Century Rio de Janeiro', in Walter Reicher (ed.), *Joseph Haydn und die 'Neue Welt': music- und kulturgeschichtliche Perspektiven* (Hollitzer, 2019) and 'Cinematic Visions of Opera in the Tropics', in *Art Research Journal* (2018).

ROSIE MCMAHON studied musicology at the University of Manchester, King's College, London, and the University of Oxford. Her doctoral thesis, 'Music in the Urban Amazon: A Historical Ethnography of the Manaus Opera House', was supervised by Prof. Jason Stanyek. She currently works as Policy Advisor for the UK Civil Service.

FRANCESCO MILELLA is a doctoral candidate at the University of Cambridge, Jesus College. His research investigates operatic networks across the Atlantic Ocean at the dawn of the nineteenth century. He is currently working on a study of the Spanish tenor Manuel García and his activity in postcolonial Mexico City. He has studied in Italy (modern literature and musicology) and the Netherlands (politics of culture). He also works as a music critic and advisor for musical magazines and cultural institutions in Europe and Latin America.

RASHNA DARIUS NICHOLSON is Assistant Professor of Theatre Studies at the University of Hong Kong, and, in 2021–2, both Barbro Klein Fellow at the Swedish Collegium for Advanced Study and Luce East Asia Fellow at the National Humanities Center. In addition to her recently published monograph *The Colonial Public and the Parsi Stage: The Making of the Theatre of Empire (1853–1893)* (Palgrave Macmillan, 2021), her work on nineteenth- and twentieth-century theatre history and historiography features in *Theatre Research International, Theatre Survey, Ethnic and Racial Studies* and *South Asia: Journal of South Asian Studies*.

DITLEV RINDOM is British Academy Postdoctoral Fellow at King's College London. He gained his PhD at the University of Cambridge and has had articles published in the *Journal of the Royal Musical Association, 19th-Century Music,* and *Cambridge Opera Journal*. He is completing a monograph examining the circulation of Italian opera between Milan, New York and Buenos Aires in the decades around 1900, and working on a critical edition of Puccini's opera *La rondine*, to be published by Ricordi. He is a regular contributor to *Opera* magazine and has also appeared as an expert commentator on BBC Radio 3.

CLAUDIO VELLUTINI is Assistant Professor of Musicology at the University of British Columbia, Vancouver (Canada). His current book project on early nineteenth-century opera and cultural exchanges between Vienna and the Italian States is supported by an Insight Development Grant from the Social Sciences and Humanities Research Council of Canada. He is the recipient of Ernst Mach Fellowship from the Österreichischer Austauschdienst, and of Alvin H. Johnson AMS 50 Dissertation Fellowship from the American Musicological Society (2014). His publications have appeared in the *Journal of the American Musicological Society, 19th-Century Music, Cambridge Opera Journal* and several collected volumes.

BENJAMIN WALTON is Professor of Music History at the University of Cambridge and Fellow of Jesus College, Cambridge. His books include *Rossini in Restoration Paris* (Cambridge University Press, 2007), *The Invention of Beethoven and Rossini: Historiography, Analysis, Criticism* (Cambridge University Press, 2013, co-edited with Nicholas Mathew) and *Nineteenth-Century Opera and the Scientific Imagination* (Cambridge University Press, 2019, co-edited with David Trippett). Between 2014 and 2019 he was the editor of *Cambridge Opera Journal*. His current research explores the movement of Italian opera and opera singers around the world during the first half of the nineteenth century.

Preface and Acknowledgements

This book examines the impact of musical exchanges on ideas of national identity associated with the production and reception of Italian opera in different parts of Europe, Latin America and Asia, with a few references to cultural exchanges with Africa and Australia. As a consequence of transnational connections between composers, impresarios, musicians and audiences, ideas of operatic *italianità* constantly changed and had to be reconfigured, reflecting the radically transformative experience of time and space that over the course of the nineteenth century turned opera into a global aesthetic commodity.

Following a cross-disciplinary approach, and involving debates in music, Italian studies and transnational and global history, our book brings together the output of an international research network which was financed over a period of three years by the Leverhulme Trust. Based at the Centre for Transnational History of University College London, we worked with partners at Brown University, the University of Cambridge and the University of Campinas in Brazil, as well as with several external collaborators in Italy and all over the world. Between 2016 and 2018, we organised three international conferences in Cambridge, Providence (RI) and Campinas, as well as numerous smaller workshops and reading groups. Our volume presents a selection from the research output that emerged from these meetings.

We are grateful to the book's contributors for sharing their research, and to our partners in the project – Francesca Vella, Suzanne Stewart-Steinberg and Benjamin Walton – for many years of most inspiring discussions. We benefitted hugely from critical feedback received from Anselm Gerhard and Roger Parker on the original project outline, and from the administrative support of Misha Enayat and Alexander Kolassa. Without their help it would have been impossible to hold together a group of researchers from all over the world. Misha Enayat played a crucial role in assembling these chapters and editing the book. Susan Rutherford, Emilio Sala and Emanuele Senici joined several of our meetings to offer advice on our conceptual framework and on preliminary versions of the chapters collected in this book. Without their ideas and encouragement, this book would not have been written.

Many colleagues not represented in this volume enriched the project by contributing their own research to our discussions or by commenting on conference papers. We express our gratitude to Rachel Becker, Harriet Boyd Bennet, Katherine Butler-Schofield, Fabio Camilletti, Alessandra Campana, Delia Casadei, Aníbal Enrique Cetrangolo, Melody Chapin, Daniele Conversi, Denise Avelino Corrêa, Gabriela Cruz, Luisa Cymbron, Enza De Francisci, Jonathan Durrant, Iara Luzia Fadel Rodriguez, Kate Ferris, Dana Gooley, Katherine Hambridge, Jens Hesselager, Artemis Ignatidou, Maurizio Isabella, Taryn Jackson, Alessandra Jones, Morris Karp, Adriana Kayama, Isaac Kerr, Gundula Kreuzer, Viviane Kubo, David Levin, Guilhermina Lopes, Valeria Lucentini, Matthew Machin Autenrith, Nicola Miller, Alberto Napoli, Danielle Padley, Silvana Patriarca, Laura Protano-Biggs, Maria Rubia Andreta, Andrea Sartori, Kim Sauberlich, Michael Sawyer, Eric Schneeman, Arman Schwartz, Danielle Simon, Harry Stopes, Alessandro Talevi, André Tavares, Alexandra van Leeuwen, Mario Videira, Maria Alice Volpe, Gavin Williams, Alexandra Wilson, Flora Wilson and Vera Wolkowicz. This list is representative of the many different academic cultures and disciplines that shaped our discussions. There were many other colleagues who contributed to our project with their expert knowledge, critical questions and comments. We also wish to express our appreciation for Emmanuele Ferrari's musical contribution to our conference in Providence, and to Angelo Fernandes and the students at the Arts Institute at Campinas for introducing us to the fascinating variety of Brazil's operatic *italianità*.

It would not have been possible to complete this project without the generous financial help of the Leverhulme Trust and the administrative support of University College London, as well as the hospitality of the Faculty of Music at Cambridge, the Department of Italian Studies at Brown and the Arts Institute at Campinas and especially the help of Angélica Oliveira and Fulvia Sannuto from the Itaú Cultural. We would like to thank the anonymous assessors who approved our original submission to the Leverhulme Trust, as well as the readers of our book manuscript for Cambridge University Press. Throughout our work on this book Kate Brett has been an exceptionally competent and encouraging editor at Cambridge University Press, who gave us the kind of support that has become rare in academic publishing. Frances Tye was a tireless, highly competent and kind copy editor during the final stages of the book's production. A draft of this introduction was presented at the Cultural Transfers seminar of the École Normale Supérieure, Paris, and the Research Centre Global Dynamics, Leipzig University, and we are grateful for the comments received on this occasion. The Leibniz Programme at Leipzig University very generously supported the final phase of work on this volume.

If opera is able to speak across national and social boundaries, we hope our book does the same.

Axel Körner and Paulo M. Kühl

1 | Opera and *Italianità* in Transnational and Global Perspective

An Introduction

AXEL KÖRNER AND PAULO M. KÜHL

Muted Slaves: On Transplanting Cultures

The cover of this book shows a square in Rio de Janeiro during the second decade of the nineteenth century, based on a drawing by the French writer, artist and traveller Jacques Arago (1790–1855; see Figure 1.1). Founded in 1565, since 1763 Rio had been the capital of the Viceroyalty of Brazil, belonging to the Portuguese Empire. In 1808, in response to the Napoleonic Wars, the Portuguese royal court made Rio its official residence. Central in the background of Arago's work one sees the majestic façade of the Theatro São João (renamed Theatro São Pedro de Alcântara after the fire on 25 March 1824), which opened in 1813 and had been built after the model of the São Carlos Theatre in Lisbon. It was certainly the most ambitious civic building in Rio de Janeiro at that time, erected to replace the old opera house and suitable for the city's new role as capital of the Portuguese Empire.[1] Arago's *Vue de la salle de spectacle sur la place do Rocio, à Rio de Janeiro* was subsequently engraved by Lerouge and Robert Bénard, and published in 1824 in the *Atlas historique* to Louis de Freycinet's *Voyage autour du monde*.[2]

The building appeared in multiple nineteenth-century drawings and engravings of Rio, including those by Thomas Ender, Jean-Baptiste Debret, Karl Wilhelm von Theremin and Friedrich Pustkow. Frequently, artists enlivened the scenery with the depiction of slaves somewhere in the square, almost so as to contrast with and underline the theatre's splendour.

---

[1] There were two opera houses in Rio de Janeiro, both built around the middle of the eighteenth century: the Opera Velha, built before 1748, and the Opera Nova, built around 1758. The term 'opera' was loosely employed, and it is hard to establish exactly what kinds of works were presented, although there were productions with music, including titles of the regular operatic repertoire. See Nireu Cavalcanti, *O Rio de Janeiro setecentista: A vida e a construção da cidade da invasão francesa até a chegada da Corte* (Rio de Janeiro: Zahar, 2004), 170–6.

[2] [Louis de Freycinet], *Voyage autour du monde* ... *exécuté sur les corvettes de S. M. 'l'Uranie' et 'la Physicienne', pendant les années 1817, 1818, 1819 et 1820* ... *publié par M. Louis de Freycinet, Atlas historique (par MM. J. Arago, A. Pellion, etc.)* (Paris: Pillet aîné, 1825), plate 7.

Figure 1.1 J. Arago, *Vue de la salle de spectacle sur la place do Rocio, à Rio de Janeiro* (engraved by Lerouge and Bénard). Banco Itaú – Edouard Fraipont/Itaú Cultural, São Paulo

If in Debret's and von Theremin's depictions the slaves appear as just one of several aspects of social life in Rio, in Arago's portrayal of the square the slaves take centre stage, clearly standing out against the orthogonal frame created by the theatre and emphasising the contrast between the great building, as a sign of the Portuguese court's civilising project, and the misery and violence of slavery, seemingly as a by-product of the continent's Europeanisation. Commenting on Arago's engraving, Freycinet only indicates that 'one could receive an idea of the exterior architecture of the Theatre San-Joaõ [sic], and of the taste that determined its construction. The inside is equally agreeable, even if it is a little too big for the city and fills itself only on the occasion of great festivities.'[3] The slaves, so prominently represented in the illustration, go without mention, as if they were to be understood as a natural aspect of life in the New World. Unlike many travellers and commentators, however, Arago lived in Brazil for long periods and died in Rio; and his ideas about the role of slavery in the New World were also different from those of many of his contemporaries.

---

[3] Ibid., 187.

1 Opera and Italianità: An Introduction 3

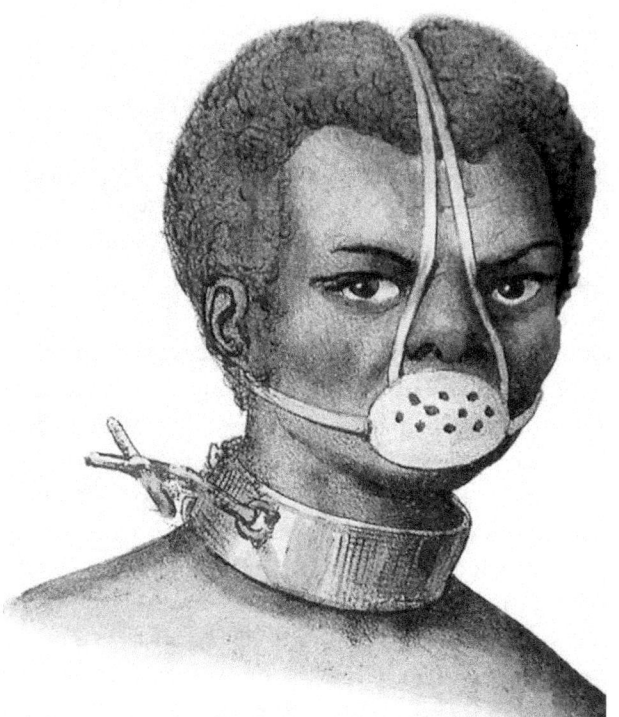

Figure 1.2 Jacques Arago (sketch), *Châtiment des esclaves (Brésil)*. Bibliothèque nationale de France

In his *Souvenirs d'un aveugle*, the author explicitly refers to the striking contrast between the beauty of the local landscape and the cruelty of slavery, a cruelty that is represented in many of the works he painted in Brazil, in which he frequently depicts the punishment of slaves.[4] As shown in his *Castigo de Escravo* (1839), the punishment of slaves also included the covering of their mouths. Although slaves were usually allowed to sing, and in some cases were even made to perform in choirs and orchestras, the depiction in his famous drawing from Rio almost seems intended to highlight this irony in its juxtaposition of a European style opera house with local slaves (see Figure 1.2). Further complicating the situation, as the

---

[4] [Jacques Arago], *Souvenirs d'un aveugle: Voyage autour du monde par M. J. Arago* (Paris: Hortet et Ozanne, 1839). The image in Figure 1.2 is from book I, plate inserted between pages 118 and 119. For his representation of slaves in Brazil, see the collection of the Museu Afro Brasil in São Paulo.

next chapter shows, some black Brazilians, usually freed slaves, appeared as patrons in some of the theatre's most highly prized seats.[5]

Written after he had lost his eyesight, Arago's memoirs placed an emphasis on contrasting visual impressions that became part of the book's dramatic strategy in representing Brazil. For instance, playing on an important topos in Italian travel writing, he notes that the impressions of natural beauty one received when entering Guanabara Bay were superior to those encountered on approaching Genoa, Naples or Venice. At the same time, however, he could not find in Rio de Janeiro many buildings that caught his attention, with the exception of the aqueduct and the opera house. The architecture of the royal palace, even that of the royal chapel with all its gold and luxury, did not seem particularly interesting to him, although he noted a strong presence of music in the city, and he was astonished to hear castrati singing in the church. Like other travellers, Arago therefore was stunned to see such an imposing theatre in this city, and mentioned that the names of Aeschylus, Sophocles and Euripides were written on the theatre curtain. Slanderously, he concluded: 'This is all that exists of Aeschylus, Sophocles and Euripides': a token reference to European civilisation, but no more. In other words, Arago seems to have been acutely aware of the contrast between the promise associated with the theatre building and the scenes of cruelty he depicted in the square in front of it.

Many contemporary writers commented on the contrast between the presence of European culture in Brazil, including the role of Italian opera, on the one hand, and the impression left on them of the country's nature and of what they referred to as savages, on the other. Arago, in his work, goes beyond this common feature, outlining in detail his experience of violence and the objectification of slaves, thus stressing the contradictions involved in transplanting cultural models from one world to another.

Opera and National Identity

Italian Opera in Global and Transnational Perspective looks beyond the role of Italian opera in the New World and in Brazil. Our book investigates the impact of transnational musical exchanges on notions of national identity associated with the production and reception of Italian opera in

[5] For a transatlantic discussion of slavery in Brazil see Natalia Bas, Kate Ferris and Nicola Miller, 'Slavery and Abolition', in Axel Körner, Nicola Miller and Adam I. P. Smith (eds.), *America Imagined: Explaining the United States in Nineteenth-Century Europe and Latin America* (New York: Palgrave Macmillan, 2012), 225–40.

the world. Covering parts of Europe, the Americas and Asia, the case studies assembled in this volume exemplify the effects of the European and global expansion of Italian opera during the long nineteenth century, and discuss the impact of this process on notions of *italianità* in different parts of the world and at home in Italy. As a consequence of transnational exchanges involving composers, impresarios, musicians and audiences, ideas of operatic *italianità* constantly changed and had to be reconfigured, reflecting the radically transformative experience of time and space that, throughout the nineteenth century, turned opera into a global aesthetic commodity.

Since the seventeenth century, music and especially opera have frequently been used as signifiers of national identity. There is a long tradition that especially associates vocal music with Italian models. The composers Michael Praetorius, Christoph Bernhard, Antoine Maugars and John Playford, among others, were all concerned with defining what they considered the Italian style or manner of singing, often referencing Giulio Caccini's *Le Nuove Musiche*, a collection of monodies and songs for solo voice and basso continuo first published in Florence in 1602. The German singer and composer Bernhard, who was a pupil of Heinrich Schütz and had travelled to Italy around the year 1650, was among the few to recognise three different Italian styles of singing (Roman, Neapolitan and Lombard), thus indicating that the Italian peninsula could not be envisioned as a monolithic culture.[6] In France, Charles de Saint-Evremond, in his book *Sur les Opera* [*sic*] (1684), took the view that 'Hispanus flet, dolet Italus, Germanus boat, Flander ululat, et solus Gallus cantat [the Spaniard weeps, the Italian suffers, the German roars, the Flemish shouts, and only the Frenchman sings]'.[7] Among many others, his work was quoted in 1708 by the German writer Barthold Feind, providing evidence of Europe's wide circulation of books on opera. Even earlier, in 1681, the French Jesuit Claude-François Menestrier had tried to identify the musical character of different nations, later used to define national styles.[8] Like many of the authors and composers quoted here, Menestrier had himself travelled to Germany and Italy, and was an expert not just on music and opera, but on ballet too.

---

[6] *Von der Singe-Kunst oder Manier* (c. 1650), Manuscript in Staatsbibliothek zu Berlin – Preußischer Kulturbesitz (Mus.ms.autogr.theor. Kuhnau, J. 1). Translation into English by Simon M. Honea, available at www.uco.edu/cfad/files/music/bernhard-kompositionslehre.pdf, last accessed 21 December 2020.

[7] Charles de Saint-Evremond, 'Sur les Opera', in *Œuvres Meslées*, vol. 11 (Paris: C. Barbin, 1684), 105.

[8] Claude-François Menestrier, *Des représentations en musique anciennes et modernes* (Paris: Chez René Guignard, 1681).

During the eighteenth century, a large number of related contributions dominated musical debates, starting with historian François Raguenet's comparison of Italian and French music of 1702,[9] continued a few years on by the early music critic Jean-Laurent Le Cerf de la Viéville. Many of these arguments were picked up later in the century by Jean-Jacques Rousseau during the famous Querelle des Bouffons, and revived again during the fights between Gluckistes and Piccinistes.[10] An idea of Italian music being mostly about performance continued to mark these debates, as demonstrated by the philosopher and co-editor (with Denis Diderot) of the *Encyclopédie*, Jean le Rond d'Alembert. Summarising the debates of the past few decades, he concluded: 'In this century, there is some sort of fatality attached to what comes to us from Italy. All gifts, good or bad, that it wants to give us are problematic.' Or even:

> In music, we [the French] write and the Italians perform [*exécutent*]. In this sense, the two nations are the image of those two architects that presented themselves to the Athenians for a monument the Republic wanted to build. One of them spoke extensively and very eloquently about his art; the other, after listening to him, said only these words: what he said, I will do.[11]

What these different authors had in common was their attempt to define what was particular to Italian singing and opera; these traits were understood as a direct reflection of Italian national character, usually without reference to local conventions, or exchanges between Italian and non-Italian traditions. While many authors idealised what they considered the Italian character in the arts, others expressed fatigue, as Eugène Delacroix suggested, many years on, when commenting on the 'eternal and often blind devotion

---

[9] François Raguenet, *Paralèle [sic] des Italiens et des François en ce qui regarde la musique et les opéra [sic]* (Paris: Jean Moreau, 1702). For the dispute between Raguenet and Le Cerf de la Viéville, see Paulo Kühl, 'A comparação entre a ópera italiana e a francesa: Raguenet e a irredutibilidade de duas tradições', *Revista Música*, 14/1 (2014), 147–95 (https://doi.org/10.11606/rm.v14i1.115251, last accessed 21 December 2020). Raguenet's book was translated into English (1709) and twice into German, by Johann Mattheson (172–5) and Friedrich Wilhelm Marpurg (1760).

[10] For a short summary of the Querelle and related bibliography see Alessandra Campana, 'Genre and Poetics', in Nicholas Till (ed.), *The Cambridge Companion to Opera Studies* (Cambridge: Cambridge University Press, 2012), 202–24, 210 f. On the wider context see David Charlton, 'Genre and Form in French Opera', in Anthony R. Del Donna and Pierpaolo Polzonetti (eds.), *The Cambridge Companion to Eighteenth-Century Opera* (Cambridge: Cambridge University Press, 2009), 155–83.

[11] Jean le Rond d'Alembert, 'De la liberté de la musique', in *Mélanges de Littérature, d'Histoire, et de Philosophie*, new edition, book IV (Amsterdam: Zacharie Chatelain et Fils, 1764), 383–462 (393, 462).

to everything that comes from Italy'.¹² Italians rarely intervened in these debates, creating what the historian Fernand Braudel, writing about Italian art in the sixteenth century, has described as an asymmetrical balance between 'the inside and the outside'.¹³ A rare exception was the eighteenth-century Florentine composer and music theorist Vincenzo Manfredini; he positioned himself against the 'Germans', who supposedly interfered in Italy's operatic scene, despite the fact that he himself wrote operas for the Russian court, and also died in Russia in 1799.¹⁴

As we have seen above, Rousseau's writings, and the responses they received, were particularly influential in associating musical styles with national identities, an idea reflecting linguistic conditions as well as the development of specific musical and operatic genres.¹⁵ During the nineteenth century, the drawing of connections between music and national character assumed new dimensions in political and aesthetic debates, partly due to the idea of reading opera as a contribution to processes of national and political emancipation. The extent to which opera was intended or understood to take a position within the political battles of national movements remains a matter of debate among opera scholars and historians.¹⁶ These controversies notwithstanding, the frequency of references to national character in nineteenth-century debates on opera and music is striking and certainly contributed to reading opera in a national key – despite the increasingly transnational movement of troupes, audiences and the repertoire; and despite the fact that most composers were influenced by a broad range of cultural and musical experiences that could hardly be reduced to one national tradition. Due to Italy's role in the invention and historical development of opera, notions of *italianità* – used with reference to different operatic genres, styles of singing or particular productions – are particularly common in the musical press, in literature and in the scholarly and pedagogical works of the time. As a consequence, these sources form an important basis for the analysis of how *italianità* was constructed and of what commentators had in mind

---

[12] Eugène Delacroix, 'Le Poussin', in *Ecrits sur l'art* (Paris: Librairie Séguier, 1988), 239.

[13] Fernand Braudel, *Le Modèle italien* (Paris: Flammarion, 1994).

[14] Manfredini criticised those who thought the preface to Gluck's *Alceste* was 'the Horace's Poetics of music ... Now the Germans come to teach us what this art is, even if it is all ours'. See Vincenzo Manfredini, *Regole armoniche, o sieno Precetti per l'apprendere i principi della musica* [1775] (Venice: A. Cesare, 1797), 22.

[15] On the international impact of Rousseau's concept of Italian singing see Claudio Vellutini, 'Interpreting the Italian Voice in London (and Elsewhere)', in Roger Parker and Susan Rutherford (eds.), *London Voices 1820–1840: Vocal Performers, Practices, Histories* (Chicago: The University of Chicago Press, 2019), 51–69 (53 f.).

[16] For a recent summary of these debates see Fabrizio Della Seta, 'Opera e Risorgimento: si può dire ancora qualcosa?', *Verdiperspektiven* 2 (2017), 81–106.

when they related notions of national character to music. While historians have investigated how ideas of Italian national character have been used in different political contexts,[17] this has not been a major topic of research in opera studies. Therefore, the construction of a relationship between music and *italianità* within the increasingly interconnected world of the nineteenth century demands critical attention from a new, transnational perspective. Our book takes a global perspective on operatic discourse, examining how notions of *italianità* were constructed in exchanges between political and cultural actors of different national origins, and how these notions related to specific local, national and in some cases imperial contexts where the Italian repertoire or Italian productions played a role. Rather than taking operatic *italianità* as a given, our book looks at how such notions were constructed and debated under the increasingly transnational and global conditions of operatic production. While recognising the extent to which *italianità* became a transnational and global commodity during the long nineteenth century, from a methodological point of view our approach questions the validity of national categories of analysis when writing the history of opera.[18]

Our book approaches this topic through a number of specific (mostly local) case studies on nineteenth-century opera production in the Americas, Europe and Asia. Latin America is particularly important in the book's geographical scope due to the early and wide diffusion of Italian opera in both Lusophone and Spanish America, and to the role played by Italian troupes in establishing opera as an art form across the Atlantic. Our focus on Latin America also allows for a critical assessment of the postcolonial condition of opera production in the former Spanish and Portuguese Empires. Studies on opera in the Americas, or on art in general, have always referred to European models, even nationalist approaches that were intended to give expression to notions of cultural independence. As former colonies, and even after the long process of seeking independence, these countries continued to maintain close relations with Europe, and especially with Portugal and Spain. Regarding the production of Italian opera, for a long time the repertoire, singers, composers and entire troupes came to

---

[17] Alberto M. Banti, *La nazione del Risorgimento: Parentela, santità e onore alle origini dell'Italia unita* (Turin: Einaudi, 2000); Silvana Patriarca, *Italian Vices: Nation and Character from the Risorgimento to the Republic* (Cambridge: Cambridge University Press, 2010); Nelson Moe, *The View from Vesuvius: Italian Culture and the Southern Question* (Berkeley, CA: University of California Press, 2002).

[18] For a programmatic outline of this approach see Axel Körner, 'Dalla storia transnazionale all'opera transnazionale. Per una critica delle categorie nazionali', *Saggiatore Musicale* 24/1 (2017/1), 81–98.

Latin America through the Iberian Peninsula, adding their own character to ideas of operatic *italianità*.[19]

As regards the European context, the role of Italian opera within the German-speaking lands of Central Europe represents a special case, not only due to the sheer number of theatres in the region where Italian opera was produced, but also because of the ways in which German music criticism used changing notions of *italianità* to articulate more general ideas about the relationship between music and national identity. Here the Habsburg monarchy is of particular interest to the study of operatic *italianità*, because of the Empire's own multinational setting and its strong tradition of seeing Italian opera as a supranational art form that speaks a cosmopolitan language. It was on this basis that Italian opera came to play a leading role in supporting Austria's supranational idea of its state.

During the nineteenth century, European musical culture became one of the issues non-European observers most frequently commented upon in the context of transcultural encounters, especially in those geographical areas where people had had very little exposure to European culture. A famous example documenting curiosity about European music are the collections of woodblock prints produced in Japan after a fleet of American warships under Commodore Matthew Perry arrived at Yokohama in 1853, forcing the Edo shogunate to open their ports to foreigners (see Figure 1.3). Many of these prints present musical instruments, and Europeans playing them in different social and political contexts.[20] Michael Facius' chapter later in this volume (Chapter 14) shows that it took a relatively long time for Japanese society to overcome its scepticism towards Europe's operatic tradition. When, at the beginning of the twentieth century, Rentarō Taki (瀧 廉太郎, 1879–1903) became the first Japanese person to study music in Europe, he did not go to Italy to learn about its operatic tradition, but to Leipzig. For Taki, engaging with Europe's musical tradition mostly meant studying the piano and the lied. Within our book's global dimension, extending our perspective from the Americas and Europe to East and South East Asia helps us to relate ideas of *italianità* to different concepts

---

[19] The research conducted at CESEM-Universidade Nova de Lisboa, especially by David Cranmer and Luísa Cymbron and also by the Caravelas research group, takes a transnational approach to the history of music. See www.caravelas.com.pt/, last accessed 21 December 2020. For Spain and Spanish America see, among many others, Álvaro Torrente and Emilio Casares (eds.), *La ópera en España e Hispanoamérica* (Madrid: ICCMU, 2001), and more recently Javier Marín (ed.), *Músicas coloniais a debate: Procesos de intercambio euroamericanos* (Madrid: ICCMU, 2018).

[20] On the introduction of Western music in Japan see Margaret Mehl, 'Western Art Music in Japan: A Success Story?', *Nineteenth-Century Music Review* 10/2 (2013), 211–22.

Figure 1.3 Utagawa Sadahide, *Female Foreigner with Western Instruments* (woodcut). Utagawa Sadahide (歌川 貞秀, 1807–c. 1878/1879) was a Japanese artist best known for his *Yokohama-e* pictures of foreigners

of Empire, but also to a more general discussion of European modernity versus non-European civilisations.

Transnationalising Opera Studies

Historians and musicologists have conventionally used national frames of analysis to explore connections between music and political-cultural meaning. In particular, music's role in the self-perception of Italians during the nineteenth century has long informed accounts of different musical genres and of specific moments of political activism, with strong implications for the general narrative of Italy's nation-making.[21] Because opera played a crucial role in defining Italy as a *Kulturnation*, the genre's connections to nationalist discourse have often provoked controversial debate among scholars.[22]

---

[21] See for instance Carlotta Sorba, 'Il 1848 e la melodrammatizzazione della politica', in Alberto M. Banti and Paul Ginsborg (eds.), *Il Risorgimento*, Storia d'Italia: Annals 22 (Turin: Einaudi, 2007), 481–508.

[22] Key contributions to this debate, taking different views, include Roger Parker, '*Arpa d'or dei fatidici vati*': *The Verdian Patriotic Chorus in the 1840s* (Parma: Istituto di studi verdiani, 1997);

While a long tradition of scholarship accepts that music, and opera in particular, played a fundamental role in articulating Italian identity, the possible implications of the transnational movement of people, goods and ideas for notions of *italianità* have been largely overlooked, ignoring a significant dimension of the nineteenth-century music industry as well as of related cultural debates. For instance, few scholars have considered how the early diffusion of Italian opera in the Western hemisphere affected notions of operatic *italianità*, in the New World as well as back home. As early as the eighteenth century, the Spanish-born writer Stefano Arteaga, an associate of the composer and influential teacher Padre Giambattista Martini in Bologna, mentioned Pietro Metastasio as 'the favourite author of the century, a name glorified from Cádiz to Ukraine and from Copenhagen to Brazil', indicating the transnational appeal of the period's most famous author of Italian libretti. When, in 1808, the Portuguese court arrived in Brazil with singers, musicians and composers, they carried with them a repertoire that even then was marked by cultural exchanges between Portugal, Italy and several other centres of European operatic life, making it difficult to assess what operatic *italianità* might have meant to constantly changing audiences and within different musical cultures.

By investigating the shifting meanings of operatic *italianità*, our collection of essays aims to take account of research that has raised critical questions over the use of 'national opera' as an analytical category.[23] Debates on national operatic styles often originated in the Old World. For instance, during the 1820s, critics on both sides of the Alps discussed the extent to which Rossini was influenced by German composers, contrary to a musicological tradition that has tended to use Rossini's music to emphasise the antagonism between Italian and German musical

---

Mary Ann Smart, *Waiting for Verdi: Opera and Political Opinion in Nineteenth-Century Italy, 1815–1848* (Berkeley, CA: University of California Press, 2018); Philipp Gossett, '"Edizioni distrutte" and the Significance of Operatic Choruses During the Risorgimento', in Victoria Johnson, Jane F. Fulcher and Thomas Ertman (eds.), *Opera and Society in Italy and France from Monteverdi to Bourdieu* (Cambridge: Cambridge University Press, 2007), 181–242; Philipp Gossett, 'Giuseppe Verdi and the Italian Risorgimento', *Proceedings of the American Philosophical Society* 156/3 (September 2012), 271–82. For the wider context of debate see Suzanne Aspden, 'Opera and National Identity', in Nicholas Till (ed.), *The Cambridge Companion to Opera Studies*. (Cambridge: Cambridge University Press, 2012), 276–97. Also Axel Körner (ed.), Opera and Nation in Nineteenth-Century Italy. Special Issue of *Journal of Modern Italian Studies* 17/4 (September 2012).

[23] Arne Stollberg, Ivana Rentsch and Anselm Gerhard (eds.), *Gefühlskraftwerke für Patrioten? Wagner und das Musiktheater zwischen Nationalismus und Globalisierung* (Würzburg: Königshausen & Neumann, 2017), 17–71, 247–516; Axel Körner, 'Beyond *Nationaloper*. For a Critique of Methodological Nationalism in Reading Nineteenth-Century Italian and German Opera', *Journal of Modern Italian Studies* 25/4 (2020), 402–19.

conventions.²⁴ In Habsburg Europe the composer's blending of different national styles could count in his favour, but on other occasions it was held against him.²⁵ During the middle decades of the nineteenth century, attempts to create German, Polish and Czech 'national operas' relied on compositional techniques associated with the Italian tradition, with French *grand opéra* or with Wagnerism, often contradicting the original aim of writing 'national' opera.²⁶ Moreover, the production of such works often relied on the involvement of musicians and impresarios versed in multiple musical styles and languages, which reflected their international careers. Despite the multi- and transnational connections of these musicians, much of the research on opera in Central Europe still focuses narrowly on tensions between German and Czech or Polish music, ignoring the huge role played by the Italian repertoire as well as the more general difficulties of distinguishing between different national idioms in music.²⁷ Related to this battle over operatic nationalism is the fact that many works on opera in Habsburg Europe still take a constant antagonism between opera and imperial politics for granted, without acknowledging the multinational foundations of the Empire's idea of the state and the implications of

---

[24] Nicholas Mathew and Benjamin Walton (eds.), *The Invention of Beethoven and Rossini: Historiography, Analysis, Criticism* (Cambridge: Cambridge University Press, 2013).

[25] Arnold Jacobshagen, *Gioachino Rossini und seine Zeit* (Laaber: Laaber-Verlag, 2015), 296; Benjamin Walton, '"More German than Beethoven": Rossini's Zelmira and Italian Style', in Nicholas Mathew and Benjamin Walton (eds.), *The Invention of Beethoven and Rossini: Historiography, Analysis, Criticism* (Cambridge: Cambridge University Press, 2013), 159–77; Claudio Vellutini, 'Cultural Engineering: Italian Opera in Vienna, 1816–1848', PhD thesis, University of Chicago, 2015, 154. For related debates during the same period see also Carolin Krahn, '"Klingklangdudeldum" – "Applaudirsünden" – "Rosinenfieber": Carl Maria von Weber, Meyerbeers *Emma* und das musikalische Italien in Dresden', *Weberiana* 28 (2018), 105–25.

[26] Natalia Nicklas, *Nationalisierung der deutschen Oper im späten Vormärz 1840–1848* (Stuttgart: Franz Steiner, 2017); Anastasia Belina-Johnson and Stephen Muir (eds.), *Wagner in Russia, Poland, and the Czech Lands* (Farnham: Ashgate, 2013); Harry Stopes, '*Lydéric, sauveur de Flandres*: décentralisation théâtrale and the local politics of the Opera in Lille, 1881–1896', *French History*, 32/3 (2018), 387–407; Ivana Rentsch, '"Keine Spur von Lohengrin": Die "verspätete" Wagner-Rezeption in Prag' and Rüdiger Ritter, 'Nationale Mission und panslawistisches Sendungsbewußtsein in der polnischen Musik des 19. Jahrhunderts', in Arne Stollberg, Ivana Rentsch and Anselm Gerhard (eds.), *Gefühlskraftwerke für Patrioten? Wagner und das Musiktheater zwischen Nationalismus und Globalisierung* (Würzburg: Königshausen & Neumann, 2017), 291–306 and 335–59.

[27] For examples of these difficulties see Vladimir Karbusicky, *Geschichte des böhmischen Musiktheaters* (Hamburg: von Bockel, 2005); Jarmila Gabrielová, 'Carl Maria von Webers Freischütz in Prag', in Jörn Peter Hieckel and Elvira Werner (eds.), *Musikkulturelle Wechselbeziehungen zwischen Böhmen und Sachsen* (Saarbrücken: Pfau, 2007), 91–8; Jiří Kopecký and Lenka Křupková, *Das Olmützer Stadttheater und seine Oper* (Regensburg: ConBrio, 2017).

these for its policies of cultural representation.²⁸ This background explains why, in addition to our focus on Latin America, several chapters in our collection of essays examine ideas of *italianità* as they were debated in Central Europe.

A field of research the authors of this volume took inspiration from when transnationalising their subject is Benjamin Walton's work on the early global diffusion of Rossini's operas, which presents a model for challenging narrowly defined national approaches in opera studies.²⁹ Recent work on *grand opéra* takes a similar approach by looking at the transnational movement of a genre that originated in a particular French operatic tradition, but then acquired new meanings due to its global appeal.³⁰ Both fields share a focus on transnational interactions in forming notions of music and national identity at a time when major technological developments led to an acceleration of global processes in cultural communication.³¹

From a methodological point of view, many of the works that helped us to define our approach have moved away from a reading of music narrowly based on philological methods, expanding instead into the analysis of music's wider social, economic, political and cultural contexts and its connections with public life.³² The contributions to our collection of essays were inspired by works that foreground the cultural analysis of opera's

---

[28] Giovanni Gavazzeni, 'Il melodramma ha fatto l'unità d'Italia', in Giovanni Gavazzeni, Armando Torno and Carlo Vitali (eds.), *O mia patria: Storia musicale del Risorgimento, tra inni, eroi e melodrammi* (Milan: Dalai, 2011), 51–183; Chiara Plazzi, *Nemico della patria! Migranti e stranieri nel melodramma italiano da Rossini a Turandot* (Acireale: Bonanno, 2007); Carlotta Sorba, 'Between Cosmopolitanism and Nationhood: Italian Opera in Early Nineteenth Century', *Journal of Modern Italian Studies*, 19/1 (2014), 53–67; Gossett, 'Giuseppe Verdi and the Italian Risorgimento'.

[29] Benjamin Walton, 'Operatic Fantasies in Latin America', *Journal of Modern Italian Studies* 17/4 (September 2012), 460–71; Benjamin Walton, 'Rossini in South America', *Tonkunst* (October 2018), 364–80. See also José Manuel Izquierdo König, 'Rossini's Reception in Latin America: Scarcity and Imagination in Two Early Chilean Sources', in Ilaria Narici, Emilio Sala, Emanuele Senici and Ben Walton (eds.), *Gioachino Rossini 1868–2018: La musica e il mondo*, Saggi e fonti, 5 (Pesaro: Fondazione Rossini, 2018), 413–35.

[30] Jens Hesselager (ed.), *Grand Opera Outside Paris. Opera on the Move in Nineteenth-Century Europe* (London and New York: Routledge, 2018); Laura Protano-Biggs (ed.), *Nineteenth-Century Grand Opéra on the Move*. Special issue: *Cambridge Opera Journal* 29/1 (2017).

[31] Jürgen Osterhammel, *The Transformation of the World: A Global History of the Nineteenth Century* (Princeton, NJ: Princeton University Press, 2014).

[32] See for instance the three very different works by Celia Applegate, Benjamin Walton and Emanuele Senici: Celia Applegate, *Bach in Berlin: Nation and Culture in Mendelssohn's Revival of the St. Matthew Passion* (Ithaca, NY: Cornell University Press, 2005); Benjamin Walton, *Rossini in Restoration Paris: The Sound of Modern Life* (Cambridge, Cambridge University Press, 2007); Emanuele Senici, *Music in the Present Tense. Rossini's Italian Operas in Their Time* (Chicago: Chicago University Press, 2019).

production, performance and reception by looking at the ways in which opera participated in the making of a modern (and increasingly globalised) public.[33] Having emerged from a close dialogue with neighbouring disciplines, in particular cultural studies, literary criticism, art history and film- and performance studies, this approach has cultural agency at its centre. Here the source base of musical research has been significantly extended: from theatre archives and materials directly related to composers, to a vast range of sources that mostly relate to the production and reception of opera, as well as to different levels of political decision-making.[34] From historical narratives focussed on particular composers and their works, many opera scholars have now turned to examining audience experiences,[35] or new spatial dimensions such as the urban, national and transnational contexts of opera production.[36] Some of these new studies pay particular attention to singers, their careers and global movements, to gender, or to the role of impresarios and their companies in challenging national readings opera.[37] Another

---

[33] Alessandra Campana, *Opera and Modern Spectatorship in Late Nineteenth-Century Italy* (Cambridge: Cambridge University Press, 2015).

[34] Michael Walter, *Oper: Geschichte einer Institution* (Stuttgart/Kassel: J. B. Metzler/Bärenreiter, 2016) makes ample use of economic and social history source materials. Axel Körner, *Politics of Culture in Liberal Italy. From Unification to Fascism* (New York: Routledge, 2009) makes use of municipal archives; Axel Körner, 'Che il pubblico non venga defraudato degli spettacoli ad esso promessi: The Venetian Premiere of *La traviata* and Austria's Imperial Administration in 1853', *Verdiperspektiven* 3 (2018), 89–106, explores the local archives of the imperial administration.

[35] Campana, *Opera and Modern Spectatorship*; James H. Johnson, *Listening in Paris: A Cultural History* (Berkeley, CA: University of California Press, 1995); Sven Oliver Müller, *Das Publikum macht die Musik: Musikleben in Berlin, London und Wien im 19. Jahrhundert* (Göttingen: Vandenhoeck & Ruprecht, 2014); Markian Prokopovych, *In the Public Eye: The Budapest Opera House, the Audience, and the Press, 1884–1918* (Vienna: Böhlau, 2014)

[36] Anselm Gerhard, *The Urbanization of Opera: Music Theater in Paris in the Nineteenth Century* (Chicago: University of Chicago Press, 1998); Christina Fuhrmann, *Foreign Opera at the London Playhouses: From Mozart to Bellini* (Cambridge: Cambridge University Press, 2015); Pierpaolo Polzonetti, *Italian Opera in the Age of the American Revolution* (Cambridge: Cambridge University Press, 2011); John Rosselli, *The Opera Industry in Italy from Cimarosa to Verdi: The Role of the Impresario* (Cambridge: Cambridge University Press, 1984); John Rosselli, 'The Opera Business and the Italian Immigrant Community in Latin America 1820–1930: The Example of Buenos Aires', *Past and Present*, 127/1, 155–82; Jutta Toelle, *Bühne der Stadt: Mailand und das Teatro alla Scala zwischen Risorgimento und Fin de Siècle* (Vienna: Böhlau, 2009); Jutta Toelle, 'Der Duft der großen weiten Welt: Ideen zum weltweiten Siegeszug der italienischen Oper im 19. Jahrhundert', in Sven Oliver Müller, Philipp Ther, Jutta Toelle and Gesa zur Nieden (eds.), *Die Oper im Wandel der Gesellschaft: Kulturtransfers und Netzwerke des Musiktheaters in Europa* (Vienna: Böhlau, 2010), 251–61.

[37] Rosselli, *The Opera Industry in Italy*; Susan Rutherford, *The Prima Donna and Opera, 1815–1930* (Cambridge: Cambridge University Press, 2006); Susan Rutherford, *Verdi, Opera, Women* (Cambridge: Cambridge University Press, 2013); Emanuele Senici, *Landscape and Gender in Italian Opera: The Alpine Virgin from Bellini to Puccini* (Cambridge: Cambridge University Press, 2009); Ian Woodfield, *Performing Operas for Mozart: Impresarios, Singers and Troupes* (Cambridge: Cambridge University Press, 2012).

important factor here is the building of new, often quite spectacular theatres in many different parts of the world. Through the global circulation of the repertoire and its performers these buildings retained close connections to Europe's operatic tradition. This development meant that in addition to musicians and the repertoire, also architects, engineers and set designers travelled around the world and through their transnational movements helped to reshape national notions of opera. Finally, whenever the repertoire travelled it was also printed in new editions; and it was adapted for use in homes across the globe, via new piano reductions, as well as in public spaces, where it was performed by brass bands, street musicians or barrel organ players, all of them translating music into new contexts.[38] In all of these cases the conditions of opera production were profoundly shaped by transnational exchanges affecting musicians, composers, impresarios and audiences, as well as the repertoire they produced.

Approaching Operatic *Italianità*

As Susan Rutherford has argued, for much of the nineteenth century 'music was regarded as an entirely idealised domain'.[39] Although it reflected the values and ambitions of composers and performers, and interacted with audiences, music existed in relative independence of the real world. The *Gazzetta musicale di Milano* argued in 1860 – notably the moment when the Italian Risorgimento had seemingly fulfilled its promise – that 'the principal aspect of music is wholly ideal; its sphere of action that of a world let us not to say unknown, but which has nothing in common with that in which we live'.[40] The underlying

---

[38] Annibale Cetrangolo, *Opera, barcos y banderas: El melodrama en la inmigración italiana de la argentina (1880–1920)* (Madrid: Biblioteca Nueva, 2015); Annibale Cetrangolo, *El melodrama italiano en Argentina entre 1880 y 1920. Un problema de identidades en el encuentro migratorio* (Padua: Imla, 2010). For the study of opera in Montevideo, see Susana Salgado, *The Teatro Solís – 150 Years of Opera, Concert, and Ballet in Montevideo* (Middletown, CT: Wesleyan University Press, 2003), and Leonardo Manzino, *La ópera uruguaya del siglo XIX – estrenos de Tomás Giribaldi en el Teatro Solís* (Montevideo: Serie Los Románticos Uruguayos / Música, 2010). John Zucchi, *Little Slaves of the Harp: Italian Child Street Musicians in Nineteenth-Century Paris, London and New York* (Montreal: McGill-Queen's University Press, 1992).

[39] Rutherford, *The Prima Donna and Opera*, 215. This marks a significant contrast to the perceptions of the eighteenth century, when an important musical tradition still argued in favour of music reflecting nature as closely as possible. See for instance Silke Leopold, *Leopold Mozart: Ein Mann von vielen Witz und Klugheit: Eine Biographie* (Kassel/Berlin: Bärenreiter/Metzler, 2019), 86–90.

[40] Quoted in Rutherford, *The Prima Donna and Opera*, 215. With regard to Verdi (and a with a focus more on theatricality than musical content) Richard Taruskin seems more sceptical about the notion of idealism, describing Verdi as 'very much a realist', whose 'subject matter

aesthetic assumptions of such ideas about music, combined with the conceptual vagueness of national and ethnic identities, make it extremely difficult to connect music to notions of national character. Despite these strains, as Suzanne Aspden has argued, 'opera's conjoining of music and words' challenged 'the universalizing tendency always present in the function and power of music'.[41] Aspden gives the example of 'Italian infiltrations' in the music of Jean-Baptiste Lully that in the seventeenth century had prompted a discussion of the musical principles distinguishing the French and Italian peoples; debates very similar to those mentioned earlier in this introduction in relation to the distinction of operatic styles in d'Alembert and Rousseau. These tensions reflected a more general philosophical debate on the relationship between universal principles and national character that marked, for instance, Johann Gottfried Herder's thoughts on the formation of humankind, which start from a universal notion of shared humanity in order to then explain how the specificity of conditions led to cultural differentiation.[42]

What was the semantic content behind musical notions of nationality as they emerged during the seventeenth and eighteenth centuries? Despite differentiating between French, German and Italian music, commentators during the eighteenth century often equated the 'Italian' with a cosmopolitan style, which served as contrast to a number of more narrowly defined national styles.[43] Other early theorists suggested that Italian and French styles be combined and this hybrid used to create a German one, which in turn could become 'universal'.[44] One element here was the weight of the Italian musical diaspora leading to the idea of a more universal musical language, although the same argument could possibly be applied to the role of Bohemian musicians within a wider European context. In these debates, however, *Italianness* was also often associated with 'the cheap and nasty', an idea further complicated by the

---

was almost always of this world'; but he concedes that 'even a stage setting in the here and now required aesthetic distancing from what was truly here and truly now'. See Richard Taruskin, *Music in the Nineteenth Century*, The Oxford History of Western Music (Oxford: Oxford University Press, 2010), 564 f.

[41] Aspden, 'Opera and National Identity', 278.

[42] Johann Gottfried von Herder, 'This Too a Philosophy of History for the Formation of Humanity' (1774), in *Philosophical Writings*, ed. Michael N. Forster (Cambridge: Cambridge University Press, 2002), 272–358.

[43] W. Dean Sutcliffe, *Instrumental Music in an Age of Sociability: Haydn, Mozart and Friends* (Cambridge: Cambridge University Press, 2020), 256. In this context it is worth mentioning that in these debates the 'English' style was often equated with a Handelian or Corellian style.

[44] Bernd Sponheuer, 'Reconstructing Ideal Types of the "German" in Music', in Celia Applegate and Pamela Potter (eds.), *Music and German National Identity* (Chicago and London: University of Chicago Press, 2002), 36–58.

fact that many representatives of the Italian/cosmopolitan style were not Italian, but 'imitators' of Italian music of any national background, including, among many lesser known figures, composers such as Haydn and Mozart.[45] The prominence of some advocates of Italian cosmopolitanism notwithstanding, Carl Ditters von Dittersdorf recounts hearing Johann Christian Bach's *Catone in Utica* in Parma and describing it as 'written very sketchily, after the Italian style'; and in his *Sinfonia nazionale nel gusto di cinque nazioni* Dittersdorf himself satirised the fashion for the Italian manner.[46] The idea of writing music in different national idioms was in no way new. As early as 1659, Lully had integrated in his *Ballet royal de la raillerie* a section in which 'la musica italiana' and 'la musique Françoise [*sic*]' are directly juxtaposed, and in dialogue with each other: according to Aspden, this was a response to the 'growing popular anti-Italianism' in French culture.[47] In Rousseau's contribution to the Querelle des Bouffons, mentioned above, the 'citoyen de Genève' turned these evaluations upside down, posing Italy's supposedly natural style against French artifice. Closer to Dittersdorf's form of musical satire, in the final act of his *Viaggio à Reims* (1825) Rossini parodies the same idea of national styles based on material taken from different national anthems. Carl Maria von Weber, although often associated with provoking tensions between the German and Italian schools in Dresden, considered the ability to write in different idioms an important quality. In this debate, Weber used the international success of Meyerbeer's Italian operas as an example.[48]

In similar ways, many of the nineteenth-century sources discussed in this book point to the fluidity of notions of *italianità*, and to the more general problem of assigning fixed meanings to opera, and to Italian opera in particular. The same has been noted by scholars outside the field of opera studies too. When Cristina Demaria and Roberta Sassatelli discuss Roland Barthes' notion of *italianicity,* rather than referring to it as anything real, they see it as 'an icon of what Italy and "things Italian" might be'.[49] Taking account of this semantic fluidity has clear implications for the validity of associating particular works with fixed political significance reflective of national character. This problem occurs, for instance, when attempting to produce 'authentic' stagings of particular

---

[45] Sutcliffe, *Instrumental Music,* 257 f.   [46] Ibid., 259 n.
[47] Aspden, 'Opera and National Identity', 279. For details see Jean-Baptiste Lully, *Ballet de la Raillerie* (LWV 11) (Versailles: André Danican Philidor, 1690).
[48] Krahn, '"Klingklangdudeldum" – "Applaudirsünden" – "Rosinenfieber"'.
[49] Cristina Demaria and Roberta Sassatelli, 'Introduction: Italianicity/Italianess', *Studi Culturali* 3 (December 2015), 311–16 (311).

works.[50] These semantic uncertainties notwithstanding, fluid and malleable notions of *italianità* continue to inform people's reading of Italian opera independently of the time and space in which productions take place. Then as well as today, notions of *italianità* were informed and reinforced by musical practice and the experience of Italian opera on stage, but also by wider debates on Italian art and history; reflections on diplomatic relations and military conflict; material culture and consumption; the knowledge of classical literature; and the country's discovery through travel writing. Although in some cases direct experience of *italianità* through travel or migration, and (especially during the Napoleonic period) through warfare, also contributed to creating images of Italy, most of these encounters were (and still are) filtered through complex transnational exchanges and often had no more than a loose connection with social and cultural life in the Italian peninsula.

Likewise, through most of the period here under investigation, most experiences of Italian opera did not take place in Italy, but in theatres at home, or during travel in third countries. Here, Italian works were often produced in translation, by singers of various national origins, with impresarios and casts playing on a wide range of images associated with Italy and Italian music.[51] These images reflected specific national and historical experiences, which in many cases tell us more about the viewer than about the viewed.[52] Frequently, the works performed were adapted to local conditions of musical production, which could differ considerably from those of the theatres in Italy, but counted as experiences of operatic *italianità* all the same. Therefore, what operatic culture stood for, north and south of the Alps, or on either side of the Atlantic, was often not the same, even at times when the Italian repertoire dominated the stages in many parts of the world. While Julian Budden associates the period from the 1850s onwards with the 'collapse of a tradition',[53] the ongoing success of Italian opera abroad suggests that the genre still responded to the expectations of its audiences. The famous Viennese critic Eduard Hanslick went so far as to suggest that the public felt a real need for

---

[50] On this problem see in particular the collection of essays by Roger Parker, *Leonora's Last Act: Essays in Verdian Discourse* (Princeton, NJ: Princeton University Press, 1997).

[51] An interesting case here is the absence of Italian singers in London during Napoleon's Continental Blockade of Britain, when their place had to be taken up by British singers: Vellutini, 'Interpreting the Italian Voice in London (and Elsewhere)', 53.

[52] On the construction of similar images see Michel de Certeau, *L'écriture de l'histoire* (Paris: Gallimard: 1975), 9f.

[53] Julian Budden, *The Operas of Verdi*, vol. 2: *From Il trovatore to La forza del destino* (London: Cassell, 1978), 3–32.

Italian opera,⁵⁴ an impression certainly confirmed by many of the case studies this volume brings together. Therefore, the perception of operatic crisis at home, partly caused by the internationalisation of the Italian repertoire and the reckoning of 'foreign' influences on Italian composers,⁵⁵ often coincided with an international perception that Italian opera was still striving. By the time Hanslick was commenting on Verdi's ongoing popularity in Vienna, the idea of a collapse of Italy's operatic tradition had long been a popular trope in music criticism, one that almost always coincided with great acclaim of Italian opera abroad. This tale started with the fights between Gluckisti and Piccinisti in the eighteenth century, mentioned above, continued with Stendhal's 'narrative of decline' to describe Rossini's stylistic development after 1815,⁵⁶ and led to the supposed 'end of the great tradition' associated with Puccini's Turandot,⁵⁷ another aspect of the same operatic crisis in which 'un-Italian' influences allegedly played their part.

Because of their transnational nature, junctures in the perception of operatic *italianità* come in many guises, which in turn left their imprint on Italian opera at home. In his contribution to this volume, Andrew Holden refers to Adriana Guarnieri Corazzol's notion of 'un fantastico mediterraneo alternativo' when describing how Italians understood Giacomo Meyerbeer's mixing of Germanic influences with Italian tradition, which in turn then left a mark on works such as Arrigo Boito's *Mefistofele*. Likewise, for Thomas Mann the final scene of Verdi's *Aida* was 'ein italienischer Liebestod', the work of a Wagnerised Italian.⁵⁸ From a musical-philological point of view, Mann might have been wrong with his analysis, but the fact that Franz Werfel, with his *Verdi: Roman der Oper*, turned the same tension into one of his greatest novels demonstrates the power of such images.⁵⁹ In international perceptions of Puccini's operas the debate on foreign influences seems to work the other way round, with audiences all over the world continuing to consider the composer's works

---

⁵⁴ Quoted in Ursula Dauth, *Verdis Opern im Spiegel der Wiener Presse von 1843–1859. Ein Beitrag zur Rezeptionsgeschichte* (Munich and Salzburg: Emil Katzbichler, 1981), 46.
⁵⁵ Axel Körner, '*Music of the Future*: Italian Theatres and the European Experience of Modernity between Unification and World War One', *European History Quarterly*, 41/2 (April 2011), 189–212.
⁵⁶ Walton, *Rossini in Restoration Paris*, 66.
⁵⁷ William Ashbrook and Harold Powers, *Puccini's Turandot: The End of the Great Tradition* (Princeton, NJ: Princeton University Press, 1991).
⁵⁸ Elisabeth Galvan, 'Thomas Mann in Italia: Thomas Mann, Gabriele D'Annunzio e Giuseppe Verdi', in Arnaldo Benini and Arno Schneider (eds.), *Thomas Mann nella storia del suo tempo* (Florence: Passigli, 2004), 151–71, 163 f, 166.
⁵⁹ Franz Werfel, *Verdi: Roman der Oper* (Berlin: Paul Zsolny, 1924).

as quintessentially Italian, despite the openness to international developments for which he was criticised by infuriated commentators at home.[60] As Emanuele Senici notes, not a single one of Puccini's operas 'is based on an Italian play, short story, novel, or poem', and only *Tosca* and *Gianni Schicchi* are set in Italy; but this did not seem to affect international ideas of *italianità* associated with the composer's work.[61] Many examples discussed in this volume show that *italianità* was not exclusively 'made in Italy', and that what was understood as *italianità* was not immune to non-Italian influences. While the argument of foreign influences shaping Italian opera is not new – as shown, in particular, by recent scholarship on Rossini and Verdi[62] – our volume goes beyond it, examining how transnational and global influences on the repertoire and its production relate to constructions of *italianità* in wider societal debates.

Experiencing Italian Opera: At Home and Abroad

Due to the multidimensional and often transnational nature of the world's encounter with operatic *italianità*, what foreign visitors saw and heard when they went to the theatre in Italy did not necessarily compare favourably to traditions of Italian operatic culture at home. In a very similar vein, two otherwise very different French authors commented on their

---

[60] On international stylistic influences see Richard Erkens, 'Konstante Aneignung: Puccini und die Opernlandschaft seiner Zeit', in Richard Erkens (ed.), *Puccini Handbuch* (Stuttgart: Metzler and Kassel: Bärenreiter, 2017), 54–66. On the Italian critics see in particular Alexandra Wilson, *The Puccini Problem. Opera, Nationalism and Modernity* (Cambridge: Cambridge University Press, 2007).

[61] Emanuele Senici, 'Introduction: Puccini, His World, and Ours', in Emanuele Senici and Arman Schwartz (eds.), *Puccini and His World* (Princeton, NJ: Princeton University Press, 2016), 1–25, 14 f. For this context of Puccini's work see also Axel Körner, 'Italien in Europa und der Welt: Opernpublikum und die Erfahrung gesellschaftlichen Wandels um 1900', in Erkens (ed.), *Puccini-Handbuch*, 30–9.

[62] The literature on such international influences is huge. For Rossini see Mathew and Walton (eds.), *The Invention of Beethoven and Rossini*. Also Benjamin Walton, 'Rossini and France', in Emanuele Senici (ed.), *The Cambridge Companion to Rossini* (Cambridge: Cambridge University Press, 2004), 25–36. Jacobshagen, *Gioacchino Rossini und seine Zeit*, 265 f. For Verdi see Fabrizio Della Seta, *Italia e Francia nell'ottocento*, Storia della musica, 9 (Turin: EDT, 1993), 219 sq. Also Andreas Giger, 'French Influences', in Scott L. Balthazar (ed.), *The Cambridge Companion to Verdi* (Cambridge: Cambridge University Press, 2004), 111–38. Gloria Staffieri, 'Da Robert le Diable a Macbeth: Influssi di Meyerbeer sulla produzione verdiana degli anni quaranta', *Studi verdiani* 13 (1998), 13–37; Gloria Staffieri, 'Verdis Frühwerk und Meyerbeers Grand opera', in Markus Engelhardt, *Giuseppe Verdi und seine Zeit* (Laaber: Laaber, 2001), 293–315. Egon Voss, 'Oberto ante portas. Zur Verdi-Rezeption in Frankreich und Belgien im 19. Jahrhundert', *Verdiperspektiven* 3 (2018), 13–27.

experience of Italian opera during their travels in the peninsula: The French composer Auguste-Louis Blondeau, a winner of the Prix de Rome, recorded detailed comments on theatres, orchestras and singers, as well as specific performances, during the four years he spent in Italy. The more famous case is the historian Hippolyte Taine, whose *Voyage in Italie* recalls in detail a performance of *Il trovatore* at the San Carlo in Naples.[63] Although writing several decades apart, their disappointment over what they witnessed closely mirrors the views of the Count d'Erfeuil in Germaine de Staël's hugely influential novel *Corinne ou l'Italie*, according to which 'every French province had a better theatre than Rome'.[64] The count's observations on Italian theatres did not necessarily reflect de Staël's personal opinion, but stood for a view that was widespread among France's upper classes and which de Staël was keen to dismantle. At the same time, these different literary traces show how difficult it is to make sense of these references: De Staël's main purpose was not to talk about the quality of Italian theatres, but to depict and critique widespread French views of other nations during the Napoleonic occupation. Within the context of de Staël's book on Italy, the count's example reflects the fact that national ideas about musical culture often served a purpose that went beyond purely aesthetic arguments. Furthermore, since the late eighteenth century, for most foreign travellers the principal motivation behind their tours of Italy had no longer been to acquire knowledge of a foreign culture, but to search their own selves, with the result that their observations often tell us relatively little about the objects of their gaze.[65]

Charles Dickens' first mention of a musical experience in his *Pictures from Italy* (1844) relates to a church service in Genoa, but expresses a similarly low opinion of Italy's musical life at the time: 'A tenor, without any voice, sang. The band played one way, the organ played another, the singer went a third, and the unfortunate conductor banged and banged, and flourished his scroll on some principle of his own: apparently well satisfied with the whole performance. I never did hear such a discordant din.' Playing on a well-established tradition of linking climatic conditions to national character, Dickens added – only seemingly out of context – that

---

[63] See Auguste-Louis Blondeau, *Voyage d'un musicien en Italie (1809–1812) précédé des observations sur les théâtres italiens*, ed. Joël-Marie Fauquet (Liège: Mardaga, 1993). Hippolyte Taine, *Voyage en Italie*. Book 1: *Naples et Rome* (Paris: Librairie de L. Hachette, 1866), 126–8.

[64] Madame de Staël, *Corinne, ou l'Italie* [1807] (Paris: Firmin Didot, 1853), 8.

[65] Irene Haberland, 'Künstlerreisen nach Rom', in Sigrid Lange and Matthias von der Bank (eds.), *Vom Rhein nach Italien – Auf den Spuren der Grand Tour im neunzehnten Jahrhundert* (Petersberg: Michael Imhof Verlag, 2019).

'the heat was intense all the time'.[66] The church service was not to be Dicken's only musical disappointment in Genoa. The first theatre he went to was the 'very splendid, commodious, and beautiful' Carlo Felice, but he soon learned that the production was 'second rate'.[67]

Dickens is not known for his musical expertise; but when the Austrian playwright Franz Grillparzer embarked on his Italian journey, in 1819, and a little closer to the setting of de Staël's novel, he was thoroughly familiar with the Italian as well as the German operatic repertoire, and had witnessed the first productions of Rossini's works in Vienna. At the time, Grillparzer had just enjoyed his first European successes as a dramatist, and his writings on theatre and culture reveal great erudition as well as a complex level of aesthetic judgement. The operatic productions he saw in Venice, Florence and Rome, however, compared poorly to what he was accustomed to north of the Alps. A performance of Giovanni Pacini's *Isabella e Florange* at Rome's Teatro Tordinona, better known as the Teatro Apollo, Grillparzer described as 'truly miserable: ordinary Italian music, poorly presented by an oversized orchestra, and mediocre or bad singers, mostly too loud'.[68] The bass reminded him of a 'quaking frog'. He described the primadonna as 'an arid and ugly creature', the buffo was 'disgusting' and the tenor had a 'stupid and ugly' face.[69] The Apollo's sets were humble, the costumes without taste, the chorus bad, the mimes miserable. The production taken as a whole struck him as poor 'to a degree not imaginable even in the lowest provincial town in Germany', an observation closely mirroring le Comte d'Erfeuil's comparisons in de Staël's *Corinne*.[70] A production of Rossini's *Cenerentola* at Florence's Teatro della Pergola seemed to him as insignificant as the work itself: 'The ballet very bad, the theatre itself neither great nor pretty', although he acknowledged the theatre's good acoustics. Ester Mombelli's performance was acceptable but mannered, reflecting ideas on Italian singers that were not uncommon in Viennese music criticism. His recollections openly expressed his disappointment over an art form he loved, and which he judged on the basis of his rich Viennese experience.[71]

In the views of these international travellers, many of whom were familiar with the splendours of Italian opera in Vienna, London or Paris, Italy had lost much of its reputation as a musical nation, if indeed musical

---

[66] Charles Dickens, *Pictures from Italy* (London: André Deutsch, 1973), 70.   [67] Ibid., 86 f.
[68] Franz Grillparzer, *Reisetagebücher* (Berlin: Rütten & Loening, 1971), 39 f. In his account, the theatre is described as *El nobile teatro di Pordenone*. We are grateful to Daniele Carnini for pointing out this mistake.
[69] Grillparzer, *Reisetagebücher*, 39 f.   [70] Ibid., 40.   [71] Ibid., 91.

content had ever been central to ideas of operatic *italianità*. Grillparzer's assessment of Italy's operatic culture was further complicated by the fact that even in opera's birthplace the best voices often originated from elsewhere: in a mediocre production of Rossini's *Barbiere di Siviglia* at the Teatro S. Simone in Venice, Grillparzer was pleased to hear Joséphine Fodor-Mainvielle, at the time one of the greatest Rossinian voices, but she was a French citizen of Hungarian-Dutch descent with close connections to Russia.[72] This background notwithstanding, when a few years later the Italian impresario Domenico Barbaja engaged Fodor for the Italian opera season in Vienna, the famous chronicler Ferdinand von Seyfried praised her for being the typical example of an Italian singer.[73] Like Grillparzer, he admired her singing, but insisted that she was extremely stingy – playing on an idea the author generally associated with the representatives of Vienna's Italian opera industry.[74] Despite the multifaceted nature of the international debate on Italian style and vocal training, discussed in Carolin Krahn's chapter below, from a musical point of view, the Italian singers at Europe's leading theatres were often held in the highest regard, as shown by the cults in London around the castrato Giovanni Battista Velluti; Giovanni David in 1820s Vienna, greatly admired by Metternich; or Luigi Lablache, considered 'indispensable to the performance of Italian opera in London and Paris' during the 1830s and 1840s.[75] As a consequence of these international movements, when Goethe's son August visited Milan in 1830 he noted that the best singers were performing in London or Paris.[76] Meanwhile, the high quality of Italian singers abroad was instrumental to the disappointment of travellers like Grillparzer once they experienced Italian opera in Italy.

The contracted focus of operatic debate on singers' performance also influenced evaluations of the Italian repertoire, often creating tensions between enthusiastic audiences and professional critics. As a consequence, some commentators criticised the public's narrow interest in vocal

---

[72] Ibid., 20.
[73] Ferdinand Ritter von Seyfried, *Rückschau in das Theaterleben Wiens seit den letzten fünfzig Jahren* (Vienna: Selbstverlag, 1864), 279 f.
[74] Ibid., 214 f. See also his comments on Balochino, ibid., 29–35. Seyfried went so far as to compare Italy's contractual exploitation of singers with the international slave trade.
[75] Sarah Fuchs, 'The Castrato as Creator: Velluti's Voice in the London Sheet-Music Market', in Parker and Rutherford (eds.), *London Voices*, 71–91. Axel Körner, 'Culture for a Cosmopolitan Empire: Rossini between Vienna and the Lands of the Bohemian Crown', in Narici, Sala, Senici and Walton (eds.), *Gioachino Rossini 1868-2018*, 357–80, 366. Sarah Hibberd, '"The Essence of Nine Trombones": Luigi Lablache and Models of Masculinity in 1830s London', in Parker and Rutherford (eds.), *London Voices*, 93–119 (93).
[76] August von Goethe, *Auf einer Reise nach Süden: Tagebuch 1830* (Munich: dtv, 2003), 23.

performance for taking precedent over critically assessing the works that appeared on stage. Making use of the Kantian terminology that had recently entered musical discourse[77], the editor of Vienna's influential *Allgemeine Musikalische Zeitung* Friedrich August Kanne argued: 'If until now all countries needed singers to perform operas, Italy now needs operas for the production of its singers. The means became the end, and the end the means. In turn, the drama itself was dissolved, nipping in the bud the sublime interest that moves humans to engage with the work of art!'[78] The consequences of this development for Europe's operatic culture, in Kanne's view, were fatal: 'Singers started to see themselves as the main thing, turning their vocal ability in such arbitrary ways to virtuosity that no real work of art was left that would allow them to play their acrobatics to their heart's content.'[79] Increasingly, this new cult of performance impacted productions beyond the Italian repertoire, not least because many of Italy's international stars also performed the works of non-Italian composers, who followed the same trend. For instance, Velluti made his 1825 debut at the London King's Theatre with Giacomo Meyerbeer's *Il crociato in Egitto* – an Italian opera by a Prussian composer who was to make his later career in French *grand opéra*. All of these developments helped to further complicate ideas of operatic *italianità* – at home as well as abroad.

While the perceived mismatch between Italian vocal stardom at home and the quality of performances in Italy was one of the issues explored by foreign commentators, many travellers were also dismayed by the behaviour of Italian audiences. As Kanne's above-mentioned argument on aesthetic ambition seems to support, in the lands where opera had been invented, going to the theatre seemed to have an altogether different meaning to that which it had at home.[80] Grillparzer criticised the Italian audience's inattentive attitude and raucous behaviour, impressions that correspond to Lord Byron's descriptions of the theatre in Milan.[81] Dickens wrote about the Carlo Felice: 'Nothing impressed me so much in my visits

---

[77] See Hans-Joachim Hinrichsen, *Ludwig van Beethoven: Musik für eine neue Zeit* (Kassel/Berlin: Metzler/Bärenreiter, 2019).

[78] Friedrich August Kanne, 'Was ist von dem jetzigen Geschmacke in der Musik zu fürchten?', *Allgemeine musikalische Zeitung mit besonderer Rücksicht auf den österreichischen Kaiserstaat* 4/91 (11 November 1820), 725–8 (727).

[79] Kanne, 'Was ist von dem jetzigen Geschmacke in der Musik zu fürchten?'

[80] On changing attitudes to the practice of theatre-going in nineteenth-century Europe see Johnson, *Listening in Paris*. Also Walter, *Oper*, 383 ff.

[81] Grillparzer, *Reisetagebücher*, 39. Peter Quennell, *Byron in Italy* (Harmondsworth: Penguin, 1955), 45.

here (which were pretty numerous) as the uncommonly hard and cruel character of the audience, who resent the slightest defect, take nothing good-humouredly, seem to be always lying in wait for an opportunity to hiss, and spare the actresses as little as the actors.'[82] Also interesting in this context is Dickens' depiction of the Piedmontese officers at the theatre. Their behaviour seemed to mirror closely what many scholars today describe as a unique feature of theatres in 'Austrian-occupied' Milan or Venice, where 'foreign' armed forces allegedly undermined Italians' cultural pastimes.[83] About Piedmontese-occupied Genoa, Dickens wrote: 'There are a great number of Piedmontese Officers too, who are allowed the privilege of kicking their heels in the pit, for next to nothing: gratuitous, or cheap accommodation for these gentlemen being insisted on, by the Governor, in all public or semi-public entertainments.'[84] At least in this case it was not 'foreign rule' that destroyed the imaginary authenticity of Italian operatic life. Dickens also dismissed the physical appearance of many of the theatres he saw. While he found Parma a rather 'cheerful' town, its theatre was 'one of the dreariest spectacles of decay that ever was seen – a grand, old, gloomy theatre, mouldering away'.[85]

Orientalising or Transnationalising *Italianità*?

Dickens wrote within a tradition of producing travelogues that orientalised the Mediterranean in order to underline the advanced civilisation of Britain, finding great pleasure in describing the dirty, 'God-forgotten towns' of Italy and the picturesque habits of their inhabitants.[86] In Grillparzer's case, on the contrary, it seems more problematic to qualify his reading of Italian culture simply as an attempt of orientalising otherness. It was principally because of his own high esteem for Italian culture that local operatic productions disappointed him. The recollections of his journeys largely lack the pejorative attitude towards Italy and its inhabitants common to other travel accounts at the time. Looking more broadly at foreign descriptions of theatrical experiences in Italy, one comes across

---

[82] Dickens, *Pictures from Italy*, 87.
[83] Giovanni Gavazzeni uses exactly these images to describe the 'palchi della Scala ... occupati dalla soldataglia e dagli austriacanti': Gavazzeni, 'Il melodramma ha fatto l'unità d'Italia', 60. For a different assessment of the Austrian administration's role see Körner, '*Che il pubblico non venga defraudato degli spettacoli ad esso promessi*'.
[84] Dickens, *Pictures from Italy*, 87.   [85] Ibid., 105 f.
[86] See in particular his descriptions of Genoa and of Tuscan villages: Dickens, *Pictures from Italy*, 77, 100–4.

many more positive accounts; and it seems partly a consequence of modern Italianists looking for orientalising descriptions, and giving preference to English-language accounts, that prejudiced descriptions have dominated debates in the field of (mostly anglophone) Italian studies. For instance, when August von Goethe saw Rossini's *Aureliano in Palmira* at Milan's Teatro della Canobiana, in 1830, he praised the production, including singers and sets, as well as the ballet given between the acts. He was even more enthused by his visit to the Teatro San Carlo in Naples; and in Venice he praised the productions of minor theatres, where he saw works by Cimarosa and, again, Rossini.[87] August von Goethe's visit to Italy was very much a restaging of his father's famous journey to the 'lands where lemons bloom'. Also, in Grillparzer's account, Italy does not appear as a backward South; and it shares little or nothing with a literary East. Instead, for Grillparzer Italy was '*Hesperia*', the West, where the Austrian arrived from Europe's Eastern periphery, after a tiresome journey through some of his beloved fatherland's most remote provinces, including the deprived heartlands of Styria and the Slovenian mountains.[88] The huts where he spent the nights had been 'bad and dirty, the people looked poor, with begging children running along the cart for half a mile'; almost recalling impressions other writers had left of Italy. But what Grillparzer describes here is not Italy, but Austria. Around him he notices nothing but rain and mud. The last leg of his journey before arriving in Trieste, seemed 'a desert', a land almost without buildings; nothing but dry chestnuts and crippled mulberry trees.[89] If in Said's analysis 'the Orient has helped to define Europe (or the West)', for Grillparzer it was his own Orient that taught him to appreciate the culturally more advanced West that so many other travellers were depicting as backward.[90]

After his tiresome journey through the Austrian mountains, how different then were his first impressions of Italy: 'Finally the customs station of Optschina, a hill ahead, and yes, there it was in front of us, large and blue and shiny, this was the sea!'[91] In Grillparzer's idea, Trieste and the *Küstenland* formed an inherent part of Austria's supranational state, but it also presented the door to Italian civilisation, a concept he associated

---

[87] Goethe, *Auf einer Reise nach Süden*, 56, 74, 81, 183. [88] Grillparzer, *Reisetagebücher*, 11.
[89] Ibid., 9 f.
[90] Edward W. Said, *Orientalism. Western Conceptions of the Orient* (London: Penguin, 1995, originally published 1978), 1. In this respect Grillparzer fits the category 'East looks West', as defined by Wendy Bracewell in her work on travel writing: Wendy Bracewell and Alex Drace-Francis (eds.), *Under Eastern Eyes: A Comparative Introduction to East European Travel Writing on Europe* (Budapest: Central European University Press, 2008).
[91] Grillparzer, *Reisetagebücher*, 11.

with the beauty of Venetian art, the majesty of Padua's cathedral, and the glory of the peninsula's ancient universities, but also with diligently cultivated plantations and the angelic beauty of the children he saw everywhere.[92] 'No language of this world is sufficient to describe the beauty of these landscapes. ... Here I wish to live and die!', he exclaims, a phrase reminiscent of Goethe's *Wilhelm Meister*, but an expression of feelings we rarely find in French or British travel accounts of the time.[93] Despite a few more mixed experiences during his journey, most of the negative stereotypes of Italians he recounted in his travel log were not of his own making but reported what Italians had told him about other Italians.[94] Even Grillparzer's misgivings over his operatic experiences do not reflect general prejudice against Italy's musical culture: his description of the church music at the Sistine Chapel reveals great aesthetic appreciation and deepest admiration.[95] The example of Grillparzer – one of Austria's most influential poets at the time – demonstrates that not all criticism of Italy's operatic culture can be reduced to another aspect of orientalising Italian culture.

Disappointment over operatic experiences in Italy suggests that opera continued to be seen, in principle, as a marker of aesthetic sophistication and of civilisation. How notions of *italianità*, and especially of operatic *italianità* were understood and employed in this sense is demonstrated by the many chapters of this volume that take a postcolonial perspective on non-European societies. The idea of opera as civilisation was especially important in Latin America. Although it often is unclear how operas were performed at the time, even for the eighteenth century its presence in the region is undisputed, supporting the idea that opera was seen as instrumental to the continent's appropriation. Within little more than a decade of the Portuguese court's arrival in Brazil, numerous European troupes had travelled to different parts of South America. In the 1820s two regular routes for travelling opera troupes were established in the Western hemisphere, both creating new conditions for cultural exchanges: one passing through Brazil and on to Uruguay, Argentina, Chile, Bolivia and Peru;

---

[92] Ibid., 25.   [93] Ibid., 83.
[94] Ibid., 30. For the inter-Italian dimension of these quarrels see Marta Petrusewicz, *Come il Meridione divenne una Questione: Rappresentazione del Sud prima e dopo il Quarantotto* (Soveria Mannelli: Rubbettino, 1998), which mirrors Said's concept of 'two geographical entities' that 'support and to an extent reflect each other': Said, *Orientalism*, 5. For a critique of how these binaries affect Risorgimento historiography see Axel Körner, 'Per una critica delle gerarchie intellettuali del pensiero politico risorgimentale. L'esempio degli Stati Uniti nell'esperienza italiana della modernità', in Fernanda Gallo (ed.), *Gli hegeliani di Napoli: il Risorgimento e la ricezione di Hegel in Italia* (Naples: Scuola di Pitagora, 2020), 29–59.
[95] Grillparzer, *Reisetagebücher*, 45.

another established between 1825 and 1827, and going back to the arrival of Manuel García's troupe in Mexico, travelling via New York.

As a consequence of these complex itineraries, the system of operatic production also changed, with travelling troupes encountering local traditions, and some of these establishing themselves permanently or for a number of years where money was to be made, a process often accompanied by the rise of music criticism and the increased construction of opera houses. Some members of these travelling troupes later returned home, bringing with them new experiences and challenging local understandings of operatic tradition. Such troupes continued to shape ideas of operatic culture, in Italy as well as in Europe's Eastern periphery. For local audiences it often did not matter that the works they produced had to be adapted to the specific conditions of their theatres or improvised stages, at times to the point of turning them into a distant relation of the original.[96] The nature of these adaptations notwithstanding, they show that theatre always had the potential to cross social boundaries as well as to bridge geographical distance. For instance, in his partly autobiographical novel *Der Pojaz* (*The Bajazzo*, 1893/1905), the Galician-Bukovinian writer Karl Emil Franzos tells us of a waitress who entertained the inhabitants of her native shtetl with stories of a theatre company from Czernowitz that once stayed at her inn. While the rabbi expressed a great deal of concern over possible infiltrations of worldly life in his community, the fact that, for the locals, Shakespeare became 'Scheckspier', and that they were unsure whether or not Schiller was still alive, did not undermine their conviction that even in the deepest provinces of the Habsburg monarchy one could take part in the Empire's cultural life. In some cases of operatic performances, or the production of *Singspiele*, female roles had all of a sudden to be taken on by male singers, or vice versa, or parts of different works were combined to make for a totally new opera. What people saw was still the same repertoire that was staged in Vienna, Budapest or Milan, or so they believed.

While similar processes resulted in the rapid diffusion of opera in South America, it turned out to be more difficult in the North, as demonstrated by Lorenzo da Ponte's attempts at establishing opera in New York, where 'Italian language and literature were . . . about as well-known as Turkish or Chinese'.[97]

---

[96] Jirí Kopecký and Lenka Křupková, *Das Olmützer Stadttheater und seine Oper* (Regensburg: ConBrio, 2017), 99. Barbara Babić, 'Rossini in Krähwinkel? Una parodia del Tancredi viennese', *Bollettino del Centro Rossiniano di Studi* LVI (2016), 9–61.

[97] Lorenzo da Ponte, *Memoirs* (New York: New York Review of Books, 2000), 345. See also Sheila Hodges, *Lorenzo Da Ponte: The Life and Times of Mozart's Librettist* (London: Granada, 1985).

For da Ponte this was less a comment on the difficulties he experienced when arriving from Vienna than a statement confirming that many in America seemed totally deprived of the intellectual and aesthetic benefits of Europe's cultural heritage.[98] While da Ponte played an important role in laying the foundations of opera in the United States, financially most of his projects turned out to be disastrous. In addition to the language barrier, and moral criticism of theatre in a predominantly protestant new country, opera was often perceived as an aristocratic art form that had no place in Republican America.[99] Moreover, as Charlotte Bentley demonstrates in her chapter below, when Italian opera arrived in New Orleans and entered into competition with the local tradition of producing French *grand opéra*, it was associated with notions of Southern-ness rather than civilisation, showing how the semantic content of these concepts always depended on local contexts. Here as well, opera served to construct a notion of Italy abroad that, in Italy, hardly played a role.

When opera started spreading in the New World, this encounter with Italian civilisation was also reflected in works written in and for the Old World. In Joseph Haydn's *Il mondo della luna* (1777), based on a popular play by the Venetian poet Carlo Goldoni, men on the moon became a metaphor for life in the New World. Another example of this genre reflecting the encounter between the Old and the New World was Alessandro Guglielmi's *La quakera spiritosa*, which da Ponte had staged for Joseph II's court theatre in Vienna and which played on gendered and religious stereotypes associated with life in the New World.[100] These works demonstrate how idealised images of American life – still rooted in Enlightenment discourse – were increasingly replaced by accounts of real-life experiences in a country that in the perspective of many of these works lacked the culture that distinguished European life, a world in which opera continued to be seen as a marker of civilisation.

---

[98] Axel Körner, 'Barbarous America', in Axel Körner, Nicola Miller and Adam I. P. Smith, eds., *America Imagined: Explaining the United States in Nineteenth-Century Europe and Latin America* (New York: Palgrave Macmillan, 2012), 125–59.

[99] See Karen E. Ahlquist, *Democracy at the Opera: Music, Theater, and Culture in New York City, 1815–60* (Urbana IL: University of Illinois Press, 1997).

[100] For a discussion of these works see Polzonetti, *Italian Opera in the Age of the American Revolution*. On the popularity of American-themed theatre see also Robert Darnton, *George Washington's False Teeth: An Unconventional Guide to the Eighteenth Century* (New York: Norton, 2003), 119–36. For a broader discussion of Italian images of America see Axel Körner, *America in Italy: The United States in the Political Thought and Imagination of the Italian Risorgimento, 1763–1865* (Princeton, NJ/Oxford: Princeton University Press, 2017).

As mentioned earlier, around the same time as the arrival of Italian opera in the Americas, it spread over large swathes of continental Europe, including its southern and eastern peripheries. In several parts of Central Europe the production of Italian opera dated back even earlier, to the seventeenth century, reflecting the Habsburgs' dynastic relations with families such as the Gonzaga or the Medici.[101] At the time, this new cultural form was understood as a direct reference to the European Renaissance and Italy's humanist tradition, which conceived of opera as the reinvention of Greek classical drama.[102] The first production of an Italian opera in Salzburg is recorded in 1614, followed by Vienna (1626), Prague (1627) and Torgau in Saxony (1627), proving those cities' affinity with Italian culture.[103] Opera's diffusion from the early eighteenth century onwards included further regions north of the Alps, but also the Balkans, which geographically were not far removed from Italian shores and were connected to Italy via the urban centres of the Venetian Republic.[104] In the 1730s, Pietro and Angelo Mignotti produced works of opera in Prague and Brünn/Brno, as well as in Laibach/Ljubljana, later expanding into many other parts of the continent.[105] Over the centuries, Italian opera in Central Europe came to reflect the political ideas that informed the Habsburgs' supranational and cosmopolitan concept of state, which meant that its production counted for much more than the national tradition of one of the monarchy's many nationalities. Aspects of this association with cosmopolitanism marked operatic *italianità* over centuries and across continents, with Italian being perceived as the natural language of music and opera. As Dina Gusejnova has argued, cosmopolitanism – whether operatic or philosophical – offers a sense of certainty during periods of change and conflict, which is why Italian opera becomes an important key to our understanding of the Napoleonic and post-Napoleonic age, an argument brilliantly exposed in Emanuele Senici's

---

[101] Otto G. Schindler, '"Die wälischen comedianten sein ja guet"... Die Anfänge des italienischen Theaters am Habsburgerhof', in Václav Bůžek and Pavel Král (eds.), *Slavnosti a zábavy na dvorech a v rezidenčních městech raného novověku* (České Budějovice: Historický ústav Jihočeské university, 2000), 107–36.

[102] Walter, *Oper*, 197. Mitchell Cohen, *The Politics of Opera: A History from Monteverdi to Mozart* (Princeton, NJ: Princeton University Press, 2017), 6–52.

[103] See John Warrack, *German Opera – From the Beginnings to Wagner* (Cambridge: Cambridge University Press, 2001), 17–33.

[104] For challenges to conventional notions of centre and periphery in European thought see Axel Körner, 'Space and Asymmetric Difference in Historical Perspective: An Introduction', in Tessa Hauswedell, Axel Körner and Ulrich Tiedau (eds.), *Remapping Centre and Periphery: Asymmetrical Encounters in European and Global Context* (London: UCL Press, 2019), 1–13.

[105] Walter, *Oper*, 116.

Music in the Present Tense.[106] At the same time, acknowledging cosmopolitanism's conceptual vagueness and its inability to establish eternal peace is not to dismiss it altogether, but to question its promise of heuristic certainty. Orlando Figes sees operatic culture as foundational to the emergence of a new European identity during an age of nationalism and railways, reaching from the Atlantic shores to Russia and beyond.[107]

Returning once more to Grillparzer's experience of operatic *italianità*, his account shows that even during the early decades of the nineteenth century the concept was a construct that existed more or less independently of the culture a music-loving traveller might encounter in Italy. The operatic productions he saw in Italy reminded the author of the ritualistic gestures he witnessed during the church services at St Peter in Rome or the performance of miracles by the priests of San Gennaro in Naples.[108] To Grillparzer, the productions he saw seemed deprived of the aesthetic truth he associated with the excellent dramatic art he knew from home or elsewhere in Europe, which was at the origin of his admiration for Tasso and Italian classicism, for Shakespeare and Cervantes. Grillparzer had similarly disappointing experiences when comparing Canova's cold sculptures with the allegedly more authentic classicism of the Dane Bertel Thorvaldsen, whose workshop he visited in Rome. For the same reason, Byron chose Thorvaldsen to sit for a portrait head.[109] Had transnationalism led to a development where foreigners had become the better Italians?

De Staël and Ideas of *Italianità* in the Age of Napoleon

Grillparzer's descriptions of Italian landscape shared much with scenes from Germaine de Staël's *Corinne, or Italy*, mentioned above. Few commentators of the early nineteenth century enjoyed greater influence in debates on national character than Germaine de Staël, and her impact on Stendhal, and on his discussion of Rossini, has often been pointed out.[110] If in recent years, Italianists have tended to look to de Staël for evidence of orientalising Italians' allegedly effeminate and indolent character, they underestimate both the contextual dimension of her work and the intellectual weight of her

---

[106] Dina Gusejnova, 'Introduction', in Dina Gusejnova (ed.), *Cosmopolitanism in Conflict: Imperial Encounters from the Seven Years' War to the Cold War* (London: Palgrave, 2018), 1–26. Senici, *Music in the Present Tense*, 211 ff.

[107] Orlando Figes, *The Europeans: Three Lives and the Making of a Cosmopolitan Culture* (London: Allen Lane, 2019). On the immense popularity of Italian opera in 1840s Russia see ibid., 9, 78.

[108] Grillparzer, *Reisetagebücher*, 48 ff.   [109] Ibid., 37. Quennell, *Byron*, 68.

[110] Senici, *Music in the Present Tense*, 134.

political thought.[111] Further to her aim of writing a novel, de Staël also went to Italy with the aim of studying the legacies of political institutions that contrasted with France's centralised tradition of state; the latter had been introduced in Italy by Napoleon, as part of what she perceived as the Emperor's antiliberal dictatorship.[112] Read as speech acts in the drama of international relations during the Napoleonic Wars, the intention behind *De l'Allemagne* and *Corinne* was only partially to speak about Germany and Italy, with de Staël's main challenge being directed at French and British politics, as well as at respective societal conventions in both countries, and how they affected Europe as a whole.[113] Her open rejection of Italy's fossilised classicism was in fact intended as a reference to the neoclassical aesthetics of Imperial France, and of what Napoleon made of Rome's artistic heritage, which she contrasts with Italians' true but suppressed aesthetic potential. This complex constellation explains why no one objected more violently to *Corinne* than the French Emperor, who even during his exile was still irritated that she had not used her novel to praise the supposedly revitalising impact of his campaign on Italians: 'Not a word about me', he howled.[114]

[111] Roberto M. Dainotto, *Europe (in Theory)* (Durham and London: Duke University Press, 2007), 134 f. More cautious about a Saidian reading is Silvana Patriarca, 'Indolence and Regeneration: Tropes and Tensions of Risorgimento Patriotism', *American Historical Review* 110 (2005), 380–408 (390). For a discussion on how stereotypes were internalised see Patriarca, *Italian Vices*. The problem with some recent accounts of de Staël's Italian gazes is their narrow concentration on *Corinne's* books 6 and 7, which deal with Italian customs and literature. However, even in these sections the 'real' Italy is represented by the heroine Corinne, who distances herself from the superficiality of the social institutions around her. For a more balanced reading see Martin Thom, *Republics, Nations and Tribes* (London: Verso, 1995). For a musicological perspective looking at intertextual references see Senici, *Music in the Present Tense*, 133 ff. Though not directly based on a reading of de Staël, Vellutini shows how emphasis on Italian creativity risks 'underpinning conceptual polarities': Vellutini, 'Interpreting the Italian Voice', 52. Assessment of de Staël's impact on discussions of Italian national character needs to take account of her role in Italy's encounter with Schiller, as well as of her discovery of Filangieri and Vico, which left a major impact on Constant and in turn on American political thought: Körner, *America in Italy*, 35, 143 f. See also Fernanda Gallo, "A Transnational Perspective on Constant's *Commentaire sur l'ouvrage de Filangieri* and the Risorgimento (1826–1860)", *Schweizerisches Jahrbuch für Wirtschafts- und Sozialgeschichte* 34 (2020), 173–188.

[112] For this tradition of the grand tour see especially Attilio Brilli, *Reisen in Italien: Die Kulturgeschichte der klassischen Italienreise vom 16. bis zum 19. Jahrhundert* (Cologne: Dumont, 1989), 31 ff. Related reflections on Italy's political institutions often took an orientalising perspective, with rather different emphasis to that of de Staël. See for instance Ferdinand Gregorovius, *Wanderjahre in Italien* [1856–1877] (Dresden: Wolfgang Jess Verlag, 1954), especially the sections on Naples.

[113] Glenda Sluga, 'Madame de Staël and the Transformation of European Politics, 1812–1817', *The International History Review* 37/1 (2015), 142–66. Also Brian E. Vick, *The Congress of Vienna: Power and Politics after Napoleon* (Cambridge, MA: Harvard University Press, 2014), ch. 3.

[114] Napoléon Bonaparte, quoted in Angelica Goodden, *Madame de Staël: The Dangerous Exile* (Oxford: Oxford University Press, 2008), 173.

De Staël's keen interest in the connection between collective passions and aesthetics generates a transnational perspective on notions of *italianità* that is directly relevant to the methodological framework behind our book. Ideas for *Corinne, or Italy* in fact predated her Italian journey, going back to her stay in Weimar, in 1804, where most of her hosts were closely familiar with Italian arts.[115] It serves as another example of the complex transnational dimensions influencing constructions of *italianità*. The idealised concept of German romanticism de Staël explored during those months in Weimar, subsequently recorded in *De l'Allemagne*, is set against the aesthetic conventions of Imperial France, but it also responds directly to Europe's romance of Italy that had developed out of the cultural practice of the Grand Tour. While some contemporaries denied that de Staël had taste in the visual arts,[116] she regularly entertained her acquaintances at the piano and impressed them with the declamation of classical drama.[117] Although opera did not play a major role during her conversations in Weimar, it allegedly was an opera she saw there – the *Singspiel Die Saalnixe* by Ferdinand Kauer – that made her decide to explore the political, social and aesthetic interdependencies informing Italians' national character.[118] Kauer's opera tells the story of a nymph abandoned by her knightly lover for a mortal, a plot best known in its later version of Antonín Dvořák's *Rusalka*. In her novel, de Staël's character Corinne takes the role of the nymph, but also carries clear features of the author's own personality: a strong and independent character of true sentiments, suppressed by foreign domination.[119] In de Staël's account, foreign intrusion is not so much a matter of physical power but of spiritual hegemony exercised through the application of cultural and social norms that de Staël associates with France's domination of Europe, but also with Britain's attempts at building an informal empire in the Mediterranean. Her analysis, therefore, needs to be read as part of her work as a political thinker, and as one of the most eloquent

---

[115] For a direct witness of her encounters in Weimar see Karl August Böttiger, *Literarische Zustände und Zeitgenossen: Begegnungen und Gespräche im klassischen Weimar* (Berlin: Aufbau, 1998), 347–96.

[116] Goodden, *Madame de Staël*, 155 f.

[117] Ibid., 351, 355 ff, 368. Renee Winegarten, *Germaine de Staël and Benjamin Constant: A Dual Biography* (New Haven, CT: Yale University Press, 2008), 14 f.

[118] Goodden, *Madame de Staël*, 156. Also known as *Das Donauweibchen*. Landesarchiv Thüringen, Theaterzettel: https://staatsarchive.thulb.uni-jena.de/rsc/viewer/ThHStAW_derivate_00047208/002194.tif, last accessed 21 December 2020.

[119] Winegarten, *Germaine de Staël and Benjamin Constant*, 280. Melanie Unseld does not refer to Kauer's work, but provides a gendered reading of the operatic nymph that is relevant to our understanding of de Staël's character: *'Man töte dieses Weib'. Weiblichkeit und Tod in der Musik der Jahrhundertwende* (Stuttgart: Metzler, 2001), 113 ff.

critics of Napoleon's imperial system. It therefore cannot be reduced to the orientalising prejudice against the allegedly effeminate Italian character that most recent commentators have extracted from her novel.

For de Staël, aesthetic sensitivity directly reflects social and cultural attitudes. In *Corinne* she juxtaposes Italy's creative abilities with the restrictive conventions commanding social relations in Northern Europe, now imposed on the peninsula by France, but also by Britain. While her hatred for Napoleon is well known, and reflected in the novel's depiction of a society under siege through its focus on Corinne's lover Oswald, Italy is also set against England, a country de Staël otherwise admired for its political institutions. England is depicted as puritanical, lifeless and repressive of individuality, and as hostile to women in particular. In this way, England serves de Staël as a canvas to develop her idea of female freedom, which she invented as a character trait of Italy, contrasting it with the paternalistic structures of English aristocratic society, as well as with the patriarchal submission she associated with Napoleonic France.[120]

De Staël's transnational approach to the analysis of collective behaviour has largely been overlooked by critics of her Italian gazes. While she considered individuals to be emotionally too different for their behaviour to be predicted, she believed in recurrent patterns of collective behaviour.[121] As she explained in *De l'Allemagne* (1810), 'national character has its influence on the literature; the literature and the philosophy on the religion; and the whole taken together can only make each distinct part properly intelligible'.[122] At the same time, de Staël was known for her sensitive approach when pursuing her experiments on collective emotions, carefully amalgamating foreign cultures into her own realm of transnational experiences and cosmopolitan ideals. In this, her attitude could not be more different from that of Byron, who spent most of his time in Italy quarrelling with the Shelleys and other expats, confirming to himself stereotypes of Italians that had been circulating among the British upper classes for generations.[123] As the Weimar-based antiquarian and literary

---

[120] Goodden, *Madame de Staël*, 162. This reading of de Staël differs considerably from that of Dainotto, who analyses her works as statements about Germany, the South and Italy rather than seeing them as ways of talking about France and Britain: Dainotto, *Europe (in Theory)*, 143 f.

[121] Biancamaria Fontana, *Germaine de Staël: A Political Portrait* (Princeton, NJ: Princeton University Press, 2016), 137 f. Julia Schmidt-Funke, "Mme de Staël und der 'Correspondent de l'Europe'. Staël-Rezeption und europäischer Kulturtransfer bei Karl August Böttiger", in Gerhard R. Kaiser / Olaf Müller (eds.), Germaine de Staël und ihr erstes deutsches Publikum. Literaturpolitik und Kulturtransfer um 1800. (Heidelberg: Universitätsverlag Winter, 2008), 241–260.

[122] Baronesse Staël-Holstein, *Germany* (trans. from the French in three volumes) (London: John Murray, 1813).

[123] Quennell, *Byron, passim*.

critique Karl August Böttiger reports, de Staël 'does not just ask, she also listens carefully; she not only hears her own voice but is serious about internalising other opinions and judgments. ... In doing so she becomes a midwife of foreign ideas, which she then knows to sense and to develop in all their complexity.'[124] Reflecting de Staël's earlier work on the influence of passions on individual and collective happiness, the basis of her art was, in Böttiger's words, the 'abandon de soi même', which allowed her to amalgamate a multitude of different ideas and cultures into new forms.[125] Spiritual renewal was what she expected from these transnational exchanges.[126]

The Italy she invents in *Corinne* is characterised by exactly such patterns. She describes Italy, and especially its port cities, as a melting pot of different peoples and cultures, where 'spirit and imagination find pleasure in the differences that characterise the nations'; at the same time, 'the art of civilisation will always tend to assimilate humankind'.[127] Nationality, in de Staël's account, therefore does not describe fixed categories, but malleable entities where culture and the arts – understood as civilisation – play a central role in shaping social and political institutions. The outcome of her exploration of national character, therefore, is not an exercise in national stereotyping but a transnational examination of collective identities that uses one national character to speak about another. As a matter of fact, the purpose of *Corinne, or Italy* is as much to talk about the British (Oswald) and the French (Count d'Erfeuil) as to talk about Italians (Corinne, who partly stands for herself). When de Staël describes the social and cultural conventions of Corinne's Italy, she points her finger at the countries that hold Italy at bay to impose their own values: in France

---

[124] Böttiger, *Literarische Zustände*, 350. In this sense Constant's character portraits of his friend are also revealing: Benjamin Constant, 'De Madame de Staël', in *Œuvres*, ed. Alfred Roulin (Paris: Gallimard, 1957), 825–52. See also Winegarten, *Germaine de Staël and Benjamin Constant*, 11, 288 f. On Böttiger see Julia A. Schmidt-Funke, *Karl August Böttiger (1760–1835). Weltmann und Gelehrter.* (Heidelberg: Universitätsverlag Winter, 2006).

[125] Böttiger, *Literarische Zustände*, 350. On her work on individual and national passions see Fontana, *Germaine de Staël*, 132–57. As de Stael said herself, as a consequence of her experience of exile and travel, she 'became European', a citizen of a Europe that Napoleon's dictatorship had almost suffocated: quoted in Goodden, *Madame de Staël*, 1. See also Madame de Staël, *Dix années d'exil* (critical edition), ed. Simone Balayé and Mariella Vianello Bonifacio (Paris: Fayard, 1996), 237, 247.

[126] 'It is thus that we are indebted for Racine to the Greeks, and to Shakespeare for many of the tragedies of Voltaire. The sterility with which our [French] literature is threatened may make it be believed that the French spirit itself has need of being renewed by a more vigorous sap; and since the elegance of society will always preserve us from certain facts, it is of the utmost importance to us, to find again the source of superior beauties.' Staël-Holstein, *Germany*, 7 f. With reference to music see ibid., 23 ff.

[127] De Staël, *Corinne*, 12.

'society is everything' and in London 'political interests absorb almost all others', she concludes in Book 1 of *Corinne*.[128] In contrast to the French and the English, Italians retain their true character through 'the arts'. In this, unfortunately, they 'are far more remarkable for what they have been and for what they could be, than for what they are now'.[129] These circumstances notwithstanding, the Italians national character is, for de Staël, more profound than the version of it that is portrayed in the present.

Stendhal's subsequent depictions of Italy lack the philosophical grounding of de Staël's studies, but distinguish in similar ways between the Italy that presents itself to the author and the idealised image he explores in defining different aesthetic and social categories. According to Dominique Fernandez, Stendhal's image of Italian attitudes reveals 'a profound contradiction between the Italy that thinks and exists, and the Italy Stendhal wanted her to be'.[130] While Stendhal shares with de Staël the purpose of contrasting Italian with French social attitudes, the principal interest behind his work on opera is to establish the complex relationship between Rossini's style and his musical debt to Mozart and Haydn,[131] understood as contrasting forms of musical practice: 'In the northern countries, of twenty pretty girls who are taught music, nineteen study the piano. Only one is shown how to sing whereas the other nineteen end up appreciating beauty solely in what is difficult. In Italy, the entire world seeks to achieve musical beauty through the voice.'[132] Here he plays on a theme de Staël had developed in almost exactly the same words: 'Instrumental music is as generally cultivated throughout Germany as vocal music in Italy. Nature has done more in this respect, as in many others, for Italy, than for Germany; for instrumental music labour is necessary, while a southern sky is enough to create a beautiful voice.'[133] It is these images that impacted nineteenth-century notions of operatic *italianità*.

With two English translations in the first year of its publication,[134] de Staël's *Corinne* became a European bestseller. While opera scholarship often relies heavily on the testimony of male agents – documents generated by

---

[128] Ibid., 17.   [129] Ibid., 18.
[130] Dominique Fernandez, 'Préface', in Stendhal [Marie-Henri Beyle], *Chroniques italiennes* (Paris: Gallimard, 1973), 7–18, 10.
[131] Arnold Jacobshagen, 'Rossini and His German Critics: A Re-evaluation', in Narici, Sala, Senici and Walton (eds.), *Gioachino Rossini 1868–2018*, 381–411 (383 f.). See also Arnold Jacobshagen's chapter below (Chapter 8).
[132] Stendhal [Marie-Henri Beyle], *Vie de Rossini* (Paris: Gallimard, 1992), 98 f. On the European image of Italian singing see also Carolin Krahn's chapter below (Chapter 3). Forms of musical sociability as they developed during the Age of Enlightenment are directly relevant to different notions of musical practice: see Sutcliffe, *Instrumental Music in an Age of Sociability*, passim.
[133] Staël-Holstein, *Germany*, 25.   [134] Goodden, *Madame de Staël*, 175.

impresarios, and music criticism in newspapers and musical periodicals – de Staël's prominent role in the discussions of collective passions and aesthetics also helps to diversify our perspective on the connection between music and national character. Not least because of the close association between music, romance and sexuality in early-nineteenth-century debates on opera, it would be misleading not to take gender, sexuality and interpersonal affection into account when analysing discourse on that musical form. As Susan Rutherford has argued, 'the relationship between love and music was nowhere more evident than in opera', and one might want to add 'in Italian opera'.[135] Her argument that 'it was passion that engendered music as much as the music itself expressed passion' sums up a debate that leads us from Rousseau's above-mentioned contributions to the Querelle des Bouffons all the way to Stendhal's engagement with de Staël's observations on Italian, French, English and German character.

Further complicating the analysis and deconstruction of notions of *italianità*, Rutherford also points out that especially 'Verdi appeared less conscious or less persuaded – of the supposed indispensability of amorous passion to opera'.[136] For instance, neither *Nabucco* nor *Macbeth* included romantic elements, and only his domestic dramas of the 1850s, especially *La traviata*, began to focus more closely on romantic sentiment.[137] While these later works certainly count as Italian treatments of the theme of love and sexuality, geographically and musically these operas also breathe a good deal of foreign air and therefore further confuse our ideas of operatic *italianità*.[138]

Globalising Italian Opera

The chapters following this introduction are arranged in roughly chronological order, taking readers on a journey that had started in Italy, but then moved from Europe to the Americas and on to South East and East Asia, with several return journeys in between, not dissimilar to the itineraries of the opera companies that are at the centre of our narrative.

Fernando Berçot's chapter investigates the life of an Italian opera company in Rio de Janeiro after the arrival, as a consequence of the Napoleonic Wars, of the Portuguese court in Brazil. During the 1820s the local press

---

[135] Rutherford, *Verdi, Opera, Women*, 93.   [136] Ibid., 93.   [137] Ibid., 111 ff.
[138] For spatial orientations in Verdi see the following studies of *La traviata* and *Un ballo in maschera*: Emilio Sala, *The Sounds of Paris in Verdi's La Traviata* (Cambridge: Cambridge University Press, 2008). Körner, *America in Italy*, 163–98.

assumed a central role in negotiating the relationship between these artists and their new audiences, revealing a growing public interest in opera and its protagonists that at the same time was reflective of shifting notions of national and social identities. Carolin Krahn examines ideas of Italian national character in Nina d'Aubigny von Engelbrunner's influential pedagogical work *Briefe an Natalie über den Gesang,* which was first published in Leipzig in 1803 and marked transnational debates on Italian vocal style for several decades. Francesco Milella's chapter looks at the role of Italian opera in negotiating Mexico's postcolonial identity. As a case study, he examines the stay of the famous Spanish tenor and composer Manuel García in Mexico City during the years 1827–9. Claudio Vellutini argues for the role of Italian opera in asserting the supranational identity of the Habsburg monarchy during the reign of Emperor Ferdinand I, when impresario Bartolomeo Merelli was able to consolidate Gaetano Donizetti's position in Vienna. Not German *Singspiel*, but Italian opera was at the core of the Habsburg's cultural policies during the years leading up to the revolutions of 1848.

Charlotte Bentley's chapter brings us back across the Atlantic to investigate the changing fortunes of Italian opera in the Americas. Her chapter looks at the competition between French and Italian opera in New Orleans during the years 1837–43, and the role of the city's operatic connections with Cuba, revealing new and different notions of Southern-ness. José Manuel Izquierdo König analyses the experiences of Italian opera singers in Chile, Peru, Bolivia and Ecuador in the 1840s, a time when opera was central to the local construction of ideas about liberalism, Europeanism, cosmopolitanism, and the all-encompassing notion of 'civilisation'.

With Arnold Jacobshagen's chapter our volume moves into the second half of the nineteenth century. He reads obituaries of Gioachino Rossini in the French, English and German language press as transnational narratives of Italian opera, reflecting the tremendous international media response generated by the composer's death, but also the continuing role of music theatre in articulating notions of transnational and national identity. The decades between Rossini's death and the outbreak of World War I saw opera in Italy absorb multiple literary and musical influences from beyond the Alps, challenging the essence of what audiences and critics believed Italian opera was all about. Andrew Holden's chapter examines this process, with special focus on how references to religious life in opera reflected changing notions of *italianità* during a time when Italian opera was increasingly influenced by international operatic forms, including *grand opéra* and Wagnerism. Similar experiences of cultural exchanges and the transformation of the operatic repertoire determined Teresa Carreño's 1887 attempt to launch an Italian opera company in Caracas, which ended in dismal failure. Ditlev Rindom's chapter uses this example to examine the problematic status of Italian opera's 'civilising' ambitions for local Venezuelan elites.

Rashna Darius Nicholson moves our transnational perspectives on operatic *italianità* to colonial Bombay and South East Asia, where from the mid-nineteenth-century residents were exposed to Italian opera, intermixed with different forms of European and American music theatre, and with a whole range of local musical traditions, including African elements. Companies involved in these entertainments travelled as far as China, Japan and Australia. The chapter then traces Parsi theatre's role in the creation of a modern South Asian 'aural culture' through the indigenisation of Italian opera. An Indian brand of opera that combined European melodies with Hindustani music became a staple not only of the theatre but also of the cinematic medium that followed. In a study based on the German reception of Alberto Franchetti's *Germania* and Ruggero Leoncavallo's *Der Roland von Berlin*, Richard Erkens raises questions about the difficult relationships between operatic style, exoticism and national identity. Franchetti and Leoncavallo, although heavily influenced by Wagnerism, employed the language of operatic *italianità* to represent German national and dynastic myths on stage. Despite the popularity of Italian opera in Germany, both works were met with remarkable levels of hostility, including direct criticism of the German Emperor and his operatic policies. Rosie McMahon investigates ideas of operatic *italianità* at the Teatro Amazonas during the belle époque and probes the extent to which the opera house became a means of engaging in a 'global fantasy of civilisation'. The final chapter, by Michael Facius, examines the search for operatic *italianità* in early-twentieth-century Japan. During the two decades between the first Japanese staging of Gluck's *Orpheus* in 1903 and the end of the Asakusa opera in the great fire of 1923, musical theatre in Japan saw a rapid process of adoption and transformation of operatic forms. Despite the well-known role of Italian choreographer Giovanni Vittorio Rosi in producing Western opera at the Imperial Theatre in Tokyo, the association between opera and Italy – so prominent in other parts of the world – never quite took hold in Japan. The chapter thus interrogates the limited appeal of *italianità* in the history of transnational operatic encounters, rooted in the difficulties of transplanting a composite cultural form to foreign settings.

Finally, Benjamin Walton's epilogue to this volume provides a critical reflection on the wider outcomes of our project for operatic *italianità* in a global and transnational context.

2 | Giving Singers a Voice

The Italian Opera Company and the Press in Rio de Janeiro, 1820–1831

FERNANDO SANTOS BERÇOT

Research on Italian opera in South America often emphasises the role of the small itinerant troupes that during the nineteenth century crossed the Atlantic with limited repertoires, basic sets and costumes, moving from city to city as if these journeys were an extension of the tours they previously undertook in Europe. Examining these small companies, their formation and the conditions behind their triumphs and failures, is essential to understanding the dynamics of the genre's dissemination in the subcontinent. They had a clear place in the local imaginary associated with operatic *italianità*. However, travelling artists were not the only exponents of opera in the region, and a fixed company of Italian singers was already active in Rio de Janeiro in the first decades of the nineteenth century. Benefitting from the arrival of a European royal court in 1808, representing a unique situation in the Americas, Rio de Janeiro stood out as a main centre of operatic life in the southern and western hemispheres, a situation which lasted at least until 1831.

The role of opera in Rio de Janeiro's cultural life increased further after the inauguration of a new opera house, the Theatro São João, in 1813 (see Figure 2.1).[1] Working with a group of business partners, the owner Fernando José de Almeida was responsible for the theatre's administration, but the house remained closely connected to the state, receiving the title of Theatro Real and enjoying special privileges such as a tax exemption and the right to promote lottery draws in order to raise funds. The city soon revealed itself as an attractive destination for foreign singers and dancers. As a result, two companies were created: an Italian opera company and a French ballet troupe. Both slowly grew in size and prominence, especially after the declaration of independence from Portugal in 1822, when the theatre changed its name to Theatro Imperial. These two companies gradually transformed the theatre into one of the most prominent houses dedicated to the two genres anywhere outside Europe. Italian opera and French-style ballet were always

---

[1] About operatic activities in eighteenth-century Brazil, see Rogério Budasz, *Opera in the Tropics: Music and Theater in Early Modern Brazil* (New York: Oxford University Press, 2019).

Figure 2.1 'Acceptation provisoire de la constitution de Lisbonne à Rio de Janeiro, en 1821', from Jean-Baptiste Debret, *Voyage pittoresque et historique au Brésil, ou Séjour d'un artiste français au Brésil, depuis 1816 jusqu'en 1831 inclusivement, epoques de l'avènement et de l'abdication de S. M. D. Pedro 1er, fondateur de l'Empire brésilien. Dédié à l'Académie des Beaux-Arts de l'Institut de France* (Paris: Firmin Didot Frères, 1839), vol. III, after 220. Prince Pedro, the future Emperor, takes his oath to the Portuguese Constitution from the terrace of the Real Theatro São João, before the crowd seen in the centre. New York Public Library

presented together, resulting in a profitable coexistence for both companies. The practice of inserting dances between the acts of an opera, or an entire ballet after the Italian performance, soon became standard in Rio de Janeiro: no evening was considered complete without the combined participation of both companies.[2] The coronation of Pedro I, for example, in December 1822, was marked by the staging of Rossini's *Elisabetta, regina d'Inghilterra*, combined with a performance of two *pas de deux*.[3]

At that time, the foreign artists still shared the stage with a company of actors who presented plays in Portuguese, which completed the range of spectacles intended to fill the season. It started after Easter Sunday and ended at Carnival. During Lent, performances were permitted under exceptional circumstances only, for instance to stage a religious drama on

[2] On the practice of combining opera and ballet in Italian theatres, see John Rosselli, *The Opera Industry in Italy from Cimarosa to Verdi: The Role of the Impresario* (Cambridge: Cambridge University Press, 1984), 3 f. On the resulting conflicts, see Axel Körner, *Politics of Culture in Liberal Italy: From Unification to Fascism* (New York: Routledge, 2009), 47–65.

[3] 'Rio de Janeiro', *O Espelho*, Rio de Janeiro, 6 December 1822, 2.

topics taken from the Bible or the lives of saints. One of those performances, organised to celebrate the proclamation of the Imperial Constitution, culminated in the accidental fire that consumed the Theatro São João during the night of 25 March 1824.[4] Over the following months, a small theatre was erected on the same grounds, serving as a provisional stage until the completion of the reconstruction works and underlining the indispensable role regular theatre performances had acquired within Imperial politics. The opening of the new opera house, now renamed Imperial Theatro São Pedro de Alcântara, took place in 1826, a crucial year for the future of opera and ballet in Rio de Janeiro.

Despite its efforts to stage complete operas and to build up its repertoire, the 'Italian Company', as it was by now officially known, was still very small during the first years after Independence; and the difficulty of finding singers explains why some of its soloists were still so young. The soprano Carlotta Anselmi, for example, arrived in the city as a child with her widowed mother, and sang regularly at the São João from the age of fourteen.[5] Her colleague Giustina Piacentini was not much older. Despite starting her career as *seconda donna*, she often had to take roles that almost certainly demanded a more mature voice, including Isabella in *L'italiana in Algeri* and Rosina in *Il barbiere di Siviglia*.[6] Among the men, the situation was slightly different, as some of the pioneers of the troupe had had previous careers in Europe. An accomplished castrato from Bergamo, Giovanni Francesco Fasciotti, was the company's leading singer. After his arrival in 1816, Fasciotti became a prominent soloist at the Rio de Janeiro Cathedral, known as Capela Real, where a regular ensemble of singers and players took part in the religious services after the transfer of the Portuguese Royal Court.[7] The theatre offered him the opportunity to demonstrate his skill in some of the most virtuosic contralto parts of that era, including the protagonist of Rossini's *Tancredi*. His role as the leader of the Italian Company, acting in tandem with the owner Fernando José de

---

[4] 'Incendio do Theatro de S. João', *A estrela brasileira*, Rio de Janeiro, 31 March 1824, 267.

[5] Arquivo Nacional (Brazil), Polícia da Corte, códice 370, v. 2, fl. 160. Carlotta was nine years old at the time of her arrival in Brazil in February 1820. After a period in Buenos Aires, she appeared as a soloist in the provisional theatre between 1824 and 1825, and took part in the performance of Rossini's *Tancredi* on the birthday of Empress Leopoldina, in January 1826. She and her mother, the ballerina Giulietta Anselmi, left the city in April 1826. Arquivo Nacional (Brazil), Polícia da Corte, códice 423, v. 3, fl. 168.

[6] Daughter of bass Fabrizio Piacentini, Giustina was registered as eighteen years old on the family's arrival in May 1820. Arquivo Nacional (Brazil). Polícia da Corte. Códice 370, v. 2, fl. 168v. Her sisters Carolina and Elisa were also employed by the theatre.

[7] About sacred music in Rio de Janeiro in the early nineteenth century, see André Cardoso, *A música na Corte de D. João VI* (São Paulo: Martins, 2008).

Almeida, is largely attested by references in newspapers. Also admired as Arsace in Rossini's *Aureliano in Palmira*, among other roles, Fasciotti remained an active singer at the cathedral services throughout the 1830s and died in Rio de Janeiro in October 1840.[8] Two other soloists who had been singing at the Capela Real since before Independence, the basses Nicola Majoranini and Salvatore Salvatori, also became leading members of the new opera troupe.

In the early days of the Empire, the Court press wrote very little about the city's opera performances. Music criticism had not yet found its place in newspapers, and only gala performances on special occasions garnered real attention. The authors of those articles usually limited themselves to descriptions of the ceremonial and external aspects of the festivities, avoiding further references to the works staged or the quality of performances. The calendar of such celebrations included the birthdays of the Emperor and the Empress, the name day of Pedro I, and the Anniversary of the Coronation. These occasions required exquisite stage decorations and abundant lighting, but higher ticket prices and the crowds filling the theatre were usually sufficient to recover the extra expense. For instance, when in early 1823 the São João's financial balance showed a higher deficit, the profit made on the birthday of Empress Leopoldina was enough, if not to revert the shortfall, then at least to mitigate the company's losses.[9]

At the time, the works of Gioachino Rossini dominated the stage. *Il barbiere di Siviglia*, *L'italiana in Algeri*, *Aureliano in Palmira* and other titles formed the core of the repertoire in Rio de Janeiro. The bills also announced works by other composers like Pietro Generali and Vincenzo Pucitta, and even performances of operas by Gaetano Donizetti and Saverio Mercadante, indicating a close relationship between the Imperial Theatro and European opera houses, mainly the São Carlos in Lisbon. Still very small until 1826, that year the Italian troupe incorporated many new members arriving from Europe. We know that Francisco Xavier Mazza, a merchant who served as Portuguese consul at Le Havre, acted as intermediary in taking the new singers under contract. Apparently, a French courier was directly responsible for choosing and engaging the soloists in Italy, a task that had to be carried out during the Carnival season.[10] Thanks to the newcomers, the São Pedro de Alcântara was able to offer a more promising opera season, and the press now started to show a regular

---

[8] 'Annuncios', *Jornal do Commercio*, Rio de Janeiro, 13 October 1840, 4.
[9] 'Declaraçoens', *Diario do Rio de Janeiro*, Rio de Janeiro, 28 January 1823, 81.
[10] 'La lettre suivante ...', *L'Écho de l'Amérique du Sud*, Rio de Janeiro, 2 January 1828, 1–2. The courier is named Téxier.

interest in the theatre, including frequent columns of criticism. Published three times per week, *O Spectador Brasileiro* was the first vehicle of such articles, which were usually printed on the paper's last page. Responsible for the publication was the French printer Pierre Plancher. His shop at the famous Rua do Ouvidor sold books, especially by French authors, pamphlets, calendars and librettos, but also theatre tickets and even medicines from Europe. The paper's first comments on local opera performances were short notes intended to describe the main qualities or imperfections of the recently arrived artists. Their tone was rarely enthusiastic. Writing in September 1826 about a performance of Rossini's *Il barbiere di Siviglia*, the editor opined:

Maria Thereza Fasciotti, just recovered from a serious discomfort she suffered, seemed weak enough to be judged in a role [Rosina] she so often had performed to the listener's complete satisfaction. We will say nothing about the Count of Almaviva, because since there was some noise in the room, we could not judge his talents, but his pretended drunkenness was too much. Figaro sang in a mediocre way, but we expect him to do better when he owns the part; the rest was executed with indifference.[11]

A double focus was discernible in these first critical remarks: passing judgement on singers and correcting what was perceived as their vices went along with admonitions against a tumultuous audience whose bad behaviour was a problem, as the spectacle risked deteriorating into disorder and immorality, thus reversing its intended civilising function. Pointing to the disturbing fractures between the supposedly riotous stalls and the ideals of an educated audience became an important purpose of the emerging genre of music criticism, all intended to create an audience formed, if not of true connoisseurs, then at least of individuals capable of understanding the basics of what they saw and heard on stage.

One of Plancher's main achievements was the publication of periodicals in French. The first was *L'Indépendant*, a short-lived gazette whose first number dated from April 1827, and included long columns about the theatre and its backstage intrigues. Its successor, *L'Écho de l'Amérique du Sud*, was produced under a different editor, but also included a regular column on the last page devoted to theatrical news and reviews. Published in Portuguese by another printer was the *Gazeta do Brasil*, whose editors also favoured articles about opera and ballet. They were sometimes presented in the form of a supplement to the regular editions. Some readers

---

[11] 'Imperial Theatro', *O Spectador brasileiro*, Rio de Janeiro, 11 September 1826, 4.

sent in letters with their own reviews, to be published under pseudonyms, and often presented controversial views about artists and the theatre.

Why did Italian singers, who could have pursued a career in Europe, feel attracted to Rio de Janeiro? The presence of the Court and the existence of a great theatre, managed by an impresario closely connected to the Emperor, was certainly an important reason for singers to come and stay. Moreover, the great number of foreigners in the Brazilian capital meant that these musicians performed for an audience that was already familiar with opera. No less important, the payment of fixed salaries, agreed in contracts that they had signed even before their departure from Europe, provided the kind of financial safety that attracted at least some of the more audacious artists in the Old World. Nevertheless, in 1825, the company counted no more than six soloists and six choristers, who all together received 800,000 réis per month.[12] Although this was unevenly distributed among the singers, the average salary could not be considered low, as it corresponded to the cost of eleven single tickets for the theatre's most expensive box.[13] During the season of 1827–8, perhaps the most successful of that decade, the Italian Company of the Imperial Theatro consisted of fifteen soloists (see Table 2.1). This was a modest but not negligible contingent, although the troupe's vocal range was not well distributed, with a clear predominance of sopranos and basses, and just two tenors. This situation demanded constant adaptations and the cutting of entire roles, but did not prevent the staging of complete operas in their original language.

For a small company, last-minute substitutions were difficult to arrange, and cancellations were common, even if the administration usually took precautions to avoid greater damage to its programme. We know that the contracts signed by the soloists imposed very strict working conditions, and sometimes these agreements were distributed to patrons as proof that performances on the dates of their subscriptions would not be cancelled. One of the clauses, for example, prohibited artists from crossing the sea at Guanabara Bay on performance days, a rule violated in August 1828 by two

[12] 'Artigos não officiaes', *Diario Fluminense*, Rio de Janeiro, 22 November 1824, 504.
[13] It seems reasonable to assume that the migration of opera singers to the New World also took place as a result of internal factors in the Italian peninsula. John Rosselli suggested that the small comic opera troupes that usually toured minor cities became less attractive to audiences who were now acquainted with Rossinian *opere serie* and their higher vocal requirements. See John Rosselli, 'The Opera Business and the Italian Immigrant Community in Latin America 1820–1930: The Example of Buenos Aires', *Past & Present*, 127 (May 1990), 155–82. In fact, the group of soloists engaged by the Imperial Theatro in 1826 seems to have been recruited from singers who had difficulties finding work in Italian theatres.

Table 2.1 Members of the Italian Company of the Imperial Theatro São Pedro de Alcântara (1827–1828)

Sopranos	Contraltos	Tenors	Baritones/Basses
- Maria Teresa Fasciotti	- Giovanni Francesco Fasciotti (castrato)	- Vittorio Isotta	- Fabrizio Piacentini
- Maria Zanetti		- Angelo Marciali	- Nicola Majoranini
- Elisa Barbieri	- Margherita Caravaglia		- Salvatore Salvatori
- Giustina Piacentini			- Gioachino Bettali
- Elisa Piacentini			- Giovanni Crespi
- Maria Tani			

soloists who, due to a sudden storm, were unable to arrive on time for Rossini's *Il barbiere di Siviglia*. Despite protests in the audience, the evening went ahead without the central roles of Figaro and Bartolo. A few days later, the singers were forced to apologise to the audience with a note published in the press.[14] Improvised solutions to the shortage of soloists included the casting of singers for roles that were unsuitable for their voices. Announced in the role of Duca Bertrando, the principal male part in Rossini's *L'inganno felice*, the recently arrived Angelo Marciali was made to explain in a notice to the local press that as *comprimario* the task of his assigned role went beyond his strength, asking to be thought of 'as a second tenor, since it was not pride that drove him to sing this role, but the needs of the company, to which all actors must concur, even with sacrifice'.[15] Moreover, the critic of *L'Écho de l'Amérique du Sud* deplored the fact that Salvatore Salvatori, described as a *basso cantante*, was the only available singer for the title role in Rossini's *Aureliano in Palmira*, and sang also Erneville in Pietro Generali's *Adelina*, two roles originally set for tenor.[16]

Despite the company's collective artistic and economic ambition, rivalry occasionally arose between its members, in which the press, either in the name of individual singers or of the audience, took position. For instance, in 1821 a group of singers criticised the social attitudes of a colleague, the bass Fabrizio Piacentini, publishing their complaint in a letter to a local daily.[17] In 1827, the

---

[14] 'Ao Respeitaval Publico', *Jornal do Commercio*, Rio de Janeiro, 12 August 1828, 4.
[15] 'Imperial Theatro de S. Pedro de Alcantara', *Diario do Rio de Janeiro*, Rio de Janeiro, 23 August 1826, 75.
[16] 'Théatre impérial', *L'Écho de l'Amérique du Sud*, Rio de Janeiro, 2 June 1827, 4.
[17] 'Noticias particulares', *Diario do Rio de Janeiro*, Rio de Janeiro, 24 November 1821, 158–9. The names of Fabrizio Piacentini and his daughter Giustina, who arrived with all the family in Rio

Gazeta do Brasil opined that Maria Teresa Fasciotti, the leader's sister, took on roles the other first soprano, Maria Zanetti, should have sung.[18] When another prima donna, Elisa Barbieri, arrived that same year, the audience split into two rival parties, a scenario well known from European theatres. The tensions between the two rival camps remained a topic for weeks, eventually leading to fierce quarrel between two politically opposed newspapers: the conservative *Gazeta do Brasil*, which then favoured Barbieri, and the liberal *Astrea*. Both papers dedicated entire pages to the issue, immediately amplifying the disputes that had arisen in the theatre's stalls, while also inciting further quarrels.[19]

At a time when public debate in Brazil was divided over the country's national question and its relationship to Europe, some voices expressed resistance to the hosting of two foreign troupes at the country's main theatre. Moreover, after the theatre reopened in 1826, the company that had previously performed plays in Portuguese on the principal stage was not reengaged, leading some papers to call for the establishment of a 'national theatre'.[20] The liberal *A Aurora Fluminense*, for example, showed no interest in opera, but acknowledged the role of theatre in popular education, complaining that the city's main stage only 'served to entertain' its audiences by supporting 'wandering foreigners'.[21] Even the *Gazeta do Brasil*, which usually praised opera and ballet performances, published a letter criticising the exclusive position of the foreign companies hosted by the Imperial Theatro, allegedly taking 'bread off fellow nationals and passing it on to foreigners'.[22] An earlier opinion piece about the organisation of the theatre, published in 1822, treated the foreign opera singers with a general sense of suspicion, employing a language that echoed contemporary political debates on the consequences of colonial exploitation:

The greatest care must be taken in [setting up] a good National Company, from which the nation extracts all the advantages. I concede that singing has its place, but within reasonable limits, because these gentlemen want to do little work while

---

de Janeiro in 1820, had appeared in the Lisbon season the previous year. A specialist in buffo roles, such as Taddeo in Rossini's *L'italiana in Algeri*, Fabrizio died in Rio de Janeiro in 1829.

[18] 'Theatro', *Gazeta do Brasil*, Rio de Janeiro, 11 July 1827, 50–1.

[19] About the rivalry between Fasciotti and Barbieri, see Luís Antonio Giron, *Minoridade crítica: a ópera e o teatro nos folhetins da Corte: 1826–1861* (São Paulo/Rio de Janeiro: Editora da Universidade de São Paulo/Ediouro, 2004).

[20] 'Artigos não officiais', *Diario Fluminense*, Rio de Janeiro, 27 August 1824, 212. The situation lasted until 1829, when a new company of Portuguese actors was engaged.

[21] 'Variedades', *A Aurora Fluminense*, Rio de Janeiro, 21 December 1827, 4.

[22] 'Theatro', *Gazeta do Brasil*, Rio de Janeiro, 30 June 1827, 39.

earning a lot; and once they have filled their pockets, they say goodbye and what remains here no longer matters to them. They leave richer and make us poorer.[23]

Some years later, the enthusiasts of the 'national theatre' would find a shelter in the stage of a smaller house erected at Rua dos Arcos, just a few blocks away from the São Pedro de Alcântara. In February 1828, when the troupe of the so-called 'Theatrinho' staged a farce entitled *Tudo à estrangeira*, the editor of a liberal newspaper noted that 'the company expressed with energy and much spirit the ridiculous nature of those nations that only absorb from foreigners what is useless and bad, thus giving the most expressive lesson of how useful and necessary it is to keep a national colour in customs always'. The writer's targets, of course, were the operas and ballets staged at the Imperial Theatro, whose principal concern was 'to cost the nation large sums [of money]'.[24]

Constructing such tensions between Brazilians and foreigners, between Europe and America, was significant to the different projects of imagined future in a young country that wished to find its own voice among the nations of the New and the Old World. Even more noticeable in press discussions, however, was a perceived conflict between barbarism and civilisation, to which the advocates of the foreign companies at the theatre usually referred. Here operatic *italianità* stood for a bastion of Enlightenment, as in the case of the editor of *L'Écho de l'Amérique du Sud*, who contrasted the cultural life around the capital's cosmopolitan court with the perceived wildness of the inner country and its native population:

At the Imperial Theatre, Rossini's music delights a distinguished society of spectators assembled in a room decorated with all the ornaments of the finest architecture. Meanwhile, a few dozen leagues from the Empire's civilised capital, located at the same latitude, the Indians gather in a forest and quarter the limbs of the lost traveller to the dissonant sounds of an ox horn serving as their trumpet ... When will come the time that you can walk through the fields without fearing the deadly tooth of the *tupinambás*?[25]

Despite the recurring criticism of the practice of employing foreign musicians, dismissing the Italian troupe altogether seemed to be out of question.

---

[23] 'Sr. Redactor', *Correio do Rio de Janeiro*, Rio de Janeiro, 28 May 1822, 164.
[24] 'Theatrinho da Rua dos Arcos', *A Aurora Fluminense*, Rio de Janeiro, 22 February 1828, 74.
[25] 'Intérieur', *L'Écho de l'Amérique du Sud*, Rio de Janeiro, 3 October 1827, 1–2. The ethnic group referred to as *tupinambás*, famous for its anthropophagic rituals, first described by Hans Staden and other early travellers in the sixteenth century, symbolised the concept of barbarism that the new country had to overcome. See Hans Staden, *Hans Staden's True History: An Account of Cannibal Captivity in Brazil* (Durham, NC: Duke University Press, 2008).

Nevertheless, this still leaves the question of how these men and women were able to start a completely new life in a foreign country. In this respect, the few sources that we have about their private lives are illuminating. We know, for example, that some of these artists remained in the city for ten years or more and acquired considerable assets. The castrato Giovanni Francesco Fasciotti, for instance, owned a rural property near the Court, including slaves, two of whom he reported as fugitives in 1829, offering a reward for their capture.[26] The master of dance, Laurent Lacombe, owned a farm across Guanabara Bay, with a garden of orange trees and accommodations for slaves and animals, which he tried to sell in January 1823.[27] Fabrizio Piacentini tried to rent a stable with horses next to his home as a means of supplementing his income as a singer.[28] Engaged as first buffo during the 1829 season, the bass Luigi Foresti took two slaves and a maidservant at his family's service upon their departure for Buenos Aires the following year.[29] These examples show that some of the foreign artists had the intention of staying in South America for a longer period to make use of their economic opportunities. Despite the politically uncertain conditions of a life in a recently independent country, these musicians were able to take advantage of their situation by dealing with property, making significant investments and ultimately adapting to local customs. Although they formed part of a company that represented them financially in their dealings with the impresario, their various economic activities became an important means of supplementing their income as singers.

Another source of additional income was the practice of organising benefit performances, which had been brought to Brazil from Europe. Here the singers acted as their own impresarios, covering all the expenses for the staging and in return retaining the entire profit from the evening. For instance, in 1828 the bass Nicola Majoranini announced a benefit performance of *L'ajo nell'imbarazzo*, a comic opera by Donizetti, premiered in Europe only four years before, and invited all interested patrons to buy tickets at his own home, located near the theatre.[30] The example speaks for a relatively close relationship between artists and their admirers, to the point that a visit to a singer's private residence became part of normal practice, although some patrons might have sent a slave to purchase tickets.

---

[26] 'Escravos fugidos', *Diario do Rio de Janeiro*, Rio de Janeiro, 13 October 1829, 44.
[27] 'Vendas', *Diario do Rio de Janeiro*, Rio de Janeiro, 31 January 1823, 93–4.
[28] 'Noticias Particulares', *Diario do Rio de Janeiro*. Rio de Janeiro, 20 November 1822, 68.
[29] Arquivo Nacional (Brazil), Polícia da Corte, códice 422, v. 4, fl. 285.
[30] 'Imperial Theatro de S. Pedro de Alcantara', *Diario do Rio de Janeiro*, Rio de Janeiro, 13 September 1828, 44.

In general, all soloists included the right of arranging a gala performance for their own benefit as part of the contract they signed with the theatre. Those evenings could generate considerable profits for the soloist at the centre of the event. For instance, in February 1828 a benefit performance for soprano Elisa Barbieri, whose Italian name concealed her French origin, was described in the papers as a very lucrative soirée.[31] One newspaper even mentioned a diamond ring she received on the occasion from the Emperor. It estimated the total amount collected at more than 2.5 million *réis*, probably enough to buy a decent house near the court or a slightly larger property just a little further away.[32] While the article might have exaggerated the profits, they certainly amounted to a considerable sum, rarely achieved by other soloists, who occasionally even made a loss. Also on those special nights, both companies were expected to collaborate in a complete soirée with opera and ballet, a set-up apparently propitious to creating a sense of solidarity and mutual support between dancers and singers. These ideals, however, do not seem to have prevailed in all cases, giving rise to some tension between Italian and French artists. In fact, a letter published by the weekly *O espelho diamantino* in February 1828 criticised the supposed unwillingness of the opera soloists to participate in benefit performances promoted by some of their French colleagues, thus generating ballet-only galas which were not very attractive to the audience, and therefore less profitable. The same commentator regretted that some soloists 'were forced to take money out of their own pockets to cover the expenses' of their benefit performances.[33] On the other hand, complaints about the large number of benefit soirées were common in the newspapers, and the critic of *L'Écho de l'Amérique du Sud* remarked, not without irony, that 'everyone in the theatre makes money, except the impresario'.[34] The article certainly overstated the case, as demonstrated by a list of performances from April 1828 to March 1829 published by the theatre and

---

[31] Despite being described as a true soprano, Elisa Barbieri started out as a contralto. Apparently, her performance as Isabella in *L'italiana in Algeri* demanded some adaptations, and included a cavatina from another opera, more suitable to her register. 'Supplemento à Gazeta', *Gazeta do Brasil*, Rio de Janeiro, 27 October 1827, supplement. In the previous season, Barbieri formed part of the troupe of Manuel García at Park Theatre, New York, where she sung, among other roles, Donna Anna in Mozart's *Don Giovanni* and Amenaide in Rossini's *Tancredi*, as mentioned in the *New-York Evening Post*. Praising Barbieri's voice, one of the critics in Rio de Janeiro cited the positive reviews in a New York weekly publication of her previous performances as a member of the García troupe. 'Théatre Impérial', *L'Écho de l'Amérique du Sud*, Rio de Janeiro, 28 November 1827, 4.
[32] 'Lettres sur le théatre. No. 1', *O Espelho Diamantino*, Rio de Janeiro, 4 February 1828, 175.
[33] 'Lettres sur le théatre. No. 2', *O Espelho Diamantino*, Rio de Janeiro, 18 February 1828, 207.
[34] 'Théatre Impérial', *L'Écho de l'Amérique du Sud*, Rio de Janeiro, 25 January 1828, 3.

consisting of 123 nights, of which only 20 (just over 16 per cent) were reserved for benefit performances.[35]

Concerts in wealthy houses, as well as private lessons, offered further opportunities of generating income in the foreign capital. Moreover, as mentioned earlier, some male singers were also members of the Capela Real, where they received a second salary for the participation in religious services. The range of economic opportunities was certainly limited, even for male performers, but there was enough to make the stay in the imperial capital attractive, at least for some years, despite the economic crisis that plagued the young country throughout the reign of Pedro I. Outshone by the foreign soloists, the theatre's ensembles also provided a living to another group of musicians. Information about the orchestra is quite sparse. It seems, however, that Pedro Teixeira de Seixas, composer and musician of the Imperial Chamber, usually conducted the opera performances from the keyboard, with first violinist Giovanni Liberali taking charge of the ensemble during ballets. The choir is rarely mentioned, but we know that its members also enjoyed the right to an annual benefit performance.[36]

Complete operas performed by a permanent troupe as part of a regular season were still a novelty for audiences in 1826. It was in those years that the newspapers became a major factor in the life of the city's main theatre, at a time when they also consolidated their role as privileged vehicles of discussion in Rio de Janeiro's emerging public sphere.[37] As part of this process, the press contributed to giving opera and ballet a new status in Brazilian society, and helped to create an audience that was growing more and more familiar with established customs of going to the theatre. Newspapers such as *O Spectador Brasileiro*, *L'Indépendant* and *Gazeta do Brasil* established a dynamic interaction with the theatre, its singers and the impresario, often also involving the readers. Furthermore, some singers did not hesitate to publish notes recommending themselves to the audience, and not only before their own benefit performances. Reverence towards

---

[35] 'Dias em que deve haver Espectaculo no Imperial Theatro de S. Pedro de Alcantara, principiando em 7 de Abril do corrente anno, até o dia 3 de Março de 1829', *O Espelho Diamantino*, Rio de Janeiro, 5 April 1828, 279–81.

[36] 'Imperial Theatro de S. Pedro de Alcantara', *Diario do Rio de Janeiro*, Rio de Janeiro, 28 February 1829, 96.

[37] According to Habermas, since the eighteenth century the art critic had 'assumed a peculiarly dialectical task: he viewed himself at the same time as the public's mandatary and as its educator'. This closely corresponds to the situation we find in early-nineteenth-century Brazil. Jürgen Habermas, *The Structural Transformation of the Public Sphere* (Cambridge, MA: The MIT Press, 1991), 41.

real or potential patrons, sometimes expressed in an exaggerated style, was the norm in such announcements, often employing *captatio benevolentiae* as a rhetorical tool. In 1821, for instance, the still-young soprano Giustina Piacentini begged the readers of a major paper for 'mercy, protection and forgiveness for any mistake she may commit, as a bad actress and a bad singer'. The note was published before her debut as Rosina in Rossini's *Il barbiere di Siviglia*, as she considered the role to be beyond her capabilities and probably feared audiences would turn against her.[38] Some years later, when opera criticism had become a regular feature in several papers, the bass Gioachino Bettali touched upon the core of public debate in the new monarchy when proclaiming to the French editor of *L'Indépendant* that 'we, you and I are Europeans, but we live with an equally enlightened people, and we must, I believe, follow our careers as if we were in Europe'.[39]

Following French models, the first anonymous articles of opera criticism in Rio de Janeiro appeared at a time when newspaper debate, hitherto restricted to politics and finance, was gradually beginning to embrace broader themes.[40] Essays on societal habits and customs, for example, were already in vogue in 1827, and new publications, such as the women's weekly *O espelho diamantino*, clearly favoured this tendency. Here, the members of the Italian opera troupe soon became central characters in reports on the city's societal life, exposing for instance their troubled relationship with the impresario, particular clauses of their contracts, and occasionally even private gossip, often giving way to subtle insinuations and malicious anecdotes. The anonymous critic of *L'Indépendant*, for example, mocked the bass Fabrizio Piacentini as a heavy drinker.[41] The *Jornal do Commercio*, some months later, contributed to a controversy surrounding the contralto Margherita Caravaglia, alluding to her supposed love affair with the impresario.[42] *O Spectador Brasileiro* printed a note

---

[38] 'Noticias Particulares', *Diario do Rio de Janeiro*, Rio de Janeiro, 31 December 1821, 90. As the Latin expression suggests, the objective of *captatio benevolentiæ* is to win the goodwill of the audience. The artist signed 'Justina Piacentini', as the Portuguese spelling of foreign given names was the norm in newspapers, a convention that also favoured the social integration of Italian artists in Rio de Janeiro.

[39] 'Monsier le Rédacteur ... ', *L'Indépendant*, Rio de Janeiro, 12 May 1827, 4.

[40] Castil-Blaze's articles for the French *Journal des débats*, for example, were published throughout the 1820s, and the first number of the *Revue musicale*, directed by François-Joseph Fétis, appeared in 1827, coinciding with the publication of *L'Indépendant*, the first French-language newspaper in Rio de Janeiro. For French opera criticism in the 1820s, see Roger Parker and Mary Ann Smart (eds.), *Reading Critics Reading: Opera and Ballet Criticism in France from the Revolution to 1848* (Oxford: Oxford University Press, 2001).

[41] 'Théatre Impérial', *L'Indépendant*, Rio de Janeiro, 24 June 1827, 4.

[42] 'Correspondencias', *Jornal do Commercio*, Rio de Janeiro, 14 February 1829, 2.

describing shouts at the home of soprano Maria Zanetti, allegedly caused by her tensions with tenor Vittorio Isotta.[43] In order to avoid a public scandal, she felt obliged to respond quickly, trying to reassure readers that the true reason for her cries was a painful toothache.[44] These examples show how the São Pedro de Alcântara became a centre of societal concern in newspapers, thereby increasing public interest in the theatre and drawing attention away from discussions over parliamentary politics and the economic fortunes of the city's port.

In the 1820s a considerable contingent of foreigners lived in Rio de Janeiro, and French was undoubtedly the city's first foreign language. Promoted by both John VI and Pedro I, the development of the arts in Rio de Janeiro largely relied on French examples, and an academy of fine arts, created by French masters established in Brazil, dates back to 1816. If the primacy of Italian models was undisputed in the operatic scene, French musicians also played an important role in music teaching, and the city had benefitted from the presence of European composers of different nationalities, such as Sigismund Neukomm (1778–1858) and Marcos Portugal (1762–1830). From 1827, local newspapers in French also played a role in the promotion of opera and ballet criticism. Italian, in contrast, never enjoyed the same prominence in the capital's societal life, despite the role of the theatre as a bastion of operatic *italianità*. This fact allows for speculation regarding the public reaction to opera libretti sung in an unfamiliar language, especially given Rio de Janeiro's socially heterogeneous theatre audience, composed of wealthy merchants and landowner, sharing the space with foreign soldiers and authorities, as well as young men of various professions, and even freed slaves of both sexes. In fact, references in the press prove the presence of black men and women in the audience. For instance, writing in 1830, the editor of a liberal paper deplored the noisy expression of hostilities towards black people and mixed-race *pardos* in the boxes, blaming people in the stalls for the uproars.[45] The example shows that the order of seats in the theatre did not necessarily reproduce the racial structure of society. Free black men and women, endowed with some wealth, could occupy a luxurious box, where they sat next to some of the country's greatest slave owners and above a predominantly white audience in the inferior stalls.

---

[43] 'Correspondencias', *O Spectador Brasileiro*, Rio de Janeiro, 22 September 1826, 4.
[44] 'Noticias particulares', *Diario do Rio de Janeiro*, Rio de Janeiro, 30 September 1826, 99.
[45] 'Reflecções', *Nova Luz Brasileira*, Rio de Janeiro, 9 March 1830, 102–3.

Since libretti and programme booklets were sold to patrons, this diverse audience increasingly familiarised itself with the Italian vocabulary it needed to follow the plots on stage.[46] In July 1827, for instance, the libretto for Ferdinando Paer's *Agnese* was available in an affordable Italian–Portuguese edition, prepared by the printer Plancher.[47] A French-language paper took an ironic stance on the audience's engagement with the Italian language:

> Sometimes we listen to complaints of our neighbours who do not understand the Italian librettos: we could congratulate them, but it is better to help their intelligence. The happy lover and his beloved always sing the words: *Adorata, la tua beltà, o me felice, il caro bene* and *la mia felicità*. The repulsed lover repeats without ceasing: *Amor, crudel tiranno, l'ingrata, perfida, misero cuore*, and, finally, *la mia fatalità*. The buffo always makes trivial jokes, and the secondary characters say nullities. Thus, as long as we know a dozen indispensable words in a play, we will be perfectly aware of the action ... There is no need to know the Italian language to understand a modern opera. It was different when composers set to music the poems of Metastasio ... But today music takes the place of everything.[48]

Such ideas reveal the different shades of meaning associated with operatic *italianità* in nineteenth-century Brazil. Moreover, the author's evocation of the Italian libretto's golden past (which most of his readers would have never experienced) reaffirmed the critic's authority as a connoisseur of the highest exponents of operatic tradition. Pointing to the precedence of music over words in contemporary Italian opera, commentators echoed a perennial debate among many of their European counterparts during those years.[49] They often acknowledged the centrality of pleasure and of pure aesthetic delight in listening to those works, and sought to combine this aesthetic experience with the pedagogical role also assigned to theatre and theatre criticism. A vocabulary of dramatic terms, published some months later by the same newspaper, revealed another attempt to mediate the relationship between works and audiences.[50] Such articles heralded the

---

[46] Paulo Kühl has argued that there 'existed a group of individuals acquainted with the vocabulary, the texts, and the way they were represented, and with ability to understand them'. Paulo Kühl, 'Tradução, adaptação e censura em libretos portugueses e brasileiros', *OuvirOUver*, 3 (2007), 17–45 (8).

[47] 'Annonce', *L'Écho de l'Amérique du Sud*, Rio de Janeiro, 22 July 1827, 4.

[48] 'Théatre Impérial', *L'Écho de l'Amérique du sud*, Rio de Janeiro, 21 November 1827, 4.

[49] See for instance F. A. Kanne, 'Was ist von dem jetzigen Geschmacke in der Musik zu fürchten?', *Allgemeine musikalische Zeitung mit besonderer Rücksicht auf den österreichischen Kaiserstaat* 4/91 (11 November 1820), 725–8.

[50] 'Petit dictionnaire dramatique', *L'Écho de l'Amérique du Sud*, Rio de Janeiro, 16 February 1828, 4.

ideals championed by the supporters of theatre and opera in Rio de Janeiro, reflecting the cultural preferences of a recently independent country, with a court eager to underline its cultural connection to Europe as a way of overcoming its colonial past.

The capital's new operatic life also resulted in the arrival of a wide range of musical commodities and a whole new material culture associated with the theatre. Commercial exchanges with the Old World resulted in the regular shipping of orchestral scores for performances, while also supplying booksellers and printers with goods destined for music lovers. Thus, when the São Pedro de Alcântara announced its first performance of Rossini's *La gazza ladra*, a newly founded bookstore seized upon the occasion by offering its customers an assortment of different arrangements, including a complete piano reduction and excerpts such as arias and duets, as well as a potpourri of the opera's most famous tunes.[51]

Despite this whole new frenzy around the theatre, from 1829 onwards various causes contributed to the rapid decline of Rio de Janeiro's main stage. The death of the impresario Fernando José de Almeida, the man behind the construction of the theatre and its development over the past fifteen years, forced the government to intervene in the affairs of the house, which was already experiencing difficulties with its contracts. The collapse of the Banco do Brasil and its subsequent liquidation process in September 1829 aggravated this scenario. The theatre owed the bank, its main lender, considerable amounts of money, which is why the building was incorporated into the bankrupt estate.[52] Furthermore, the political instability which culminated in the abdication of Pedro I and the instauration of the regency in 1831 seriously threatened the survival of regular theatrical performances in the capital. At first, the theatre's financial crisis affected the payment of wages and the quality of performances. Therefore, only a few operas were staged during the 1829 season. One of them was the house premiere of Rossini's *Matilde di Shabran*, with the sets taking a long time to be completed, most likely due to the theatre's financial difficulties. As the situation worsened, some singers decided to leave the city, perceiving Europe or Buenos Aires as more promising destinations. Other artists insisted upon

---

[51] 'Livros á venda', *Jornal do Commercio*, Rio de Janeiro, 30 July 1830, 2.

[52] For a deep analysis of the events around the collapse of Banco do Brasil, see Kurt E. von Mettenheim and Maria Antonieta del Tedesco Lins, 'The Banco do Brasil', in K. E. Mettenheim, *Federal Banking in Brazil* (London: Pickering & Chatto, 2010), 59–100.

staying, and eventually reunited in a new company. In a last effort, in 1831, they took control of the theatre and started a subscription for a new season. In spite of their attempts, the atmosphere of dispute and uncertainty that loomed over the capital in the last days of Pedro I's reign proved fatal to the theatre's survival. For security reasons, it was forced to close its doors during the first days of the regency. The company's dissolution was inescapable, and the city remained deprived of complete opera performances for the next twelve years.

The decline of the theatre in Rio de Janeiro contributed to a flow of singers moving towards the River Plate, with some of the former soloists joining a travelling troupe that toured various cities in Latin America and ultimately reached as far as Macao and Calcutta.[53] Speaking for the city's music lovers, however, throughout the 1830s the newspapers continued to echo the public demand for opera performances, a desire that would only be satisfied in 1844 with the arrival of a new Italian company. Only after the turbulent years of the regency had come to an end did opera begin flourishing once more in Rio de Janeiro, now under the patronage of Pedro II, a revival that would be witnessed by some of the pioneers of the old troupe that had taken roots in the capital.

The paths of early-nineteenth-century theatre in Rio de Janeiro show how Italian opera played a central role in the cultural imaginary that helped to establish Brazil as an independent nation state, with its fortunes being closely related to the country's political and economic stability. Within this process, the genre embodied the idea of European civilisation to which the leaders of the Independence movement wished to relate, although the role assigned to foreign artists remained contested. Critics also sought to discuss the principles of operatic *italianità* with the audience, grounding their authority in examples and opinions from the Old World. The pioneer Italians who brought opera to Brazil had to find their way between opportunities and threats, and some of them increasingly adopted the habits and strategies of either wealthy or ordinary locals: some became landowners, others opened their own business, and even the least successful provided a keen audience of observers with societal

---

[53] Former soloists of the Italian Company, including the bass Gioachino Bettali and contralto Margherita Caravaglia, toured many cities in South America and performed in Macao and Calcutta in the 1830s. Teresa Schieroni and Domenico Pizzoni, leading figures of that group, also had sung in Rio de Janeiro during their brief stay at the city before going to Buenos Aires. See Benjamin Walton, 'L'italiana in Calcutta', in S. Aspden (ed.), *Operatic Geographies: The Place of Opera and the Opera House* (Chicago: University of Chicago Press, 2019), 119–32.

gossip. In many ways, Italian opera had become a vibrant topic of discussion in the public sphere. To current scholars, the lives of those protagonists can still raise exciting questions: could an Italian castrato, who owned slaves and ran a farm, still identify himself with his counterparts in Europe? And what did Italian operatic tradition represent to free black people who were able to afford seats in the theatre's expensive boxes?

3 | Nina d'Aubigny's 'Italian Voice'

A Musical Projection Screen in German National Discourse

CAROLIN KRAHN

Nina d'Aubigny's *Briefe an Natalie über den Gesang* is known as a popular source on German-language music pedagogy for the systematic education of the voice.[1] The thirty-one letters to the fictive character Natalie contained in the volume provide a practical instruction to German-speaking readers on (primarily female) vocal education. In its epistolary form, the volume stands in the tradition of educational literature around 1800. Situated at the intersection of women's emancipation, voice and musical education in the German-speaking lands, this source is an early example of a German-language pedagogical music treatise by a female author.[2] The name 'Nina d'Aubigny' served as the *nom de plume* of Jana Wynandine Gertraud d'Aubigny (14 April 1770, Kassel, Germany – 29 January 1847, Nestelbach, Austria). According to the biographical sketch provided by Sigrid Nieberle, d'Aubigny was a writer, singer, music educator and composer who published some of her works.[3] As the daughter of a Legation Councillor and aristocratic educator at the court of Hesse, she grew up in Kassel and received vocal training from, among others, Pompeo Sales. In 1794, d'Aubigny moved to Bückeburg, where she wrote the *Briefe an Natalie* for her newly married sister Susette. After five years

---

[*] I cordially thank Axel Körner and Misha Enayat for their many thoughtful comments and editions of the manuscript, and I am grateful to Scott Edwards as well as Jeremy Llewellyn for sharing the fine nuances of their mother tongue with me.

[1] In this chapter, I quote from the second revised edition: Nina d'Aubigny von Engelbrunner, *Briefe an Natalie über den Gesang, als Beförderung der häuslichen Glückseligkeit und des geselligen Vergnügens: Ein Handbuch für Freunde des Gesanges, die sich selbst, oder für Mütter und Erzieherinnen, die ihre Zöglinge für die Kunst bilden möchten*, 2nd ed. (Leipzig: Voß, 1824 (1st ed. 1803)). For an overview of the main differences between the two editions, see Manfred Elsberger, *Nina d'Aubigny von Engelbrunner: Eine adelige Musikpädagogin am Übergang vom 18. zum 19. Jahrhundert. Untersuchungen zu ihrem Hauptwerk* Briefe an Natalie über den Gesang (Munich: Allitera, 2000), PhD thesis University of Passau 2000, 223–37.

[2] Sigrid Nieberle, 'Aubigny von Engelbrunner, Jana Wynandine Gertraud d', gen. Nina', in A. Kreutziger-Herr and M. Unseld (eds.), *Lexikon Musik und Gender* (Kassel/Stuttgart/Weimar: J. B. Metzler, 2010), 126–7, here 127; for other versions of her name, see also Ingeborg Harer, 'Nina d'Aubigny von Engelbrunner', in B. Borchard and N. Noeske (eds.), *MUGI: Musikvermittlung und Genderforschung: Lexikon und multimediale Präsentationen* (Hamburg: Hochschule für Musik und Theater), 2003ff. www.mugi.hfmt-hamburg.de/Artikel/Nina_d'_Aubigny_von_Engelbrunner (last accessed 5 November 2020).

[3] See Nieberle, 'Aubigny von Engelbrunner', 126–7.

(1803–7) in England, mainly in London, she and her sister Emilie lived in Calcutta from 1807 through 1818. Thereafter, d'Aubigny embarked on a longer journey through Italy before moving to Vienna in the 1820s and then, beginning in 1828, spending the remainder of her life at the castle of Erko near Graz. Manfred Elsberger sketched out many details of her presence in Germany and her travels to France, Italy and the Netherlands, as well as a substantial journey through Italy in 1823–4.[4] In spite of the fact that mobility was common within the courtly context of Europe, d'Aubigny's mobility is quite remarkable in terms of her status as a single woman, and had a significant impact on the geographical scope covered by her literary output.[5] Scholarship, however, has not paid much attention to the entanglement of her mobility and her musical and literary activities.[6]

In regard to *Briefe an Natalie*, at first glance, d'Aubigny's principal goal seems simply to be the fostering of beautiful voices within society at large, as noted towards the end of the volume.[7] A closer examination of the source, however, reveals a more complex narrative related to this goal, which should be considered against the background of national musical discourse. For one, *Briefe an Natalie* integrates for the first time the abovementioned thematic strands in a comprehensive form in order to address the central function of mothers in musical education within German society. This in turn is intertwined with contemporary and often polemically charged aesthetic debates on music, in particular those that were being negotiated transnationally between clichés of German versus Italian musical characters. In this context, the idea of the 'Italian voice', which is often somewhat subliminally or casually woven into d'Aubigny's text, represents a key concept in terms of the development of the ideal voice, a notion situated on the horizon of d'Aubigny's pedagogical aspirations. In turn, as a result of the link between mothers as educators, music pedagogy and national musical thought, this chapter argues that *Briefe an Natalie* is not just any music pedagogical guide written by a female author, but an aspiring medium for conveying national ideas on music, one that contributed to the shaping of Italian stereotypes within German-speaking society.

In order to understand this process, this chapter will proceed in two complementary steps. In the first section of this chapter, *Briefe an Natalie*

---

[4] See Elsberger, 'Nina d'Aubigny von Engelbrunner', 29–76.
[5] See the overview in Elsberger, 'Nina d'Aubigny von Engelbrunner', 283–96.
[6] Among the few publications on d'Aubigny and especially her experiences abroad:
Helen Metzelaar, 'A Young German Girl Visits Holland: Nina d'Aubigny von Engelbrunner's Travel Journal, 1790–1791', in R. Grotjahn and F. Hoffmann (eds.), *Geschlechterpolaritäten in der Musikgeschichte des 18. bis 20. Jahrhunderts*, Beiträge zur Kultur- und Sozialgeschichte der Musik 3 (Herbolzheim: Centaurus, 2002), 177–86.
[7] D'Aubigny von Engelbrunner, *Briefe an Natalie über den Gesang*, 213.

is placed within a perspective beyond its pedagogical context, which is in turn realised by bringing together several strands of relevant scholarship. A brief explanation of the re-evaluation of the role of mothers in Germany's musical culture around 1800 is followed by critical reflection on the scholarly reception of *Briefe an Natalie*, which has hitherto been limited primarily to its German context. That makes it difficult to appreciate its transnational dimensions between the German and Italian musical worlds in light of national music historiography. The section also examines connections between domestic music and voice training in a national context. The second part of this chapter traces the concept of the Italian voice in *Briefe an Natalie*. By analysing selected passages from the letters of Nina d'Aubigny, the chapter will show how voice serves as a wide-ranging projection screen that expands beyond strictly musical topics, tackling above all anthropological, moral, societal and aesthetic questions, all of which propagate clichés of Italian music into German everyday life. Finally, these considerations on the meaning and content of *Briefe an Natalie* are brought together in order to reflect on the relevance of the concept of the Italian voice in German music historiography. Ultimately, this chapter investigates the multiple levels on which the idea of an Italian voice is constructed and shaped; it does so against a transnational backdrop, thus broadening perspectives on *Briefe an Natalie* beyond its reception in the realm of Germany's (female) music pedagogy.[8] The chapter will illustrate how the cultivation of the voice in Italy, as assessed by d'Aubigny, serves not just as a contrasting foil for the situation in the German-speaking lands, but in fact also as a musical model to be overcome.

Musical Mothers in Europe's Living Rooms: Readjusting the View

Aside from reflection upon the work's focus on women and especially on mothers, a deeper understanding of *Briefe an Natalie* within the context of an emerging educated middle class requires a transdisciplinary as well as

---

[8] As, for instance, in Dimitra Will's recently published PhD dissertation (2018) at the University of Bayreuth. The author enforces the focus on the operatic aspects of vocal education, due to the main focus of her dissertation topic. Thereby, the broader societal function of musical education in a national context is put in the background. See chapter 3.1, 'Körper oder Karriere: Nina d'Aubigny von Engelbrunner', in Dimitra Will, *'Geisterstimme aus höheren Welten': Untersuchungen zum Alt-Diskurs des 19. Jahrhunderts* (Würzburg: Königshausen & Neumann, 2020), 69–72.

a transnational perspective. As literacy rates in Germany increased around the turn of the century, mothers assumed a central function in educating their children – and thus in enabling the 'society of the future'.[9] This undertaking clearly entailed more than the physical, psychological and moral aspects of education. As Friedrich Kittler and Sigrid Nieberle have argued, mothers became the biographical nucleus of literary and musical education.[10] Indeed, the central role of mothers in their daughter's education is already adumbrated in the dedication to the first edition of *Briefe an Natalie* (see Figure 3.1).

In addition to its dedication to the Empress of Russia, the Queen of Prussia and the Princess of Wales, the book directly addresses 'Europe's most sublime mothers of the most hopeful daughters'.[11] Despite the dedication's reference to Europe, the polyglot background of the work's author and the general focus on Italian musical life at the time, *Briefe an Natalie* has hardly been discussed in the context of a transnational history of music. The dominant focus in scholarship has been on the work's reception, read as a historical source for music education and the theory of singing, and appreciated by the likes of Beethoven, among others.[12] Critical reflection on the work's national-historiographical dimension within the context of German music history has played a minor role in scholarly debates.[13]

---

[9] The idea of societal progress cannot be considered a specifically German phenomenon, but needs to be seen in the wider European context of the time. Above all, Jean-Jacques Rousseau's writings in search of a natural, unadulterated and moral societal vision as culminating in his *Émile* come to mind here, especially the fifth book, describing Émile's encounter with Sophie as the *femme parfaite*, a book which likewise marks Émile's entrance into proper social life. See Jean-Jacques Rousseau, *Émile ou De l'éducation: Texte établi par Charles Wirz, présenté et annoté par Pierre Burgelin* (Paris: Gallimard, 1969), for example 528–9. For Rousseau, the understanding of Sophie as wife and mother-to-be was closely linked to the striving for moral development within bourgeois contexts, as Barbara Vinken has outlined in more detail in her book *Die deutsche Mutter: Der lange Schatten eines Mythos*, 2nd ed. (Frankfurt am Main: Fischer Taschenbuch, 2011), 133–43.

[10] Friedrich Kittler, *Aufschreibesysteme 1800/1900* (Munich: Wilhelm Fink, 1985) (4th ed. 2003), 37–42; Sigrid Nieberle, *FrauenMusikLiteratur. Deutschsprachige Schriftstellerinnen im 19. Jahrhundert*, Ergebnisse der Frauenforschung 51 (Stuttgart and Weimar: J. B. Metzler, 1999), 29–35.

[11] D'Aubigny von Engelbrunner, *Briefe an Natalie über den Gesang* (unpaginated).

[12] In this context, references to Beethoven tend to serve as a means to prove the work's overall impact, or to defend the (female) author's quality. For instance, see Eva Rieger, *Frau, Musik und Männerherrschaft: Zum Ausschluß der Frau aus der deutschen Musikpädagogik, Musikwissenschaft und Musikausübung*, 2nd ed. (Kassel: Furore, 1988), 59.

[13] See Elsberger's consideration in his chapter 'Vokalmusik führender Nationen und ihr Verhältnis zueinander', in Elsberger, 'Nina d'Aubigny von Engelbrunner', 206–17, here 217. On the general problem of rewriting national histories in the later twentieth century across disciplines and nation states within Europe, and on lacking the plurality required in order to overcome national master narratives, see Stefan Berger, 'A Return to the National Paradigm?

Figure 3.1 Nina d'Aubigny von Engelbrunner, *Briefe an Natalie über den Gesang* (Leipzig: Voß, 1803), unpaginated. © Bayerische Staatsbibliothek, Mus.th. 214, urn:nbn: de:bvb:12-bsb10598218-5

The goal of female education at the time was essentially to prepare girls for their future societal duties, thus the musical activities of wives and mothers have mainly been discussed within a historiographical framework of gender and women's studies.[14] In this context, research into European and in particular German-language music history of the early nineteenth century has so far focused primarily on the role of the 'higher daughter', meaning young women of a middle-class background, who were expected to play the piano or sing for the household. As shown by the literary scholar Adrian Daub in his cultural history of four-hand piano playing, 'the daughter of the household', usually average in talent, 'pays musical homage

National History Writing in Germany, Italy, France, and Britain from 1945 to the Present', *The Journal of Modern History*, 77/3 (September 2005), 629–78; on methodological nationalism with a particular focus on opera see Axel Körner, 'Beyond Nationaloper: For a Critique of Methodological Nationalism in Reading Nineteenth-Century Italian and German Opera', *Journal of Modern Italian Studies*, 25/4 (2020), 402–19.

[14] For instance, Rebecca Grotjahn, 'Alltag im Innenraum: Die "höhere Tochter" am Klavier', in S. Keym and K. Stöck (eds.), *Musik in Leipzig, Wien und anderen Städten im 19. und 20. Jahrhundert: Verlage, Konservatorien, Salons, Vereine, Konzerte* (Bericht über den XIV. Internationalen Kongress der Gesellschaft für Musikforschung vom 28. September bis 3. Oktober 2008 am Institut für Musikwissenschaft der Universität Leipzig), Musik-Stadt: Traditionen und Perspektiven urbaner Musikkulturen 3 (Leipzig: Gudrun Schröder Verlag, 2011), 431–41; Adrian Daub, *Four-Handed Monsters: Four-Hand Piano Playing and Nineteenth-Century Culture* (Oxford: Oxford University Press, 2014), for example 44ff. or 181–2.

to the bust of Beethoven' and other 'old masters' of music only to a limited extent.[15] She therefore appears as an average 'musical subject', rather than as an established artistic personality. In addition to playing the piano, singing was usually also a pursuit available to young ladies.[16] The function and significance of female domestic singers in the early nineteenth century seemed intended above all to be that of entertainment for social pastimes. As the century progressed, the situation of an artist confined by domestic or marital restrictions has been epitomised primarily by such figures as Fanny Hensel, Felix Mendelssohn's sister, or by Alma Mahler-Werfel, who both were relegated to the shadows of male composers.[17] Apart from providing uplifting music for the home, the primary roles of most female musicians seemed limited to those of wife and mother. As a consequence, motherhood, musical education and female voices have rarely been discussed together more in depth, nor has this nexus proven to be a key area within national music histories or the study thereof.[18]

---

[15] Daub, 'Four-Handed Monsters', 95.

[16] Beyond the domestic use of female voices, of course the opera stage was reserved for outstanding female singers around 1800. This topic has been thoroughly researched and is also reflected in the music criticism of the time. Most recently, this has been dealt with in more detail in musicological and theatrical research, for example in the volume by Saskia Maria Woyke, Katrin Losleben, Stephan Mösch and Anno Mungen (eds.), *Singstimmen: Ästhetik, Geschlecht, Vokalprofil*, Thurnauer Schriften zum Musiktheater 28 (Würzburg: Königshausen & Neumann, 2017); in addition, there is research on selected female singers in the environment of famous composers in the eighteenth and nineteenth centuries, for instance Suzanne Aspden, *The Rival Sirens: Performance and Identity on Handel's Operatic Stage*, Cambridge Studies in Opera (Cambridge: Cambridge University Press, 2013); Giorgio Appolonia, 'Angelica Catalani musa di Vincenzo Pucitta', in A. Bonsante and Ph. Gossett (eds.), *Vincenzo Pucitta: Il tumulto del gran mondo*, Le vie dei suoni 1 (Barletta: Cafagna, 2014), 109–50. In general, case studies of outstanding Italian singers such as Faustina Bordoni, Angelica Catalani, Henrietta Sontag and so on have been the main focus so far, for example Saskia Maria Woyke, *Faustina Bordoni: Biographie, Vokalprofil, Rezeption* (Frankfurt am Main: Peter Lang, 2010); Carola Bebermeier, *Celeste Coltellini (1760–1828) – Lebensbilder einer Sängerin und Malerin* (Biographik. Theorie – Kritik – Praxis 4) (Cologne/Vienna/Weimar: Böhlau, 2015). For a more comprehensive approach to the 'voice' as a trope linked to the topic of women in music across genres, countries and social spheres, see the essay collection by Jane A. Bernstein (ed.), *Women's Voices Across Musical Worlds* (Boston, MA: Northeastern University Press, 2004).

[17] As a consequence, especially in Germany several musicologists in the field of 'women's studies on music' have tried to correct the non-perception of female composers within historiography and scholarship. See for instance the series *Europäische Komponistinnen*, edited by Melanie Unseld and Anette Kreutziger-Herr. Also see Peter Schleuning, *Fanny Hensel, geb. Mendelssohn: Musikerin der Romantik*, Europäische Komponistinnen 6 (Cologne, Vienna and Weimar: Böhlau, 2007). Also Susanne Rode-Breymann, *Alma Mahler-Werfel: Muse, Gattin, Witwe* (Munich: C. H. Beck, 2014).

[18] Although her focus is mostly on opera, an exception needs to be made for Susan Rutherford's work. See Susan Rutherford, *The Prima Donna and Opera 1815–1930*, Cambridge Studies in Opera (Cambridge: Cambridge University Press, 2006), especially 120–60; see also Rutherford's

The relationship between women, education and the singing voice during the nineteenth century cannot be limited to either domestic musical entertainment or to opera. Instead, it represents a core theme of music-sociological debate. Various reviews of d'Aubigny's book in leading contemporary periodicals illustrate this claim. For instance, on 23 August 1807 the *Zeitung für die elegante Welt* underlined the significance of the *Briefe an Natalie* for society more broadly:

> In short, if the ladies all follow the good advice and teachings that are scattered here in abundance; if they listen attentively to exemplary singers and try to observe the advantages to which reference is here given: so it cannot but happen that better singing will soon be more widespread, and our living rooms and parlours will resound with the echo of purer voices and more beautiful, more refined singing.[19]

In addition, the *Neue Bibliothek für Pädagogik und Schulwesen* emphasised that d'Aubigny's book for the first time addressed neither just virtuosos – as the 'elderly Italians' Pier Francesco Tosi,[20] Johann Friedrich Agricola[21] [sic] and Nicola Porpora[22] did – nor merely schoolteachers – as had Johann Adam Hiller with his *Anweisung zum richtigen Gesang* – but that it was intended as a more general educational instruction for women.[23] Moreover, Leipzig's *Allgemeine musikalische Zeitung* of 14 September 1803 underscored

---

chapter 'Marriage' in her monograph *Verdi, Opera, Women*, Cambridge Studies in Opera (Cambridge: Cambridge University Press, 2013), 142–77.

[19] See the original German quote in: 'Musik: Bildung zum Gesange', *Zeitung für die elegante Welt*, 3/101 (23 August 1803), cols. 799–803, here col. 803.

[20] Pier Francesco Tosi, *Opinioni de' cantori antichi e moderni, o sieno osservazioni sopra il canto figurato* (Bologna: Lelio dalla Volpe, 1723).

[21] Agricola is presented as Italian, most likely on the basis of his considerably expanded, annotated translation of Tosi's aforementioned treatise: Johann Friedrich Agricola, *Anleitung zur Singkunst: Aus dem Italiänischen des Herrn Peter Franz Tosi, Mitglieds der philarmonischen Akademie: mit Erläuterungen und Zusätzen von Johann Friedrich Agricola, Königl. Preuß. Hofcomponisten* (Berlin: Winter, 1757). See also Thomas Seedorf (ed.), *Agricola, Johann Friedrich: Anleitung zur Singkunst. Reprint der Ausgabe Berlin 1757 mit neu gesetzten, modern geschlüsselten Notenbeispielen* (Kassel: Bärenreiter, 2002).

[22] This probably refers to a circulating anecdote by François-Joseph Fétis contained in his *Curiosités historiques de la musique. Complément nécessaire de la musique mise à la portée de tout le monde* (Paris: Janet et Cotelle, 1830). It relates to a sheet of paper with singing exercises that Porpora is said to have given to his student Gaetano Majorano. The anecdote by Fétis, which has not been proven with certainty to date, was given further attention by music teacher Marcia Harris's edition *Porpora's Elements of Singing* (London: Addison, Hollier and Lucas, 1858), which according to her is based on a copy of the aforementioned sheet. I am grateful to Livio Marcaletti for pointing me to the discussion of this anecdote in Thomas Seedorf (ed.), *Handbuch: Aufführungspraxis Sologesang* (Kassel: Bärenreiter, 2019), 128–9.

[23] See Johann Christoph Friedrich GutsMuths (ed.), *Neue Bibliothek für Pädagogik, Schulwesen und die gesammte neueste pädagogische Literatur Deutschlands, als Fortsetzung der Zeitschrift für Pädagogik*, 2/5–8 (1810), 233.

the importance of *Briefe an Natalie* as a reflection upon its own time, highlighting how the book took an international perspective, which included shedding light on the musical lives of the three nations of Germany, Italy and France. The review highlights the book's representative status:

> The book, by the way, offers many good things; it contains so much that it could be called a word of its time; it is so suitable that it should achieve its next important purpose – our wish that it be included in the reference library of every educated woman. For that purpose, and for that audience, there is no book yet available, neither in German, nor in French, nor in Italian literature.[24]

In light of the apparent widespread demand for the work's further dissemination, it seems necessary to clarify the extent to which this form of national music historiography was brought into public consciousness by addressing the issue of the 'Italian voice' within German musical society.[25]

Where Is Nina's 'Italian Voice'?

D'Aubigny's elaborations are charged with mainly positive notions of 'the Italian voice', on musical as well as cultural levels. These notions are used to develop an image of the ideal voice for the book's German-speaking readers that might serve as a model in national musical education – in fact, one that significantly draws from Italian musical culture and thus conceals a transnational perspective. By and large, the concept of an ideal voice and its proper education is scattered throughout the letters to the fictive Natalie. At the very beginning, in the second letter, it is made unmistakably clear that Italy serves as the central reference point for the development of German vocal culture in general, which will be the subject of the following letters:

> Why should a good, pure organ not be the dowry of every human being in Germany, as is the case with the Italians? Admittedly, this nation enjoys some

---

[24] See the original German quote in the review 'Briefe an Natalie über den Gesang, als Beförderung der häuslichen Glückseligkeit und des geselligen Vergnügens. Ein Handbuch für Freunde des Gesanges, die sich selbst, oder für Mütter und Erzieherinnen, die ihre Zöglinge für die Kunst bilden möchten. Von Nina d'Aubigny von Engelbrunner. Leipzig, bey Voss und Compagn. 1803 (Pr. 1 Thlr. 16 Gr.)', in *Allgemeine musikalische Zeitung*, 5/51 (14 September 1803), cols. 837–48, here col. 838.

[25] Regarding the fascination with 'Italian singing' in London and Italy's position, according to the author, as a 'locus classicus' within the British musical imagination that fuelled the formation of a national 'operatic voice', see Claudio Vellutini : 'Interpreting the Italian Voice in London (and Elsewhere)', in R. Parker and S. Rutherford (eds.), *London Voices 1820–1840: Vocal Performers, Practices, Histories* (Chicago and London: University of Chicago Press, 2019), 51–69.

advantages that we do not yet savour. Others we will never enjoy, like the language of the Italians, which naturally invites good singing.[26]

Already here, the idea – which was widespread at that time – that the Italians had a supposedly 'natural disposition' for singing is made explicit. Meanwhile, it is made clear at an early stage that the state of contemporary Italian music with its 'frequent everyday fare of sweet melodies' is considered inferior to that of German music with its 'inventive spirit, genius and thoroughness'.[27] Thereby, d'Aubigny takes part in an ambivalent, value-charged aesthetic opposition pervasive at the time of her book's publication, and which would form the basis for much German music historiography in the decades to come.[28] In the following letters, d'Aubigny abstains from sketching out a comprehensive concept of the 'Italian voice' – from physiognomy through to singing technique and the repertoire. Instead, she uses her references mostly as an indistinct screen for projecting an idea of the Italian voice that she imagines to be naturally cultivated within Italian society and central to the nation's outstanding musical qualities, without parallel in the world. Any technical details of vocal training – regarding the proper production of tones, the intonation of scales, timbre or musical style, and the physical treatment of the voice – are outlined on the basis of an imagined ideal voice, inspired by what d'Aubigny considers typical of Italian national character, on which she also comments throughout the book.

Yet, as the following examples will demonstrate, this ideal voice ultimately no longer comes across as limited to the Italian realm, even though its description so heavily relies on references to Italy. Instead, it becomes a blueprint for a future musical culture at large, the achievement of which represents the true aim of the book, understood as a profound challenge to the German-speaking world. It is with this aim in mind that d'Aubigny alludes to an imaginary musical culture of Italy, based on historical examples, ideas of the particular vocal qualities of Italians and excellent infrastructure for musical education. Examples of particular composers of vocal music such as Niccolò Piccinni and Antonio Sacchini form part of her argument, as do references to prominent sopranos like Angelica Catalani, or highly sought-after castrati such as Farinelli and Luigi

---

[26] D'Aubigny von Engelbrunner, *Briefe an Natalie über den Gesang*, 9.
[27] D'Aubigny von Engelbrunner, *Briefe an Natalie über den Gesang*, 3.
[28] For a brief summary of the main trains of thought on the opposition of German versus Italian music see Frank Hentschel, *Bürgerliche Ideologie und Musik: Politik der Musikgeschichtsschreibung in Deutschland 1776–1871* (Frankfurt am Main and New York: Campus, 2006), 340–56.

Marchesi.²⁹ A characteristic feature of these references is their ambivalence: on the one hand, these figures are worthy of admiration; on the other hand, they set the bar for what is considered musical achievement, against which German music making has to measure.

The Voice Between Social Structures and National Ideas

Nina d'Aubigny's idea of the social significance of the voice pursues at least two directions: writing from a German point of view, as demarcation against other 'musical nations', and as a means of national cohesion. On the one hand, the more nationally oriented passages of her work, which describe the general qualities of voices and their roles within society, draw a clear line between the German-speaking and the Italian worlds; to a lesser extent, the French, English and Dutch also come into play when contemplating locally shaped sound production and overall vocal development. Here the voice serves as a tool to draw and define discursive boundaries between different ideas of 'musical nations'. On the other hand, d'Aubigny's elaborations on the positive effects of vocal training underscore the voice's potential to bind society together, to foster social cohesion. Here the voice and vocal education serve as a key to forming the musical character of specific social groups. For instance, in her tenth letter, d'Aubigny shifts her emphasis from motherly vocality to the aural and vocal organs of children that depend on it. At first glance, Italy seems to serve as a national role model of such musical culture:

[I]n the future, I want every mother to be naturally a good singer; I want her to start teaching the child singing when it is still a baby. I want her to understand the development of the ear and the throat in order to enable her to form her children's ears and throats.... In a word, in a few decades I want the town and country, the forest and meadows of our fatherland to resound with melodious and joyful song just like in Italy, for I am convinced that as soon as the taste for it will be commonplace, good singing will pass from the elders to the children, and with more ease than the little feet of the Chinese.³⁰

It seems important to keep in mind that the idea of Italy's imagined 'natural affinity' with song was a double-edged sword in this context. There were two main points related to the idea of the 'typically Italian' gift for vocal

---

²⁹ D'Aubigny von Engelbrunner, *Briefe an Natalie über den Gesang*, 200, 207 (Piccinni, Sacchini); 190, 193 (Catalani); 224–5 (Farinelli); 192–4 (Marchesi).
³⁰ D'Aubigny von Engelbrunner, *Briefe an Natalie über den Gesang*, 60–1.

music that frequently recurred, unmasking this discourse as both polemically and anthropologically charged: for one, the fact that Italians were supposed to be particularly at ease with anything vocal was considered the result of the proximity between their language and singing.[31] In other words, early on in their lives Italians supposedly undertook constant training in forming the 'right' sounds when simply cultivating their mother tongue, hence they did so without great effort. Secondly, Italians' outstanding vocal qualities were allegedly cultivated in a public network of musical conservatories: singing was purportedly taught on a regular basis through prayer in church services, hence a form of public music education across the peninsula. Thus, vocal training was believed to be so deeply anchored both socially and culturally in Italy that Italians almost automatically developed their voices on a daily basis. Furthermore, d'Aubigny stresses that the quality of voices and vocal music in Italy benefitted from the southern climate and its impact on the Italian people, which, according to her, apparently resulted in the transformation of happy moods into song:

The beautiful climate, the clear sky of Italy, awakens a cheerfulness in its inhabitants, which was already described as characteristic of the people at the time of the Romans, if one translated its main needs into the two words, 'bread and circus games!', and helped them bear the many oppressions under which the people groaned. The Italian sings his stanzas at the rudder of the gondola, he sings before and after work, and feels happy, as if he actually were happy![32]

D'Aubigny's motivation to strengthen vocal education in Germany went beyond purely musical aims, however. Vocal development, as a gift available to any human being, would presumably foster the general fabric of society regardless of social class, and help bridge social differences, affecting even those who might not be in a position to afford to learn musical instruments:

It was the duty of the Italian people to go almost daily to the temples of God, which were at the same time temples of music, where, from childhood on, their ears were unconsciously formed; and how easily the throat tunes up when it is guided by

---

[31] A key source on the link between music and language is certainly Jean-Jacques Rousseau's *Essai sur l'origine des langues* published in 1781. For reflections on the essay against the Italian musical background from a wider cultural perspective, see Alexander Kolassa and Axel Körner (eds.), *Opera in Transnational Context: Reading Rousseau's 'Essay on the Origin of Languages'*: www.ucl.ac.uk/centre-transnational-history/sites/centre-transnational-history/files/rousseau_italianita_essays2.pdf (last accessed 5 November 2020); see also Axel Körner, *Le Devin du Village: Language and the Aesthetics of Music*: http://passionatepolitics.co.uk/rousseau-devin-du-village/ (last accessed 5 November 2020).

[32] D'Aubigny von Engelbrunner, *Briefe an Natalie über den Gesang*, 15.

a correct ear and a melodious language. The educated classes, as well as the lower classes, enjoyed the same benefits of attending the most outstanding performances of musical masses and singing to the innumerable saints in all sorts of ways. How could a general taste for singing not spread across this nation?[33]

This idea of public musical training in Italy was also reflected in subsequent reviews of her book. Here the positive effects of well-developed vocal cords became entangled with both physiological and societal aspects that had, in fact, very little to do with music. For instance, the reviewer for the *Allgemeine musikalische Zeitung* related his appreciation of the book to medical reports that emphasised the voice's positive impact on health in Italy. Quoting a passage from the *Briefe*, the reviewer claimed that the reduction in the rate of tuberculosis in Italy was ostensibly due not just to the country's pleasant climate, or to the comparatively mobile lifestyle of Italians, but to the early vocal training of children.[34] D'Aubigny also stressed numerous advantages of singing related to mental well-being and the stability of social structures – in particular its power to quell boredom and to foster serenity in households. This aspect did not go unnoticed by reviewers, too, and was disseminated beyond Germany. For instance, in his *Dizionario e bibliografia della musica,* published in Milan 1836, the Austrian physician and music scholar Peter (or Pietro) Lichtenthal refers to d'Aubigny's understanding of singing as a means of promoting domestic felicity and social entertainment (see Figure 3.2).[35]

Early on in her writing, d'Aubigny provides another example of this by recommending 'Pergolesi's, Graun's, or Haydn's and Mozart's heart-moving melodies'[36] in order to cheer up a group of friends spending time together. Remarkably, her choice of composers reflects a popular distinction between the musical past and present, with the 'old Italian master' Pergolesi on one side and three leading representatives of recent Austro-German music on the other. In other words, not only the operatic voice but also amateur voices in private settings became associated with particular repertoires, or at least with the names of certain composers. Another central though not strictly musical topic regards d'Aubigny's insistence on the moral effects of vocal education. She refers to considerations on music by Plato, Cicero, Rousseau, Linguet, Voltaire and Shakespeare in order to assert that music makes people not only happier, but also morally better.[37] In doing so, the author argues

---

[33] D'Aubigny von Engelbrunner, *Briefe an Natalie über den Gesang*, 1.
[34] See the original German quote in the review 'Briefe an Natalie über den Gesang', 840.
[35] I thank Barbara Babić for bringing the *Dizionario e bibliografia della musica* to my attention.
[36] D'Aubigny von Engelbrunner, *Briefe an Natalie über den Gesang*, 28.
[37] See the seventh letter in d'Aubigny von Engelbrunner, *Briefe an Natalie über den Gesang*, 44–5.

> D'AUBIGNY (VON ENGELBRUNNER NINA), figlia d'un Maggiore a Cassel: *Brief an Natalia über den Gesang, als Beförderung der häusslichen Glückseligkeit des geselligen Vergnügens. Ein Handbuch für Freunde des Gesangs die sich selbst, oder für Mütter und Erzieherinnen, die ihre Zöglinge für diese Kunst bilden möchten.* Leipzig, bei Voss, 1803, gr. 8. mit 5 *Musiktafeln. Zweite vermehrte Auflage*, ibid., 1824, gr. 8.
>
> Sono 31 Lettere sul canto, dirette a Natalia, scritte con istile vivace, e le quali contengono ottime osservazioni. L'Autore considera il canto come mezzo di promuovere la domestica felicità del sociale piacere.

Figure 3.2 Pietro [Peter] Lichtenthal, *Dizionario e bibliografia della musica*, vol. 4 (Milan: Antonio Fontana, 1836), 151. © Bayerische Staatsbibliothek, Mus.th. 2011–4, urn:nbn:de:bvb:12-bsb10598918-8

against the diminished esteem for vocal music within non-sacred contexts that still prevailed in the German lands at the turn of the century, thus underlining the moral grounding of her writing and demonstrating its contribution to a long tradition of moral thought on music.

The Italian Voice and the Competition for Musical Hegemony

While the 'grace of Italian singing' is highlighted throughout *Briefe an Natalie*, towards the end of the book this idea of Italian musical culture is increasingly challenged. While Italians are presented as the leaders in global cultures of singing – mainly due to the public and domestic circumstances explained in the book – d'Aubigny also points to a certain one-sidedness of this argument, as well as to the limitations of vocal education in Italy and the performance of Italian singers. For instance, she describes the contemporary situation of Italian vocal training as an uninspiring ordeal, arguing that Italian singing teachers supposedly 'torture their pupils in a merciless way through so-called solmization to make them secure in hitting the right pitches'.[38] The assumed result of this ultimately thoughtless overemphasis on virtuosity – a core motif of German music history and its polemic against 'welsh' music[39] – is illustrated by such prominent

---

[38] D'Aubigny von Engelbrunner, *Briefe an Natalie über den Gesang*, 140.
[39] I have outlined this polemical core motif in discourse on Italian music in German music historiography in more detail in chapters 12.1 ('Sänger – Virtuosen – Komponisten – Publikum') and 15.1 ('Oberflächlichkeit statt Tiefe – Verzierung statt Kontrapunkt – Melodie statt Harmonie') of my recent book. See Carolin Krahn, *Topographie der Imaginationen: Johann*

singers as Luigi Marchesi. His mode of singing in the 'Italian style', which is contrasted with the idea of supposedly more thoughtful, profound and harmoniously rich German instrumental music, makes him an outright defiler of contemporary musical taste, according to the author:

> Marchese [*sic*], an Italian singer, whose throat had every kind of dexterity for the most brilliant passages, combined an equally inventive genius with an original gift for transformation. As a consequence, he was able to vary the simplest melody, prepared many years ago, perhaps without knowing it or intending to, reflecting the one-sided training for the Italian kind of performance. The army of his imitators believed that they achieved everything by just countering the wise sobriety of the older method with a lavish waste of embellishments. Not only did this run against the power of expression but also against all principles of harmony, because by far the greater number of singers tend to have too little insight into the score to be able to determine how far they may surrender themselves to their addiction to shine, regardless of the higher laws of composition.[40]

Based on similar arguments, d'Aubigny also blames performers such as Marchesi for the contemporary decline of *portamento*. According to this view, contemporary Italian singing – in contrast to the more noble style of *portamento* – seems shallow, amazing listeners by the mere movement of the throat, which she considers 'soulless nonsense'[41]; according to d'Aubigny, the trend has affected even church and instrumental music in Italy due to the misguided imitation of its vocal styles.

Finally, d'Aubigny complements her criticism with a sharp condemnation of the alleged sense of musical superiority common among Italians, which seemingly is reflected in their own way of singing and their long-standing global dominance in the field, as well as in their disregard for German vocal music:

> Italians, with their monopolizing attitudes, previously considered it beneath their dignity to appreciate the vocal music of other nations ... feeling far superior to them. Even now, when German vocal music has undergone such great improvements, one will very rarely hear an Italian sing a German aria. In part, his ear, accustomed to gentle vibrations, finds the German language too barbaric; in part, the wealth of our harmony, which the better composers work on as diligently and as thoroughly, does not speak to his musical sense, which is more accustomed to sweet, or even often dull, soft melodies. In addition, the Italian, like any other

---

Friedrich Rochlitz' musikalisches Italien um 1800, Wiener Veröffentlichungen zur Musikwissenschaft 54 (Vienna: Hollitzer, 2021), 156–207 and 293–317.

[40] D'Aubigny von Engelbrunner, *Briefe an Natalie über den Gesang*, 192.
[41] D'Aubigny von Engelbrunner, *Briefe an Natalie über den Gesang*, 193.

compatriot whose mother tongue is particularly soft and light, has in some way pampered his linguistic organ, thus lacking the ability to speak harder languages successfully, and even less to sing those which require effort and expression of strength.[42]

Central to this argument is the idea of the Germans' linguistic superiority, which often appears in comparisons between German and Italian vocal music:

> As singers Italians have spread all over the world, when other nations in Europe still had low levels of vocal education. They have become their masters. Now, of course, many things have changed to bring a better balance to the musical world. But the Italian is still at the top of the list in terms of taste and grace, in terms of tone, and our singers are formed by him; for the best taste in German singing always remains a 'mixo-Italian'. Germans and Italians therefore have felt musically related and have appreciated each other for as long as they have known each other. The former are modest enough to grant the Italian the advantages of the natural sound of his throat and the superiority of taste; the latter finds in the German the best qualities of the most perfect singer, if he allows himself to be educated by him.[43]

The idea of the Germans' special versatility in adapting national musical styles, as expressed by d'Aubigny's concept of 'mixo-Italian', existed within a tradition that has been described by Johann Joachim Quantz. In his *Versuch einer Anweisung die Flöte traversiere zu spielen*, for instance, Quantz explains his popular idea of German 'mixed taste':

> If one knows how to choose from different peoples the best of their tastes in music, with due assessment, then a mixed taste follows from it, which, without going beyond the limits of modesty, one could very well call the German taste.[44]

Finally, d'Aubigny stresses the idea that the German language also carries a comparable softness that might serve as the basis for further developing German vocal music in the future: 'The beautiful Italian language counts in many cases the same advantage; its words, barbaro, scempio, squarciar etc. are not softer than German expressions.'[45] In this context, the allegedly lesser capabilities of German singers, compared to Italian virtuosos, are not

---

[42] D'Aubigny von Engelbrunner, *Briefe an Natalie über den Gesang*, 203–4.
[43] D'Aubigny von Engelbrunner, *Briefe an Natalie über den Gesang*, 204–5.
[44] Johann Joachim Quantz, *Versuch einer Anweisung die Flöte traversière zu spielen; mit verschiedenen zur Beförderung des guten Geschmackes in der praktischen Musik dienlichen Anmerkungen begleitet, und mit Exempeln erläutert. Nebst XXIV Kupfertafeln* (Berlin: Johann Friedrich Voß, 1752), 332.
[45] D'Aubigny von Engelbrunner, *Briefe an Natalie über den Gesang*, 160–1.

considered due to the possibly more limited musicality of Germans, but to the effects emanating from a complex language, which ultimately leads to rapid 'mechanical' fatigue:

> There is no doubt that the cause of this difference lies in the language itself; ... He [i.e. the German singer] has to struggle with so many letters and syllables, and while he is sacrificing himself to this first duty, the time and calmness which, in the Italian language, invites the singer to use these advantages to disseminate the brilliant artistry of his throat, has already partially passed.[46]

Aiming to stir German musicians to make use of their unique propensity for making the best of any musical tradition their own, d'Aubigny even calls on German 'patriotic poets' to invest in verses that might form the basis of more superior forms of German music, in a position to compete with Italian (or French) song: 'Gentlemen, remember the daughters of your country, and pick for them in the Heliconian fields the flowers of glazed colour, of joy and fine wit, so that when you rest, we may decorate and delight you with them in your own country.'[47]

The examples show how, ultimately, *Briefe an Natalie* questions the idea of Italian supremacy in the field of vocal music, which is presented as a model to be overcome. The ambiguity of the 'German views' on Italy's musical qualities needs to be placed in the context of nationalist debates. The polemic contained in these examples aimed to enhance the quality of 'German music'. As Barbara Eichner has argued:

> In view of the hegemony of Italian and French models it is hardly surprising that many attempts at a stylistic definition went little beyond anti-foreign polemics: German composers should neither imitate the florid and 'superficial' virtuosity of Italian singing nor the cool elegance or 'frivolous' effects of French opera. As Sebastian Werr has noted, 'the perceived shortcomings of Italian opera were used as a backdrop to demonstrate the strength of German music'.[48]

Beyond this description of the state of affairs in transnational musical relations, it seems important to emphasise the future-oriented perspective of this polemic, especially in the case of d'Aubigny's work. Taking the form of a pedagogical treatise, her work aimed to initiate a comprehensive musical development of German vocal culture. As such, her work took

---

[46] D'Aubigny von Engelbrunner, *Briefe an Natalie über den Gesang*, 201–2.
[47] D'Aubigny von Engelbrunner, *Briefe an Natalie über den Gesang*, 169.
[48] Barbara Eichner, *History in Mighty Sounds. Musical Constructions of German National Identity 1848–1914*, Music in Society and Culture 1 (Woodbridge and Rochester, NY: Boydell, 2012), 43–4.

part in a debate that had existed for decades, and which persists into the present.

The Italian Voice as the Boon and Bane of German Musical Culture

In his anthropological and sociological considerations on national identity as a means of human identification rather than given fact, Joep Leerssen has stressed the role of imagological reflection in cultural history:

> Imagology cannot hope to cure this deep-seated tendency towards anachronistic reification; but it demonstrates from case to case that nations and national categories, thrown up as they are by the varying contingencies of history, are in fact little else than projecting screens, blank categories which we fill with projections, images, characterological rationalizations of the world's diversity.[49]

Read against this theoretical framework, d'Aubigny's idea of the 'Italian voice' shows how transnationally circulating notions of musical 'Italianness' shaped a much wider societal discourse, thus taking up an important theme discussed in the introduction to this volume.[50] These ideas were not only held by the author herself, but were confirmed in the public reception of the *Briefe*. The voice proffered a fertile means of characterising Italy superficially as a nation with a flair for melody, and

---

[49] Joep Leerssen, 'Nation, Ethnie, People' in M. Beller and J. Leerssen (eds.), *Imagology: The Cultural Construction and Literary Representation of National Characters: A Critical Survey*, Studia Imagologica 13 (Amsterdam and New York: Brill Rodopi, 2007), 377–81, here 380.

[50] The idea of a particular 'Italianness' as reflected, among other ways, in the arts, is often coined by the term *italianità*, in both scholarship and everyday speech. In addition to the issues raised in the introduction to this volume, I suggest taking this term with a grain of salt in light of the concept's prominence during the period of Italian fascism. See Silvana Patriarca, *Italianità: La costruzione del carattere nazionale*, Storia e Società (Bari: Laterza, 2010). On the inflationary construction of the image of Italy and Italians during the nineteenth and twentieth centuries, see Giovanni Aliberti, *La resa di Cavour: Il carattere nazionale italiano tra mito e cronaca (1820–1976)* (Florence: Le Monnier, 2000); Gino Bedani and Bruce Haddock (eds.), *The Politics of Italian National Identity: A Multidisciplinary Perspective* (Cardiff: University of Wales Press, 2000); Albert Russell Ascoli and Krystyna von Henneberg (eds.), *Making and Remaking Italy. The Cultivation of National Identity around the Risorgimento* (Oxford: Berg, 2001);
Suzanne Stewart-Steinberg, *The Pinocchio Effect: On Making Italians (1860–1930)* (Chicago and London: Chicago University Press, 2008); Eva Garau, *Politics of National Identity in Italy: Immigration and 'Italianità'*, Routledge Studies in Extremism and Democracy 20 (New York: Routledge, 2015). The fascination with the mother as social nucleus saw a major revival through the myth of the Italian 'mamma' that was emphatically stylized as a pillar of Italian vernacular culture in the mid-twentieth century. See Marina D'Amelia, *La mamma*, L'identità italiana (Bologna: Il Mulino 2005).

Italians as a people 'of an enchanting spirit', while also hinting at a certain contemporary 'decay' of Italy's grand musical culture. Nina d'Aubigny's description of the Italian voice, including its particular qualities and its effects in the cultural framework of society, serves as a blueprint of Germany's musical culture of the future. It adds an important facet to established views, especially in the fields of German studies and comparative literature, that in the age of Goethe images of Italians were by and large defined by travel writings.[51]

Reading sources such as Nina d'Aubigny's *Briefe an Natalie* beyond the existing framework of debates in music pedagogy helps to unveil new aspects of imagological constructions in German and European music historiography. The examples outlined above illustrate how examining one specific treatise on vocal education advances our understanding of how musical ideas were constructed, articulated and received in society. Especially by addressing mothers as the primary recipients of her work, d'Aubigny's concept of the 'Italian voice' bridges gaps between social classes, between public and private and between the arts and society at large. Through her reflections on the voice and its embeddedness in society across nations, d'Aubigny played a part in paving the way for images of Italian musical culture, Italian musicians and, ultimately, Italian music as a whole to be broadened. By speaking about the voice, she aims to connect a people to their music while also challenging the Italian model she draws up in order to use the resultant image as an inspiration to foster vocal culture within Germany. In consequence, d'Aubigny's characterisations of the Italian voice and its rootedness within a specific musical culture were meant to become a public image as well as a national aspiration for her German readers – and hence remained a double-edged sword, not only for musical mothers and their hopeful daughters in Europe's most sublime households.

---

[51] See for example Frank-Rutger Hausmann (ed.), *'Italien in Germanien'. Deutsche Italien-Rezeption von 1750–1850* (Tübingen: G. Narr, 1996); Sandro M. Moraldo (ed.), *Das Land der Sehnsucht: E. T. A. Hoffmann und Italien*, Beiträge zur neueren Literaturgeschichte 186 (Heidelberg: C. Winter, 2002).

4 | Italian Opera and Creole Identities

Manuel García in Independent Mexico (1826–1829)

FRANCESCO MILELLA

On the night of 29 June 1827, after lengthy preparations, the new Compañía de Ópera Italiana of Mexico City was finally ready to make its debut with *Il barbiere di Siviglia* by Gioachino Rossini. Local elites and operagoers had waited a long time for this premiere. Rossinian opera was already familiar in Mexico City, having arrived in 1823, soon after independence from Spain was declared two years before, and having been performed several times by local companies and circulating in the domestic sphere in the form of guitar or piano transcription. Nevertheless, the arrival of a foreign opera company was an exciting novelty for the Mexican capital and its audiences. The Teatro de los Gallos had sold out fast, and the local elites who filled the boxes and the stalls had high expectations: the first European company to reach Mexico after independence was about to stage one of the audience's favourite operas. The opera's star was none other than Manuel García (1775–1832), the very tenor who had premiered the role of Conte d'Almaviva at the Teatro Argentina in Rome back in 1816 under the supervision of Rossini himself. The performance, though, did not achieve the success everyone expected.[1] The reasons became clear a few days later when an anonymous report was published in the newspaper *El Sol*:

of course, this is the best show we have ever seen in the operatic arena. But García made things worse when he decided to sing the opera in a foreign language. The most ridiculous thing was that, despite being an opera with a Spanish plot, we were forced to see it performed in Italian. Many Americans in the theatre disliked it as they could not understand most of it.[2]

Until then, Mexican theatres had always staged *Il barbiere* in Spanish, in accordance with the Bourbon law of 1799 that required any theatrical work performed anywhere in the Empire to be translated. Likewise, that night,

---

[1] According to the Mexican historian Luis Reyes de la Maza, 'shortly after the beginning, a loud murmuring swept the theatre and some members of the audience started to leave the hall well before the performance was over'. Luis Reyes de la Maza, *El teatro en México durante la independencia (1810–1839)* (Mexico City: Instituto de investigaciones estéticas UNAM, 1969), 26.

[2] *El Sol*, 5 July 1827, 4.

given also the Andalusian setting of the opera and the nationality of the leader of the company, Mexicans expected to see *El barbero de Sevilla*. But when Fiorello took to the stage with the other singers and players to accompany the Count's serenade, singing the Italian words 'Piano pianissimo, senza parlar' the audience was perplexed: that was not the opera Mexican elites knew and loved; it was not the *Barbero* that they had paid for and wanted to see.

Though critical of the linguistic decisions made by García, these press reports entail more than the question of translation and communication between the stage and the audience of the Teatro de los Gallos. In fact, by singing the whole *Barbiere* in Italian, Manuel García unwittingly overturned a cultural Bourbon world that Mexicans felt themselves familiar with: what they thought they would easily recognise and enjoy suddenly became incomprehensible and unpleasant. These reactions confront us with issues and questions that situate the relationship between early independent Mexico and Italian opera in a wider cultural and historical context, well beyond the evanescence and immediacy of a theatrical performance. Indeed, the arrival and operatic debut of Manuel García in Mexico City marked one of the first and at the same time one of the most problematic cultural encounters between non-Spanish Europe and the young Mexican nation after independence in 1821: his operatic activity, whether in the composition, performance or reception of his operas, disclosed a complex cultural scenario where different cultures (colonial and liberal), perceptions, expectations and illusions coexisted, interacting and colliding on the same stage. On these premises, this chapter aims to explore the operatic seasons of Manuel García in Mexico City in order to see how the transnational encounter between his operatic *italianità* and the cultural milieu of early independent Mexico not only altered the musical tastes and theatrical routines of its elites and operagoers, but also contributed significantly to a cultural and social reconfiguration of its creole identities.

Addressing García in Mexico City

Despite the weighty questions raised by his operatic performances overseas, Western musicology of the twentieth century approached García's Mexican (1826–9) years from a teleological perspective, as a necessary yet weak and transitory step towards the rooting and spread of Italian operatic cultures in Mexico during the 1830s. Indeed, the dominance of postcolonial uncertainties over theatrical practices, while raising questions about the local musical and cultural challenges of early independent Mexico, ended up situating Manuel García in the background of a national history that was often claimed to have begun officially only in the 1830s, with the arrival of the Rossinian bass Filippo Galli and his company from Milan.[3] Throughout the twentieth century, there were, nonetheless, a few attempts to investigate the activity of García in Mexico, mostly drawing on the *Reseña histórica del teatro en México* of Enrique Olavarría y Ferrari (1895).[4] Following the publication of James Radomski's biography in 2000, however, further contributions have begun to shed new light on García's short operatic season, revealing unexpected details on the arrival of Italian opera in post-independence Mexico. Yet, while such work has successfully pulled Mexico and Manuel García out of the musicological periphery, there remains much more to say about the wider implications of this operatic encounter.

While European and American musicologists have approached these years mostly in biographical terms (e.g. Radomski, or Mengíbar and Ferrer),[5] those from Mexico have instead analysed them from a national perspective, with a strong focus on the reception of García's operas among the Mexican capital's elites (e.g. De Pablo Hammeken).[6] Either way, both paths acted to restrict this operatic phase within historical and geographical boundaries, limited by personal or nationalistic factors. In doing so, they therefore omitted an array of wider national processes and transnational networks that actively contributed to the arrival and spread of Italian opera in Mexico during the 1820s. These ranged from the intertwined process of decolonisation from Spain, with the unforeseen persistence of colonial patterns, and the subsequent rise of connections with non-Spanish

---

[3] Filippo Galli (1783–1853) was an Italian bass who premiered most of the Rossinian operas of the Italian period (1812–23). For a more detailed overview of his Mexican years (1831–8), see Áurea Maya Alcántara 'La Producción de Ópera Italiana En México Durante La Primera Mitad Del Siglo XIX', unpublished PhD thesis, Universidad Autónoma de México (2019).

[4] Enrique Olavarría y Ferrari, *Reseña Histórica Del Teatro En México* (Mexico City: La Europea, 1895). See also Gerónimo Baqueiro Foster 'De cómo vino a México en 1827 el cantante español Manuel García, primer tenor del mundo', *El Nacional* (Mexico City, 3 April 1949), 10; Otto Meyer-Sierra, *Panorama de la música mexicana, desde la independencia hasta la actualidad* (Mexico City: El Colegio de México, 1941).

[5] James Radomski, *Manuel García (1775–1832): Chronicle of the Life of a Bel Canto Tenor at the Dawn of Romanticism* (Oxford: Oxford University Press, 2000); Alberto Romero Ferrer, Andrés Moreno Mengíbar (eds.), *Manuel García: de la tonadilla escénica a la ópera española (1775–1832)* (Cadiz: University of Cadiz, 2006).

[6] Alberto Romero Ferrer, Andrés Moreno Mengíbar (eds.), *Manuel García: de la tonadilla escénica a la ópera española (1775–1832)* (Cadiz: University of Cadiz, 2006); Luis de Pablo Hammeken, 'Don Giovanni en el Palenque: el tenor Manuel García y la prensa de la Ciudad de México 1827–1828', *Historia Mexicana* 1/61 (2011), 231–73.

Europe to, also, the new position achieved by Mexico in the new Atlantic system: perspectives and factors that seem worth taking into consideration in viewing the encounter between García and Mexico as the outcome of a range of different political, social and cultural processes.

Transnational and postcolonial studies have already explored these processes and connections and opened the way to a cultural reconceptualisation of Latin American spaces. Although defined in historic and geopolitical terms, their focus on concepts of hegemony, identity and nation (and their permutations over time and space) has enriched understandings of nineteenth-century opera: the inclusion of this vocabulary in the musicological arena pushed the narrow European focus of much musicology towards a radical rethinking of operatic geographies in more hybrid and globalised terms. 'Beyond Europe' has therefore become the motto of a new musicological turn aimed both at revealing global networks and connections and at critically investigating the spread of European musical traditions and the ways in which they adapted to specific urbanised contexts on a global scale, from Calcutta to Lima and New Orleans.[7] By moving towards a redefinition of opera's cultural meaning in relationship to 'the specific historic context of its performance and reception', new operatic scholarship has gradually approached the genre as a 'nomadic medium', liable to being continuously transformed by and through the frameworks, concerns and experiences of specific European and non-European contexts.[8] While focused on decentralising operatic histories, this debate has raised new questions concerning also the spatial dimension of European cultural power: indeed, as Suzanne Aspden has recently suggested in *Operatic Geographies*, 'opera's adaptation to new environments inevitably called into question European

---

[7] My analysis refers to Axel Körner's essay 'From Transnational History to Transnational Opera: Questioning National Categories of Analysis' (available online on the website www.ucl.ac.uk/centre-transnational-history, last accessed 25 October 2021), translated from the Italian version 'Dalla storia transnazionale all'opera transnazionale: Per una critica delle categorie nazionali', *Saggiatore Musicale* 24 (2017/1), 81–98. Calcutta, Lima and New Orleans have been recently included in the debate on global operatic networks during the first half of the nineteenth century by new contributions: Benjamin Walton, 'L'italiana in Calcutta', in Suzanne Aspden (ed.), *Operatic Geographies* (Chicago: Chicago University Press, 2019), 119–32; José Manuel Izquierdo König, 'Rossinian Opera in Translation: José Bernardo Alzedo's Church Music in Mid-Nineteenth-Century Chile', *The Opera Quarterly* 35/4 (Autumn 2019), 251–75; and Charlotte Bentley, 'Resituating Transatlantic Opera: The Case of the Théâtre d'Orléans, New Orleans, 1819–1859', unpublished PhD thesis, University of Cambridge (2018).

[8] Ibid., 5. The definition of opera as a 'nomadic medium' has been recently used by Benjamin Walton in 'Teresa Schieroni and the Beginnings of Global Opera' (in press), drawing on John Plunkett, 'Moving Panoramas c.1800–1840: The Spaces of Nineteenth Century Picture Going', *Interdisciplinary Studies in the Long Nineteenth Century*, 17 (2013), 1–34 (9).

hegemony, destabilising narratives of cultural superiority'.[9] Likewise, the spread of Italian opera in independent Latin America at the beginning of the nineteenth century not only drew attention to its role as a fashionable and easily portable form of entertainment, but also shed light on its ability to be invested with the values and discourses of Restoration Europe, thus becoming viewed as nothing less than a vessel for the values of modernity and civilisation.[10]

All that said, however, the independence of Latin America did not lead to a straightforwardly postcolonial situation, with emancipated nations struggling to overcome the legacies of the former colonial power by replacing them with alternative and more prestigious cultures. What this analysis wants to propose here, instead, is a more nuanced cultural analysis that takes into account also what the historian Jeremy Adelman defined as 'the stamina' of colonial legacies after 1821 and their interaction with the independent cultural and social scenario.[11] Indeed, as recently suggested by the Spanish historian Tomás Pérez Vejo, Latin American independence processes, like those of Mexico, were underpinned and fuelled, at least in their early years, by the explicit intention of Spanish colonies to be considered as the 'rightful heirs' to Bourbon power after the French invasion of Spain, rather than by any nationalistic impetus against their motherland.[12] The resulting cultural scenario of the newborn nations reveals a much smoother transition from coloniality to nationalism than the sort of rift implied by the rhetoric of independence, where cultures and ideas moved fluidly between spaces (Europe and America) and times (from Bourbon domination to independence). In light of this, the premises of Mexican operatic culture (and of García's activity) need to be radically reconsidered from a broader perspective which also takes account of colonial legacies and the role they played in nation building and the formation of identities.

---

[9] Suzanne Aspden, 'Introduction: Opera and the (Urban) Geography of Culture', in Aspden (ed.), *Operatic Geographies*, 1–11 (7).

[10] Benjamin Walton, 'Italian Operatic Fantasies in Latin America', *Journal of Modern Italian Studies* 17/4 (2012), 460–71.

[11] Jeremy Adelman, *Sovereignty and Revolution in the Iberian Atlantic* (Princeton, NJ: Princeton University Press, 2006), 4.

[12] Tomás Pérez Vejo, 'Nación e independencia nacional: México y España', in Hilda Hiparaguirre, Massimo de Giuseppe and Ana María González Luna (eds.), *Otras miradas de las revoluciones mexicanas (1810-1910)* (Mexico City: Escuela Nacional de Antropología e historia, 2015), 59–70, 68. See also Pérez Vejo, *Elegía Criolla* (Mexico City: Crítica México, 2019).

Opera and the Atlantic in the 1820s

By the time of García's journey, Atlantic nations were already undergoing structural transformations by gradually opening up to new commercial networks. As suggested by Matthew Brown and Gabriel Paquette, what once had been a monopoly of the Spanish and British maritime empires started during the 1820s to stimulate wider and more flexible connections between Europe and the Americas.[13] However, although primarily linked to commercial and political needs, these connections soon resulted in cultural dialogues on a large scale, fuelled by questions of national identity and social expectations that the withdrawal of Spain was making much more pressing. After more than three centuries of Spanish domination, the newborn Latin American nations were on the one hand gradually reinventing themselves on new cultural and political bases while, on the other, trying to deal with an ever-present and rooted colonial past. While some elites continued to consider Spain and Iberian culture as their main interlocutor, others – soon to become the majority – started to look to non-Spanish Europe (namely France, England and Italy) as the supposed cradle of civilisation and as the bearer of a new modernity.

These complex, often conflicting, connections between the two shores of the Atlantic drew upon Italian opera from early on. From the 1820s, Latin American nations from Mexico to Chile started to import Italian repertoires in the hope of providing their own elites with fashionable and civilising models and of being accepted by Europe as modern and autonomous entities. Operas by Rossini, Cimarosa and Mozart, among others, spread rapidly through the theatres and private venues both in the capitals and in minor peripherical cities, while local newspapers began to create their own narratives by providing their readers, on a weekly basis, with portraits of European opera houses and anecdotal sketches of famous composers.[14] Yet the bulk of the seasons still consisted of a solid tradition of Iberian theatrical works imported during the colony. When the Teatro Principal of Mexico City reopened in 1821 after the independence turmoil, a long list of *sainetes, tonadillas* and Spanish *operetas* continued to be

---

[13] Matthew Brown and Gabriel Paquette (eds.), *Connections after Colonialism. Europe and Latin America in the 1820s* (Tuscaloosa, AL: Alabama University Press, 2013).

[14] As recently pointed out by the musicologist Yael Bitrán Goren, operatic repertories played a seminal role in the development of private musical practices of the elites in early republican Mexico. See Yael Bitrán Goren, 'La buena educación, la finura y el talento: Música doméstica en las priméras décadas del México independiente', in Ricardo Miranda and Aurelio Tello (eds.), *La música en los siglos XIX y XX* (Mexico City: Conaculta, 2013), 112–53.

performed on a regular basis alongside the new, appealing operas of Gioachino Rossini.[15]

This colonial tradition was probably too familiar to be celebrated by local newspapers or mentioned in the urban discourses of the elites; yet it smoothly coexisted for decades with the new Italian operas coming from Europe, often conditioning the way in which those new operas were performed and listened: for instance, Italian operas were usually sung in Spanish (*La Italiana en Argel, La Urraca Ladrona, El Tancredo, Otelo* and *El barbero de Sevilla*), imported in translation from Cuba, Bourbons' only remaining colony in Spanish America. Even the performers were still embedded in Iberian musical theatre, having little or no experience with Italian bel canto: those who were born in Mexico or arrived before independence to sing Spanish theatrical works had to reinvent themselves after independence to meet the new needs of the creole elites, improvising or relying on what they had learned about Italian opera in Spain before 1799, when the Bourbon government had banned foreign operatic repertoires and companies from the Empire. And even those who instead crossed the Atlantic after 1820 to start a new career in Mexico City and take advantage of the new cultural impulse given by creole elites came also from Spain without therefore bringing any external innovation in the way Italian operas were staged. So, before García's arrival, the continuous interconnection between the two theatrical traditions had thus consolidated a stable and rather successful scenario in which European fashion coexisted with colonial traditions: a balance that the arrival of Manuel García was soon to upset.

Manuel García from New York to Mexico City

Manuel García sailed towards America in the autumn of 1825. At the dawn of his fiftieth birthday, after almost thirty years of operatic triumphs divided between Madrid, Paris, Naples and Rome, García realised he had already passed the peak of his operatic career. Over the last ten years, he had crossed different countries and musical cultures, from Spanish *tonadillas* to French *grand opéras*, to become a groundbreaking figure of the nineteenth-century cosmopolitan culture that Orlando Figes has recently explored through the life of García's youngest daughter, Pauline Viardot (1821–1910).[16] Yet, by

---

[15] Archivo Histórico de la Ciudad de México: Secc. Teatros, vol. 4016, exp. 24.
[16] Orlando Figes, *The Europeans: Three Lives and the Making of a Cosmopolitan Culture* (London: Allen Lane, 2019).

that time, the world his reputation was more closely linked to was Italian opera: his career at the Teatro San Carlo in Naples starring in two Rossinian premieres – as Norfolk in *Elisabetta Regina d'Inghilterra* (Naples, 1815) and as Conte d'Almaviva in *Il barbiere di Siviglia* (Rome, 1816) – turned his name into an international byword of operatic *italianità* around Europe. Since 1816, Rossini, Mozart, Cimarosa and Paisiello became the core repertoire of his transnational trajectory from the Théâtre Italien in Paris to London, where he eventually settled in 1824 as *primo tenore* of the King's Theatre. From there, as soon as he realised that operatic Europe had nothing more to offer him, he set out to seek new stages to bring his musical trajectory to a respectable conclusion, while also giving a solid future to his operatically talented offspring, Manuel Patricio, María Felicia Anna (later María Malibran) and the already mentioned Pauline (born Paulina). Though he was fifty years old, he hoped that, for an operatic star like him, age would not be an obstacle to charting a new path as an Italianate tenor, especially outside Europe. And indeed, a new opportunity soon arose. In spring 1825, Dominick Lynch, an American tycoon and opera lover, who was based in London for business, offered him the intriguing and quite unexpected opportunity to introduce Italian opera to North America. Supported by Lynch and the old Mozartian librettist Lorenzo da Ponte, who had been living in New York since 1805, García embarked with his three sons and his second wife Joaquina Sitchez Briones on a new adventure.[17] They landed in Philadelphia before moving on to New York in November 1825, with a small operatic company assembled in Europe and a repertoire including operas by Mozart, Rossini, Vaccaj and Zingarelli. Despite initial successes, however, the American scheme did not go according to plan: the unwanted marriage of García's elder daughter María to the Swiss banker Eugène Malibran, the poor quality of the local theatre and its audience, and a succession of illnesses soon turned New York into a difficult place, far from the long-dreamed *terra promessa* he had originally described it as when trying to convince the famous soprano Giuditta Pasta to follow him across the Atlantic Ocean.[18] By the beginning of 1826 a new move had therefore become necessary for the Garcías.

---

[17] For further information about Da Ponte's operatic adventures in North America, see John Dizikes, *Opera in America: A Cultural History* (New Haven, CT: Yale University Press, 1995); Pierpaolo Polzonetti, *Italian Opera in the Age of the American Revolution* (Cambridge: Cambridge University Press, 2011); and Axel Körner, *America in Italy: The United States in the Political Thought and Imagination of the Italian Risorgimento, 1763–1865* (Princeton, NJ and Oxford: Princeton University Press, 2017).

[18] Maria Ferranti Nob. Giulini (ed.), *Giuditta Pasta e i suoi tempi: Memorie e lettere* (Milan: Ettore Sormani, 1935), 83: 'Everyone agrees that people in New York are crazy about music, especially

Not a return, though: by that time, García's voice was no longer as flexible and brilliant as it used to be during the 1810s, when he had been one of the most admired tenors of Europe. Moreover, his children were still too young to take his place in the company and to successfully embrace operatic careers of their own. In the spring of 1826 García began to look, once again, for a new stage: after abandoning the plans of going to Florence and New Orleans, he got in contact with Luis Castrejón, a Mexican businessman and impresario he had met in London a few years before, to explore the operatic opportunities that Mexico City could offer to him.[19] By June he had made his decision and, once again, he informed his friend Giuditta Pasta in Italy.[20] The project in Mexico City might have raised new hopes for García and his family of an opportunity to revive old successes without too much effort for the rest of his and his children's lives, while staying close enough to his daughter María, who had at that point decided to remain in New York with her husband.

In the meanwhile, Mexico City and its creole elites readied themselves to welcome Manuel García and inaugurate the new opera season. When his arrival was confirmed during the summer of 1826, the theatrical life of Mexico City was already undergoing a swift process of structural renovation: the Teatro de los Gallos, previously used as an outdoor venue for cockfights, was fully refurbished, thus becoming the second theatre of the city after the Teatro Principal, the New Coliseum, built in 1753 under the Bourbon domination. In addition, after appointing Castrejón as the new impresario and opera manager, the town council approved a series of measures to establish a set price for tickets and subscriptions, to redecorate the hall and, eventually, to take measures to improve the conduct of the audience. Local public opinion, however, was not universally in favour of García's arrival. While some members of the elite, led by Castrejón himself, hoped that García could become a potential driving force to enhance the culture of the city, others were more suspicious: according to them, not

---

if Italian. That country is a promised land. No other Italian theatre has decided to establish Italian opera under happier auspices.' The letter was written and sent during the summer of 1825, but the exact date is unknown.

[19] Anonymous, *Manifestación que hace un ciudadano amigo de los adelantamientos de su patria, del mérito y de la justicia* (n.p.: Imprenta de Galván, 1827).

[20] On 10 June 1826 García wrote to Giuditta Pasta: 'I think it might be a ruse in order to make use of money for a while longer. In fact, since the money is here, and myself having decided to go on to Mexico (perhaps, for the rest of my days), I thought it is more convenient to take it here and now, and not to give you the pain of returning it once more.' James Radomski, *Manuel García (1775–1832): Chronicle of the Life of a Bel Canto Tenor at the Dawn of Romanticism* (Oxford: Oxford University Press, 2000), 207. See also *The Harmonicon*, 40, April 1826, p. 81.

only did García's arrival require significant expenditure to renovate the city's theatrical assets, but his Iberian origins also seemed problematic at a time when Spanish people, especially those residing in the newly independent republic, were becoming an unwanted demographic and a target of anti-colonial attitudes.

Unaware of such local disputes, García and his family landed in Veracruz on 2 November 1826. Despite the efforts of Castrejón and local politicians, delays with work permits and financial disagreements with the company postponed their debut at the Teatro Provisional to 27 June 1827, which finally took place with the staging of Il barbiere di Siviglia by Gioachino Rossini. Two weeks later, García made his first local appearance as a composer with the opera L'Abufar, ossia La famiglia araba.[21] With these performances, public opinion in the capital split again, not least because, as we said, García ignored the tradition of translating any theatrical piece into Spanish. A debate on the virtues of translation ensued: taking advantage of the country's Hispanophobia and the ongoing attempts to expel any Spanish residents living in Mexico, the two main political parties, namely the masonic lodges of the Yorkinos (Yorkists) and the Escoceses (Scots), used García's Andalusian origins and his musical decisions as a way to undermine the power and reputation of their enemies in relation to upcoming national elections that took place in 1828. For the Yorkinos, a federalist and *antiespañol* party, García deserved to be expelled along with all his Spanish compatriots as a potential threat to the political stability of the newborn nation. On the opposite side, the Escoceses, a more centralist, moderate and philohispanic party, believed that he was adding new value to the cultural life of Mexico City and should therefore be protected by the authorities. The ascendancy of the Yorkino lodge, however, brought García's activity in Mexico City to a sudden conclusion. Although he had obtained a permit to live in Mexico and had started to translate all his operatic repertoire into Spanish, by the end of 1828 had García decided to leave Mexico and go back to Paris to resume his career there.[22] By the time he left Mexico City in January 1829 he had composed six theatrical works –

---

[21] The libretto by Felice Romani was first used by the Italian composer Michele Carafa in 1823 (Vienna, Kärntnertortheater).

[22] The Yorquino leader José María de Tornel y Mendívil (1795–1853) added a short clause to the decree of expulsion, implicitly intended for García himself, but addressed to all Spanish residents, announcing that 'the government will exclude from the decree all those Spaniards who had previously stood out for the support they gave to the independence of the Mexican nation, and showed their respect and affection for our institutions'. It eventually specified that 'this clause will be applied to sons and daughters who have not contradicted the behaviours of their parents and who still live in the republican territory, [and] to professors of any science, art

the Italian operas *Un'ora di matrimonio*, *L'Abufar* and *Semiramis* and the Spanish operas *Acendi*, *Los maridos solteros* and *Xaira* – plus one opera previously written for New York (*L'amante astuto*) and had staged four operas by other composers: *Il barbiere di Siviglia*, *La Cenerentola* and *Otello* by Rossini and *Don Giovanni* by Mozart.[23]

García's Operas: Hybridisation on Stage

By the time of his arrival, Manuel García was not unknown to the Mexican elites. They were surely aware of the success and reputation he had gained in Europe, given that Luis Castrejón and other key figures of Mexican political and cultural life had visited and lived in London and Paris while García was singing at the King's Theatre and the Théâtre Italien. The Manuel García Mexicans knew was therefore an outstanding representative of the Italian bel canto; the leading tenor of the successful European premieres of operas by Ferdinando Paër, Nicola Manfroce, Giovanni Simone Mayr, Pietro Generali and, of course, Gioachino Rossini, among others; but also the composer of his own Italian operas.[24] Meanwhile, however, he was also thought of as a Spanish singer who had cultivated his exotic Andalusian aura across Europe with *canciones* and *tonadillas* praised by Romantic poets and composers.[25] Between the 1810s and the time of his arrival in 1826, some of these compositions had already crossed the ocean to be staged in Mexico either anonymously or under a different title.[26] For the Mexican elites, therefore, he seemed to be the right singer:

---

or business useful for the nation'; in José María de Tornel y Mendívil, *Breve reseña histórica de los acontecimientos más notables de la nación mexicana* (Mexico City: Cumplido, 1852), 168.

[23] Alongside the operatic performances at the Teatro de los Gallos, Manuel García also gave private recitals in the hall of La Lonja and the Palacio de Minería at the end of 1827 and composed a *Salve Regina* for a local religious festivity in the Cathedral of Mexico City in honour of Nuestra Señora de los Remedios in 1828. It was eventually prohibited by the canonry for being too operatic.

[24] García's Italian operas are: *Il califfo di Bagdad* (Naples 1813), *Jella e Dallaton* (Naples, 1814), *Il fazzoletto* (Paris, 1820) and *La figlia dell'aria* and *L'amante astuto* (New York, 1826).

[25] The *polo* 'Yo que soy contrabandista' from the *tonadilla El Poeta Calculista* (1805) became famous across Europe, captivating composers like Franz Liszt (*Rondeau fantastique sur un thème espagnol 'El Contrabandista'*, 1836), and writers like Victor Hugo (*Bug Jargal*, 1826) and George Sand (*Histoire Lyrique 'Le Contrebandier'*). See *Revue et Gazette musicale de Paris*, 26 February 1837.

[26] Only two Spanish *operetas* by García are proven to have been staged in Mexico before his arrival, *Quien porfía mucho alcanza* (Madrid, 1802; Mexico, 1823) and *El Hablador* (Madrid, 1805; Mexico, 1823).

'European' enough to improve local theatres, and yet moderately Spanish, so as to smoothly communicate with the Mexican elites.

García's own perspective when arriving in Mexico, however, was very different from the expectations of the Mexican elites. Although no documents have been found about García's ideas on Mexico before his journey, it is likely, however, that he formed his own opinion through various means circulating in Europe at that time: the reports of singers who had previously crossed the Atlantic, diaries and travelogues of European explorers who had visited Mexico and also news reports, letters and even public events. As the British traveller William Bullock wrote in 1824 to introduce an exhibition on Mexico at the Egyptian Hall near Piccadilly in London, the new Latin American nation was becoming 'an object of great European consideration', becoming a popular destination for European travellers and thinkers drawn from France and England to its exotic surprises and opportunities.[27] García, who lived between Paris and London from 1816 to 1825, was probably intrigued by these new discourses about Mexico, a nation that he had previously, though indirectly, known as a key territory of the Bourbon Empire where he was born. Conscious of Mexico's cultural opportunities but, arguably, unaware of its wider context and post-independence challenges, García eventually convinced himself that it was the right place for him and his family: a Spanish-speaking and potentially rich nation full of theatres and curious audiences, waiting to be civilised with new Italian operas.[28] His perception of Mexico on his arrival in Veracruz did not appear to have been much different from what *Le Journal des Débats* wrote about him on his way back to Paris in January 1829, after a performance of Ilo in Rossini's *Zelmira*. 'He returns to us from the other world: the memory of his exploits, his adventurous and distant travels ... surround García with mysterious myths of Romanticism.

---

[27] William Bullock, *Catalogue of the Exhibition, Called 'Modern Mexico'; Containing a Panoramic View of the City, with Specimens of the Natural History of New Spain and Models of the Vegetable Produce, Costume, Etc, Now Open for Public Inspection at the Egyptian Hall, Piccadilly* (London: n.p., 1824).

[28] Between 1824 and 1826 William Bullock published a diary of his journey: *Six Months in Mexico; Containing Remarks on the Present State of New Spain, Its Natural Productions, State of Society, Manufacturers, Trade, Agriculture, Antiquities, Etc.* (London: John Murray, 1825), 2 vols; and a *Description of a View of the City of Mexico and Surrounding Country, Now Exhibiting in the Panorama, Leicester-Square* (London: Adlard, 1826). See also George Francis Lyon, *Journal of a Residence and Tour in the Republic of Mexico in the Year 1826, with Some Account of the Mines of That Country*, 2 vols (London: John Murray, 1828) and Robert William Hale Hardy, *Travels in the Interior of Mexico in 1825, 1826, 1827 & 1828* (London: Colburn & Bentley, 1829).

He carried musical civilisation to the cities conquered by Hernán Cortés, he fought against the rebels, against yellow fever.'[29]

When García's *italianità* and the hybrid operatic traditions of independent Mexico met for the first time on the stage of the Teatro de los Gallos that night in June 1827, the contrasts, differences and misperceptions between these two cultures came at last to the fore. The staging of *Il barbiere* revealed the shocking size of the cultural distance between García and the elites of Mexico City at the instant of the performance. The effects of this encounter, however, became manifest not only on the stage and among the audiences, but also through the score, in the composing and revisioning that took place prior to the performance: the composer's surviving manuscripts reveal, in fact, the long and deep processes of transformation and adaptation that García's style and dramaturgy had to undergo in order to meet local needs and expectations. From this perspective, his operas can help us to interrogate the encounter between his operatic background and the elites of Mexico City from a different standpoint beyond a reception-focused approach and examine new sources and ways of thinking about the production and staging of Italian opera in early nineteenth-century Mexico.[30]

Un'ora di Matrimonio

The first operas García composed in Mexico City are, in this regard, particularly revealing given their chronological proximity to his problematic debut with *Il barbiere*. Of the two or three operas he probably composed between 1826 and 1827, the manuscript of *Un'ora di matrimonio* offers the most instructive indications regarding his efforts to adapt the score to the expectations of local audiences.[31] Likely composed during the

---

[29] *Le Journal des Débats*, 21 September 1829. The report refers also to the famous incident that befell the Garcías on their way back to Veracruz, when they were robbed by local brigands.

[30] The manuscript of the Mexican operas returned to Paris in 1829 with García. After his death in 1832, his daughter Paulina inherited them. In 1910 the collection moved to the archive of the Conservatoire de musique in Paris and, from there, to the Bibliothèque nationale de France after World War II.

[31] Manuscript F-Pn MS-6621 (in some local newspapers the opera appears with the title *Un día de matrimonio*). According to Radomski the opera *Zemira ed Azor* was also composed and staged in Mexico in the same period together with *L'Abufar*. As proved by Bruno Cagli's investigation of Domenico Barbaja's letters, the opera was instead composed in Naples in 1814; it is thought that it was eventually reused in Mexico City, but no evidence has been found in this regard. See Bruno Cagli and Sergio Ragni (eds.), *Rossini: Lettere e Documenti*, 4 vols (Pesaro: Fondazione Rossini Pesaro, 1992), vol. 1, 102.

eight-month period of inactivity between his arrival in November 1826 and his debut in June 1827, the opera was meant to be staged at the very beginning of the season, but unforeseen events laid a different path and forced García to withdraw the score and rearrange it for a later debut. *Un'ora di matrimonio* is based on the one-act *Une heure de marriage*, an *opéra comique* composed by Nicholas Dalayrac with a libretto by Charles-Guillaume Étienne that premiered at the Théâtre de l'Opéra-Comique in Paris on 20 March 1804. García knew this work very well since he had sung its Spanish translation, *Una hora de matrimonio*, in Madrid back in 1805 and probably attended some performances of the Italian *commedia* translated by the poet Camillo Giordani in 1815, staged in Rome and Naples. Between 1826 and 1827, when Manuel García decided to compose a new opera on this plot, he eventually used an unknown Italian version of the libretto. By that time Mexican audiences too were familiar with this opera: like many other French operas by Méhul, Boieldieu, Berton and Isouard, after being successfully translated and arranged for Spanish theatres, the Spanish version of Dalayrac's opera might have been staged in Seville and Cadiz to then sail off to Cuba and, from there, to Mexico, although no records of performances have been found so far.

After the negative critiques of *Il barbiere* and the unlucky debut of his *L'Abufar* García withdrew the score of *Un'ora di matrimonio*: the work then disappeared until 8 February 1828, when it finally premiered at the Teatro de los Gallos with the Spanish title *Una hora de matrimonio*.[32] The opera performed that night was, however, radically different from the first version García had in mind eight months earlier. By then, the political situation had become heated and, after the enactment of the Expulsion Law against Spanish residents, García had become more conciliatory than he had been at first. Instead of stubbornly forcing Mexicans to get used to 'his' way of performing opera, he decided to look for a compromise. By the end of 1827 he started to translate the librettos of the operas he had already composed. The case of *Un'ora di matrimonio* was, however, more challenging: it was not only about translating the libretto into Spanish and rewriting it over the Italian score. Rather, the opera had to undergo a process of adaptation that had a major impact both on the structure of the whole composition and on the internal rearrangement of the sections.

---

[32] *El Correo de la Federación Mexicana*, 9 February 1828, 3.

First, García composed a new overture to replace the short instrumental *introduzione* of twenty-one bars that had opened the first version of *Un'ora di matrimonio*. No documents have yet been found to explain the reasons why García had decided not to include overtures to his first Mexican operas (*L'Abufar* too began with a similar introduction) and, eventually, to compose a new one for *Un'ora di matrimonio*. It is, however, likely that García had initially underestimated some local circumstances prior to his debut. He might have considered composing a new overture an unnecessary and unappreciated effort for audiences that, according to him, were likely to have little or no experience of 'authentic' performances of Italian opera. But we can also assume that he deemed the twenty-one musicians of the theatre incapable of playing a long instrumental composition properly as the European orchestras of Paris, London and Naples usually did. However, after the premieres of *Il barbiere* and *L'Abufar*, the reality appeared to be quite different from what the European imagination of Manuel García had pictured before his debut. Not only were Mexican elites already familiar with Italian overtures, relishing the opportunity to listen their melodies inside and outside the theatres, as shown by *Il barbiere* and its domestic circulation prior to 1827: also local musicians, mainly creoles and Spanish, were skilled enough and used to playing a wide variety of repertoires from Italian instrumental music to the German classical symphony, both imported from Spain after the end of the eighteenth century. Under these new and unexpected circumstances, García changed his mind and composed a new *obertura* following the Italian bipartite form – Adagietto and Allegro – making all his annotations in Spanish.

García then replaced all the Italian spoken dialogue of the first version with new *recitativi con basso* translated into Spanish (Figure 4.1). All the original dialogue is now lost, but we can still trace its presence in the first version of the manuscript through the legible marks it left on the top of the first page of each scene. These marks were the last words of the previous spoken dialogue and were originally meant to support the conductor or *primer violín* who, without the harmonic support of the traditional *recitativo*, used them as a reference to know exactly when to start the following scene (Figure 4.2, 'ultima moda'). But let us dwell a little more on this page, for it provides further details that are worth analysing in order to understand the transformations that the manuscript of *Un'ora di matrimonio* had to undergo to meet the expectations of Mexican audiences. The mark 'ultima moda' suggest in fact that the 'ariettina D. Marco' was originally preceded by spoken dialogue and was therefore inserted somewhere in the middle of the first one-act

Figure 4.1 First page of one of the new *recitativi* in Spanish (Scene V, Act II) composed by García to replace the previous spoken dialogue in Italian of the first version of *Un'ora di matrimonio* (Bibliothèque Nationale de France, Département de la Musique, MS 6621, autograph, 455)

manuscript, presumably in scene n. 8 (top-right corner). Yet today it appears at the opening of the second act as shown by the note in Spanish 'Acto 2°' added at a later time (and, probably by another person) at the top centre of the page. This shows that, in addition to the translation into Spanish and the replacement of the Italian spoken dialogues, García also had to split the original one-act version of the opera into two different acts. Once again, the reasons for this readjustment are to be found in the Mexican theatrical habits of the time. As a matter of fact, late colonial and early independent theatrical performances in Mexico used to be rather short and heterogeneous in order to include popular dances, arias and *tonadillas* during the intermissions. This tradition influenced the staging and reception of Italian operas early on: these shows were included to make operatic performances shorter and more appealing to the audience. After independence, this colonial habit forced García to divide the

4 Italian Opera and Creole Identities: Manuel García

Figure 4.2 First page of the 'Ariettina D. Marco', the opening scene of Act II of the new version of *Un'ora di matrimonio*. The spoken Italian dialogue ending with the words 'ultima moda' (top-left corner) was removed and the Italian text was translated (lower-right corner). (Bibliothèque Nationale de France, Département de la Musique, MS 6621, autograph, 276)

manuscript into two acts and make room for an intermission with shows, songs and dances. But there is still one more detail that deserves our attention in this page. This *ariettina* gives us, in fact, a glimpse at the translation into Spanish of the Italian libretto of the first version. The process of translation, which appears throughout the whole manuscript of the opera (with the exception, of course, of the new *recitativi*), can be clearly observed at the end of the page (Figure 4.2) where the Spanish new version ('Por ejemplo estamos viendo') was added over the Italian original text ('Per esempio voi vedrete'). These structural changes notwithstanding, *Una hora de matrimonio* did not achieve the success García had hoped for. The day after its premiere at the Teatro de los Gallos an operagoer summarised in a local newspaper: 'I wouldn't like my wedding day to be like that!'[33]

The analysis of this manuscript places the operatic activity of Manuel García between 1826 and 1829 within the complex cultural and historical context of early independent Mexico, in an attempt to move beyond the simplistic narrative of a straightforward Europeanisation of Mexican theatrical life. The difficult interaction between García and the Mexican elites created a hybrid space of contacts between different cultures and expectations that, alongside political and press debates, transformed opera and *italianità* into an 'unstable commodity ... unpredictable in (its) effects', a consequence recently evoked by Benjamin Walton in his historical and theoretical framing of the early globalisation of Italian opera: what was supposed to satisfy local needs and fashions ended up offending the identity and cultural project of an entire nation.[34] In other words, García's operas and performances created a new space of interaction where, for the first time, Mexico came into direct contact with the European operatic tradition. The persistence of colonial models did not, however, lead towards a hegemonic dialogue between new colonising forces – namely France, Britain and Italy – and a young nation like Mexico, which would passively and uniformly take over European values. Instead, the arrival of Manuel García and his *italianità* generated a more complex panorama where colonial and European musical cultures critically interacted on the stage and behind.

The consequences of this interaction became rapidly perceptible. While Italian opera in Mexico underwent a substantial transformation in terms of its production and reception on stage, the elites found themselves embedded in their own creole identity, suddenly becoming aware, as Walter Mignolo

---

[33] Ibid.   [34] Walton, 'Teresa Schieroni and the Beginnings of Global Opera'.

observes, of 'not being who they were supposed to be'.³⁵ After García, however, rather than leading to a rethinking of its colonial past, operatic Mexico moved closer towards a non-Spanish understanding of European culture. In 1831, when Filippo Galli arrived from Milan to take over García's role as the leader of new opera company of Mexico City, he staged the entire Rossinian catalogue of works alongside several new Italian operas by Pacini, Mercadante, Coccia and Meyerbeer, all in their original Italian version. His productions, perhaps surprisingly, aroused a new enthusiasm among the elites of Mexico City, as though the previous tensions with García had never happened. Mexico soon forgot García's name and his operas, but local operatic life continued to be marked by the consequences of a transition he had begun: his operatic *italianità* had shaken Mexico's identity by revealing, for the first time since independence, its difference and cultural distance from Europe.

[35] Walter Mignolo, *The Idea of Latin America* (Hoboken, NJ: Blackwell Publishing, 2006), 63.

5 | Italian Opera in *Vormärz* Vienna

Gaetano Donizetti, Bartolomeo Merelli and Habsburg Cultural Policies in the Mid-1830s

CLAUDIO VELLUTINI

Gaetano Donizetti's first visit to Vienna in the spring of 1842 was the culmination of a long-coveted project. Aged forty-five, he embarked on the journey to the Austrian capital to supervise the first production of *Linda di Chamounix*, his first opera for the Kärntnertortheater, the city's court opera, then managed by two Italian impresarios, Bartolomeo Merelli and Carlo Balocchino.[1] For a number of years, the composer had repeatedly expressed his wish to obtain a commission from the Kärntnertortheater. On 13 August 1837, Donizetti had written to his publisher, Giovanni Ricordi, requesting that one of the firm's employees mediate with Merelli on his behalf.[2] The impresario was an old acquaintance of Donizetti's. Both were natives of Bergamo, a town in Lombardy, which belonged to the Austrian Empire at the time, and both had studied with the Bavarian composer Johann Simon Mayr, who had settled in Bergamo after having made a name for himself throughout the Italian peninsula as an author of Italian operas. After a few unsuccessful attempts as an opera composer and librettist, Merelli amassed a considerable fortune as a theatrical agent and impresario.[3] The circumstances that eventually allowed the composer and the impresario to come to an agreement

---

[*] This chapter draws on research generously supported by the University of Chicago, the University of British Columbia and the Social Sciences and Humanities Research Council of Canada.

[1] For a discussion of the two impresarios' management of the Kärntnertortheater, see Michael Jahn, *Die Wiener Hofoper von 1836 bis 1848: Die Ära Balochino–Merelli* (Vienna: Der Apfel, 2004).

[2] 'Tell Pedroni that I wish to see Vienna, and that he should speak with Merelli, because it is not worthwhile if I do it myself.' The original letter is published in Guido Zavadini, *Donizetti. Vita – Musiche – Epistolario* (Bergamo: Istituto Italiano d'Arti Grafiche, 1948), 437–8. In the rest of this chapter, the letters quoted from Zavadini's work will be labelled with a Z followed by their number of publication (in this case, for instance, Z249). Giacomo Pedroni, a friend of Donizetti, was an accomplished musician and employee of Ricordi. He was frequently in charge of the piano arrangements of Donizetti's operas.

[3] See Francesco Regli, *Dizionario biografico dei più celebri poeti e artisti melodrammatici* (Turin: Dalmazzo, 1860), 323–4; and Angelo Rusconi, 'Merelli, Bartolomeo', *Dizionario Biografico degli Italiani*, vol. 73 (Rome: Istituto della Enciclopedia Italiana, 2009), 629–32.

over *Linda di Chamounix* have been examined in great detail.[4] But why did Donizetti feel reluctant to reach out directly to Merelli in 1837?

William Ashbrook laments a lack of documentary evidence to address this question, and speculates that Merelli had personal resentment towards Donizetti.[5] Previously overlooked documents from Viennese archives, however, suggest a different explanation, revealing that Donizetti had been in negotiations with Merelli and Balocchino as soon as they took control of the Kärntnertortheater at the end of 1835. Because the three of them did not reach an agreement on this occasion, the composer might have decided to cautiously resume the negotiations in 1837. Whatever the case, these documents show that, no matter what their personal relationship might have been, discussions between Donizetti and Merelli had taken place on a regular basis since the impresario took control of Vienna's court opera house. In this essay, I propose that reconsidering this early negotiation may help us to shed light not only on this apparently minor aspect of Donizetti's biography (one that has nonetheless important implications for a full understanding of the composer's late operatic output) but also on a relatively neglected moment of Viennese musical life. Reconsidering Donizetti's systematic attempts to become involved in Vienna's operatic life addresses a central theme of this volume: it provides a case study for understanding the extent to which ideas of operatic *italianità* underpinned the transnational dissemination of opera even at a time when – and despite the fact that – national ideologies had come to dominate the local discourse on it. As we shall see, such ongoing interest in *italianità* was a crucial component of Austrian cultural policies.

While the recent surge of scholarly interest in Italian opera in early nineteenth-century Vienna has focused mostly on Rossini and his role in steering musical debates in the 1810s and 1820s, the following two decades have remained comparatively underexplored, at least up to the 1848 Revolution.[6] This oversight is in part due to the historiographical

---

[4] On Donizetti's attempts to write for Vienna, see William Ashbrook, *Donizetti and His Operas* (Cambridge: Cambridge University Press, 1982), 160–2. Ashbrook's reconstruction informs the discussion in Gabriele Dotto, 'Historical Introduction', in Gaetano Donizetti, *Linda di Chamounix*, ed. Gabriele Dotto (Milan/Bergamo: Ricordi – Fondazione Donizetti, 2005), xxxi–xxxii. I have discussed the changing reception of Donizetti's operas in Vienna prior to 1842 in my article 'Donizetti, Vienna, Cosmopolitanism', *Journal of the American Musicological Society*, 73/1 (2020), 1–52.

[5] See Ashbrook, *Donizetti*, 162.

[6] Among the works on the years immediately following the Congress of Vienna, see Alice Hanson, *Musical Life in Biedermeier Vienna* (Cambridge: Cambridge University Press, 1985); Leopold Kantner and Michael Jahn, 'Il viaggio a Vienna', in M. Bucarelli (ed.), *Rossini 1792–1992: Mostra storico-documentaria* (Perugia: Electa, 1992), 197–204; Leopold Kantner, 'Rossini nello specchio della cultura musicale dell'impero asburgico', in *La recezione di Rossini ieri e oggi* (Rome:

paradigms that catalysed research after Carl Dahlhaus proposed an understanding of European nineteenth-century music as the development of a duality of styles (*Stildualismus*) epitomised by Beethoven's symphonies and Rossini's operas. Concerning Viennese musical life, Dahlhaus has enriched, but not fundamentally altered, established approaches to an already well-trodden field of investigation, with Rossini now functioning as a 'foreign' complement to a local tradition marked by Beethoven and Schubert.[7] Adding Rossini to the Viennese musical landscape only reinforces the sense that, by the end of the 1820s, the city had lost its centrality. Certainly, the close death dates of Beethoven and Schubert in 1827 and 1828, respectively, have been regularly held up as a watershed in the musical history of the city. According to Henri-Louis de la Grange, for instance:

> With Schubert's death, the most fertile musical age that Vienna ever knew came to an end . . . . [F]or more than forty years thereafter, Vienna ceases to be a center of musical creation. The capital of Austria, which up to this point could claim to be the capital of music, must content itself to experience the echo and repercussions of phenomena that, henceforth, take place elsewhere.[8]

Accademia dei Lincei, 1994), 215–22; Michele Leigh Clark, 'The Performances and Reception of Rossini's Operas in Vienna, 1822–1825', unpublished PhD dissertation, University of North Carolina (2005); Michael Jahn, 'Rossinis Opern in Wien von 1816 bis 1822' in his *Di tanti palpiti . . . : Italiener in Wien* (Vienna: Der Apfel, 2006), 61–116; Benjamin Walton, '"More German than Beethoven": Rossini's Zelmira and Italian Style', in N. Mathew and B. Walton (eds.), *The Invention of Beethoven and Rossini: Historiography, Analysis, Criticism* (Cambridge: Cambridge University Press, 2013), 159–77; Claudio Vellutini, 'Rossini's Operas and the Politics of Translation' and Axel Körner, 'Culture for a Cosmopolitan Empire: Rossini between Vienna and the lands of the Bohemia Crown', both in I. Narici, E. Sala, E. Senici and B. Walton (eds.), *Gioachino Rossini 1868–2018: La musica e il mondo* (Pesaro: Fondazione Rossini, 2018), 337–55 and 357–80, respectively; and Axel Körner, 'Beyond Nationaloper: For a Critique of Methodological Nationalism in Reading Nineteenth-Century Italian and German Opera', *Journal of Modern Italian Studies* 25/4 (2020), 402–19 (402–6). In comparison, the literature on the two decades before 1848 is relatively scant. In addition to a few, short and often wanting general overviews, see Ursula Dauth, *Verdis Opern im Spiegel der Wiener Presse von 1843 bis 1859: Ein Beitrag zur Rezeptionsgeschichte* (Munich/Salzburg: Katzbichler, 1981); Michael Jahn (ed.), *Donizetti und seine Zeit in Wien* (Vienna: Der Apfel, 2010); and my own works: 'Adina *Par* Excellence: Eugenia Tadolini and the Performing Tradition of Donizetti's L'elisir d'amore in Vienna', *19th-Century Music* 38/1 (2014), 3–29; 'Opera and Monuments: Verdi's *Ernani* in Vienna and the Construction of Dynastic Memory', *Cambridge Opera Journal* 29/2 (2017), 215–39; and ' Fanny Tacchinardi-Persiani, Carlo Balocchino, and Italian Opera Business in Vienna, Paris and London (1837–1845)', *Cambridge Opera Journal* 30/2–3 (2018), 259–304.

[7] See Carl Dahlhaus, *Nineteenth-Century Music*, trans. by J. Bradford Robinson (Berkeley/Los Angeles: University of California Press, 1989), 8–15. See also Richard Taruskin, *Music in the Nineteenth Century* (New York: Oxford University Press, 2005), 7.

[8] Henry-Louis de la Grange, *Vienne: Une histoire musicale* (Paris: Fayard, 1995), 143.

Similarly, Theophil Antonicek writes about a 'creative paralysis' (*eine Krise des Schöpferischen*) after Schubert's and Beethoven's deaths.[9] Furthermore, in a generalist publication, Franz Endler labels the years after the two composers' passing as 'The Time of Minor Masters'.[10] While recent responses to Dahlhaus have called for a more nuanced understanding of the musical cultures Beethoven and Rossini represent – one that emphasises their interaction rather than their opposition – the chronological focus of all of these approaches has remained anchored to roughly the fifteen years following the Congress of Vienna.[11] The Italian impresario Domenico Barbaja, who had brought Rossini to Vienna in 1822, resigned from his post at the helm of the Kärntnertortheater in 1828. Moreover, albeit far from Vienna, Rossini himself quit composing operas the following year, a circumstance that reinforces the perception that the late 1820s constitute the close of an era in the city's musical life.

This approach, however, leaves a considerable part of the picture unexplored. Because of Vienna's musical tradition, its status as the capital of a multinational empire and the specific sociopolitical conditions of the Empire after Napoleon's fall, the musical life in the city and the discourse around it were both characterised by a multiplicity of intersecting – and at times conflicting – events and forces. One might argue that the resulting tensions, which were evident to contemporary observers, testify to the city's ongoing vitality rather than to its immobility. Some of these tensions, of course, have already been examined in relation to Rossini.[12] In what follows, however, I wish to address some of the continuities that characterised the official cultural policies of the Austrian state towards Italian culture across the 'watershed' years of 1827–30, proposing that, up to the late 1840s, the Habsburg court sustained an idea of *italianità* that was integral to the supranational conception of the Austrian Empire at large. Donizetti's early negotiations with Merelli reveal some of the strategies behind these cultural policies. They occurred in conjunction with an administrative reorganisation of the Kärntnertortheater aimed at reinforcing Vienna's musical ties to the

---

[9] Theophil Antonicek (with contributions by Rudolf Flotzinger, Rudolf Hopfner and Alfons Hubner), 'Biedermeierzeit und Vormärz', in R. Flotzinger and G. Gruber (eds.), *Musikgeschichte Österreichs*, vol. 2: *Vom Barock zum Vormärz* (Vienna: Böhlau, 1995), 279–351 (280).

[10] Franz Endler, *Vienna: A Guide to Its Music and Musicians*, trans. Leo Jecny (Portland, OR: Amadeus Press, 1989), 40.

[11] See, in particular, Mathew and Walton (eds.), *The Invention of Beethoven and Rossini*. For an earlier critique of Dahlhaus, see Philip Gossett, 'Carl Dahlhaus and the "Ideal Type"', *19th-Century Music* 13/1 (1989), 49–56.

[12] See, in particular, Walton, '"More German than Beethoven"'; Vellutini, 'Rossini's Operas'; and Körner, 'Culture for a Cosmopolitan Empire'.

Italian states, which the Habsburg court had been cultivating systematically since the seventeenth century and again after the Congress of Vienna. Focusing on this overlooked moment of nineteenth-century opera history in Vienna ultimately shows the flexibility with which the Habsburg court persevered in promoting *italianità* within the cultural and ideological project in defence of the supranational identity of the Empire.

In Search of an Italian Opera Composer

On 17 December 1835, the Viennese newspaper *Der Wanderer* announced that two days earlier Emperor Ferdinand I had signed a resolution to entrust the management of the Kärntnertortheater to Bartolomeo Merelli and Carlo Balocchino.[13] Balocchino would reside in Vienna, take care of the daily errands of the opera house and be responsible for the German opera seasons, which ran between July of each year and March of the following year. Merelli, who was also in charge of the administration of Milan's Teatro alla Scala, would remain in Italy for most of the year and supervise the organisation of Vienna's Italian opera seasons, which ran from April to June. This task included selecting operas and arranging an Italian opera company to be sent to the Kärntnertortheater every spring.[14]

As soon as they closed their contract with the court, the two impresarios entered into negotiations with Donizetti. Three undated documents written in the composer's hand, now kept in the library of Vienna's City Hall, reveal the details of their bargaining. According to these documents, Donizetti planned to prepare a revision of *Francesca di Foix* (a one-act *farsa* that needed to be expanded into two acts) for the 1836 Italian opera season and a new *opera seria* for the following year.[15] It is likely Donizetti was setting the conditions for different agreements, either for the two operas separately (with no strings attached to the other project), or for both at a reduced price. In one document, the composer sets the price for the new opera at 12,000 francs, in addition to free accommodation in Vienna, shared property of the autograph full score

---

[13] *Der Wanderer*, 'Kurier der Theater und Spektakel', 17 December 1835, n.p.

[14] See Jahn, *Die Wiener Hofoper von 1836 to 1848*, 17–23.

[15] Wienbibliothek im Rathaus (henceforth, A-Wst), Handschriftensammlung, H.I.N. 10223, 10224 and 10225. The three documents come from Carlo Balocchino's business archive. The first one was published, with a few omissions, in Leopold Kantner, 'Donizetti a Vienna', in G. Tintori (ed.), *Gaetano Donizetti* (Milan: Nuove Edizioni, 1983), 49–60 (56). Kantner ascribes the document to the years 1840–1. As explained in this essay, however, the content of these documents invalidates this hypothesis. To my knowledge, the other two documents have never been published.

and exclusive rights to sell it to music publishers.[16] Another document contains only Donizetti's demands for the revision of *Francesca di Foix*: a remuneration of 5,000 *lire* for himself in addition to the expenses for his collaborator, Giacomo Pedroni, who would stage the opera in Vienna in Donizetti's stead.[17] Finally, for both projects, Donizetti demanded 16,000 francs and envisioned the cast for *Francesca di Foix*.[18]

This negotiation anticipates any previously known remark about Donizetti's intentions to write for Vienna. Despite the lack of any dates in the documents, there is no doubt that they were written sometime between the end of 1835 and the beginning of 1836 – enough time for the composer to work on the planned revisions to *Francesca di Foix*. This chronological attribution is further confirmed by yet another undated document, a draft letter from Balocchino to Merelli confirming that the impresarios and Donizetti had settled several details:

I thought about yesterday's project, and I find your maestro's proposition about the *opera seria* for spring 1837 sensible, and indeed it should be accepted. That is, we should wait until we have a company, inquire whether the maestro is satisfied with it and then sign the contract with him. So, let's not do otherwise, taking for granted that your Donizetti keep his word and ensure that he is free. Regarding the opera

---

[16] 'For a new opera specifically composed for the Vienna opera house, owned by Merelli and Co., bearing myself the cost of the new libretto and composed for the company upon which we secretly agreed – twelve thousand Francs. Lodging in Vienna provided, shared ownership of the manuscript score, exclusive rights to reductions. I commit myself to go to Vienna to stage the new opera and I submit myself to the usual duties, obligations, etc. etc.': A-Wst, H.I.N. 10223. The *verso* of the document contains Balocchino's own indication 'Dimanda del Sig.^r Maestro Donizetti'. The transcription of the three Donizetti documents discussed in this section is provided in my 'Cultural Engineering: Italian Opera in Vienna, 1816–1848', unpublished PhD dissertation, University of Chicago (2015), 231–2, footnotes 7–9.

[17] 'To expand *Francesca di Foix* into two acts and submit it on time: five thousand Austrian Lire, to be paid in Naples. To Maestro Pedroni, who will go to Vienna to stage the opera: travel costs and lodging provided, as well as a hundred Thaler of remuneration. No other additional costs either for the price of the opera, nor for Pedroni. Exclusive rights of said expanded version of *Francesca di Foix* to be shared with the composer': A-Wst, H.I.N. 10225.

[18] 'To rework the opera *Francesca di Foix*, originally given at the San Carlo in Naples, in two acts for Tadolini, Genero, Ronconi or Marini and Domenico Galli, as well as a contralto (Page); and for a new opera for Vienna for Spring 1837 for the company upon which we secretly agreed; bearing myself the cost for both librettos (i.e. expanding *Francesca* from one to two acts, as well as for the new libretto for the opera seria) – sixteen thousand Francs. Exclusive rights for the manuscript score as well as for reductions for voice and piano, instruments etc. shared with the *Impresa*. Lodging in Vienna provided': A-Wst, H.I.N. 10224. The singers mentioned in this letter (soprano Eugenia Tadolini, tenor Giovanni Battista Genero and basses Sebastiano Ronconi and Ignazio Marini) all sang in Vienna during the 1836. The company also included Vincenzo Galli, whose first name Donizetti probably got wrong. See Michael Jahn, 'Die Sänger der italienischen Stagione in Wien von 1835 bis 1847', in his *Di tanti palpiti . . . : Italiener in Wien* (Vienna: Verlag Der Apfel, 2006), 214–41.

buffa for the upcoming spring, I authorise you to close [the contract], but do not offer more than four thousand Austrian Liras – in fact, keep the price lower if you can. He will take care of the libretto and will own half of the score for both publication of the vocal score and rental to other theaters. It seems to me that this is a considerable offer, which shows the esteem of the impresa for your maestro, for he won't have to travel and will stay home, while we will not be able to enjoy his useful presence in Vienna to stage the opera. Furthermore, this *farsa* is already known and this also needs to be taken into consideration, just as we have to take into account the cost for maestro Pedroni, which is ours to cover, and for which I ask you instead to stipulate a forfeit for his journey to and from Vienna, and his lodging.[19]

As soon as the two Italian impresarios took on the management of the Kärntnertortheater at the end of 1835, they made concrete plans to have Donizetti in Vienna. If the reasons for the failure of these projects remain unclear, the tone of Balocchino's letter leaves some room for hypotheses.

In addressing Merelli, Balocchino appears somewhat cautious about yielding to Donizetti's demand. Not only did the impresario insist on according Donizetti a lower remuneration for *Francesca di Foix*; he also did not seem comfortable with committing the money for a new opera by the composer right off the bat. Balocchino, who was in charge of the Kärntnertortheater bookkeeping and had the last word on financial matters, was famously intransigent in his business negotiations. This attitude might have induced Donizetti to walk away from a disadvantageous deal.[20] That money was an issue is evident from Donizetti's blunt rejection of another offer he received from Merelli a few years later.[21] By the time of his first negotiation with Balocchino and Merelli, Donizetti was undoubtedly the most sought-after Italian opera composer: of his chief competitors, Vincenzo Bellini had died in

---

[19] Undated draft letter from Carlo Balocchino to Bartolomeo Merelli: A-Wst, H.I.N. 10399. The original document, written in the hand of Balocchino's secretary, is transcribed in Vellutini, 'Cultural Engineering', 233, fn. 10.

[20] The journalist and music critic Ferdinand Ritter von Seyfried reported that 'Merelli had no firm personality, while Balocchino distinguished himself for his diligence in fulfilling all his duties but also for his stubborn determination. He used to say: "*Io pago – io voglio*" (I pay, I want it), and no further objection could follow, as every other word would have been useless': Ferdinand Ritter von Seyfried, *Rückschau in das Theaterleben Wien's seit den letzten fünfzig Jahren* (Vienna: Selbstverlage des Verfassers, 1864), 30.

[21] Letter to Paolo Branca, 26 September 1840, Z348. Merelli likely acted as a broker between the composer and Balocchino. In this letter, Donizetti declares himself ready to go to Vienna for 10,000 Austrian *lire* – significantly less than the 12,000 francs demanded previously – if the *Impresa* covered the cost for the trip and for his accommodation.

September 1835, Saverio Mercadante was kept busy by his post as *maestro di cappella* of the Novara cathedral and Giovanni Pacini had temporarily retired from the operatic arena. This situation entitled him to demand generous remuneration for his works. But a glance at the Viennese operatic repertoire up to 1836 suggests that Balocchino had some reasons to be prudent. Only seven operas by Donizetti had been performed in Vienna up to that point, and of these, only *L'elisir d'amore* had scored an undisputed success.[22] It is likely that, at the beginning of their enterprise, Balocchino and Merelli thought of Donizetti as a risky investment and looked for alternatives elsewhere.

For their opening Italian opera season at the Kärntnertortheater (the same for which Donizetti was expected to revise *Francesca di Foix*), the two impresarios turned to Pietro Antonio Coppola (1793–1877), whose opera *La pazza per amore* had made a sensation in Rome the previous year, and who was to compose a new opera, *Enrichetta di Baienfeld*.[23] The Viennese, however, were far from gripped by it. *La pazza per amore* received a mere eight performances in Vienna, three of which took place during a revival of the opera in 1839. The new opera Coppola specifically wrote for the Kärntnertortheater, *Enrichetta di Baienfeld*, fared even worse; it foundered after only four evenings and was never revived.[24] After this fiasco, Balocchino tried to lure other Italian composers to Vienna. In 1837 he beseeched a reticent Rossini to consider writing a new work for the Kärntnertortheater.[25] Equally unsuccessful was Balocchino's attempt at closing a deal with the elderly composer Francesco Morlacchi.[26] In sum, Balocchino and Merelli were making substantial efforts not only to bring new Italian operas and singers to Vienna, but also to secure the presence of composers who would write works specifically conceived for the local audience.

This strategy reveals an important aspect of ideas of operatic *italianità* – the concern that these works would meet the expectations of particular non-Italian spectators. The operas in question, in other words, were meant to blur cultural divides. As Benjamin Walton has shown, Rossini had set an

---

[22] See Vellutini, 'Adina *par excellence*'; and Michael Jahn, 'Donizettis Opern in Wien: Von 1827 zum Ende des Zweiten Welkrieges', in his *Donizetti und seine Zeit in Wien*, 113–238.

[23] See Maria Giordano, *Pietro Antonio Coppola: Operista siciliano dell'Ottocento* (Lucca: LIM, 2003), 31–8.

[24] See Jahn, *Die Wiener Hofoper von 1836 bis 1848*, 444–5.

[25] A-Wst, H.I.N. 10403. The letter was first published in Franco Schlitzer, *Un piccolo carteggio inedito di Rossini con un impresario italiano di Vienna* (Florence: Sansoni, 1954).

[26] For the correspondence between Balocchino and Morlacchi, see A-Wst, H.I.N. 10268, 10463, 10269 and 10464.

important precedent in Vienna. His *Zelmira* (premiered in Naples in 1822, but conceived for Vienna, where it opened that same year) engaged critics in an intense debate, as the work eschewed clear categorisation as either Italian or German.[27] But what were the motivations that induced the two impresarios to make the Kärntnertortheater a centre of production for Italian opera, and not a mere centre for consumption of imported operatic goods? Answering this question requires digging into the reasons that brought Merelli and Balocchino to Vienna in the first place, exploring the role of opera impresarios within the Empire's cultural politics and discussing the strategies that different impresarios adopted to fulfil this role.

Imperial Aspirations on a Tight Budget

Since the end of the Napoleonic Wars, Emperor Franz I, some of his ministers and some high-ranking civil servants had been considering several approaches to the management of the Kärntnertortheater, with two distinct but complementary objectives in mind. The first one was financial efficiency, the lack of which had severely compromised the functioning of the institution up to the Congress of Vienna. The other was the integration of the opera house within a strategic vision of imperial culture that would take into account the profound changes the Austrian Empire had been undergoing since the beginning of the century.[28] Particularly important among these changes was the Empire's transformation into a dynastic realm in 1804 and its continuously shifting borders until Napoleon's ultimate defeat in 1815.[29] The latter event ushered in the return of Italian territories under Austrian authority and opened a new phase in the political and cultural relationships between Vienna and the Italian States. With all of this in mind, Emperor Franz and his entourage discussed at length whether the Kärntnertortheater should be administered by court officials or by private impresarios, and whether it should include an Italian opera company in addition to a permanent group of German singers and

---

[27] See Walton, '"More German than Beethoven"'.

[28] See Andreas Gottsmann, *Staatskunst oder Kulturstaat? Staatliche Kunstpolitik in Österreich 1848-1914* (Vienna: Böhlau, 2017), 9-17. For the administrative foundations of this process, see John Deak, *Forging the Multinational State. State Making in Imperial Austria from the Enlightenment to the First World War* (Stanford, CA: Stanford University Press, 2015).

[29] On the creation of the Austrian Empire in 1804, see Robert J. W. Evans, 'Communicating Empire: The Habsburgs and Their Critics, 1700-1919 (The Prothero Lecture)', *Transactions of the Royal Historical Society*, Sixth Series, XIX (2009), 117-38.

a ballet company. Different parties voiced alternative and, at times, radically contrasting opinions. Eventually, the line that prevailed was the one advocated by Franz's Minister of Finance, Johann Philip Stadion.[30]

Stadion first formulated his vision of the political and cultural function of the Kärntnertortheater in a long report from 11 July 1817.[31] As one of the court theatres, the Kärntnertortheater was foundational to the promotion of values that contributed to the definition of an imperial collective identity. The court opera house, in Stadion's view, catered to the 'many foreigners [that] live in Vienna and seek entertainment, but neither understand German nor like German opera, and thus would have no access to any public spectacle'.[32] The inclusion of different genres on the court stages, in other words, was functional to the representation of Vienna as the cultural, as well as administrative, capital of a multinational Empire – one in which German drama and opera had to coexist with other forms of cultural expression.

While Stadion did not immediately endorse the formation of a new Italian opera company at the Kärntnertortheater, it soon became clear to him that finding a profitable balance between audience demands and diversified cultural offerings required firmer entrepreneurial skills than those possessed by civil servants. In 1819, he communicated to the Emperor that the management of the opera house required an entrepreneurial mindset, which included knowledge of the market, readiness to take advantage of the opportunities it offered and complete dedication to the business.[33] The minister's openness to a market-oriented administration of the Kärntnertortheater did not necessarily emerge from a personal belief in liberal ideas; rather, Stadion believed that a market-oriented management of the theatre had to be reconciled with opera's educational and moral function – a central concern of the Empire's cultural policies. Within a year, he had worked out these discrepancies, settling on a coherent proposal that recognised Italy as the land with the most developed taste

---

[30] For a detailed picture of these debates, see Vellutini, 'Cultural Engineering', 37–102. On Stadion's position, see also Theresa Reichenberger, 'Italienische Opernstagioni im Wiener Vormärz', in P. Chiarini and H. Zeman (eds.), Österreich-Italien: Auf der Suche nach der gemeinsamen Vergangenheit/Italia-Austria: Alla ricerca del passato comune (Rome: Istituto Italiano di Studi Germanici, 2002), 213–24.

[31] Stadion to Emperor Franz, 11 July 1817: Vienna, Haus- Hof- und Staatsarchiv, General Intendanz der Hoftheater (henceforth abbreviated as HHStA, Gen. Int.), Box 8, 1817, ad 220, Beil. 1.

[32] Ibid. Original quoted in Vellutini, 'Cultural Engineering', 64, fn. 50.

[33] See Stadion's report to Emperor Franz from 28 March 1819: HHStA, Gen.Int., Box 10 (1819–20), 1819, 318 (olim 2947).

for sumptuous spectacles and that ranked the opera houses in Milan and Venice among the highest cultural institutions of the Empire.

Stadion singled out these venues not only as models for managing the Kärntnertortheater but also as pivotal to a much more ambitious – and cost-effective – plan: the joint administrative and artistic direction of the Empire's principal opera houses.[34] This project suggests that the financial and artistic stability provided by private impresarios did not conflict with the government's aim of exercising control over cultural production; quite the contrary, it was preparatory to the creation of a centralised system embracing cultural institutions from various regions of the Empire – a system that ultimately reinforced the state's multinational character. To be sure, this plan did not materialise exactly in these terms, especially since the main opera house in Venice, La Fenice, was the property of private box owners rather than the government. Nevertheless, it did set the groundwork for the integration of the Kärntnertortheater within an Italian operatic network, as negotiations to entrust the theatre to the impresario Domenico Barbaja – at that time in charge of the Teatro San Carlo in Naples, and later of La Scala – began soon thereafter.

During his tenure at the Kärntnertortheater (1822–8), Barbaja furthered Stadion's cultural project by creating the conditions for a more intensive circulation of operatic works and artists across the Alps. The unprecedented financial backing the impresario received from the court outraged many supporters of German opera.[35] Yet, despite the outcries prophesising the twilight of German operatic culture in Vienna, Barbaja hardly turned into the harbinger of an Italian invasion. Sure enough, the overlapping presence of Weber and Rossini in Vienna between 1822 and 1823 has rightly been described as one of

---

[34] This plan is outlined in an unsigned document included in Stadion's report to Emperor Franz from 13 January 1820: HHStA, Gen. Int., Box 10 (1819–20), 1820, *ad* 350, Beil. 6 (*olim: ad* 1934/ M 820). See also Reichenberger, 'Italienische Opernstagioni', 214–15. Jutta Toelle has pointed out that a remarkably similar plan was proposed again in 1857: see her *Bühne der Stadt: Mailand und das Teatro alla Scala zwischen Risorgimento und Fin de siècle* (Vienna: Böhlau and Oldenbourg, 2009), 46–9.

[35] See, for instance, the copy of Ignaz von Mosel's report (on behalf of, and endorsed by, the Director of the Court Theaters Moritz von Dietrichstein) to the Emperor, 26 October 1821: HHStA, Gen.Int., Sonderreihe 55/I, Pachtakten Barbaja 1821, Fasz. 10: 'Against my objections, the impresario has been granted so many benefits which *I*, your Majesty's Theater Director, would have never dared to request'. Dietrichstein and Mosel had been temporarily put in charge of the Kärntnertortheater while negotiations with Barbaja were carried on, and they openly discouraged Emperor Franz from placing the opera house in the impresario's hands: see Franz Hadamowsky, *Wien: Theater Geschichte* (Vienna: Jugend und Volk, 1988), 332–3.

the greatest achievements of Barbaja's business instinct.³⁶ In following that instinct, however, he also acted for practical reasons. His contract with the Habsburg court obliged him to produce German operas and to maintain a German opera company, while his obligations in Naples required that his Italian troupe in Vienna be reduced in number and that his most prominent singers spend only a limited amount of time north of the Alps.³⁷ He thus organised the calendar of the Kärntnertortheater into two distinct, but at times overlapping, seasons: a longer German season, made up of German operas as well as Italian and French works in German translation, and an Italian season, exclusively dedicated to operas in Italian and featuring the artists who visited Vienna from Naples.

Barbaja faced major challenges in maintaining this system. One of them was the deterioration of his professional relationship with Rossini after his first season at the Kärntnertortheater, due to a dispute over the rights of *Zelmira*.³⁸ Rossini did not renew the contract that bound him to Barbaja and the San Carlo, and the impresario lost one of his major trump cards. Barbaja invited to Vienna a string of Italian younger composers – Michele Carafa in 1823, Saverio Mercadante in 1824 and Giovanni Pacini in 1827 – but to no avail. Their works hardly survived their first run at the Kärntnertortheater.³⁹ Moreover, Barbaja received major complaints in Naples due to the prolonged absence of the company's leading singers from the San Carlo.⁴⁰ This negative trend changed only when the impresario brought Vincenzo Bellini's *Il pirata* to the Kärntnertortheater in 1828. The production, however, marked the impresario's swansong in Vienna. Worsening financial conditions and declining health persuaded him to

---

[36] See, for instance, Hanson, *Musical Life*, 66; and Philip Eisenbeiss, *Bel Canto Bully: The Life and Times of the Legendary Opera Impresario Domenico Barbaja* (London: Haus Publishing, 2013), 122.

[37] Barbaja's contract is published in full in Paologiovanni Maione and Francesca Seller, 'Da Napoli a Vienna: Barbaja e l'esportazione di un nuovo modello impresariale', *Römische Historische Mitteilungen* 44 (2002), 493–508. On Barbaja and German opera, see also Thomas A. Denny, 'Schubert's *Fierrabras* and Barbaja's Opera Business', *Schubert: Perspektiven* 5/1 (2005), 19–45 (26–36).

[38] See Richard Osborne, *Rossini: His Life and Works*, 2nd ed. (New York: Oxford University Press, 2007), 73–4; and Philip Eisenbeiss, *Bel Canto Bully: The Life and Times of the Legendary Opera Impresario Domenico Barbaja* (London: Haus Publishing, 2013), 141–4.

[39] See Michael Jahn, 'Saverio Mercadante an der Wiener Hofoper (1824–1856)', in his *Di tanti palpiti ...*, 117–39, and Odo Aberham, 'Zwei vergessene Donizetti-Zeitgenossen in Wien', in Jahn (ed.), *Donizetti und seine Zeit in Wien*, 245–66.

[40] Bass Luigi Lablache, in particular, became the object of a legal dispute between the impresario and the Neapolitan court: see Maione and Seller, 'Da Napoli a Vienna', 498.

withdraw from his obligations with the Habsburg court and focus on his business in Italy.

Barbaja's departure created a void that proved hard to fill. His immediate successor was Robert Wenzel von Gallenberg, an aristocrat and ballet composer who had assisted Barbaja in the administration of the Teatro San Carlo in Naples and had helped him broker his agreement with the Habsburg court.[41] Without a well-established business network, Gallenberg maintained the presence of Italian opera only through occasional guest appearances that outstripped his financial circumstances.[42] Within a few months, he had lost most of his fortune and had to terminate his contract. On 1 September 1830, Barbaja's former associate in Vienna, the ballet master Louis Duport, stepped in and took over the management of the Kärntnertortheater, but only after he successfully negotiated his exemption from the obligation to organise Italian opera seasons.[43] Yet this very clause, which endangered the cultural edifice the Habsburg court had painstakingly built over the previous decade, became Duport's thorn in the flesh. Even before taking office, he lamented that he had been chastised 'for proposing to give only German opera as a regular spectacle' and blackmailed by opera patrons who had 'manifested their willingness not to renew their subscriptions'.[44] Five years later, Duport's failure to carry out the court's cultural policies is mentioned in a report from Count Joseph von Sedlnitzky, the Austrian Chief of Police.[45] Shortly thereafter the French impresario stepped down from his post.

As soon as Duport communicated the conditions of his resignation, Merelli submitted his proposal to take on the administration of the Kärntnertortheater in partnership with Carlo Balocchino.[46] This turnover

---

[41] See Michael Jahn, *Die Wiener Hofoper von 1810 bis 1836: Das Kärnthnerthortheater als Hofoper* (Vienna: Der Apfel, 2007), 20–6; and Rosa Cafiero, 'Il "grande industriale internazionale del balletto" a Napoli nell'età di Rossini: Wenzel Robert Gallenberg', in P. Fabbri (ed.), *Di sì felice innesto: Rossini, la danza e il ballo teatrale in Italia* (Pesaro: Fondazione Rossini, 1996), 1–40.

[42] See, for instance, Gallenberg's request for additional contributions to cover the costs for Giuditta Pasta's performances in his letter to the *Oberstkämmerer* Count Johann Rudolf von Czernin, 17 February 1829: HHStA, Gen.Int., Box 71 (1828–9), 1829, 11.

[43] See the documents filed as 'Pachtakten Duport 1830', in HHStA, Gen.Int., Sonderreihe, 55/1.

[44] Duport to Czernin, 4 June 1830: HHStA, Gen.Int., Sonderreihe, 55/1, Pachtakten Duport 1830, unnumbered.

[45] 'Duport's administration... does not conform in any way to the dignity of the Court and of the City': Sedlnitzky to Czernin, official report, 5 June 1835: HHStA, Gen.Int., Sonderreihe, 55/II, Pacht-Auflösung mit Duport und Pacht-Vertrag mit Balochino und Merelli 1835–6, 1063.

[46] On 25 May 1835, Duport submitted to Czernin a copy of a letter the impresario had addressed to the Minister of Inner Affairs, Franz Anton von Kolowrat, outlining his demands (HHStA, Gen.Int., Sonderreihe, 55/II, Pacht-Auflösung mit Duport und Pacht-Vertrag mit Balochino und Merelli 1835–6, unnumbered). According to Sedlnitzky, Merelli had been negotiating his agreement with the court since 2 June 1835. See Sedlnitzki's official report to Czernin,

brought along important innovations. As John Rosselli explains, Merelli was among the first Italian businessmen to exploit extensively a model of artistic management whereby the control of opera houses was subordinated to that of their artistic forces. Whereas Barbaja built his opera empire on the lucrative monopoly of gambling tables in opera houses, Merelli entered the business as an agent.[47] He closed long-term contracts with singers to whom he paid a regular salary, with the provision that he could hire them out to other impresarios on his own terms. Merelli benefitted from the difference between the remuneration he had accorded to his artists and the amount he charged other impresarios for them. Once this system proved efficient, Merelli began negotiating directly with local authorities, and sold opera seasons as 'package deals' consisting of a full company as well as a repertory of old and new works.[48]

This is indeed how Merelli reached Vienna. In 1835, thanks to the mediation of Count Ferdinand Pállfy (manager of the Kärntnertortheater from 1812 to 1817, and then owner of the Theater an der Wien) and of a Bohemian aristocrat, Count Johann Joseph Pachta, Merelli organised the first proper Italian opera season since the times of Barbaja, lasting three full months, from early April to the end of June.[49] For this first season, Merelli officially acted as a subcontractor to Duport and made remarkable profit. Ferdinand von Seyfried reported that Merelli would negotiate a fee of 12,000 Austrian lire for the singers he brought to the Kärntnertortheater, but that cost him only 4,000 lire; the rest was agency fees.[50] While Seyfried's numbers are likely misleading, Merelli's business practices allowed him to capitalise on the allocation the Habsburg court had accorded to the impresarios of the Kärntnertortheater.[51] At the same time, he provided what neither Duport nor Gallenberg had managed to secure: regular Italian opera seasons.

---

9 December 1835: HHStA, Gen.Int., Sonderreihe, 55/II, Pacht-Auflösung mit Duport und Pacht–Vertrag mit Balochino und Merelli 1835-6, 2250.

[47] See John Rosselli, *The Opera Industry from Cimarosa to Verdi: The Role of the Impresario* (Cambridge: Cambridge University Press, 1984), 147. According to Barbaja's biographer Eisenbeiss (*Bel Canto Bully*, 162–70), after 1820, when legislation against gambling in opera houses passed in most of the Italian states, the impresario maintained his international network thanks to his skills as a talent scout and agent of young singers. As Rosselli points out, however, this hardly became the core of his business, as it was for Merelli.

[48] See Rosselli, *Opera Industry*, 147–8.

[49] Negotiations between Duport and Merelli emerge from a series of letters that Duport sent to the Chief of State Police, Count Joseph Sedlnitzky, and which are now preserved in Vienna, Österreichisches Staatsarchiv, Allgemeines Verwaltungsarchiv, Polizei Hofstelle, fasc. 8493/1834.

[50] Seyfried, *Rückschau*, 33–4.

[51] Michael Walter has explained Seyfried's inaccuracies as a result of the complex currency system in use in the Austrian empire: see his *Oper: Geschichte einer Institution* (Stuttgart: Metzler, 2016), 202–3.

Shifting Politics

The beginning of Balocchino's and Merelli's administration of the Kärntnertortheater coincided with important changes at the head of the Austrian Empire itself. The death of Emperor Franz I on March 2, 1835, marked the conclusion of a forty-three-year-long reign, most of which had been dedicated to the creation and consolidation of the new, dynastic imperial state that had succeeded the Holy Roman Empire after the latter's demise in 1806 under the pressures of the Napoleonic Wars. Over the following decades, Franz I had stressed the need for recognition of the ruling dynasty as the unifying force of an otherwise heterogeneous conglomeration of possessions by insisting that the legitimate heir of his crown be his eldest son Ferdinand, despite the fact that the latter had been suffering from epilepsy, hydrocephalus and other neurological conditions. Taking account of these circumstances, Franz I had provided guidelines for the creation of a state cabinet that would govern the Empire on behalf of Ferdinand. After inner struggles within the court's top echelons, the council included Prince Clemens von Metternich, one of Franz's closest advisors, and another minister, the younger Count Franz Anton von Kolowrat.[52] The continuous disagreements between these two men, which ultimately took a heavy toll on the functioning of the imperial government, were reflected in their different operatic tastes: Metternich was famous for his enthusiastic support of Italian opera, while Kolowrat privileged German opera.[53] The structure of Balocchino and Merelli's administration, with clearly defined German and Italian opera seasons, reflected these differences, and thus managed to endure for twelve years, despite continuously shifting power dynamics.

Yet it is during this period that modernising reforms profoundly transformed the Empire, from growing industrialisation to the enhancement of the banking system, from railroad building to expanded transportation

---

[52] See the documentary reconstruction of Ferdinand's succession in Friedrich Walter, *Österreichische Verfassungs- und Verwaltungsgeschichte von 1500–1955*, ed. Adam Wadruszka (Vienna: Böhlau, 1972), 137–8. On Kolowrat, see Isabella Schüler, *Franz Anton Graf von Kolowrat-Liebsteinksy (1778–1861): Der Prager Oberstburggraf und Wiener Staats- und Konferenzminister* (Munich: Herbert Utz, 2016).

[53] Metternich's passion for Italian opera is discussed in Bernd Rüdiger Kern, 'Rossini e Metternich', *Bollettino del Centro Rossiniano di Studi* 39, no. 1 (1999), 5–20; Körner, 'Culture for a Cosmopolitan Empire', 659–9; and Körner, 'Beyond *Nationaloper*', 405–6. On Kolowrat, see Erich Schenk, 'Robert Schumann und Peter Lindpaintner in Wien: Ein musikgeschichtlicher Beitrag zum romantischen Nationalismus', in D. Weise (ed.), *Festschrift Joseph Schmidt-Görg zum 60. Geburtstag* (Bonn: Beethoven-Haus, 1957), 267–82 (270).

infrastructure. While private entrepreneurs or lobbies often prompted these projects, the imperial government played a crucial role in supporting them and carrying them forth.[54] As I have argued elsewhere, these changes stimulated ideas about a new cosmopolitan culture that had a considerable impact on the perception of Donizetti's operas in Vienna and set the ground for his ultimate arrival in the city in 1842. Central to this process were Donizetti's successes in Paris, which demonstrated his stylistic adaptability and showed the extent to which he might support a project of cultural policies that aimed at transcending national boundaries. Between 1842 and 1845, Donizetti wrote two operas for the Kärntnertortheater (*Linda di Chamounix*, 1842, and *Maria di Rohan*, 1843) and supervised the local premieres of a number of other works he had originally written for Paris (*Don Pasquale*, 1843, *Dom Sébastien*, 1844, revived in Vienna in a German translation in 1845 under Donizetti's baton). These productions, as well as his appointment as Vienna's Court Composer and Director of Chamber Music (*Hofcompositeur und Kammerkapellmeister*) contributed to his image in Vienna as a versatile, cosmopolitan musician, one who embodied transnational cultural ideals in line with Austrian imperial ideology.[55]

The years separating the composer's early negotiations with Balocchino and Merelli and his arrival in Vienna coincided with a phase of major cultural, administrative and political readjustments in the ways the Empire was run. Because of the rivalry between Metternich and Kolowrat, the reign of Emperor Ferdinand went down in history as a long period of political deadlock, often presented as inevitably leading to the 1848 Revolution. The expression *Vormärz* ('pre-March', with reference to the outbreak of the insurrection in Vienna on 13 March 1848) has come to indicate a period of gradual build-up of the forces that instigated the revolution. While its closing term is unquestionable, historians have proposed alternative options as to when the *Vormärz* begins. Pieter Judson, for instance, proposes that it starts with the conclusion of the Congress of Vienna in 1815, while Wolfram Siemann identifies its *terminus post quem* in France's July Revolution of 1830.[56] Judson, however, rejects the teleological implications of the term *Vormärz*, accepting it only as a heuristic tool. He portrays post-Napoleonic Austria as a state in search of its path to

---

[54] See Pieter M. Judson, *The Habsburg Empire: A New History* (Cambridge, MA: The Belknap Press of Harvard University Press, 2016), 112–20.
[55] See Vellutini, 'Donizetti, Vienna, Cosmopolitanism'.
[56] Judson, *The Habsburg Empire*, 102; Wolfram Siemann, *Metternich: Strategist and Visionary*, trans. Daniel Steuer (Cambridge, MA: The Belknap Press of Harvard University Press, 2019), 665.

modernity, with all the contradictions and dead ends that such a search entails. While acknowledging the 'serious power vacuum at the top of the system' following the coronation of Emperor Ferdinand, he identifies 'new forms of activism in order to solve ... problems that the paralyzed government seemed unwilling to address'.[57] Albeit grudgingly, Judson claims, the central government did not prevent, but rather encouraged, support of private enterprises that could benefit the economic and social development of the state as a whole.[58]

The management of the Kärntnertortheater exemplifies how, since the years following the Congress of Vienna, this cautious openness to entrepreneurial initiatives came to involve cultural production as well. Italian impresarios such as Barbaja, Merelli and Balocchino introduced different administrative practices that, taken together, helped the Habsburg court outsource the costs for opera seasons while ensuring the presence of Italian opera in a diversified cultural landscape. Doing so was no mere capitulation to foreign influence. Since the seventeenth century, cultural life at the Habsburg court had been deeply marked by references to *italianità* – its open disposition towards Italian influences. Central to this phenomenon was a multifaceted process of *reception* of Italian culture grounded in a set of ideas (and, at times, veritable fantasies) projected onto it from outside.[59] *Italianità* did not designate the mere implantation of Italian culture into a foreign context, but rather its adaptation and transformation for purposes *specific* to the new context. As we saw, this process underpinned Habsburg cultural policies once the Congress of Vienna had established the reintegration of several territories in the Italian peninsula within the Austrian Empire.

In Vienna, Italian opera acquired a meaning that was specific to that city and that was constantly negotiated, as the vicissitudes surrounding Donizetti's early negotiations with Merelli and Balocchino and his later involvement in Viennese musical life aptly demonstrate. More importantly, though, these ever-changing processes of signification provide us with additional clues for questioning the trope of the *Vormärz* as an age of paralysis – political, social and cultural – and reconsidering instead the transformations brought about by a regime whose ambitions, concerns and conflicts have until recently been more the target of demonisation than the object of critical investigation.

---

[57] Judson, *The Habsburg Empire*, 104–5. [58] Ibid., 120.
[59] See Corinna Herr, Herbert Seifert, Andrea Sommer-Mathis and Reinhard Strohm, 'Italianità – Image and Perception in the Musical Theatre of Central Europe in the Seventeenth and Eighteenth Centuries', in C. Herr, H. Seifert, A. Sommer-Mathis and R. Strohm (eds.), *Italianità: Image and Practice* (Berlin: Berliner Wissenschafts-Verlag, 2008), 1–4. For a reconsideration of operatic *italianità* from a transnational perspective, see Körner, 'Beyond Nationaloper', 404–8.

6 | Southern Exchanges

Italian Opera in New Orleans, 1836–1842

CHARLOTTE BENTLEY

> We have now in this place what no city in America, and few cities in the world, can boast of: strong companies of actors in the English, French and Italian languages, and, what is more, they are all extremely well patronised ... We can support more theatres than any other city of its size in the world. Give us but good companies, and we can ensure all of them success.[1]

The New Orleans *Daily Picayune*, like most emerging local newspapers of the first half of the nineteenth century, proudly and frequently heralded its city as being exceptionally cultured. But, in the case of this passage, the writer may well have had as much of a sense of awed bewilderment as self-congratulation: April 1837 proved to be an extraordinarily busy month in New Orleans's theatrical life. On any given night, theatregoers had the opportunity to see English-language theatre (musical and spoken) at the Camp Street and more recently opened St Charles theatres; French opera or drama at the long-established Théâtre d'Orléans; or attend one of the myriad concerts, magic shows, demonstrations, lectures or equestrian entertainments that occupied venues across the city.[2] Most important for the *Daily Picayune*'s writer at this particular juncture, however, was the presence of an Italian opera troupe, which had opened at the huge, 4,000-seat St Charles Theatre the previous evening. This was, in fact, the second Italian company to grace the theatre's stage since the beginning of 1837, and the third in just a little over twelve months: New Orleans was experiencing a craze for Italian opera.

Responsible in large part for this sudden enthusiasm was the English-born impresario, James Caldwell. Having arrived in New Orleans in 1820 as the manager of a travelling theatre troupe that rented the Théâtre d'Orléans for its performances, he opened the city's first anglophone theatre – the Camp Street Theatre – in 1824. He went on to own theatres all over the southern United States, in cities such as St Louis, Mobile and

---

[1] 'Theatres', *Daily Picayune*, 5 April 1837.
[2] For an exploration of the richness of New Orleans' musical life in this period, see John Baron, *Concert Life in Nineteenth-Century New Orleans: A Comprehensive Reference* (Baton Rouge: Louisiana State University Press, 2013).

Nashville, but it was New Orleans that he made his home, opening a second theatre – the enormous St Charles – at a cost of $300,000 in November 1835.³ It was to his new theatre that he brought a series of visiting Italian troupes between 1836 and 1842.

Before 1836, audiences in New Orleans had little experience of Italian opera, and there is no evidence to suggest they felt they were missing out. Having been founded as a French colonial town in 1718, French remained the dominant cultural and linguistic force in New Orleans into the early nineteenth century, with francophones outnumbering anglophone residents until the late 1830s.⁴ Audiences there enjoyed a regular diet of French operatic works: the earliest documented operatic performance – of André Grétry's *Sylvain* – took place in 1796, and by the first decade of the nineteenth century New Orleans supported two francophone theatres.⁵ In 1819, Paris-born businessman John Davis opened his Théâtre d'Orléans; from that time on the city had a resident opera company, sourced through annual recruitment in Europe, and it consequently had a more sustained operatic life than any other city in the United States. French *operas comiques* by Grétry, François-Adrien Boieldieu and Étienne Méhul formed the mainstay of the Théâtre d'Orléans' repertoire until the early 1830s, when the works of a new generation of composers – among them Ferdinand Hérold and Daniel Auber – were introduced.

Caldwell's Camp Street Theatre opened in 1824 to cater to the growing number of English speakers who had started to relocate to New Orleans in the years after the Louisiana Purchase of 1803; with it, the city's theatrical life diversified to include abridged Shakespeare and other English plays, as well as some musical works (principally solo instrumental pieces and orchestral overtures) and heavily rearranged English or 'Englished' operas.⁶ There was

---

³ Felicia Hardison Londré and Daniel J. Watermeier, *History of the North American Theater: The United States, Canada and Mexico – From Pre-Columbian Times to the Present* (New York: Continuum, 1998), 114. For more on the history of the St Charles Theatre, see Lucille Gafford, 'A History of the St Charles Theatre in New Orleans, 1835–43', unpublished PhD thesis, University of Chicago (1930).

⁴ For more of an overview of the city's demographics in the nineteenth century, see the essays by Joseph G. Tregle, Jr., Paul F. Lachance and Caryn Cossé Bell in *Creole New Orleans: Race and Americanization*, ed. Arnold R. Hirsch and Joseph Logsdon (Baton Rouge: Louisiana State University Press, 1992). For a detailed account of the history of New Orleans from its founding to 1812, when Louisiana gained statehood, see Lawrence N. Powell, *The Accidental City: Improvising New Orleans* (Cambridge, MA: Harvard University Press, 2012).

⁵ John Dizikes, *Opera in America: A Cultural History* (New Haven, CT: Yale University Press, 1993), 25.

⁶ 'Englished' is a term Katherine K. Preston uses to describe foreign operas that were translated into English (and often heavily rearranged) in *Opera for the People: English-Language Opera and Women Managers in Late 19th-Century America* (New York: Oxford University Press, 2017).

still, however, little by way of Italian opera. The limited familiarity audiences at the Camp Street Theatre had with Italian opera came largely in the form of two very popular English-language works based on Sir Walter Scott's *Guy Mannering* and *The Lady of the Lake*, which had scores constructed out of a patchwork of excerpts from Rossini's operas and original pieces by the English composer Henry Bishop.[7] Although the small number of Italian works performed in translation at the Théâtre d'Orléans or the English-language theatres (principally *Le barbier de Séville/The Barber of Seville* and *La pie voleuse/The Thieving Magpie*) achieved a measure of success with audiences, the 'Rossini fever' that struck many other cities around the world in the 1820s and 1830s largely seems to have passed New Orleans by.

This chapter focuses on the introduction of Italian opera to New Orleans between 1836 and 1842, exploring responses to the visiting companies' performances in the local francophone and anglophone press and the ways in which Italian opera continued to permeate the musical and theatrical consciousness after the troupes' departures. While Henry Kmen, Juliane Braun and others have emphasised the continued importance of French culture in the construction of New Orleans' postcolonial identity in the nineteenth century, and they have at various times placed this francophone heritage in conflict with developing anglophone culture in the city, the significance of the Italian opera seasons has remained little explored.[8] Meanwhile, recent work has both problematised methodological nationalism in present-day studies of opera and suggested that the transnational circulation of ideas helped shape perceptions of national identity for people in the nineteenth century.[9] Here, then, I will investigate the Italian seasons through the lens of such ideas, in order to suggest that the New Orleans critics' self-conscious focus on 'other' national characters (i.e. the Italian rather than French or Anglo-American) became a way of selectively embracing and denying their own city's international cultural allegiances,

---

[7] Henry Kmen, *Music in New Orleans: The Formative Years, 1791–1841* (Baton Rouge: Louisiana State University Press, 1966), 94.

[8] Kmen, *Music in New Orleans*, Juliane Braun, 'Petit Paris en Amérique? French Theatrical Culture in Nineteenth-Century Louisiana' (PhD diss., Julius-Maximilians-Universität Würzburg, 2013). See also Charlotte Bentley, 'The Race for *Robert* and other Rivalries: Negotiating the Local and (Inter)national in Nineteenth-Century New Orleans', *Cambridge Opera Journal*, 29/1 (2017), 94–112.

[9] See, for instance, Axel Körner, 'Beyond Nationaloper: For a Critique of Methodological Nationalism in Reading Nineteenth-Century Italian and German Opera', *Journal of Modern Italian Studies*, 25/4 (2020), 402–19 and Axel Körner, *America in Italy: The United States in the Political Thought and Imagination of the Risorgimento, 1763–1865* (Princeton, NJ: Princeton University Press, 2017). See also Benjamin Walton, 'Italian Operatic Fantasies in Latin America', *Journal of Modern Italian Studies*, 17/4 (2012), 460–71.

and thereby negotiating a desirable global self-image for it. In particular, I wish to highlight the discourses surrounding the relationship between Italian character and music that reviewers developed and the ways in which the reception of Italian opera in New Orleans became entangled in discussions of the city's connections with a perceived global south.

The Italian Troupes

When James Caldwell decided to engage an Italian company, he was seeking to fill what he perceived to be a gap in the market. Caldwell had long made a modernising agenda a fundamental part of his theatrical management strategy – the Camp Street Theatre had been the third theatre in the United States to use gaslights both on stage and in the auditorium – and in the second half of the 1830s, novelty was at the forefront of both his and his audiences' minds.[10] Nowhere was this more evident than in April 1835, just under a year before the first Italian troupe's arrival, when Caldwell's company at the Camp Street Theatre had raced the Théâtre d'Orléans troupe to produce Meyerbeer's *Robert le diable* in their respective languages.[11] This was the first real challenge to the Théâtre d'Orléans' operatic dominance, and it was especially shocking to francophone critics that not only did the anglophone troupe beat the French theatre to the work's premiere in the city by six weeks, but that the anglophone production was of an unexpectedly high quality.

In a decade in which French hegemony in New Orleans was seriously threatened for the first time – English speakers outnumbered French speakers in the city by the time of the 1840 census and tensions between the two groups ran high in commerce and government – the anglophones' impressive performance was interpreted in some quarters as a sign that the francophone hold on New Orleans' cultural sphere was loosening.[12] Nonetheless, while *grand opéra* became a key part of the Théâtre d'Orléans' repertoire, after his success with *Robert*, Caldwell never again attempted to compete with the French theatre in this genre; having captured the attention of the French-language press and devotees of the Théâtre d'Orléans, and shaken their cultural self-assurance, he soon sought to introduce a new novelty: the first Italian company to visit the city.

[10] Geddeth Smith, *Thomas Abthorpe Cooper: America's Premier Tragedian* (London: Associated University Presses, 1996), 207.
[11] For a full exploration of this incident, see Bentley, 'The Race for *Robert* and other Rivalries'.
[12] For more, see Joseph G. Tregle, Jr., 'Creoles and Americans', in *Creole New Orleans*, 153–60.

Table 6.1 lays out much of the key information about the four Italian troupes Caldwell brought to New Orleans over the seven-year period between 1836 and 1842, including the length of the seasons, the works staged and the principal performers. Since Henry Kmen and Katherine Preston have both touched on the repertoire and nightly reception of these tours, I want to use this information as a stepping-off point for a more detailed exploration of the notions of operatic *italianità* that emerged in relation to the troupes' visits.[13] Nonetheless, it seems worth highlighting some salient features from the table in order to sketch out a little further context.

The four troupes were run by different managers, and all came to New Orleans from Havana, Cuba (the significance of which I shall explore later in this chapter).[14] Giovanni Montresor, manager of the first troupe to visit New Orleans, was the son of Giacomo Montresor, who had run an Italian opera season in New York in 1832–3.[15] The second troupe – which gave only nine performances in a two-month residency at the St Charles – was closely connected to the first: many of the performers had been members of the Montresor troupe for the first season in 1836, but, having spent the summer performing in Louisville, Kentucky, they returned to New Orleans under the direction of Antonio de Rosa, one of the troupe's basses. Montresor was not among them.[16]

Even while they were still in New Orleans, it appears that Caldwell set his sights on a larger and more prestigious group, and he dismissed the de Rosa troupe in February. His new company, under the management of Francesco Brichta, arrived from Havana in early April. Unlike the earlier troupes Caldwell had secured, Brichta's troupe had not been set up as a touring company, but was the resident company at Havana's Teatro Tacón, which had been under his management since 1833. The final troupe of the four Caldwell brought to New Orleans was also from Havana's Teatro Tacón, but now under the direction of Francisco Martí y Torrens, Brichta's successor. This was the largest of all the troupes, comprising some fifty-seven singers and orchestral musicians.[17]

---

[13] See Kmen, *Music in New Orleans*, 140–65 and Preston, *Opera on the Road: Traveling Opera Troupes in the United States, 1825–60* (Urbana, IL: University of Illinois Press, 1993), 113–22.

[14] There was a fifth visit by an Italian troupe from Havana in April 1843, again under Martí y Torrens' direction, but I have chosen not to include it in my discussions here because it was not arranged with Caldwell, who retired from the theatre business in January that year. The 1843 visit formed the basis of a much larger tour of the United States undertaken by the Havana company, which Preston mentions in *Opera on the Road*, 118.

[15] Preston, *Opera on the Road*, 106–13.   [16] Kmen, *Music in New Orleans*, 146.

[17] Preston, *Opera on the Road*, 117.

Table 6.1 Italian troupes' visits to New Orleans, 1836–42

The Italian troupes' visits, 1836–42	Season	Dates of visit	Venue	Number of performances	Works performed	Manager	Key performers
1.	1835–6	6 March 1836–30 May 1836	St Charles Theatre	28	Bellini – *Il pirata* Bellini – *Norma* Bellini – *La straniera* Rossini – *Otello* Rossini – *Zelmira* Rossini – *Il barbiere di Siviglia*	G. B. Montresor	Adolaide Pedrotti G.B. Montresor Antonio de Rosa Signora Marozzi Signora Ravaglia M. Orlandi
2.	1836–7	4 December 1836–February 1837	St Charles Theatre	9	Rossini – *La Cenerentola* Rossini – *Il barbiere di Siviglia* Rossini – *L'inganno felice* Rossini – *Il turco in Italia* Bellini – *I Capuleti e i Montecchi* Rossini – *Semiramide* Mercadante – *Caritea, regna di Spagna* Ricci – *Chiara di Rosemberg* Donizetti – *Parisina* Bellini – *Norma* Rossini – *Tancredi* Rossini – *Il barbiere di Siviglia*	Antonio de Rosa Francesco Brichta	Signora Marozzi Antonio de Rosa Luigi Gabici (conductor) Clorinda Pantanelli Teresa Rossi Pietro Candi Paolo Ceresini Signora Papanti Signor Forsonari
3.		4 April 1837–6 June 1837 10 June 1837–14 July 1837	St Charles Theatre Théâtre d'Orléans	29 10			

4.	1837–41	No Italian troupe			
	1841–2	22 February 1842–16 March 1842	St Charles Theatre	9	Donizetti – *Marino Faliero* Bellini – *Beatrice di Tenda* Ricci – *Chiara di Rosemberg* Donizetti – *Lucia di Lammermoor*	Francisco Martí y Torrens
		17 March 1842–18 April 1842	Théâtre d'Orléans	12	Donizetti – *Il furioso all'isola di San Domingo* Bellini – *La sonnambula* Donizetti – *Belisario*	Mme Rossi Celestin Salvatori Alessandro Cecconi Perozzi

Caldwell worked hard to ensure that each of the four troupes received considerable press attention. When Giovanni Montresor's troupe arrived in New Orleans from Havana in early March 1836, Caldwell immediately encouraged press representatives to attend the troupe's rehearsals, in order to generate publicity and excitement for their upcoming performances.[18] All the troupes received an enthusiastic welcome from both anglophone and francophone sections of the New Orleans public, although this did not always translate into exceptional box-office receipts. Caldwell, in fact, claimed after the departure of the Montresor troupe in May 1836 that he had lost the huge sum of $10,000 on the enterprise, owing to the high costs of securing the performers.[19]

While Caldwell certainly viewed Italian opera as having considerable potential to bring him financial success, in practice none of the four troupes made him the money he had hoped. In early June 1837, for instance, following a disagreement between Caldwell, the star contralto Clorinda Corradi Pantanelli and Brichta, the Italian troupe broke their contract with the St Charles Theatre and moved to the Théâtre d'Orléans to give ten further performances.[20] If the earlier competition between Caldwell and the French theatre to produce Meyerbeer's *Robert* had cemented an open rivalry between the theatres, the Italian troupe's move underscored continuing tensions.

For the next four summers, no Italian troupes came to either the francophone or anglophone theatres of New Orleans: perhaps Caldwell had been put off by his argument with Brichta and the financial losses it had caused him. And yet there is evidence that, at least in 1840, he did try to find an Italian troupe for the city, with the *Daily Picayune* carrying a short notice reporting that Caldwell had sent his agent on the Natchez steamboat to Havana with 'a carte blanche to bring [the Italian troupe] over'.[21] The newspaper stated that 'they will remain in the city, should they see fit to pay us a visit, until the beginning of June'. For whatever reason, the troupe did not ultimately come to New Orleans that year, and nor did Caldwell manage to secure an Italian troupe for 1841.

That is not to say, however, that New Orleans was completely bereft of Italian opera in those years. In April 1840, Italian singers from Havana organised a 'grand vocal concert'. Three singers – Signora Majocchi (soprano), Signors Giamboni (tenor) and Vattellina (basso) – and a violinist (Ludovico Gabici, who went on remain in New Orleans as a music teacher

---

[18] Kmen, *Music in New Orleans*, 141. [19] Ibid., 143. [20] Ibid., 155–6.
[21] *Daily Picayune*, 4 April 1840.

and composer for many years) performed excerpts from works by Rossini, Donizetti, Bellini, Mercadante and Ricci for audiences at the Verandah Hotel.[22] The people of New Orleans, therefore, had opportunities to hear Italian music, but not full works.

Even when Caldwell did succeed in negotiating another Italian troupe in 1842, financial success again eluded him. He had negotiated a six-week run at the St Charles with Martí y Torrens, the manager of the fifty-seven-strong Italian troupe from Havana's Teatro Tacón. On 13 March, however, only minutes before curtain up on the Italians' performance, the St Charles Theatre caught fire. Within hours, the magnificent building had been reduced to a smouldering heap of rubble. Luckily for the Italians, most of their equipment had been stored off-site and, in the end, their losses amounted to little more than the costumes for that evening's performance.[23] They finished the rest of their run at the Théâtre d'Orléans, leaving Caldwell in a financial mess from which he never fully recovered; he cut his losses and retired from the theatre business early the following year.[24]

Italian vs French Opera in the New Orleans Press

The Italian troupes' repertoire expanded over the years from the Rossini- and Bellini-dominated repertoire of the Montresor and de Rosa troupes' visits, to encompass works by Donizetti, Mercadante and Rossi. The troupes' performances were, of course, not the only ways in which people in New Orleans could become familiar with Italian operas: sheet music imported from Europe was offered for sale at the city's music shops, and visiting performers also gave excerpts from operas that had not been staged in the city. For instance, when the visiting Italian singers from Havana organised their aforementioned 'grand vocal concert' in April 1840, they sang excerpts from Donizetti's *Belisario*, Mercadante's *I normanni a Parigi* and Bellini's *I puritani*, none of which had been performed by earlier visiting companies, as well as other more familiar works.[25] Nonetheless, the troupes' performances provided a focus for discussions in the press.

---

[22] 'Grand Vocal and Instrumental Concert', *Daily Picayune*, 20 April 1840.
[23] *La lorgnette*, 17 March 1842.
[24] On Caldwell's retirement, see *Daily Picayune*, 8 January 1843 and 14 January 1843.
[25] Audiences in New Orleans also had the unusual opportunity during this concert of hearing excerpts from Rossini's *Le siège de Corinthe* (which they had been familiar with in the original French since 1830) performed in Italian (as *Il assedio di Corinto*).

Since audiences in New Orleans were so accustomed to French opera, the arrival of the Italians inevitably encouraged direct comparisons between the two national schools; the city, therefore, is a significant case study for understanding global constructions of operatic *italianità*. Critics expressed delight that they were now able to comment on Italian opera in its original language, rather than in translation: various authors celebrated the fact that the Italian troupes afforded them the opportunity to hear Rossini's *Barber* as the composer had conceived of it, and they therefore no longer had to rely on the much-altered French arrangement by Castil-Blaze.[26] The apparent 'authenticity' of the troupes' repertoire and the high quality of the performers (the critic for *La lorgnette* suggested that Antonini, a tenor in Martí y Torrens' troupe, was surpassed in brilliance only by Duprez and Rubini) created particular focus for comments in the press, as well as being an attractive prospect for audiences.

For others, the arrival of the Italian troupes served as an important reminder to the management and performers of the French theatre that they needed to work hard to maintain their reputation. They positioned the arrival of the Italians as a much-needed 'wake-up call' to the city's French speakers, who were apparently taking their theatre for granted. The critic for *La lorgnette*, for instance, complained regularly that audience numbers were low at the Théâtre d'Orléans. He suggested that, while performances at the French theatre were generally good and deserving of more support, the French theatre could learn much from the attention to detail (musical and in terms of staging) shown by the Italian troupe.[27]

Such rallying cries, for all their rhetorical fervour, were not unusual in the New Orleans press: similar comments had emerged in the debates surrounding the twin performances of *Robert le diable* in 1835, and changes to the management of the Théâtre d'Orléans between 1836 and 1843 prompted ongoing cries to support French opera.[28] In a way, Italian opera became part of a rescue narrative surrounding French opera in the city: it was held up as a shining example to which the French theatre and its audiences should aspire.

In other respects, however, critics used faults they perceived in Italian opera as a means of highlighting the merits of French opera, thereby

---

[26] 'Cette fois ce n'était plus le triste pastiche arrangé par Castil-Blaze; c'était l'opéra, tel que l'a conçu et que l'a écrit Rossini, et joué comme aucun des assistans [sic] de cette soirée ne peut espérer de le revoir encore'. 'Bulletin dramatique: opéra italien', *Le moqueur*, 25 June 1837.

[27] *La lorgnette*, 24 February 1842.

[28] Charlotte Bentley, 'Resituating Transatlantic Opera: The Case of the Théâtre d'Orléans, New Orleans, 1819–1859', unpublished PhD thesis, University of Cambridge (2017), 36–9.

encouraging audiences in New Orleans to support the French theatre. Italian comedy, in particular, came in for criticism.²⁹ On 31 March 1842, the critic for the magazine *La lorgnette* commented on the Italian troupe's performance three days earlier of Donizetti's *Il furioso all'isola di San Domingo*. The libretto, he remarked, was not at all to his liking, and he found it unworthy of Donizetti's talents: 'these are exaggerations upon exaggerations and if ever a libretto resembled a dishevelled melodrama, it is certainly the one I am concerned with today'.³⁰

The lack of sophistication was clearly part of the problem here, but perhaps so too was the unbelievability of the character and the setting at large. *Il furioso* takes place on Santo Domingo, the Spanish-occupied part of the island of Hispaniola, which bordered Haiti in the west; this semi-serious opera had a Caribbean setting and featured among its characters black islanders, a plantation overseer and Spanish colonists. While for Donizetti, his librettist Jacopo Ferretti and audiences across Italy, this might have seemed engagingly exotic, audiences in New Orleans were more intimately familiar with Saint-Domingue and its inhabitants. After all, a good proportion of New Orleans' population had connections with Saint-Domingue: more than 20,000 refugees – black and white, free and (previously) enslaved – came to the city between 1791 and 1810, fleeing the violence of the slave revolution on the former French sugar colony, and their descendants still lived in the city in the 1830s and 1840s.³¹ What may have seemed to be an exotic 'elsewhere' to European audiences was rather closer to home for those in New Orleans.

The critic's principal source of discomfort was the characterisation of Kaidamà, the black slave (although carefully labelled a 'servant' in the libretto), who bears the brunt of the madman's rage on more than one occasion. The critic for *La lorgnette* wrote angrily of 'this cursed role of the fool who comes into the middle of the most pathos-laden scenes ... This cursed role of Kaidamah [*sic*] is the most insipid creation, the falsest that one could imagine'.³² Although there is little sense from the critic's words

---

²⁹ On various occasions, Italian tragedy, too, was criticised: the reviewer for *La lorgnette* found the libretto for *Beatrice di Tenda* to be particularly poor. 'Troupe italien', *La lorgnette*, 10 March 1842.

³⁰ 'Il est fort peu de mon goût: ce sont exagérations sur exagérations, et si jamais libretto ressembla à un mélodrame échevelé, c'est certainement celui dont je m'occupe aujourd'hui'. 'Théâtre italien', *La lorgnette*, 31 March 1842.

³¹ Carl Brasseaux, *French, Cajun, Creole, Houma: A Primer on Francophone Louisiana* (Baton Rouge: Louisiana State University Press, 2005), 22.

³² 'Ce maudit rôle de bouffon qui vient au milieu des scènes les plus pathétiques ... Ce maudit rôle de Kaidamah [*sic*] est la création la plus insipide, la plus fausse que l'on puisse imaginer'. Ibid.

that he found the choice of setting or characterisation upsetting or insulting, it may well have been that he found the portrayal of the slave character (perhaps the only character in the opera to see the situation and other characters with clear eyes) and the opera's evocation of a hurricane unbelievable. He would not have been alone among New Orleans' critics in finding Italian opera a little too far-fetched for his liking: other reviewers suggested at various points in their discussions that French audiences perhaps demanded a greater degree of plausibility from a work than their Italian counterparts.[33]

Nonetheless, the critic goes on to suggest that his concern was motivated less by the subject itself than by issues of genre. He clearly disliked the mixture of tragedy (encapsulated in the opera's themes of infidelity, madness, a shipwreck and a tender reconciliation of lovers) and low comedy (the capering of the slave character, played in blackface by the *basso buffo*) within the work. Far from setting the tragic elements of the work in sharper relief, such juxtapositions seemed to him to undermine them to the point of ridiculousness, creating only 'exaggerations upon exaggerations'.[34]

Eventually, his thoughts seem to have crystallised around the notion that comedy might have particular national forms, and he observed that 'in this respect, the Italians are well behind, and their comedy does not come close to ours. They are two centuries late'.[35] The idea of *commedia dell'arte* stock characters was clearly in his mind as he reflected on the character of Kaidamà –he would not have been alone in drawing such associations, as Martin Deasy has observed of the Neapolitan reception of the opera in the 1830s – and it seems to have clashed with what he perceived to be the more fleshed-out characterisations in some of the Théâtre d'Orléans' favourite *operas comiques*.[36] National styles of comedy, then, did not necessarily translate successfully between cultures, and they encouraged reflection on opera as not simply a cosmopolitan product but as representative of certain national qualities of the culture that produced them.

---

[33] See, for instance, *Le moqueur*, 25 June 1837.
[34] 'Théâtre italien', *La lorgnette*, 31 March 1842.
[35] 'Certes, de ce côté, les Italiens sont bien en arrière, et leur genre comique est loin d'approcher du notre. Ils sont en retard de deux siècles.' 'Théâtre italien', *La lorgnette*, 31 March 1842.
[36] Martin Deasy, 'Local Color: Donizetti's *Il furioso* in Naples', *19th-Century Music* 32/1 (2008), 11–14.

'Italia's Sunny Clime': Evoking National Character

In spite of such criticisms of the perceived inferiority of Italian comedy in comparison with its French counterpart, critics regularly stressed the extent to which the Italian troupes' presence had changed life in New Orleans. In November 1838, for instance, a writer for the *Daily Picayune* remarked: 'when the Italian opera was introduced among us, the entire musical world was astir. You heard people at every corner talking of notes (so you do now, but they are notes given for swamp lots) – Basso buffo, soprano, contralto, and prima donna were on the tongues of the people "familiar as household words".'[37] The presence of the Italian troupes in this account is characterised as exciting and also inspiring fevered discussion, as being educational (bringing with it previously unfamiliar vocabulary), and as increasing cultural sophistication (as is highlighted by the difference in meaning of the word 'notes' that the author lays out). And yet, when this article appeared in print, there was no Italian troupe in the city: by November 1838, there had been no troupe for over a year. It seems worthwhile, then, to focus on the discussions that were had in the New Orleans press during times in which there was no Italian opera to see how discourses emerged as much in times of absence as in times where Italian opera was readily accessible.

Critics articulated the sense of loss felt by the people of New Orleans at the departure of the Italian troupes particularly clearly. The article of 1 November 1838 continued: 'As at a touch all vanished – it was as though Italia's sunny clime, light music, and dancing waters, had sunk into the bosom of some vast abyss.'[38] The sense of immediate grief and the depth of despair following the troupes' departure are evident; in other articles, critics referred to the departure as 'bidding adieu to a band of friends'.[39] What is more, the author articulates those feelings through a very particular set of adjectives: 'sunny clime', 'light music' and 'dancing waters'. Painting as they do a picture of the Italian character as being steeped in sunshine and melody, these descriptors were inherited from European discourses of national styles, stemming, if not directly from the work of Jean-Jacques Rousseau, from the filtering of his ideas through more popular fiction or journalism.

Indeed, discussions of national character emerged in other articles from late in 1838. On 17 December, the *Daily Picayune* carried an article

---

[37] 'Théâtre d'Orléans', *Daily Picayune*, 1 November 1838.   [38] Ibid.
[39] 'Italian Opera Company', *Daily Picayune*, 17 December 1838.

reporting on a plan to raise capital for a resident Italian opera company and a dedicated Italian theatre in New Orleans: a group of music lovers had decided that they were no longer willing to wait for visiting troupes, but wanted an Italian opera of their own.[40] The plans ultimately never came to fruition, but the article took ideas of national or regional character further, discussing their relevance for New Orleans itself. Reflecting on the Brichta troupe's visit and the potential for maintaining Italian opera in New Orleans permanently, the writer for the *Daily Picayune* mused:

> The city of New Orleans is with us, both in an appreciation of the troupe under consideration, and in a love for Italian operas in the abstract. To the praise of our citizens it can be said that they form the first community in this country who have supported them, from a taste at once musical and deeply refined.[41]

The anglophone author clearly viewed New Orleans as exceptional (a common trope in the city's press) and was somewhat scathing about the reception Italian opera had received elsewhere in the United States. Only in New Orleans, the author asserts, did a love for opera come from a genuine, cultivated love for music. As Katherine Preston has shown, there may well have been reason for the critic to think that love for Italian opera shown elsewhere in the 1830s was not so genuine: in the early 1830s, there had been efforts to establish an Italian opera scene in New York (and, to a lesser extent, Philadelphia), with the Montresor troupe (then run by Giovanni's father) providing a season in 1832–3, and then a company run by Vincenzo Ravafinoli giving the first-ever season at a newly founded (but short-lived) Italian opera house in New York.[42] In 1834, however, the whole enterprise collapsed, and Preston ventures to suggest that it was because 'wealthy New Yorkers were not interested in importing Italian opera because of their innate love of music, but because it could be transformed into an exclusive and elite pastime that could lend to its auditors – merely by attendance – some of those attributes'.[43] The people of New Orleans, in contrast, the writer for the *Picayune* was keen to stress, enjoyed Italian opera (and not just the performances of any particular star singer) because of their sophisticated musical taste, rather than any sense of social elitism.

---

[40] Ibid. [41] Ibid.

[42] Preston, *Opera on the Road*, 106–13. Lorenzo da Ponte, best known as Mozart's librettist for *Le nozze di Figaro*, *Don Giovanni* and *Così fan tutte*, helped to fund the Montresor tour, which proved to be of no financial benefit to him and only reinforced his disillusionment with New Yorkers and their apparent lack of interest in Italian culture. See Karen Ahlquist, *Democracy at the Opera: Music, Theater and Culture in New York City, 1815–60* (Urbana, IL: University of Illinois Press, 1997), 123.

[43] Preston, *Opera on the Road*, 111.

The reasons for this superior taste seemed obvious to the author:

> We need not go into a consideration of the causes of this – they are known to every child. We are a Southern people – our city is the central point for all nations, and the proportion of those who come here, with a taste for sweet sounds, is to those who 'have no music in their souls', as ten to three – voilà tout. The Frenchman, the German, the Neapolitan and the Spaniard, form two thirds of our population, and the two last named nations, would, in the person of the lowest labourer, give their last dollar to the characters of their native airs.[44]

Such identification of the city's population as 'southern' not only signals its geographical location in the United States, but also reflects an attitude shared with the above-mentioned article from 1 November 1838 in its Rousseauian undertones. Unlike the earlier article, however, it mentions not just hypothetical Italian characteristics, but actual Italians living in New Orleans ('the Neapolitan').

New Orleans did have an Italian population from relatively early on in its history, and Italians were involved in musical and theatrical life; the Theatre d'Orleans' first set designer, Jean Baptiste Fogliardi, was born in Italy.[45] In contrast to the city's francophone residents, however, there was little sense of a distinct Italian identity in the city until after the Civil War, when the first waves of Sicilian immigrants started to make their way across the Atlantic, swelling the city's Italian population dramatically.[46] Like Fogliardi, many Italians adopted French forenames and identified themselves with the francophone population. The history of Italian opera in New Orleans, then, is less to do with an Italian minority in the city than it is to do with the connections that were drawn between Italianness and associated attitudes of and towards southernness.

Although the author of the article specifically mentions the 'Neapolitan' in the passage quoted above, when the New Orleans press of this period wrote of Italian opera and national character, articles often evoked – consciously or not – a sense of pan-Italian identity, rather than a fixation on any particular place. Other articles, for instance, referred not to Neapolitans, but to the 'language of Venice' and the 'Banks of the Arno', bringing the Veneto and Tuscany into

---

[44] 'Italian Opera Company', *Daily Picayune*, 17 December 1838.
[45] For more on the history of Italians in New Orleans, see Joseph Maselli and Dominic Candeloro, *Italians in New Orleans* (Charleston, SC: Arcadia, 2004).
[46] Maselli and Candeloro state that there 'were more Italians in New Orleans than in any other US city in the period between 1850 and 1870', and that there were likely roughly 30,000 Italians resident there by the late 1890s, as a result of direct trading links between New Orleans and Sicily. Ibid., 13.

their image of Italy.[47] While there is no guarantee that the Anglo-American writers for the *Daily Picayune* actually had any direct experience of Italy and its regional diversity, it is interesting to note that their image of Italy involved places across the country and cut across the north and south. What is more, the writer chooses to bring in discussions of Italy and Italian character not in relation to specific performances in New Orleans and the troupes that gave them, but rather, in their absence, to a broader concept of Italian opera that existed partly independently of the visit of any particular troupe.

The connections between Italianness and southernness more broadly conceived seem to be key here. In the above-mentioned article of 17 December, southernness is not presented as being the preserve of a single nation or linguistic origin, but as something explicitly musical. Indeed, the evocation of southernness points to something more than simply Italianness. There is even a sense that the author of the article, an anglophone in New Orleans, considered himself to be southern, alongside those from the named nations. Perhaps more significantly, when talking of our 'sunny South', articles in the *Daily Picayune* seemed to think of the city's French occupants as being a fundamental part of any southern identity. Indeed, they concluded that although they deeply regretted the departure of the Italian troupe, their need for 'delicious melody' was amply fulfilled by the French music of the Théâtre d'Orléans: this article's author reflected on how melody inspired the attitude of 'loving languor' displayed by the beautiful women who frequented the theatre.

For the anglophone critics of the *Daily Picayune*, this 'southernness' in the character of New Orleans's residents was both desirable and connected to good taste and a high level of cultural appreciation.

Exoticised *Italianità*: Cuban Connections

'Southernness' was not always perceived as a desirable trait, however, as emerged in other comments related to Italian opera in the New Orleans press. The way that New Orleans was introduced to Italian opera meant that the connection between America and Italy was not a direct one: all of the Italian troupes that gave major seasons in New Orleans between 1836 and 1842 came to the city not from Italy itself (or even from the northern United States), but from Cuba. The singers – some Italian by birth and

---

[47] *Daily Picayune*, 1 November 1838.

others trained in the Italian tradition – arrived in New Orleans from Havana, leaving Cuba and Italy inextricably entwined in the minds of audiences and critics. In this way, the images of *italianità* that critics and audiences in New Orleans developed were inevitably filtered, at least in part, through the lens of Cuba; the narratives they created about Cuba, therefore, came to stand in for representations of Italy.

The operatic connection with Cuba, however, was rarely addressed explicitly. While there were numerous articles about shipping and commercial connections with Havana in the New Orleans press, there were few references to music. Comments on the troupes' origins in Havana were often limited to notices remarking on their departure from or arrival in Cuba, and there were also occasional reports on the progress of the theatrical season at the Italianate Teatro Tacón, Havana's principal theatre. Even such brief comments as there were, however, suggested that New Orleans' residents (especially in francophone circles) viewed Havana as exotic. For instance, *La lorgnette* reported on the departure of Martí y Torrens' troupe on the ship *The Alabama* in April 1842, with the following remarks:

The Alabama has pulled them tight into its wooden depths (as a pure-blooded romantic would say) and taken them towards the climate, as hot as it is tedious, of Havana. They have passed like the flight of a bird, the breath of a breeze, like the mangoes.[48]

In emphasising the heat and the lack of activity in Havana, these comments display typical strategies for presenting the 'Otherness' of a place and its people. The reference to mangoes is another deliberate attempt to create a sense of the exotic, as although it is possible that mangoes arrived on the dockside in New Orleans in shipments from further south for limited periods of the year, the city's climate is not consistently hot enough for them to grow locally and they were, therefore, a transient luxury at best. Cuba, as much as Italy, then, emerges in such comments as being viewed as part of a global south, but Cuba presents us with an intensified version of the characterisation: while descriptions of Italian character referred to sunshine and melody, in Cuban terms this was exaggerated and linked to scorching heat and boredom.

---

[48] L'Alabama les a resserrés dans ses entrailles de bois (comme dirait un romantique pur sang) et les a emportés vers le climat aussi chaud qu'ennuyeux de la Havane. Ils ont passé comme le vol d'un oiseau, comme le souffle de la brise, comme les mangots [sic]'. 'Théâtre italien', *La lorgnette*, 21 April 1842.

Cuban southernness, however, did not necessarily equate to musicality in the way that Rousseau had drawn connections between the Italian language and melody, and which critics in New Orleans echoed in their comments about Italian character. This is perhaps not surprising, as the question of whether Spain (and, by extension, its empire) could be considered a musical south in its own right had been a topic of debate among Spanish theorists since the late eighteenth century, as José Manuel Izquierdo König has shown; while some believed Italian and Spanish were both musical languages (the underlying implication being that Spanish composers should separate themselves from the influence of Italian opera), others believed that Italy was the only true musical south.[49] As a Spanish colony, but with a good portion of its musical life imported from Italy, Cuba seems to have inspired similar considerations among the New Orleans press.

On the relatively rare occasions that the New Orleans press did mention Cuba's operatic life more than in passing, they revealed somewhat disparaging attitudes. In the summer of 1843, the *Daily Picayune* ran a series of articles called 'Hieroglyphics on Havana'. While many parts of this series focused on aspects of city life and complained heartily about the 'political degradation' of the island and the lack of a free press there,[50] opera did eventually come into play. Writing about the city's markets, the author came to focus specifically on the fish market, saying

> As in Havana monopolies or exclusive privileges pervade all departments of business, Martí, who has a monopoly of the opera, has also a monopoly of the fish market – or has the exclusive privilege of saying how much or at what rate the Habaneros shall be supplied with fish. We suppose he so manages it that when the taste for Italian songs decline[s] salmon rises, and when there is a glut of mullet in the market music is made cheap.[51]

Martí y Torrens, the manager of the Teatro Tacón, whose troupe came to New Orleans in 1841, did indeed have a monopoly on both fish and opera in the city.[52] While this proved lucrative business for him (both were

---

[49] José Manuel Izquierdo, 'Opera in Transnational Context: Reading Rousseau's Essay on the Origin of Languages', ed. Alexander Kolassa and Axel Körner, UCL Passionate Politics (accessed 24 February 2020), www.ucl.ac.uk/centre-transnational-history/sites/centre-transnational-history/files/rousseau_italianita_essays2.pdf and Ellen Lockhart, 'Pimmalione: Rousseau and the Melodramatisation of Italian Opera', *Cambridge Opera Journal* 26/1 (2014), 1–39.
[50] D.C., 'Hieroglyphics on Havana, no. XV', *Daily Picayune*, 21 June 1843.   [51] Ibid.
[52] Max Maretzek discusses Martí y Torrens and his various professions in *Crotchets and Quavers: Or, Revelations of an Opera Manager in America* (New York: S. French, 1855), 149–59.

perhaps more salubrious professions than his earlier occupation as a pirate), for the author writing in the *Daily Picayune*, opera is somehow cheapened in Havana through its association with the fish market: in the author's words, it is stripped of its specific status as 'opera' and reduced to simply 'Italian songs'. The somewhat disdainful attitude displayed in this article towards the connection between opera and lowly commerce like the fish trade is entirely different from the praise the same newspaper afforded to the troupe's performances in New Orleans the previous year, when Italian opera was heralded as the height of refinement. In the author's perception, the Cubans do not appreciate opera 'from a taste once musical and deeply refined', as that same newspaper had earlier argued that New Orleans' residents did, but rather that opera was a commodity to be had either at a premium or as a bargain by the people of Havana, depending on the sale of other goods. Critics in New Orleans seemed, then, to prefer to separate their experience of Italian opera from the Cuban context that brought it to them.[53]

This, therefore, highlights the paradox that lay at the heart of conceptions of operatic *italianità* in nineteenth-century New Orleans: it signified both the refined or cosmopolitan and, at the same time, the Other, free from the trappings of refinement. If the balance were to shift too far either way, the contradictions inherent in the concept would come to the fore and cause the meanings attached to it began to collapse. That is to say, the New Orleans press could neither tolerate pretensions to cultural grandeur (which they perceived in other cities, but not in New Orleans, where they believed people appreciated Italian opera out of genuine cultural appreciation), nor could they make room for an appreciation of Italian opera that removed all veneer of cultivation and musical sensibility.

***

The story of Italian opera's early days in New Orleans, then, was bound up in local desires for cosmopolitanism and anxieties about being perceived as part of the global south. The New Orleans press dangled Italian opera as a threat to the francophone theatre and audiences in the city, and as representing cosmopolitan musical possibilities; and it prophesied doom if those francophone impresarios and patrons did not rise to the

---

[53] Disdainful attitudes to Cuba and its musical life were also expressed clearly in relation to an invitation the francophone Théâtre d'Orléans troupe received to spend the spring of 1843 in Havana. The critic for *La lorgnette* expressed alarm at the prospect, suggesting that if the French troupe were to undertake a trip to Cuba they would never be able to recruit high-quality performers from France ever again. See *La lorgnette*, 26 January 1843 and 9 February 1843.

challenge of producing higher-quality theatre and patronising it with more commitment. As for Italian opera itself, it was something that could be either elevated to a marker of cultural refinement or lowered to the level of cheap songs, depending on the behaviours of the people with which it was associated.

Although the Italian troupes' visits were few in number and only reflected a very small part of theatrical activity in New Orleans during the late 1830s and early 1840s, their impact was lasting and seems to have cemented Italian opera's place in the Théâtre d'Orléans repertoire. By the late 1840s when Louis Fiot, the Théâtre d'Orléans regisseur, started to release his series of bilingual libretti of favourite works performed at the French theatre, Italian operas were firmly among the repertoire he chose to highlight: mainly Donizetti, but with select works by Rossini, Bellini and early Verdi among them.[54] As Italian opera was integrated into the city's musical life, however, the works were translated into French and then again into English, gradually weakening their Italian connections.

There is perhaps a sense, then, that operatic *italianità* became bifurcated in New Orleans through the Havana troupe's visits. Italian works gained an important place in the city's operatic repertoire, and the visiting troupes were seen as something to which the resident French troupe could aspire. However, ideas of Italian national character and the melodiousness of the Italian language seem to have blurred into concerns about associations with Havana as a representative of the global south. Although Italian opera did ultimately find a more stable place in New Orleans's operatic life, the way it did so was in translation, through a sidestepping of the question of language and the associations with character and behaviour that it brought with it.

---

[54] For more on Fiot's libretti, see Bentley, 'Resituating Transatlantic Opera', 134–47 and Catherine Jones, *Literature and Music in the Atlantic World, 1767–1867* (Edinburgh: Edinburgh University Press, 2014), 91.

7 | 'For a Moment, I Felt Like I Was Back in Italy'

Early South American Experiences of Italian Opera Singers (1840–1860)

JOSÉ MANUEL IZQUIERDO KÖNIG

In 1845, the Bolognese journal *Teatri, arti e letteratura* published a letter sent by Raffaele Pantanelli, Italian conductor and impresario, who was then working with a new opera company in Valparaíso. It is not clear whether the letter was meant to be published, since it was addressed to Gaetano Fiori – violin maker and editor of the journal – in the manner of a letter to a personal friend.[1] The letter is the first one we know to have been written by Pantanelli after his arrival in the Americas in the late 1830s. It was written at a particularly important moment for him and his family. Pantanelli had travelled to the Americas with his wife, the celebrated contralto Clorinda Corradi Pantanelli; the couple had lived in Havana, and performed in New Orleans and New York, before taking up the suggestion of tenor Vincenzo Zapucci that they lead a new opera company in Lima, the capital of Peru.[2] Zapucci, who had been living in South America since the 1820s as an opera singer and teacher, knew the region well, and the prospect made sense: although one company had performed there in the early 1830s, since then no new company had filled the desire for opera productions in the Andean region.

Pantanelli and his family had moved to Lima in early 1840, and then to Chile in 1844, where they had received an invitation to inaugurate a new opera house in Valparaíso. Thus, the letter was written during their first year in Chile, and set out the details of the project that moved the Pantanellis into these lands. Readers in Italy would have known by then, through other newspapers, about the new opera house in Valparaíso (Teatro Victoria), and the growing operatic scene in South America. The Teatro Victoria was built by Italian businessman Pietro Alessandri and was

---

[*] This chapter was written with the support of funding from Fondecyt, Project 11170265. I am grateful for the support, help and ideas of Macarena Robledo, Macarena Aguayo and Colomba Nómez, who contributed greatly to the chapter with their suggestions and the information they provided. Also, I would like to thank Paulo Kühl, Susan Rutherford, Benjamin Walton and Alessandra Jones for their comments at various stages of the writing of this chapter.

[1] *Teatri, Arti e Letteratura*, Bologna, 2 October 1845.
[2] *El Amigo del Pueblo*, Lima, 4 August 1840.

depicted in Italian newspapers as a triumph for the global projection of Italian culture: a sign that 'our Italian opera is always expanding'.[3] Pantanelli, in his own letter, seems to agree with those portrayals: for him, the fact that so many Italians – like Alessandri or designer Raffaele Giorgi – were involved in the construction of this new building only served to demonstrate that the Victoria, and their own performances there, were signs 'to the musical world [of] the progress Italian Opera is making in the New World'.

As part of that migration, Italian opera, too, was read in part as a projection of Empire, always accompanied by notions of 'progress' and 'civilisation' in European terms. But opera also fostered local perspectives that contributed to new understandings of the modern world. Opera, considered in local terms, embodied one of the most important cultural transformations for Latin America during the nineteenth century: it came to represent many of the desires of postcolonial elites associated with ideas of modernity, civilisation, free trade, cosmopolitanism and the 'Westernisation' of values and high culture. By the 1850s there was a veritable opera fever in the region, with large opera houses being built with local funding as state or private projects: they were becoming the most tangible projections of an imagined Europe.[4] Opera houses, like the Teatro Victoria in Valparaíso, were the signposts of the liberal political stability gained by the new American nations in mid-century, the architectural and social projection of their major cities in an imagined transatlantic 'civilised' sphere.

However, these assumptions can obscure some of the more specific ways that opera – and Italian opera in particular – was being read in Latin America at the time, during opera's mid-century ascendance to elite cultural Parnassus. For example, it is not easy to understand whether Italian opera was primarily read as Italian, or rather as cosmopolitan, or as something else altogether. Indeed, one could argue some writers considered it as more specifically Parisian, reflecting the importance of Paris in the imagination of local elites, and the Parisian connections of the core Italian repertoire of Rossini, Bellini and Donizetti. The problem of the 'locus' of opera becomes evident when comparing contemporary discourse. For instance, a review of the first opera performance in Guayaquil

---

[3] *Il Pirata*, Milan, 4 January 1844.
[4] Verónica Zárate and Serge Gruzinski, 'Ópera, imaginación y sociedad: México y Brasil, Siglo XIX', *Historia Mexicana* 58/230 (2008), 803–60. Miguel Farías, 'Pretensiones culturales de la oligarquía chilena en el siglo XIX, el caso de la ópera', *Neuma* 8/2 (2015), 110–32.

(Ecuador), given in 1842 by a group joining forces between Lima and Havana, argued:

It must be some sorcery from the goddess of Opera, when we can feel, for a night, as if we were in Lima, or Janeiro, or Paris, London, Madrid or Milan, three thousand leagues from here, when we have not left Guayaquil. Isn't that wonderful? The Empire of Opera.[5]

For comparison, here is a section of the review of the first performances of a similar company (with many of the same singers) in Valparaíso, two years later:

[We have seen] the triumph of Italy and the ostentation of its masterworks. To hear the melodies of the bard of Italy, and his sublime tragedy, performed by Italian voices, on a stage made live by the hand of an Italian painter. Our cosmopolitan town was transported to Italy, the queen of the world.[6]

Attempting to observe and comprehend the many ways in which these new operatic experiences and their early reception in Latin America were being read and discussed is no easy task. This chapter deals with the private experience of Italians involved in opera in Latin America during this early period of modern operatic reception. The subject is particularly difficult because it forces us to search for sources beyond those that have been central to the study of opera in the region until now – in particular newspapers, the most common resource for scholars of operatic reception. Newspapers contribute much in terms of who sang what, when and where, but are of limited use elsewhere. I believe there is a strong need for new frameworks and additional sources, to measure and understand newspapers – still a fundamental source – within a larger context of operatic culture.

In particular, newspapers, by definition, cannot give us more than glimpses of private experiences, and always through a prism of censorship, taste and moderation. How did singers in this period compare their lives in South America with their previous experience of singing in Italy? Why did some of them stay, and others leave? How did they adapt the business and interpersonal models of Italian operatic practices to the Latin American context? And a crucial question: beyond the prospect of financial gain, what made singers in mid-nineteenth-century Europe go to places as foreign to them as Bolivia or Colombia, which didn't have a standardised

---

[5] *Correo Semanal de Guayaquil*, 25 September 1842.
[6] *El Mercurio de Valparaíso*, 17 December 1844.

and regulated operatic scene?[7] Was there something of that 'last frontier' spirit behind such decisions, as Pantanelli's letter seems to imply?

This chapter, of course, will not be able to fully answer those questions; I doubt it is even possible to do such a thing. But these questions invite us to examine new sources and explore new readings for old ones. In this case, my focus is on the Andean region, and particularly on the private experience as brought forward through letters. As Julian Johnson has suggested, European music 'migrated across the world on the back of imperial and colonial networks, and with the promise of new opportunities'.[8] Those networks, of course, were neither abstract nor neutral: they were shaped by people; by specific individuals and their decisions.

Networks of Private Experience

Opera was made possible in the region by interpersonal connections, and many of those were private in character. Due to the complex transnational nature of these connections, I have not been able to find many documents that allow us to trace how these networks sustained the production of opera at the time, but one key letter is in the large collection of the correspondence of impresario Alessandro Lanari, which can now be found in the National Library in Florence.[9] Sent from Valparaíso in February 1847, it offers clues as to their relationship. Apparently, Pantanelli had sought to obtain the music from a new unspecified opera, in Bordeaux. The local agent, Briau, had decided not to pay for the rights of sending the work to South America, thus cancelling Pantanelli's plans. For this reason, he asked Lanari for help, while also announcing some of his company's recent successes in Chile, with Verdi's *Ernani*, as well as with Donizetti's *Lucrezia Borgia*. He described the beauty of Alessandri's Victoria theatre in Valparaíso, and reported that the company's repertoire now comprised twenty-seven operas. He also asked for further news of Verdi's successes (particularly with *Macbeth*) and enquired as to the *figurini* (costume designs) for Pacini's *Saffo*, perhaps the opera he was waiting to receive from Bordeaux. The letter reflects the need of companies like Pantanelli's

---

[7] On this question also see the chapter by Fernando Berçot (Chapter 2).
[8] Julian Johnson, *Out of Time: Music and the Making of Modernity* (Oxford: Oxford University Press, 2015), 125.
[9] At the National Library in Florence there are a handful of letters sent by Raffaelle Pantanelli, but these mostly date from the time he spent in Italy before travelling to the Americas.

(fixed in a single place in the Americas) to constantly expand their repertoire.[10]

Many other impresarios worked along similar lines. Antonio Neumane presents an interesting case. Neumane had been an arranger for Ricordi in Milan in the 1830s and subsequently worked as a conductor in South America. He arrived in Ecuador in 1842, where he died in 1871. He wrote the National Anthem for his new nation and set up the first national conservatoire. Despite this close connection with his new homeland, he never lost contact with Italy. In 1847 and in 1852, for example, he returned to hire new singers for seasons in Ecuador, Chile and Peru. His daughter Rosa, who was born in Guayaquil, remembered the trip in an interview given decades later. She was seven years old when her father decided to leave his children and wife, Idalide Turri, behind in order to once again undertake the perilous trip to Europe, now during the age of early regular steamers; the anxiety was evident among the family members.[11]

There was a strong network of Italian singers and artists who became agents and impresarios, working through Italian and American networks. An important example is Luigi Bazzani, who in the 1840s and 1850s often used Italian newspapers to announce opportunities for Italian singers to perform in South America.[12] Bazzani might have been the most important broker for Italian singers on the Pacific coast during this period, and more research is certainly needed on him. Working alongside Amato Ricci, his contact in Italy, he organised companies to visit places as far-flung as Peru and California.[13] Bazzani and Neumane are symptomatic of a growing consciousness of the importance of networks to solidifying opera as a business in the Andean region. In order to build up those networks, people who knew the local scene were needed, alongside the Italians creating clusters of migration that were essential to the development of the genre. In consequence, the migrants' private lives were also reshaped by these experiences.

For instance, in 1846 Paolo Ferretti, an Italian tenor who had arrived in the Andean region via Cuba in the early 1840s, married María España, the only Peruvian soprano working at the time for these companies. Together they travelled for three decades performing operas and opera scenes up and down the Andean region. Soon Ferretti became the agent of his own tours. They were the first singers to stage operas in La Paz, Bolivia (in 1847), as

---

[10] National Central Library of Florence, Papers, Lanari 31^{II}, 31.
[11] *El Telégrafo*, Guayaquil, 14 August 1930.   [12] *Il Pirata*, Milan, 14 July 1846.
[13] *Il Pirata*, Milan, 8 April 1854. At the time of writing, Alexander Klein is working on a book on Bazzani.

well as in Lambayeque (1851), Arequipa in Peru (1859) and Quito in Ecuador (1857), to name just a few of the cities they visited. In January 1850, they gave the American premiere of Verdi's *Alzira* in Lima for a benefit performance by María España, 'dedicated to my homeland', as she wrote in a long column in the local newspaper. The project was highly emotional for the couple, as the action of the opera took place in Lima, with Ferretti, the European, performing Gusmano and María España, the local, appearing in the title role of an Inca princess.[14] Ferretti died in Ica, Peru, an old man and 'retired music teacher', in September 1889.[15]

When over four decades earlier España and Ferretti were married in Arequipa, in 1846, Paolo, being a foreigner, had to provide proof that he was Catholic. He presented seven letters from his Italian family, dated from 1840 to 1846, clearly selected for their references to his Catholicism. Mostly penned by his sister, all of them concluded with prayers for him.[16] Today those letters highlight the ways in which Ferretti reconnected with Italy, how his private and commercial interests were related, and how these connections changed over the years. Over time, the letters gradually leave off discussing his return, of which they were initially confident. The first of these letters, sent to Ferretti in Cuba in May 1840, was written by his father from his deathbed. In a letter from July 1843, a few months after Ferretti had arrived in Peru, his mother asks him for a relic of Saint Rosa of Lima upon his return. In April 1845 his sister thanks him for money he sent back to Italy, used to support the education of his brothers, still boys when their father died. In the last letter, from July 1846, his sister shares some positive news: that another member of the Ferretti family of Sinigaglia had been elected Pope (Pius IX), and that the Pope's brothers send their regards; unquestionable proof of his well-connected Catholicism.

The comings and goings of these singers, the complex decisions they made and the way different categories of Italian operatic life echoed in the Andes, such as the role of impresarios and agents, invite us to think about these people in more personal ways beyond their professions: their sense of belonging, the ways in which they constructed their nationhood, their political views and so on. Did some of them begin to see themselves as

---

[14] *El Comercio*, Lima, 17 January 1850.

[15] 'Perú, defunciones, 1750–1930', database, *FamilySearch*: https://familysearch.org/ark:/61903/1:1:FNBQ-5L2, last accessed 8 February 2020, Pablo Ferretti, 1889.

[16] 'Expediente matrimonial de Pablo Ferretti pretende contraer matrimonio con Doña María España. 24 de octubre de 1846'. Archivo Arzobispal de Arequipa, Expedientes Matrimoniales 72 (9 January 1846–30 June 1847).

Americans? And if not: what was the situation for their families and children, many of whom were born in the Americas? How much did this changing sense of belonging affect their decisions as artists and musicians?

Two Italian Sopranos in the Andes

It would be impossible to answer all these questions here. But the issues they raise are important not only in terms of the negotiations involved in being Italian abroad: they also concern the ways locals perceived these artists, and how they related to them. Take, as an example, the cases of Teresa Rossi and Clorinda Corradi, two female singers of the original Pantanelli Company, who worked in Peru and Chile during the 1840s.[17] They had an interesting relationship to one another: Clorinda Corradi, wife of Pantanelli, was the real star. As Paola Ciarlantini has shown, Clorinda started her career in 1823, and for more than a decade she performed in all the large theatres of Italy.[18] For example, she had premiered the role of Luigi in Donizetti's *Ugo, conte di Parigi* at La Scala in 1832 (with Giuditta Pasta as Bianca and Giulia Grisi as Adelia).[19]

Teresa Rossi, on the other hand, seems to have had only a short career – mainly as a dilettante – before departing European shores: she made her debut in Venice, in 1834, singing Isolina in Gaetano Rossi's *Teobaldo e Isolina*,[20] the first review praising her 'natural gifts that merited attention and applause at the Apollo'.[21] For three years she sang mostly minor roles, in addition to appearing in symphonic concerts, mostly in the north of Italy (Milan, Ferrara). In the late 1830s she left for Cuba, then the main arrival point for Italian singers in the Americas. From there she joined the

---

[17] Idalide Turri, a 'dilettante' and the wife of Antonio Neumane, also joined the company on a few occasions, as did Alaide Pantanelli (daughter of Clorinda and Raffaelle), and María España, the Peruvian soprano.

[18] Paola Ciarlantini, 'Il percorso biografico-artistico di Clorinda Corradi Pantanelli, "musa" di Carlo Leopardi', *Quaderni Musicali Marchigiani* 10 (2010), 73–86.

[19] William Ashbrook, *Donizetti and His Operas* (Cambridge: Cambridge University Press, 1983), 552. A sonnet for her, published in *Teatri, arti e letteratura*, was also recently discussed in a paper by Francesco Izzo : 'Divas and Sonnets: Poetry for Female Singers in Teatri Arti e Letteratura', in Rachel Cowgill and Hilary Poriss (eds.), *The Arts of the Prima Donna in the Long Nineteenth Century* (Oxford: Oxford University Press, 2012), 8–9 and 16.

[20] I have not been able to trace Teresa Rossi's family history and ascertain whether she might have been related to Gaetano. But given that Rossi is such a common surname, it is probably just a coincidence.

[21] *Il censore universale dei Teatri*, 12 April 1834.

Pantanellis as part of the Havana Opera Company that visited New Orleans.[22]

There are two sources for letters from both singers written during this period: one is the collection of the German painter Moritz Rugendas, at the Iberoamerikanisches Institut in Berlin; the other is a personal album *amicorum*, a collection of letters, poems, lithographs, drawings and concert programmes,[23] belonging to Spanish-Chilean singer Isidora Zegers at the University of Chile, which includes several letters, scores, newspapers and other private documents from her career and personal relationships. Zegers was well known as a supporter of artists, always welcoming them on their arrival to Chile. Rugendas, who was travelling the region in the 1840s, lived with the singers in the same house in Lima and became a close friend. Both collections shed important light on how Corradi Pantanelli and Rossi perceived their experiences in the Andes.

A powerful moment in one of the early letters from Rossi to Rugendas is when the former acknowledges that 'while we two [Rossi and Corradi] are celebrated the same, in *Tancredi* the audience preferred her: she has the best role, but also her husband, who speaks a lot and has good connections here, whereas I don't have anyone'.[24] What appears in newspapers as an equal partnership between the singers may not have been so simple behind the stage. Indeed, both singers also had very different experiences of social life while living in Chile. Clorinda hoped to join high society and was invited to the homes of prominent families, which she considered an essential part of her personal life in Lima and in Santiago.[25] In one of the letters to Rugendas she uses a full paragraph to comment on 'the families we visit, which are the Zegers, Tocornal, Valdés, Vicuña, Herrera and Solar', all members of the elite in Santiago.[26]

These depictions in Corradi's letters are intriguing, because on the one hand, as a married woman (unlike Teresa Rossi), it would have been easier for her to be invited to gatherings of the conservative and Catholic elite. In

---

[22] Katherine Preston, *Opera on the Road: Traveling Opera Troupes in the United States, 1825–60* (Urbana: University of Illinois Press, 2001), 320. See also Charlotte Bentley's chapter above (Chapter 6).

[23] I would like to thank Fernanda Vera for her insights on album culture in this period in South America.

[24] Gertrud Richert, 'La correspondencia del pintor alemán Juan Mauricio Rugendas', *Revista Chilena de Historia y Geografía* 47 (1954), 151–2 (the letters are collected in volumes 47–51, but those mentioned here are all in volume 47, so I will use the dates from the letters to facilitate finding them, both in the volumes and in the originals in Berlin. This letter is from Rossi to Rugendas, 18 June 1844).

[25] Corradi to Rugendas, 28 May 1844.   [26] Corradi to Rugendas, 15 July 1844.

that sense, one could think of a certain convergence between Italy and South America at this time, based not only on shared political interests (as Garibaldi would prove), but also on their Catholicism, an aspect of everyday life that profoundly connected both countries and shaped operatic experiences at the time. On the other hand, and expressing perhaps a radical difference between the experience of Italian singers in South America and those back home, constant mingling with the social elites (becoming one of them rather than merely being invited as a performing star) would probably have been much rarer for a professional singer in Italy.

Rossi, however, seems much less interested in this social landscape. Her letters focus mostly on passing foreigners and those she calls 'kindred spirits', in particular Isidora Zegers, whom she describes from very early on as a 'good friend', in part because of her total lack of interest in high society but also because she sees her as a fellow romantic, a kindred and informal spirit.[27] In another letter she wrote about having spent the entire evening with Isidora in her garden, the Chilean woman 'always tireless, in a frenzy to sing'.[28] As Rossi puts it, she is interested in people with whom she can relate through music and the arts, while the increasing number of polite social visits can easily become 'fastidious', particularly because they consume time otherwise better used for rehearsals and practice.[29] Perhaps, however, this 'artistic' connection was bent towards seeking out other Italians in Rossi's life, considering that in the late 1850s she decided to return to Italy, unlike the Pantanelli family. It seems as if she never managed to feel as though she actually belonged to Chilean society, even though she had been presented with some very similar opportunities to those encountered by the Pantanellis.

What Rossi and Corradi were hinting at in those letters from 1844 and 1845 is their change of status: from travellers to migrants, adapting to a new host society and culture. They welcomed people into their houses, they shared a life with certain families and friends, while still living, for months at a time, in hotels and other temporary residences. During their transition from travellers to migrants, the relationship to Italy always continued to be a complex one for Italian singers and artists. On the one hand, as Rossi shows, there was a desire to reproduce the experiences of Italian opera in a new geographic setting. On the other hand, the experience of South America quickly changed these singers, as the examples of Rossi and

---

[27] Rossi to Rugendas, 2 May 1844.   [28] Rossi to Rugendas, 12 October 1844.
[29] Rossi to Rugendas, 5 August 1844.

Corradi demonstrate. In a letter to Rugendas, Corradi apologised for using a few Spanish expressions, being conscious that Spanish had become her main language.[30] Rossi began one of her letters to Isidora Zegers in 1849 in Spanish before stopping halfway and stating: 'how stupid am I, that I started this letter in Spanish when I'm lucky you understand Italian so well, but I'm easily distracted'.[31]

By the 1850s, more than a decade after their arrival in the Americas and after having lived for years in Chile, both singers were transitioning from being migrants to being locals. A letter from Rossi to Zegers from 1851 shows how true this was. Rossi was living in Valparaíso, the Pantanellis in Santiago and Zegers in Copiapó, a mining town in the north, when a large earthquake struck central Chile. Rossi's letter shows her desire to know what has happened to everyone else, that the Pantanellis, as well as some other Italian artists (the Bastoggis, Ubaldi, stage painter Giorgi) were safe, and she tells Zegers all about them. Certainly, one could say most of the people she mentioned were Italians, but they were all Italians who had been living for years in the Andean region. Indeed, many of these early Italian artists who visited Chile and Peru (unlike later generations of singers) stayed to live and die there, reshaping their identities and, also, surpassing the career prospects they had had when they arrived.

Private and Public Lives

In one of her letters to Rugendas, Rossi comments on the albums she and Corradi kept at their homes.[32] To those who visited them, those albums represented, in a physical and material way, their complex status as both travellers and migrants; but they also portrayed the thin line between their private and their public lives. For example, in 1848 in *El Comercio*, the main Peruvian newspaper of the period, there is a long commentary on the album of Lucrezia Micciarelli, a soprano who arrived in 1848, hired by Antonio Neumane to sing in Lima, Valparaíso and Santiago. The commentary is signed by *unas limeñas*, a group of women from Lima, who went to her house in December that year. They saw Micciarelli's album and considered it intriguing since it spoke both of 'the actress we see on the stage'

---

[30] Corradi to Rugendas, 15 July 1844.
[31] Rossi to Isidora Zegers, 20 September 1849. The letters from Rossi and Corradi-Pantanelli to Isidora Zegers are all found in the Album de Isidora Zegers (no catalogue number or document numbers), which is preserved in the Archivo Central Andrés Bello at the University of Chile.
[32] Rossi to Rugendas, 12 October 1844.

and of 'the woman . . ., the tender mother, and the one who exposes herself to the fury of the seas . . ., remote countries, and the inconveniences of a long journey'.[33] In other words, the woman in that album is both one of them (a contemporary woman of society) and also a completely different person, one they only partially grasp when seeing her as an artist on stage.

In Corradi and Rossi's letters, however, this difference is not so obviously perceived. Their stage and professional experiences converge as private ones, and we can glimpse both sides of the same woman as one, as is the case for Micciarelli, or Corradi or Rossi. For example, when Rossi writes in a letter to Rugendas about one of her benefits in Santiago, when 'so many wreaths were thrown to the stage . . . and they followed us to our house, in the midst of the shouts from the crowd. For a moment, I felt like I was in Italy, surrounded by a very Italian enthusiasm. How I cried for happiness!'[34]

There were, of course, important limitations to those boundaries between public and private lives. When, in a letter to the newspaper, a group of critics complained in February 1847 about one of Clorinda Corradi's performances, her husband attacked the critics, defending 'his' wife.[35] The debate continued for a few days, but the key comment came at the very end, when the critics wrote: 'The problem [Mr. Pantanelli] is that you don't understand that there is a big difference between your wife and the actress on stage, whom we have the right to attack.'[36]

The case of the aforementioned soprano Lucrezia Micciarelli, who arrived in Lima in 1848, also illustrates the complex relationship between public and private personas. Her original contract in Spanish, signed in November 1847 in Milan, survives in Lima, with Antonio Neumane representing Francisco Coya as impresario in Chile and Peru, and Alberto Torri as the Italian agent for the singers. The original contract shows many changes made in different inks at the moment of signing, and it included a monthly allowance of 400 pesos, plus a benefit each year. The impresarios would pay for the journey as well as for a return to Italy after the Carnival of 1850, making it a two-year contract. Torri received a commission as agent.[37]

---

[33] *El Comercio*, 28 December 1848.   [34] *El Mercurio de Valparaiso*, 12 February 1847.
[35] Sadly, we can only guess from a comment made by the editor on 15 February what that letter might have said, since that number (from 13 February) was missing from the collections I searched.
[36] *El Mercurio de Valparaiso*, 16 February 1847.
[37] Archivo Nacional del Perú, Sección Republicana, RPJ428.

The contract survived together with other materials from Micciarelli because in 1849 she and her husband Giuseppe Marconi filed a court case against Coya, the impresario in Lima, for unpaid wages. She won the case, and thanks to these legal documents alongside private letters and newspapers, it is possible to gain a better understanding of her time in Lima. Micciarelli had arrived in Lima in March 1848, as the prima donna of a small company of singers, and all her early reviews were extremely encouraging. But by early April rumours had begun to appear in newspapers regarding a supposed affair between her and the conductor Antonio Neumane. For weeks this issue attracted more attention than her performances. One article, signed by 'the Italians', explicitly addressed this very public scandal, describing Micciarelli's attitude as un-Italian and speaking out in favour of her husband.[38] In response to these attacks, she decided to publish a long letter, which certainly must have shocked local audiences. In this letter, she gave very personal insights into her life in Lima, explaining that her husband relied entirely on her income, and also beat her and had at least once attacked her with a knife in public in Lima. It was for these reasons that she had asked for divorce after eleven years of marriage.[39]

Another layer of her personal circumstances is revealed in the private diaries of further witnesses to her life in Lima. Heinrich Witt, who lived for decades in Lima and kept a private diary, worked as an assistant for the theatre. In his entry of 17 April 1848, he speaks of his excitement at listening, for the first time, to the new singers hired by Neumane, who were paid through 'a subscription enabling Mr. Newman [sic], the Director of the Orchestra, to bring a new company over from Europe'. Commenting on the singers, he states:

> Those who believed themselves connoisseurs considered Lucrezia Micciarelli, who sang Elvira, superior to Rossi. On every occasion, they insisted that her voice was more powerful. However, the majority of listeners, and I was one of them, preferred the old favourite, Rossi, who was younger, better-looking, and a better actress.[40]

Taking account of the many problems around Micciarelli's reputation, affecting in particular the theatre's Catholic audience's reception, the old members of the Pantanelli Company were invited to return and save the season, including Rossi, who had left Lima in 1844. Newspapers, and most probably the impresarios, recognised in this development a chance to have both singers in the city at the same time, thus fuelling a rivalry between

---

[38] *El Comercio*, 29 April 1848.   [39] *El Comercio*, 27 April 1848.
[40] Heinrich Witt, *The Diary of Heinrich Witt*, vol. 4 (Leiden: Brill, 2016), p. 164 (Monday 17 April 1848).

Micciarelli and Rossi. Both of them were so crudely attacked by the other's group of supporters that by late 1848 they published a joint letter in the newspaper to stop this flood of attacks, stating that they were 'in perfect harmony, in friendship and mutual consideration. Please stop praising one in the intention of attacking the other one, because we are both sensitive to the feelings of each other.'

We also have a few letters from Rossi to Isidora Zegers dating from this period. A letter from December 1848 sets out its intention of putting personal problems aside in order to 'speak about theatre'. In her correspondence, Rossi comments on everyone in Lima, including individual musicians in the orchestra, as well as on new works being premiered that she had not yet studied or heard before, like Donizetti's *Maria di Rohan* (premiered in Vienna in 1843). According to Rossi, the real reason for bringing her over from Chile was not necessarily Micciarelli's supposed affair with her 'adored Neumane' but rather the fact that Micciarelli was constantly sick, with symptoms including bleeding from her mouth, which accounts for the comments about her being 'indisposed' in the newspapers. Rossi explains how she had had to take on Micciarelli's role in *I Due Foscari*, resulting in a group of Micciarelli's supporters constantly disrupting her singing with fifes, until she finally managed to overcome her own fears and eventually won over the audience.[41]

Her rivalry with Micciarelli occupies an extensive section of the letter, which considers the newspapers' portrayal of their relationship as a competition between the 'old' and the 'new' soprano unfair. She also expresses her belief that Micciarelli herself had published some of those comments anonymously in the newspaper. Nevertheless, Rossi admits that there might be something true about their supposed technical and stylistic differences, adding that she is scared of being surpassed by a new, younger singer. She also acknowledges that Micciarelli's technique, being very different from her own, might reflect a new vocal style in Italy: 'In a way [listening to Micciarelli's *Ernani*], it seems that her singing is quite unique, and she herself says that it stands for a new method, but I don't see the other [incoming singers] doing it like her. She is quite agile, and very loud, but not very musical.'[42]

Conclusions

For the majority of audiences in the Andes, the voices of Pantanelli and Rossi embedded, during the 1840s, the idea of operatic voice, and projected

---

[41] Rossi to Zegers, 12 December 1848.   [42] Rossi to Zegers, 12 December 1848.

almost single-handedly a notion of *italianità* as defined by opera. But the arrival of Micciarelli, as well as of other singers from the late 1840s on, transformed that notion. Increasingly, perceptions of what an 'Italian' voice was and how it defined opera began to change. Did this mean that this was a mobile and constantly changing quality, rather than standing for an operatic convention that stood for a certain continuity in the style of singing? Rossi herself had not returned to Italy in more than a decade, and in her private letters she expressed her realisation that notions of operatic *italianità* were changing, as well as the anxiety that she might not necessarily embody them for Andean audiences for much longer. Opera, thus, was not eternal.

Rossi returned to Italy by the end of the 1850s. Her final letter to Isidora Zegers, sent from Milan in September 1860, portrays the writer as a woman who had long left behind the 'happy' years of her life: those times in the Andes, as she tells her old friend. She feels disconnected from her former world, without news from the Pantanellis, without a companion to attend La Scala, and with no professional life to speak of, her only interest being the political developments of the peninsula's unification and her support for Garibaldi, reflecting the fact that one of her nephews was fighting alongside him.[43]

Rossi, who had left Italy for the Americas at the very beginning of her career, had first exchanged a life as a minor singer in Italy for one as a star in the Americas; but two decades later, she exchanged her life as an admired soprano and central figure of Chilean musical life for a retirement in personal and public isolation in Italy. Was this the right decision for her? How did she feel about it? Should we even ask these questions? How much of an Italian soprano was she, if her entire career and professional experience were bound to the Americas? How significant was her Latin and South American experience to her own understanding of her life as a singer? And what role did such transatlantic experiences play for ideas about opera at home in Italy? As I have mentioned before, it is difficult to know the answers to these questions; but asking them might lead us to more nuanced explorations of the ways in which opera was experienced not only in the Americas, but also in those private and public borderlands of what had become global 'Italian' opera.

---

[43] Rossi to Zegers, 10 September 1860.

8 | Reimagining Rossini

Obituaries as Transnational Narratives of Italian Opera

ARNOLD JACOBSHAGEN

Composers' obituaries have so far been largely neglected by music historians. In view of the relevance of biographical literature for the field as a whole, this may come as a surprise. As the first textual document after a person's death, the obituary is the starting point of any biography, which – if it is to be complete – needs to begin from the point of a completed life.[1] Its source value is underlined by the fact that the obituary is one of the oldest genres in the history of literature. A number of rhetorical elements shape its formal structure and content: traditionally divided into the sections *lamentatio, vita, laudatio* and *consolatio*, other rhetorical categories are used, especially *comparatio* (the comparison with other personalities) and *auctoritas* (the use of judgements of recognised authorities).[2] Not all of these features are regularly to be found in the age of the mass press, and especially in the modern feuilleton one can generally observe 'an easing of the formal rules of discourse'.[3] For the historian, these characteristics of the modern obituary make a careful textual analysis even more revealing.

Nevertheless, even in the heated musicological debates about the process of canonisation of composers and musical works, obituaries have received only exceptional attention, despite the fact that they explicitly aim at memorialisation and therefore play a significant role in the formation of a cultural memory.[4] The main reason for the 'downright stupendous ignorance of the long and rich history of necrology' may lie in the 'supposedly unreasonable haste and at the same time cause-relatedness of

---

[1] Thomas Goetz, *Poetik des Nachrufs: Zur Kultur der Nekrologie und zur Nachrufszene auf dem Theater* (Vienna: Böhlau, 2008), 51.
[2] Ralf Georg Bogner, *Der Autor im Nachruf: Formen und Funktionen der literarischen Memorialkultur von der Reformation bis zum Vormärz* (Tübingen: De Gruyter, 2006), 25.
[3] Ibid., 129.
[4] Cf. Jan Assmann, *Cultural Memory and Early Civilization. Writing, Remembrance, and Political Imagination* (Cambridge: Cambridge University Press, 2012); Bridget Fowler, *The Obituary as Collective Memory* (London: Routledge, 2007); Klaus Pietschmann and Melanie Wald-Fuhrmann (ed.), *Der Kanon der Musik: Theorie und Geschichte: Ein Handbuch* (Munich: edition text + kritik, 2013).

production'.[5] The difficult procurement of sources may also have played a role in the low level of consideration in research in the past. Thanks to the digital humanities and the resulting online availability of a huge range of newspapers and the most important music journals of the nineteenth century, obituaries can nowadays be easily located and analysed. For the analysis of notions of national identity in relation to musical styles they offer extremely rich source material, especially when read in transnational perspective.

The death of Gioachino Rossini on 13 November 1868 in Passy near Paris incited a tremendous international media response, the extent of which can only be approximated at the current state of research. Within a few weeks of his death, thousands of articles about Rossini had appeared worldwide. As James William Davison commented in *The Musical World*: 'Columns upon columns of biography and eulogy have appeared in every civilized language; so many columns that most probably laborious triflers are at this moment computing how far they would reach if put in line on some king's highway.'[6] The extraordinary prominence of the deceased, about whom not only numerous biographies in various languages but also novels and plays had appeared decades before his death, may explain part of the phenomenon.[7] The rapid development of print media, especially since the middle of the nineteenth century, also contributed significantly to this early manifestation of modern celebrity culture.

This chapter examines and compares obituaries of the composer from the British, French, German, Austrian and Swiss press, bringing to light in condensed form some of the then-predominant narratives of Rossini's life and personality outside his Italian homeland.[8] Despite their different

---

[5] Bogner, *Der Autor im Nachruf*, 2.

[6] Thaddeus Egg [James William Davison], 'Rossini Commemorations', *The Musical World*, 19 December 1868, 859.

[7] See, for example, Eugène Scribe, *Rossini à Paris ou le Grand Diner* (Paris: Baudouin Frères, 1823); Stendhal [Henri Beyle], *Vie de Rossini, orné des portraits de Rossini et de Mozart* (Paris: Boulland, 1824 [first published in autumn 1823]); Amadeus Wendt, *Rossini's Leben und Treiben: Vornehmlich nach den Nachrichten des Herrn v. Stendhal geschildert und mit Urtheilen der Zeitgenossen über seinen musikalischen Charakter begleitet von Amadeus Wendt* (Leipzig: Leopold Voß, 1824, reprint Hildesheim: Olms, 2003); Giuseppe Carpani, *Le Rossiniane, ossia Lettere musico-teatrali* (Padua: Forni, 1824); Pietro Brighenti, *Della musica rossiniana e del suo autore* (Bologna: Emidio Dall'Olmo, 1830); Antonio Zanolini, *Biografia di Gioachino Rossini* [Paris 1836] (Bologna: Zanichelli, 1875); Eduard Maria Oettinger, *Rossini* (Leipzig: Costenoble und Remmelmann, 1851); Alexis Azevedo, *Rossini: Sa vie et ses œuvres* (Paris: Heugel, 1864).

[8] The text selection makes no claim to completeness. I only considered contributions from British, French, German, Austrian and Swiss print media that directly refer to Rossini's death, published by the end of 1868 and available online in digital form via the British Newspaper Archives and British Periodicals, the French National Library (*gallica*), the Austrian National Library (*anno*), the Swiss National Library (*e-newspaperarchives*) and the Bavarian State Library (*digipress*). Cf.

origins and perspectives, all authors of these obituaries seem to agree that Rossini led an extraordinarily happy life, which was not marked by any kind of sadness. This presumed earthly happiness is attributed above all to his Italian origins, which allegedly also had a decisive influence on his musical compositions. Comparing these obituaries reveals a certain standard of perspective on Italian opera that was typical of transnational operatic debates during the first half of the nineteenth century, as well as specific concepts of *italianità* associated with Rossini.

Greatness, Happiness and *Italianità*

British critics commenting on Rossini's death outbid each other with superlatives. According to *The Globe*, Rossini was 'one of the very few absolute and supreme geniuses of the world', and he had 'passed away to join the immortals among whose highest nobility his name has long been enrolled'.[9] In the view of the *Morning Post*, Rossini was 'the greatest of Italian composers', and his biography 'comprised the history of operatic music during the present century'.[10] For *The Musical World*, he was 'one of the most remarkable geniuses and one of the kindliest spirits of the nineteenth century', and the founder of a school that had 'more disciples, good, bad, and indifferent, than probably any other in any art'.[11] *The Sun* stated that 'among modern musicians there is none who has the slightest pretence to take his place',[12] the *East London Observer* mourned the loss of 'one of the greatest musical geniuses and composers the world ever produced'[13] and the *Illustrated Times* spoke of Rossini as 'one of the most remarkable geniuses and one of the kindliest spirits of the nineteenth century'.[14] While *The Athenæum* thought of him as 'one of the most original artists in every sense of the word',[15] for the *Penny Illustrated Paper* 'the great Rossini' was 'the last of the mighty men of music'.[16]

---

www.britishnewspaperarchive.co.uk; https://search.proquest.com/britishperiodicals/index; https://gallica.bnf.fr; http://anno.onb.ac.at; www.e-newspaperarchives.ch; www.bsb-muenchen.de/sammlungen/zeitungen/ (last accessed 17 December 2019). An overview of the French and German obituaries can be found in Arnold Jacobshagen, 'Der Nachruf als Kanonisierungsinstanz: Gedenken an Rossini anno 1868', *Die Tonkunst*, 12/4 (2018), 348–63.

[9] 'Rossini Is Dead', *The Globe*, 16 November 1868, 3.
[10] 'London, Monday Nov. 16, 1868', *Morning Post*, 16 November 1868, 4.
[11] 'Rossini', *The Musical World*, 21 November 1868, 789.
[12] 'Correspondence from Paris', *The Sun*, 16 November 1868, 8.
[13] 'Death of Rossini', *East London Observer*, 21 November 1868, 2.
[14] 'Rossini', *Illustrated Times*, 21 November 1868, 14.
[15] 'Gioachino Rossini', *The Athenæum*, 21 November 1868, 686.
[16] 'Rossini', *Penny Illustrated Paper* – Saturday 21 November 1868, 11.

The French press was equally enthusiastic about the composer. Ambroise Thomas, who gave the first speech at the funeral, called Rossini 'one of those flames that illuminated an entire century'.[17] Henri Vignaud described Rossini in *Le Mémorial diplomatique* as 'the greatest opera composer of the present and the past' ('le plus grand compositeur lyrique des temps modernes et des temps passés'),[18] whereas for Thomas Grimm, of the *Revue pour tous*, he was 'the most famous dramatic composer of the 19th century, the greatest modern melodist and the god of contemporary music'.[19] Gustave Stradina saw in him 'one of the most famous masters known to mankind';[20] and according to Jacques-Léopold Heugel, writing in *Le Ménestrel*, 'no fame could be more popular and aristocratic at the same time' than that of Rossini, 'whose songs are engraved in the memory of all time'.[21]

Similar hymns of praise were also attributed to individual operas. Charles Clarette in *L'Illustration* calls *Guillaume Tell* 'an immortal work', and states that Rossini's genius would also survive 'with just as much strength as charm'.[22] Henri Vignaud praises Rossini's last opera in even more exuberant terms, describing it as 'the masterpiece of all masterpieces, the mighty, all-powerful, supernatural Guillaume' and a true 'miracle'.[23] For reasons that have frequently been discussed, Rossini was undoubtedly more highly regarded in the French and the British than in the German press, as the *Neue Berliner Musikzeitung* registered: 'Perhaps no composer has been celebrated like Rossini in France, where the Rossini cult does not date from his death, and one wonders what remains of great opera composers after Halévy's, Meyerbeer's and Rossini's departure?'[24]

German critics were generally more reserved than their French and British colleagues. Eduard Hanslick's judgement that Rossini was 'Italy's most brilliant and popular composer'[25] can be considered representative of the German-language press – limiting his fame exclusively to the field of *Italian* music. Similar ratings can be found in many variations, describing

---

[17] 'Discours de M. Ambroise Thomas', *Le Ménestrel*, 22 November 1868, 409.
[18] Henri Vignaud, 'Rossini', *Le Mémorial diplomatique*, 19 November 1868, 765.
[19] Thomas Grimm, 'Histoire de la semaine', *Revue pour tous*, 21 November 1868, 1.
[20] G. Stradina, 'Rossini', *Le Moniteur des pianistes*, 20 November 1868, 45.
[21] Jacques-Léopold Heugel, 'G. Rossini', *Le Ménestrel*, 22 November 1868, 409.
[22] Charles Clarette, 'Courrier de Campagne', *L'Illustration*, 21 November 1868, 322.
[23] Henri Vignaud, 'Rossini', *Le Mémorial diplomatique*, 19 November 1868, 765.
[24] 'Correspondenzen', *Neue Berliner Musikzeitung*, 25 November 1868, 386.
[25] Eduard Hanslick, 'Rossini', *Neue freie Presse: Morgenblatt*, 17 November 1868, 1–3; reprint in: Hanslick, *Die moderne Oper: Kritiken und Studien* (Berlin: Hofmann, 1875), 101–22 (101).

him as 'Italy's most famous composer',[26] as 'almost idolized in Italy' or simply calling him 'the master of Italian opera'.[27] Even those authors who were by no means in favour of Rossini and his music, especially in the Protestant parts of Germany, did not question his leading position within Italian music during the first half of the nineteenth century.

National stereotypes of Italian music were prominently represented in German-language obituaries.[28] The Viennese periodical *Die Debatte*, for example, referred to Rossini 'as an Italian, a man of fashion and acquisition, [who] drove the melodic element, the vocal virtuosity to its peak with the utmost ruthlessness against the dramatic truth'.[29] When Rossini is described as 'the once-praised composer' and 'maestro of modern pompous opera', it suggests that the present now judged him differently, for 'his talent and, above all, his early successes drove him to gimmickry, so that only a small part of his works could stand up to severe criticism; and, at least in German theatres, [his operas] were soon pushed aside by more solid and profound works'.[30] The *Neue Berliner Musikzeitung* reports with a significant mixture of respect and contempt that 'with him a system, an entire musical epoch, the age of sweet Italian music, of coloratura and fioritura singing, was buried'.[31]

Rossini had left Italy as early as 1823, at the age of just thirty-one, and then lived abroad for the longest part of his life, including more than twenty-five years in Paris, where in the words of *The Globe* he became 'one of the pets of polite and intellectual society'[32] and 'one of the idols of the modern world'.[33] Nevertheless, more than any other composer of his generation, he was associated with Italy and was regarded as its leading musical representative until his death. In numerous obituaries the image of Rossini is mixed with that of a more general idea of *italianità* to form an overall picture of a supposedly Mediterranean way of life. This conflation of Rossini with *italianità* creates the impression that the composer's long absence from his homeland, in retrospect, even strengthened observers' perceptions of the Italian character, which it was thought he had first received in his youth. The image of the idle old master in the metropolis of Paris served as a counterpoint to the enraptured imagination of the

---

[26] 'Rossini', *Pfälzer Zeitung*, Speyer, 20 November 1868, 2.
[27] 'Giacomo Rossini', *Die Neue Zeit*, Olomouc, 18 November 1868, 1.
[28] Cf. Arnold Jacobshagen, 'Rossini and His German Critics', in Ilaria Narici, Emilio Sala, Emanuele Senici and Benjamin Walton (eds.), *Gioachino Rossini 1868–2018: La musica e il mondo* (Pesaro: Fondazione Rossini, 2018), 381–411.
[29] H. W., 'Joachim Rossini', *Die Debatte*, Vienna, 17 November 1868, 1.
[30] 'Gioachino Rossini', *Illustrirtes Kreuzblatt*, Augsburg, 1 December 1868, 189.
[31] 'Correspondenzen, *Neue Berliner Musikzeitung*, 25 November 1868, 385.
[32] 'Rossini Is Dead', *The Globe*, 16 November 1868, 3.   [33] Ibid.

young Rossini in Italy, who was brimming with an almost immeasurable creative power. In this way, the anonymous author of the Vienna daily *Die Debatte* contrasted two opposing images of the composer in an article entitled 'Rossini at Thirty':

When I think of Rossini, I remember the picture he had himself produced in Vienna in 1820, during his brilliant period: Wrapped in a military coat, a Polish cap on his head, the carefree look of the big, protruding eyes, the small moustache that was usual at that time, the cheerfully sensual mouth with the gourmet lips, a facial expression of satisfaction with the whole world and one's own self, a smile of the beautiful man, that is so the true type of the successful man from the restoration period. Carefree, cheerful, happy and a little vain, his life turned out to be the most completely successful artist's existence.

If you enter Italy for the first time on the southwestern sea route, you will be surprised by the happy appearance of the country, whether you climb up in Naples, Genoa, Spezia or one of the other small ports on the western coast. The whole landscape appears blue and pink, the bay is surrounded by hills that descend to the horizon, flirtatious villas are scattered along the coast. The slopes are covered in a charming mixture of grey olive trees with their lightly moving foliage and dark leafy orange trees; from this green background stand out, here and there, plant-covered houses with intensely red tiled roofs, rosy, green, ochre patches. . . . .

In such a country one feels at the first moment immediately pervaded by physical well-being; it is as if our spirit, free of all worries, happily floats in this sea of light and colour. In order to suffer, one must withdraw into oneself, concentrate within oneself, but here the spirit turns outward; the sight remains always the same, but this uniformity does not tire, because one is always in the same joyful mood. Here suffering, sorrow, sadness cannot take root, this environment only allows serenity, pleasant thoughts, here is no birthplace of gigantic wrestling souls, like those of Beethoven or even more seriously intimate, like those of Mozart, here grows and grants only a happily unconcerned sense, with some egoism, like Rossini.[34]

The British also loved imagining Rossini's career in terms of pastoral landscapes, as *The Musical World* suggested:

We can look with complacency at the long life just terminated. It was an example of the unbroken sunshine in which some favoured mortals bask. Almost without effort Rossini became famous. From the time when he wrote his first opera, to the day when *Guillaume Tell* consummated his work and his renown, he travelled an easy and flower-strewn path. Content with the success thus achieved, he lived in keenest enjoyment of whatever it brought, the centre of a circle which included all that was famous in literature and art. A career such as his excites no strong

---

[34] 'Rossini mit dreißig Jahren', *Die Debatte*, 5 December 1868, 1.

emotions, and possesses no absorbing interest. It can be looked at as one looks at a pastoral landscape, or a summer sea.[35]

And the same goes for his music, the critic concluded: 'His music reflects the joyousness of the life he led. Bright, sparkling, even in its melancholy like the grief of a child behind which laughter is ever lurking, it will always be the cause, as it is the result, of happiness.'[36]

Rossini is almost without exception described as a 'lucky child' favoured by fate, who died in old age, carefree and 'in full enjoyment of life'. The Austrian poet Sigmund Kolisch, for example, who had met the composer in Paris some time before, drew the following picture of him:

If ever a person could be called happy on earth, it was Gioachino Rossini . . ., for the much-favoured musician has always been torn away from the violence of changeable fate. He died in full enjoyment of life, in full possession of mental power and receptivity to the joys of the world, the glory wreath fresh and green on his head, sought and celebrated, in the look a smile, on his lips a joke. Only flowers, but no tears, were to fall on the grave of this merry son on earth. He has never cried himself, and may every sorrow of his enviable temper be chuckled away.[37]

The *Neues Wiener Tagblatt* commented very similarly on the news of his death:

At the fresh grave, our fellow world will have no reproaches to make of having misjudged the one who has just sunk down, that it has tortured him and left him to worry and sorrow for his existence; the funeral speech will not cast a glance at a life full of tears, for the life that was exhaled in the tumult of the noisy metropolis was one full of sunshine and happiness.[38]

Such portrayals of unclouded earthly happiness can be encountered in many variations: for example, 'The "Swan of Pesaro" has ended his long life, which has not been clouded by any mishaps.'[39] The Parisian journals, which were usually much better informed about biographical details, came to an equally clear conclusion about the composer's life, so richly blessed by earthly happiness. According to the *Moniteur des pianistes*, 'everything radiated towards him at an early age, love, fame and happiness', and in old age 'the entire musical world was at his feet'.[40]

---

[35] 'Rossini', *The Musical World*, 21 November 1868, 794.   [36] Ibid., 795.
[37] Sigmund Kolisch, 'Rossini in Paris', *Beilage zur Allgemeinen Zeitung*, Munich, 5 December 1868, 5175.
[38] Fr., 'Rossini †', *Neues Wiener Tagblatt*, 16 November 1868, 3.
[39] 'Rossini †', *Der Erzähler am Main*, Aschaffenburg, 21 November 1868, 564.
[40] G. Stradina, 'Rossini', *Le Moniteur des pianistes*, 20 November 1868, 45.

According to the *London Evening Standard*, Rossini's happiness could also be recognised in the multitude of honours he received during his lifetime: 'If success and worldly honours could bring happiness, he ought to have been one of the happiest of men. His fame was world-wide; his wealth was enormous; and his collection of orders, medals, and ribands is believed to be nearly, if not quite, the largest in the world.'[41] Overall more critical in its assessment, the *Manchester Courier and Lancashire General Advertiser* declared that Rossini was at least 'the most popular, if not the greatest composer of the Italian lyric stage in the present century'.[42]

Popularity and simplicity were among the most important qualities attributed to him by the *London Evening Standard*: 'If to be "a man of the people" be a claim to distinction in the present day, the great Italian musician whose death is just reported had assuredly a more than ordinary title to respect.'[43] His origins in the simplest of circumstances may have contributed to his popularity, as the *London Daily News* suggested: 'Scarcely any man ever achieved speedy fortune and renown with less adventitious aids than those which attended the youth of this great composer';[44] and the critic of the Sheffield *Daily Telegraph* assumed that 'Rossini, by his delicious melodies, dashing style, and rich dramatic effects, has, in spite of his frequent carelessness in harmony, and of his frequent repetition of himself, succeeded in delighting more auditors than any lyric composer of modern times.'[45]

The 'Second Death' of the Artist

Every obituary commented on the fact that Rossini's career as a composer of operas had ended as early as 1829. As Edouard Lockroy astutely pointed out in *Le Diable à quatre*: 'The artist dies for the general public on the day on which he no longer cultivates his art. Rossini's funeral took place forty years ago.'[46] The recurring narrative of the artist's 'second death' leads to a weakening of the lament, with reference to the four decades that had passed since the end of his activity as an opera composer: 'With him a rich

---

[41] 'Rossini', *London Evening Standard*, 16 November 1868, 5.
[42] 'Death of Rossini', *Manchester Courier and Lancashire General Advertiser*, 21 November 1868, 12.
[43] 'Rossini', *London Evening Standard*, 16 November 1868, 5.
[44] 'Rossini', *London Daily News*, 16 November 1868, 5.
[45] 'Death of Rossini', *Sheffield Daily Telegraph*, 16 November 1868, 4.
[46] Edouard Lockroy, 'Chronique théâtrale', *Le Diable à Quatre*, 21 November 1868, 13.

playing of strings has faded away. If this loss does not touch the world as painfully as it did with the death of Mendelssohn or Schumann, this is only because the swan of Pesaro had been silent for some time and no new songs were expected of him.'[47] According to the *Allgemeine Zeitung* from Augsburg, Rossini 'stopped suddenly at the height of his creativity' and thus practised an example of self-criticism and self-denial that can only be found in a few composers:

> Whether Rossini could have achieved even more than his 'Tell' – who is in a position to make a judgement about that? ... Rossini did not want to give the world the impression of an ageing and diminishing power of production. This is why we have kept such a youthfully fresh and unclouded picture of him as of no other Italian composer.[48]

In a similar sense, the *Didaskalia* from Heidelberg wrote that 'the world-famous Maestro Rossini' was 'one of the few mortals who was allowed to experience his own immortality'.[49] At times similar views were expressed in even more drastic words. For instance, *Le Figaro* reported that Rossini's death had occurred four decades ago: 'Before he came to rest in the vaults of La Madeleine, he had already been dormant in the crypt of his private life for forty years. It came as a complete surprise to learn that he had to be embalmed again.'[50] The satirical magazine *Le Lapin indépendant* claimed that it could even ignore Rossini's death altogether, because 'when the nightingale no longer sings, she's just a common bird. Rossini had taken his own life in cold blood.'[51] Most journals formulated similar thoughts with somewhat greater reverence, such as *Le Moniteur des pianistes*: 'Rossini had long been immortal, which means dead. This great genius produced nothing more. They didn't cry at his memorial – they came to look!'[52] Ange-Henri Blaze reported that compared to Meyerbeer's death, which had occurred in 1864, Rossini's death left only half as strong an impression on the public eye: 'This was because Meyerbeer was uprooted in the midst of his struggle of life', while Rossini had 'renounced the pomp of the world and the theatre for about forty years, and limited himself entirely to domestic relationships and pleasures'.[53]

---

[47] 'Rossini †', *Blätter für Musik, Theater und bildende Kunst*, Vienna, 17 November 1868, 4.
[48] 'Der Tod Rossini's', *Allgemeine Zeitung*, Augsburg, 18 November 1868, 4898.
[49] 'Gioachino Rossini', *Didaskalia*, Heidelberg, 17 November 1868, 2.
[50] 'Gazette de Paris', *Le Figaro*, 19 November 1868, 1.
[51] 'La Semaine', *Le Lapin indépendant*, 21 November 1868, 2.
[52] G. Stradina, 'Rossini', *Le Moniteur des pianistes*, 20 November 1868, 46.
[53] Ange-Henri Blaze [F. de Lagenevais], 'Revue musicale', *Revue des deux mondes*, 1, 1868, 766.

His 'second death' caused the press to speculate once more about the motivation behind his premature artistic retirement:

> What were the actual reasons for his comparative cessation from labour his most intimate friends would find it difficult to explain, for he himself could never be brought to talk seriously on the subject. The loss to art through the obstinate reticence of so great a genius may be readily imagined; but he had purchased leisure by hard toil and working of the brain enough to wear a stronger frame.[54]

The British music journal *The Orchestra* had a clear opinion on exactly this issue: 'What stopped Rossini? Not fear of work; not dread of failure. But he was in no situation to advance, and he knew it.'[55]

Transfer of Genius

Two very different authors, Richard Wagner and Eduard Hanslick, published extensive obituaries of Rossini. Particularly striking here is the fact that both authors conclude with a reference to Mozart. On Wagner, who had met Rossini in Paris in 1860, Rossini 'made the impression of the first truly great and revered man', placing the 'Swan of Pesaro' in one line with Palestrina, Bach and Mozart: Like them, 'Rossini belonged to his own time.'[56] Hanslick also made several references to Mozart in his obituary: 'Rossini was born in Pesaro on 29 February 1792, three months after Mozart's death, as if his spirit had sought a new incarnation, like God Vishnu so as to walk again on earth.'[57] Hanslick then tried to artistically justify the affinities between the two: 'Just as he is musically related to Mozart through a fine sense of form, a restrained grace, a beautiful sensuality, so he also shared many other things with him.'[58] Finally, Hanslick even gave this close relationship a genealogical underpinning by declaring Mozart Rossini's metaphorical father: Rossini had left 'his beloved Champs Elysées to visit those legendary Elysian fields where the shadows of the great dead wander in blissful peace and serenity. He will not hope in vain that Mozart will meet him there and call out to him: My dear son!'[59]

---

[54] 'Rossini', *The Musical World*, 21 November 1868, 789.
[55] 'Who Was Rossini?', *The Orchestra*, 21 November 1868, 138.
[56] Richard Wagner, 'Eine Erinnerung an Rossini', *Allgemeine Zeitung*, Augsburg, 17 December 1868, 5375f.; trans. William Ashton Ellis, ' A Remembrance of Rossini', in *Richard Wagner's Prose Works*, vol. 4 (1895) (London: Kegan Paul, Trench and Trübner, 1892–1899), 271–3.
[57] Eduard Hanslick, 'Rossini', *Neue Freie Presse: Morgenblatt*, 17 November 1868, 1–3; reprint in Hanslick, *Die moderne Oper: Kritiken und Studien* (Berlin: Hofmann, 1875), 101–22 (102).
[58] Ibid., 122.   [59] Ibid.

Establishing these parallels between Mozart and Rossini, Hanslick followed a long tradition that has received little attention in nineteenth-century music history. Stendhal, Rossini's first biographer, had used the same comparison with Mozart as a leitmotif as early as 1823.[60] The title pages of the two volumes of the first edition of his *Vie de Rossini* (1823–4), which had immediately been translated into several languages, were both adorned with portraits of Rossini and Mozart.[61] As a model for his book on Rossini Stendhal had used the well-established genre of the literary double portrait, which he had previously employed in his *Racine et Shakespeare* (1823) as a way of illustrating the relationship between classical and romantic aesthetics.[62] At the same time, this literary technique followed on from the recent Parisian musical *querelle* which had related the opposing camps of 'Mozartistes' and 'Rossinistes' at the beginning of the 1820s to those of the 'Lullistes' and 'Ramistes' and of the 'Gluckistes' and 'Piccinnistes', which at the time had given rise to most vehemently fought controversies.[63]

As Benjamin Walton has recently demonstrated, the proximity of Mozart's death to Rossini's birth had prompted the painter Eugène Delacroix, in 1825, to speak of 'a transfer of genius from one to the other'.[64] Parallels between Mozart and Rossini can also be found in the historiographical accounts of time. For instance, Heinrich Heine's idea of a 'musical interregnum'[65] after Mozart's death, which only ended with Felix

---

[60] For Stendhal's image of Rossini, see, among others, Pierluigi Petrobelli, 'Balzac, Stendhal e il Mosè di Rossini', in Petrobelli, *Annuario 1965–70 del Conservatorio di musica G. B. Martini di Bologna* (Bologna: Casa editrice Patron, 1971), 205–19; Kurt Ringger and Christof Weiand (eds.), *Stendhal und Deutschland* (Tübingen: Narr, 1986); Benjamin Walton, *Rossini in Restoration Paris: The Sound of Modern Life* (Cambridge: Cambridge University Press, 2007), 24–67; Olivier Bara, 'Du nouveau dans le beau idéal: Stendhal, Vie de Rossini', in Bara, *Être moderne: Les écrivains face aux nouveautés artistiques, littéraires et technologiques* (Paris: Euredit, 2011), 65–78; Xavier Bourdenet, 'Nord/Sud, ou imaginaire géographique du romantisme chez Stendhal (à propos de la Vie de Rossini)', in Olivier Bara and Alban Ramaut (eds.), *Généalogies du romantisme musical français* (Paris: Vrin, 2012), 225–38; Anna Opiela, *La musique dans l'œuvre de Stendhal et de Nerval* (Paris: Honoré Champion, 2015).

[61] Stendhal, *Vie de Rossini*.

[62] Stendhal [Henri Beyle], *Racine et Shakespeare* (Paris: Bossange, 1823). On the literary tradition of the double portrait as used by Stendhal, see Francesco Manzini, *Stendhal's Parallel Lives* (Oxford: Peter Lang, 2004).

[63] Cf. Paolo Fabbri, 'Rossini in Paris vor Rossinis Ankunft: Einige Bemerkungen zur Debatte über Rossinis Musik von 1821–1823', in Bernd-Rüdiger Kern and Reto Müller (eds.), *Rossini in Paris* (Leipzig: Leipziger Universitätsverlag, 2002), 201–51.

[64] Cfr. Walton, *Rossini in Restoration Paris*, 210–11.

[65] In his 'Ninth Letter on the French Stage', Heine mocks the 'Rossinism' condemned in Berlin, naming Adolf Bernhard Marx in particular, 'who at the time belonged to a certain musical reign which, during the minority of a certain young genius, who was regarded as Mozart's legitimate heir to the throne, constantly paid homage to Sebastian Bach'. Heinrich Heine, 'Über die französische Bühne: Vertraute Briefe an August Lewald: Neunter Brief', in Heine, *Historisch-*

Mendelssohn's appearance, refers directly to a historical construction by Stendhal, according to which an 'interregnum' after Domenico Cimarosas's death was overcome with Rossini's appearance.[66] The Austrian historian of music Raphael Georg Kiesewetter also regarded Rossini as Mozart's legitimate successor. In his view, 'nobody had surpassed Mozart in the field of opera'; but Rossini 'appropriated the now recognised effects of German instrumental music (known to him through and through). Defeating the prejudice of the nation and the vanity of its singers, he now translated them into Italian opera with a felicity hitherto unheard of.'[67]

The imaginative notion of a transfer of genius between Mozart and Rossini also inspired the former director of the Paris opera Nestor Roqueplan in the very extensive obituary he wrote for *Le Constitutionnel*: 'In 1791 the author of *Don Juan* died; in 1792 the future author of *Guillaume Tell* was born in Pesaro. For the joy of mankind and in order to perfectionate the masterpiece of grand opera, the chain that had been torn off since Mozart's death was renewed.'[68] Roqueplan drew an outline of the history of opera from Monteverdi to the present day, with Mozart and Rossini as the two irrefutable highlights; but while Mozart found a worthy successor in Rossini, with Rossini an epoch came to an end for which there could no longer be an equivalent sequel.[69] Similar judgements are to be found in the British press: 'No one has done so much for the opera since Mozart.'[70] The parallel between Mozart and Rossini was often equated to that of the two 'immortal masterpieces', *Don Giovanni* and *Guillaume Tell*.[71] In his eulogy to Rossini, the composer Ambroise Thomas also mentioned Mozart, to whom Rossini owed above anything his greatness as a thinker and musician: 'By diligently studying the models of all schools, by meditating above all between Haydn and Mozart, of whom he made a true cult all his life, this spontaneous genius subjected himself to healthy traditions and acquired this feeling of beauty, this love of form and contours, this science of architectural order which makes a work of art imperishable.'[72]

---

kritische Gesamtausgabe der Werke, ed. Manfred Windfuhr, vol. 12/1 (Hamburg: Hoffmann und Campe, 1980), 273–83 (275).

[66] Stendhal, *Vie de Rossini*, 18–30, cf. Arnold Jacobshagen, *Opera semiseria. Gattungskonvergenz und Kulturtransfer im Musiktheater* (Stuttgart: Franz Steiner, 2005), 7; Jacobshagen, *Gioachino Rossini und seine Zeit* (Laaber: Laaber-Verlag, 2015, 2nd ed. 2018), 280–3.

[67] Raphael Georg Kiesewetter, *Geschichte der europäisch-abendländischen oder unserer heutigen Musik: Darstellung ihres Ursprungs, ihres Wachsthums und ihrer stufenweisen Entwicklung von dem ersten Jahrhundert des Christenthums bis auf unsere heutige Zeit* (Leipzig: Breitkopf & Härtel, 1834), 97.

[68] Nestor Roqueplan, 'Rossini', *Le Constitutionnel*, 22 November 1868, 2.   [69] Ibid.

[70] *Shipping and Mercantile Gazette*, 16 November 1868, 8.

[71] Benoît Jouvin, *Gioachino Rossini*, *La Presse*, 23 November 1868, 2.

[72] 'Discours de M. Ambroise Thomas', *Le Ménestrel*, 22 November 1868, 409.

For Rossini's funeral on 21 November 1868, at the church of La Trinité in Paris, the eighty-seven-year-old Daniel-François Auber arranged a *Requiem* based on Mozart's *Lacrimosa* and framed by five compositions by Rossini, as well as two other works by Jommelli and Pergolesi, both of whom Rossini particularly admired. At the same time, a funeral service *in absentia* of the deceased took place in Florence with an enormous musical line-up, bringing together an orchestra of 200 musicians and a chorus several times more numerous, to produce a performance of Mozart's *Requiem*. As one English periodical commented, 'the execution of the Requiem was in the highest degree creditable, considering the short time employed in the rehearsal; it was even the finest display of choral music which I have heard for a long time in Florence'.[73]

Other authors discovered parallels between Mozart's and Rossini's childhood, even though Rossini was never explicitly regarded as a 'child prodigy'. Eduard Schelle, Hanslick's successor as music editor of the *Wiener Presse* since 1864, wrote: 'Rossini was a thoroughbred musician like Mozart. Already in his early childhood he revealed an unusual musical talent.'[74] Various journals quoted a well-known anecdote with the intention of testifying to Rossini's fondness for Mozart and German music: 'Once asked whom he considered the greatest of the three great masters Haydn, Mozart and Beethoven, he replied: It was certainly not for him to judge, but as far as his individual view was concerned, he could only say that he played Beethoven twice a week, Haydn four times, but Mozart every day!'[75] Finally, the critic of *Saunders's News-Letter* compared the deaths of the two composers, stating that 'Rossini did not die, like his great rival in renown, Mozart, singing a sad and sweet death-song. For nearly a generation he had been silent; and yet men had not forgotten.'[76]

Negative Press and *Damnatio Memoriae*

Apart from mentioning Mozart, the obituaries rarely compared Rossini to other composers. Meyerbeer and Auber are occasionally referred to, but without being considered worthy of detailed stylistic analysis. Not surprisingly, even Giuseppe Verdi is absent in the French and German articles,

---

[73] 'Rossini's Funeral in Florence', *The Orchestra*, 28 November 1868, 213–14.
[74] E[duard] Schelle, 'Gioachino Rossini', *Die Presse*, 17 November 1868, 3.
[75] Thus, in the anonymous contribution 'Gioachino Antonio Rossini', *Neues Fremden-Blatt*, Vienna, 17 November 1868, 6.
[76] 'Death of Rossini', *Saunders's News-Letter and Daily Advertiser*, 17 November 1868, 1.

though his name occasionally appeared in British magazines such as *The Musical World*: 'The professors abused his [Rossini's] music as they do that of Verdi to this hour; and yet Verdi is incomparably the greatest composer living, and has the honour of being the best vilified dramatic writer by our acute and discriminating journalists.'[77]

Very often, however, Rossini was associated with a personality from a completely different profession, namely the banker James Rothschild. It was not only the fact that Rossini 'still in his last years made the impression of a highly witty and kind personality, whose excellent qualities were somewhat distorted only by a too far driven preference for the sounding metal', as Eduard Schelle was able to report.[78] The immediate cause for the Rothschild comparisons stems from the coincidence that France's leading banker died almost simultaneously with Rossini in Paris on the morning of 15 November 1868. Since Rothschild, like Rossini, was born in 1792 and was also close friends with him, it seemed natural to look for further parallels in the biographies of the 'prince of money' and the 'music prince', as the Viennese *Morgen-Post* suggested:

There is no doubt that Joachim Rossini and James Rothschild were kindred spirits. Both lived in the realm of melodies, only the melodies of one were sounded in music, the other by the clink of coins. We haven't had time to count Rossini's golden notes, but it's not impossible that he leaves 700 million note heads, like Rothschild's 700 million francs. Both were born in 1792, both chose Paris for their permanent residence, both liked each other, both were gourmets, and both are mentioned in one and the same volume of the Encyclopedia of conversation, both died in 1868, one on November 14, the other, presumably because he took the medio as his expiration date as a merchant, only the following November 15.[79]

Also, from the point of view of hedonism, Rothschild's eventful life and indescribable prosperity were predestined to be compared to those of Rossini:

If in common terms both were happy people, Rossini was undoubtedly the happier one. Not only because he had the earthly means to fully enjoy life, and at the same time also had the heavenly means to transfigure life, but also because, since the beginnings of this world, there had been no mortal who during his lifetime had been granted to sunbathe in the glory of his glory as long as he had. He witnessed his glory for forty years. He saw his own monument erected, his bust erected in the most distinguished Paris theatre, among the immortal greats of past centuries. He

---

[77] 'Who Was Rossini?', *The Orchestra*, 21 November 1868, 137.
[78] E[duard] Schelle, 'Gioachino Rossini', *Die Presse*, Vienna, 17 November 1868, 3.
[79] 'Aus dem Leben zweier Todten', *Morgen-Post*, Vienna, 18 November 1868, 1.

had already seen all the splendour and honours pour over him in abundance, which usually only pour over immortals after their earthly death.[80]

Not only did the Paris journals report that Rossini and Rothschild had been close personal friends, but also that the banker had received music lessons from Rossini for some time.[81]

The Rossini–Rothschild comparison was picked up again and again in the German press, not least because the family of Jewish bankers had originally come from Frankfurt and continued to have headquarters there. With reference to Rothschild, numerous negative attributions were condensed into a conflict-laden semantic field associated with money, sensuality and (Jewish) identity. In the musical terrain, this identity was associated especially with Paris and the names of Meyerbeer, Halévy and Offenbach, who were now joined, via Rothschild, by Rossini. 'Money is the God of our time, and Rothschild is his prophet', as Heinrich Heine had noted.[82] In his 1860 essay on 'Rossini and the Principle of Sensual Pleasure in Music', August Wilhelm Ambros complained that Rossini had degraded music 'with an almost frivolous ruthlessness to an ear-twinkling smouldering'.[83] These stereotypes employed a feedback effect associated with the idea of purely sensual musical pleasure, caricatures of Rossini's obese appearance (see Figures 8.1 and 8.2) and anecdotes about his sophisticated lifestyle and the commercial orientation of his composing. In these images, bourgeois morality's 'anti-culinary self-understanding and the anorexic hostility to the body' seemingly reinforced each other.[84] After all, the direct comparison between Rossini and Rothschild produced a clear winner, as Jacques-Léopold Heugel observed in *Le Ménestrel*: 'Rossini's death was the European event of the week, so much so that the funeral of Rothschild, the great king of finance, will have gone almost unnoticed.'[85]

Even where no direct comparison to Rothschild was made, Rossini's material prosperity and his interest in financial matters were mentioned in numerous obituaries. Only exceptionally, however, was he described as stingy

---

[80] Ibid. [81] 'Chronique Parisienne', *Le Gaulois*, 18 November 1868, 1.
[82] 'Denn das Geld ist der Gott unserer Zeit und Rothschild sein Prophet.' Cf. Heinrich Heine, *Lutezia: Berichte über Politik, Kunst und Volksleben* [1841] (Hamburg: Hoffmann & Campe, 1854); Heine, *Historisch-kritische Gesamtausgabeder Werke*, vol. 13/1 (Hamburg: Hoffmann & Campe, 1988), 123.
[83] August Wilhelm Ambros, 'Rossini und das Prinzip des sinnlichen Genusses in der Musik', in Ambros, *Culturhistorische Bilder aus dem Musikleben der Gegenwart* (Leipzig: Matthes, 1865), 33–41 (33).
[84] Cf. Iris Därmann, *Kulturtheorien zur Einführung* (Hamburg: Junius, 2011), 19–27 (23).
[85] Jacques-Léopold Heugel, 'G. Rossini', *Le Ménestrel*, 22 November 1868, 409.

Figure 8.1 Benjamin Roubaud, *Rossini* (Paris: Imprimérie d'Aubert & Cie, 1839)

or hard-hearted. For instance, the critic of the *Morning Advertiser* sharply condemned Rossini's alleged miserliness and his handling of finances:

Rossini was sordidly avaricious, and did not hesitate to gratify his thirst for gold in streams which were not of the purest or most pellucid water. His love of lucre, however filthy the lucre might be, carried him far beyond that of the Roman Emperor, who pocketed the proceeds of the sewers with the grim reflection that money stinks. His two marriages were sad instances of this good old gentlemanly vice; both of the ladies whom he married were richer in wealth than in honour. They had the *ceinture dorée*, but the *bonne renommée* was not theirs. It is hardbound to say these things of one who has filled so high a place in the world's admiration; but when we look still farther into his character, we see this great composer, enriched by his works and by two marriages, walking about the

Figure 8.2 Étienne Cajart, *Rossini* (Paris: Imprimérie Bertauts c. 1855)

boulevards in a greasy, threadbare great coat, and writing bad music – such as the cantata played at the close of the Exhibition – making worse jokes, at the close of a glorious career, and even refusing to contribute to the Patriotic Fund when his countrymen came forth with their offerings to the great cause of emancipation. For this, his great offence, his countrymen have never forgiven him. He was compelled to fly from Bologna in 1855, and has lived here and at Passy ever since.[86]

This representation of course had little to do with Rossini's actual biography. On the whole, Rossini was given numerous honours in Bologna both before and after 1855. This negative portrayal also contrasts with numerous other tributes that characterise Rossini as particularly charitable

[86] 'Death of Rossini', *Morning Advertiser*, 16 November 1868, 5.

and lovable. *The Illustrated Times* praised him 'not merely on account of his fame as composer, but for his wit, his humour, his amiability, and general goodness',[87] and according to *The Musical World*, he was 'one of the kindliest spirits of the nineteenth century'.[88] Nevertheless, the wording here seemed characteristic of an essential tendency to link aesthetic and moral judgements, and to so mutually justify them.

Another form of negative reporting was to refuse the publication of an obituary altogether. This was the case for the two leading music magazines at Leipzig, the Protestant centre of German music publishing: both the *Allgemeine musikalische Zeitung* and the *Neue Zeitschrift für Musik* renounced a formal obituary. The latter published a poorly researched report on 20 November 1868, according to which Rossini had died at noon 'from the consequences of pneumonia'.[89] The reservations of the two leading German music journals towards Rossini were based on a long-standing tradition.[90] Nevertheless, the irritating silence of the two papers still seems to require explanation. While the *Allgemeine musikalische Zeitung* eventually reported in great detail about Rossini's funeral, mentioning among other things that there had been much less public mourning than after the death of Meyerbeer,[91] the restraint of the *Neue Zeitschrift* might have been connected to the death of its editor-in-chief: on 25 November 1868, two weeks after Rossini, Franz Brendel, a particularly severe opponent of Rossini and of nineteenth-century Italian music in general, had died. Brendel himself perhaps would not have missed the opportunity of writing an obituary on Rossini. His *History of Music in Italy, Germany and France* (1850) contained a detailed chapter on the composer,

---

[87] 'Rossini', *Illustrated Times*, 21 November 1868, 14.
[88] 'Rossini', *The Musical World*, 21 November 1868, 789.
[89] 'Todesfälle', *Neue Zeitschrift für Musik*, 20 November 1868, 415.
[90] Cfr., among others, Josef Loschelder, 'Rossinis Bild und Zerrbild in der Allgemeinen musikalischen Zeitung Leipzig', *Bollettino del Centro Rossiniani di Studi* (1973), 1, 23–42 and 2, 23–42; (1977), 3, 17–40; Sieghart Döhring, 'Rossini nel giudizio del mondo tedesco', in Paolo Fabbri (ed.), *Gioachino Rossini, 1792-1992: Il Testo e la Scena* (Pesaro: Fondazione Rossini, 1994), 93–104; Michael Wittmann, 'Das Bild der italienischen Oper im Spiegel der Kritik der Leipziger Allgemeine Musikalische Zeitung', in Fiamma Nicolodi and Paolo Trovato (eds.), *Le parole della musica. Studi sulla lingua della letteratura musicale in onore di Gianfranco Folena*, vol. 2 (Florence: Olschki, 1994), 195–226; Claudio Toscani, 'Dem Italiener ist Melodie Eins und Alles': Italienische Oper in der Leipziger 'Allgemeinen musikalischen Zeitung', in Sebastian Werr and Daniel Brandenburg (eds.), *Das Bild der italienischen Oper in Deutschland* (Münster: LIT Verlag, 2004), 137–49; Arnold Jacobshagen, 'Rossini and His German Critics', in Ilaria Narici, Emilio Sala, Emanuele Senici and Benjamin Walton (eds.), *Gioachino Rossini 1868-2018: La musica e il mondo* (Pesaro: Fondazione Rossini, 2018), 381–411.
[91] 'Tod und Leichenbegräbnis Rossini's', *Allgemeine musikalische Zeitung*, 23 December 1868, 414–15.

which would have offered enough material for such a piece.⁹² Rossini was described here as 'the composer of restoration', a concept that allegedly had come to precedence 'when since 1830 a new spirit had taken hold'.⁹³ The readers of the *Neue Zeitschrift für Musik* had to wait until 26 February 1869 to reflect on Rossini's death, when the journal reprinted Richard Wagner's *In Remembrance of Rossini*.⁹⁴

Celebrity and Canonisation

In the history of music, Rossini was one of the first personalities to become a global celebrity, in the modern sense of the word; his celebrity was closely linked to the rapid development of the print media at the time.⁹⁵ A special biographical feature of Rossini's worldwide fame and media presence was that it began to unfold at a time when his career as an opera composer was already drawing to a close. The extent to which obituaries played a role in representing Rossini as an example of the musical canon, as well as a phenomenon of a 'celebrity culture', cannot be addressed conclusively. In fact, it seems that the necrologists had nothing fundamentally new to add to the information, images and assessments already published during his lifetime. As some obituaries were ready to concede:

What can be said about Rossini that has not already been said? What eulogy for his immortal works could be more eloquent than the many already known? All conceivable compliments and eulogies were already given during Rossini's lifetime. Nothing more can be said about the man who has just died, and the wreaths of honour now to be placed on his statue do nothing new to the glory of the name.⁹⁶

The significance of the obituary in establishing a musical canon does not, of course, diminish such a finding to any significant extent. For only the composer's death was able to generate this level of simultaneous omnipresence in the

---

[92] Franz Brendel, *Geschichte der Musik in Italien, Deutschland und Frankreich* (Leipzig: Matthes 1868), 402–8.

[93] According to Brendel (and a considerable part of German music criticism), Rossini's 'great importance and at the same time his great lack' lies 'in the one directed towards sensory stimulation and ear tingling' (ibid.)

[94] Richard Wagner, 'Eine Erinnerung an Rossini', *Neue Zeitschrift für Musik*, 26 February 1869, 71–2.

[95] On the historical constitution of 'celebrity' around the middle of the nineteenth century, see, among others, Robert van Krieken, 'Celebrity's Histories', in Anthony Elliott (ed.), *Routledge Handbook of Celebrity Studies* (New York: Routledge, 2018), 26–43 (27). Rossini would undoubtedly be a particularly fruitful object of research for the still-young discipline of 'celebrity studies'.

[96] G. Stradina, 'Rossini', *Le Moniteur des pianistes*, 20 November 1868, 45.

international press, which in turn then anchored this image in the collective memory of a global public. To conclude with *Le Ménestrel*,

Rossini's highly revered image, his biography praised for the price of five centimes on the streets, has spread with almost no effort throughout the people, while the world of the salons still fights over the smallest remains of this great personality. Rossini's name is on everyone's lips; he lies in the air like a magical vibration that no man can escape.[97]

At the same time, however, sublime examples of undermining the maxim *de mortuis nil nisi bene* can also be observed, whether through hidden or open criticism or the almost demonstrative refusal to publish an obituary. In the case of the *Allgemeine musikalische Zeitung* and the *Neue Zeitschrift für Musik* this attitude can also be interpreted as an example of *damnatio memoriae* and as an attempt to exclude Rossini from the canon of great composers. In their aesthetic evaluation, many German-language critics may have diverged markedly from the views of their British and French colleagues; but their judgement hardly makes a difference to the transnational narrative about the famous, happy and supposedly carefree Italian composer, which thus contributed to an idea of operatic *italianità* that, in this form, could only be constructed far from Rossini's homeland.

[97] Jacques-Léopold Heugel, 'G. Rossini', *Le Ménestrel*, 22 November 1868, 409.

9 | From Heaven and Hell to the Grail Hall via Sant'Andrea della Valle

Religious Identity and the Internationalisation of Operatic Styles in Liberal Italy

ANDREW HOLDEN

> the other evening I went to hear *Mefistofele* ... I had been told that the Prologue in Heaven was a burst of inspiration, of genius, but hearing the harmonies of that number, based almost always on dissonances, I thought I was in ... surely not heaven. You see what it means not to be *dans le mouvement!!*[1]
>
> - Giuseppe Verdi to Count Opprandino Arrivabene, 30 March 1879

The first half century of the new Kingdom of Italy, after its foundation in 1861, was dominated by three fundamental questions of nation-building, bequeathed by the Risorgimento, which preoccupied early generations of Italian statesmen. First, the perceived imperative to construct a sense of citizenship and nationhood from the peninsula's bewildering inheritance of local, regional and transnational cultures. The second challenge was the need to modernise the economy to compete as a major European power, and attempt to integrate the more prosperous and industrialising northern regions with the semi-feudal south. Finally, the Catholic Church did not recognise the new kingdom, yet dominated provision of charity and education across the peninsula, and held wider social influence through the overwhelmingly Catholic adherence of the Italian population. Resolving the religious question of the institutional power of the Church therefore assumed huge importance, both for ideological and social reasons.

These questions can all be seen reflected in debates about the condition and future of Italian art, literature and music, including opera. The economic travails and social and demographic trends of the new nation state accelerated the decay of the model of opera-going inherited from the pre-unification period, which had been dominated by aristocratic elites and

---

[1] *Verdi intimo: carteggio di Giuseppe Verdi con il conte Opprandino Arrivabene, 1861–1886/ raccolto e annotato da Annibale Alberti; con prefazione di Alessandro Luzio* (Milan: A. Mondadori, 1931), 226.

court theatres. The publishing houses of Ricordi and later Sonzogno became the principal mediators of public tastes, the diviners of the commercial potential of new operas, and the filter for the importation of foreign repertoire. The emergence of repertory opera which could reliably support opera's economic model both calcified public expectations and narrowed the opportunities for emerging composers and stylistic innovation.[2]

The direction of artistic trends was often seen as evidence of the problems the country faced in seeking to mould a new national Italian identity. For De Sanctis, his fellow countrymen's predilection for music over literature was a manifestation of insincerity, born of an inheritance of religious hypocrisy which required an exterior cover for internal vacuity: 'Melodrama and musical drama are the popular genre, where scenery, mimicry, song and music work on the imagination far more powerfully than an insipid word, a vacuous sonority, which has turned into a mere supplement.'[3] Other leading figures of the Risorgimento generation saw the role of music in the new Italy in a more positive light. Cavour recognised that the tradition and pervasiveness of music in Italian culture meant the need for a 'national music' could not be ignored.[4]

A reinvigoration of the *bel canto* tradition of Italian operatic art, which could embody a modern sense of *italianità* in the face of the growing influence of ultramontane opera, therefore became a key field of controversy for music critics and the intellectual class after unification. Mazzini had prefigured this debate, arguing that Italian music was mired in materialism, while German music was consumed by mysticism. Through their fusion, he proclaimed 'musical expression will distil these two fundamental concepts: individuality and the idea of the universe – God and man'.[5]

It is easy enough to read in Giuseppe Verdi's response to the celestial music from Arrigo Boito's *Mefistofele* the niggling wound caused by the

---

[2] See, for example, Jutte Tolle, 'Opera as Business? From Impresari to the Publishing Industry', *Journal of Modern Italian Studies*, 17/4 (2012), 448–59. The role of Casa Ricordi in the evolution of the opera industry has long been well documented and discussed, partly through its patronage of Verdi and Puccini, but also because of the want of archival material related to Sonzogno, as the latter company's records were destroyed in a fire in World War II. Mario Morini, Nandi Ostali and Piero Ostali Jr., *Casa Musicale Sonzogno: Cronologie, saggi, testimonianze*, 2 vols. (Milan: Casa Musicale Sonzogno, 1995). Silvia Valisa, 'Casa editrice Sonzogno: Mediazione culturale, circuiti del sapere ed innovazione tecnologica nell'Italia unificata (1861–1900)', in Ann Hallamore Caesar, Gabriella Romani and Jennifer Burns (eds.), *The Printed Media in Fin-de-siècle Italy: Publishers, Writers and Readers* (London: Legenda, 2011), 90–106.

[3] Francesco De Sanctis, *La Storia della Letteratura Italiana* (Turin: Einaudi, 1996), 615.

[4] Quoted in Alexandra Wilson, *The Puccini Problem* (Cambridge: Cambridge University Press, 2006), 13–14.

[5] Giuseppe Mazzini, *La Filosofia della Musica* (Florence: Guaraldi, 1977), 100–1.

poetic slight Boito had offered as a youthful *scapigliato*, which Verdi had probably misinterpreted as directed at himself.[6] The generational rupture was eventually reconciled, leading to the most celebrated collaboration between librettist and composer of the nineteenth century. However, the more significant subtext was the structural crisis which afflicted Italian opera in the post-Risorgimento period – the impetus to rejuvenate the bel canto tradition, and embody a modern sense of *italianità* for the new nation, in the face of the influence of German and French opera, as the output of Verdi himself slackened. Of course, the relationship between supposed national operatic styles had long been more complex than the binaries implied in heated contemporary debates, or among subsequent musicological assumptions about the penetration of Italy by French and German opera. Ideas of Italy as a monolithic bastion of Verdian works have increasingly been shed in favour of a less linear and more transnational understanding of the production, circulation and reception of opera in nineteenth-century Italy.[7]

A number of distinct but overlapping developments contributed to an abundance of religious material in operas performed in Italy during the period between 1840 and 1870. Musical actions and devices established in the first half of the nineteenth century to represent religious rites formed a broader vocabulary of ritual staging and musical language which underpinned the performative force of opera in sonic, visual and verbal dimensions.[8] As Gloria Staffieri has argued, the *grand opéra* model of contrasting public and private conflicts, in which religious division and sublimity were prominent, offered Italian composers and audiences

---

[6] 'Perhaps the man is already born, modest and pure, who will set art erect once more on that altar, befouled like a brothel wall.' Quoted in William Weaver, *The Verdi–Boito Correspondence* (Chicago: University of Chicago Press, 1994), xix. The exponents of the *scapigliatura* artistic movement of the first post-Risorgimento decades, 'the dishevelled', sought to invigorate Italian art, partly through greater openness to foreign influences. *Mefistofele* was its foremost operatic success. Verdi's ironical slight on the 'Prologue in Heaven' in this letter, about a younger contemporary's work, should be read in the context of other later evidence about Verdi's good opinion of *Mefistofele*, including the fact that Verdi lobbied to overcome Boito and Ricordi's hesitance to propose *Mefistofele* for La Scala in 1881 when the theatre was in need of new blood, and the composer's comments as reported by Amilcare Ponchielli to his wife in a letter following a visit to Verdi in 1885, about some, but by no means all parts of the opera. Ibid., 14–15, 82.

[7] See, for example, Axel Körner, *Politics of Culture in Liberal Italy: From Unification to Fascism* (New York: Routledge, 2009); Anna Tedesco, 'Opera a macchina': La fortuna di Giacomo Meyerbeer in Italia dal 1840 al 1870', doctoral thesis, University of Bologna (1999); Tedesco, 'Il Grand Opéra e i teatri italiani: un caso emblematico "Il Profeta a Parma 28 dicembre 1853"', *Musica e storia*, 11/1 (2003), 139–60.

[8] Marco Beghelli, *La retorica del rituale nel melodramma ottocentesco* (Parma: Istituto nazionale di studi verdiani, 2004), 38–45.

opportunities for dramatic innovation which chimed with aspirations for Italian art, not least in Mazzini's *Filosofia della musica*.[9]

A further source for heightened religious colouring of Italian opera came from the literary flourishing of the Catholic revival, defined by Francesco De Sanctis in 1870 as the Catholic-Liberal school (*scuola cattolico-liberale*).[10] This was epitomised by Alessandro Manzoni's *I promessi sposi* (1827), in which the innate goodness of its eponymous peasant lovers, Renzo and Lucia, is tested in the face of persecution by immoral characters of aristocratic status, culminating at the Lazzaretto hospital in Milan during the plague of 1630, where their forbearance is finally rewarded.[11] The consistent quality which De Sanctis identifies in the body of religiously inspired texts encompassing Manzoni, Tommaso Grossi and Massimo D'Azeglio was a religious attitude of *mansuetudine* – meekness and endurance – in the face of personal trials and political oppression. This was seen in contrast to the 'democratic' school expounded by Mazzini, to whom action and resistance were the route to national and spiritual liberation.[12]

Meanwhile, Wagner's juxtaposition of Christian and pagan myth in *Tannhäuser* (1845) and *Lohengrin* (1850) made Christian virtues such as repentance, forgiveness and redemption central to their musical and dramaturgical language, though the first Italian premiere of any Wagner opera had to wait until 1871, when *Lohengrin* was staged at the Teatro Comunale in Bologna.[13] By this time, Meyerbeer's *grands opéras* had already enjoyed a period of popularity which often matched even those of Verdi.[14] Though the staging requirements taxed even the best-resourced

---

[9] Gloria Staffieri, *Musicare la storia: il giovane Verdi e il grand opéra* (Parma: Istituto nazionale di studi verdiani, 2017), 7–17.

[10] Francesco de Sanctis, *Opere di Francesco de Sanctis 11: La scuola cattolico-liberale e il Romanticismo a Napoli / Francesco De Sanctis; a cura di Carlo Muscetta e Giorgio Candeloro* (Turin: Einaudi, 1958).

[11] Alessandro Manzoni, *I promessi sposi a cura di Stefano Verdino* (Milan: Gruppo editoriale Fabbri, Bompiani, Sonzogno, Etas, 1990).

[12] Jonathan Lee Cheskin, 'Catholic-Liberal Opera: Outline of a Hidden Musical Romanticism', unpublished PhD thesis, University of Chicago (1999), 7–18.

[13] Robert Ignatius Letellier, *The Bible in Music* (Cambridge: Cambridge Scholars Publishing, 2017), 20, 91–2; Körner, *Politics of Culture*, 234–7.

[14] Tedesco, 'Opera a macchina', and '"Queste opere eminentemente sinfoniche e spettacolose": Giacomo Meyerbeer's Influence on Italian Opera Orchestras', in Niels Martin Jensen and Franco Piperno (eds.), *The Opera Orchestra in Eighteenth and Nineteenth-Century Europe*, vol. 2: *The Orchestra in the Theatre – Composers, Works, and Performance* (Berlin: Berliner Wissenschaftsverlag, 2008), 185–227; '"Le Prophète" in Italy', in Matthias Brzoska, Andreas Jacob and Nicole K. Strohmann (eds.), *Giacomo Meyerbeer: Le Prophète: Edition – Konzeption – Rezeption* (Hildesheim: Olms, 2009), 565–602; Fabrizio Della Seta, 'Un aspetto della ricezione di Meyerbeer in Italia: Le traduzioni dei "grands operas"', in Sieghart Döhring and Arnold Jacobshagen (eds.), *Meyerbeer und das Europäische Musiktheater* (Laaber: Laaber-Verlag,

theatres, through three decades from 1860 Italy saw over 260 productions of his 6 mature operas, mostly following the composer's death in 1864.[15] Two years before Meyerbeer's death, Milan's La Scala gave the Italian premiere of Charles Gounod's *Faust*, which would rival most foreign or even Verdian operas for popularity in Liberal Italy.[16]

This chapter positions these international currents of operatic styles in post-Risorgimento Italy in the context of the religious question, particularly focusing on examples from Turin and Rome, twin poles of political change and religious identity in the new kingdom. As well as stimulating cultures of municipal cosmopolitanism, these influences heralded new directions for the use of religious themes in operas written in Italy in the second half of the nineteenth century.[17] I will suggest that librettists and composers approaching religious themes within very different musical and dramatic styles were keenly aware of the need to create a vocabulary of religious images and sounds which the predominantly Catholic audiences across Italy could recognise, even when adopting ideas from French or German literary and musical models. Strategies included the archaic quotation or imitation of plainsong and chorales, the interpolation of ecclesiastical scenes, attempts to follow Wagner in dissolving boundaries between stage music and orchestral sound and locating recognisable religious music within exoticised settings. This vocabulary represented, therefore, a vital component of the narratives about operatic *italianità* in Liberal Italy, the extent of stylistic continuity and distinctiveness and the range of responses among Italian audiences and critics.

Audience Reception of Religious Themes

Weighing evidence about the reception of religious themes in nineteenth-century Italy raises similar questions to the hoary debate about the political

---

1998), 309–51; *Not without Madness: Perspectives on Opera* (Chicago: University of Chicago Press, 2012), 158–77.

[15] Tedesco, 'Il Grand Opéra e i teatri italiani', 141.

[16] For example at Bologna's Teatro Comunale, *Faust* was revived more frequently than any opera apart from *Lohengrin* and *Mefistofele*, alongside Verdi's *Aida*. See Körner, *Politics of Culture*, 258; in Turin *Faust* was also among the most popular operas in the whole city by number of productions, of which it had nineteen in the fifty years after its premiere in 1864 across five different theatres. See Giorgio Rampone, 'Le prime rappresentazioni e l'opera a Torino', in *Faust Production Programme* (Turin: Teatro Regio, 2014), 86.

[17] See, for example, Körner, 'From Hindustan to Brabant: Meyerbeer's *L'Africana* and Municipal Cosmopolitanism in Post-Unification Italy', *Cambridge Opera Journal*, 29/1 (2017), 74–93.

agency ascribed to opera during the Risorgimento.[18] Cheskin's surfacing of the importance of the Catholic-Liberal school of literature offers an important correction to the focus on the political message which might be read through opera, particularly when *giobertian* sentiment was at its height, before Pius IX's renunciation of liberalism.[19] Mary Ann Smart acknowledges opera's potential for political engagement among a diversity of contemporary responses, and posits a more diffuse relationship between opera and the wider intellectual climate.[20] If the idea of Romantic melodrama having a direct political impact during the Risorgimento needs to be treated with extreme caution, what effect on audiences' sense of piety, scepticism or fidelity to the Catholic Church might be measurable from the seeping of religion into opera? Leopardi had bemoaned the passivity of opera audiences, and seen a direct connection with their subjection from the pulpit, perhaps reflecting his self-confessed imperviousness to theatrical effect.[21] But as Carlotta Sorba has written, 'it is as problematical to speak in the singular about an Italian theatre public as of an Italian aristocracy, bourgeoisie, or lower class'.[22] So if we follow a more nuanced interpretation of audience reception specific to local, social and intellectual context, we can see religion in opera as a crucial way in which the Italian public, amidst the political confrontation between the Church and the new state, engaged with the contemporary question of the place of religion in society and their own cultural milieu, while becoming increasingly receptive to cosmopolitan musical trends. In this sense the religious question as encountered in opera became a significant challenge to conventional ideas of operatic *italianità* dominating Italian stages.

Language like '*fanatismo*', a word which, in the early part of the century, was used to indicate an enthusiasm bordering on the ecstatic and religious,

---

[18] Roger Parker, *Leonora's Last Act: Essays in Verdian Discourse* (Princeton: Princeton University Press, 1997), 33. Carlotta Sorba, *Teatri: L'Italia del melodrama nell'età del Risorgimento* (Bologna: Il Mulino, 2001), 190–225; Philip Gossett, 'Becoming a Citizen: The Chorus in "Risorgimento" Opera', *Cambridge Opera Journal*, 2/1 (March 1990), 41–64; Körner, *Politics of Culture*, 224.

[19] Cheskin, 'Catholic-Liberal Opera', 18.

[20] Peter Stamatov, 'Interpretive Activism and the Political Uses of Verdi's Operas in the 1840s', *American Sociological Review*, 67/3 (June 2002), 345–66; Mary Ann Smart, 'How Political Were Verdi's Operas? Metaphors of Progress in *I Lombardi alla* prima crociata', *Journal of Modern Italian Studies*, 18/2 (2013), 190–204; *Waiting for Verdi: Opera and Political Opinion in Nineteenth-Century Italy 1815–1848* (Oakland: University of California Press, 2018).

[21] Suzanne Stewart-Steinberg, *The Pinocchio Effect: On Making Italians 1860–1920* (Chicago: University of California Press, 2007), 14–15.

[22] Carlotta Sorba, 'To Please the Public: Composers and Audiences in Nineteenth-Century Italy', *Journal of Interdisciplinary History*, 36/4, Opera and Society: Part II (Spring, 2006), 598–9.

was commonly deployed by composers and critics describing public reactions to opera.[23] Contrary to Leopardi, we can find ample evidence in the reception of religious themes in the decades leading up to World War I that even secular critics and audiences were beginning to focus on the spiritual purpose and message of many operas. These critics often indicate an intense engagement with theatrical experience, coloured by religious atmosphere, which spoke to the Mazzinian project for opera's unifying vision. Critic Benedetto Bermani, writing in 1846, observed that religion was one of four essential components of serious opera.[24] In *La Moda*, Carlo Tenca opined of Verdi's two recent operas that 'even love itself must connect to something more exalted that surpasses vulgar complacency, as occurs in *Nabucco* and *I Lombardi*, where it is elevated by religious exaltation'.[25] Verdi's setting of an Italianised version of the 'Ave Maria' as a *preghiera* for Giselda in *I Lombardi* elicited contrasting responses to its religious authenticity. Retitled 'Salve Maria' to satisfy the pedantic Milanese censors, the aria failed to convince the agent and founder of *L'Arpa*, Raffaele Vitali, that the setting of the words of the prayer was appropriate: 'a musical thought so sweet, so tranquil, so rich in affecting modulations, that distances it from any idea of profane song'.[26] The Bolognese critic Enrico Panzacchi recalled with rapt enthusiasm, writing in the year of Wagner's death in 1883, the Italian premiere of *Lohengrin*, conducted by Angelo Mariani in 1871:

And look, Angelo Mariani has climbed on to his conductor's podium; slowly turns his handsome head to left and right ... enters into the prelude with the orchestra ... a choir of angels slowly descends from the heavens and restores to earth the miraculous chalice in which the Saviour blessed the wine during the last supper with the Apostles.[27]

We might note here the seamless transition from the reportage style with which Mariani's own performance as conductor is witnessed, to the painting of the stage picture of the realisation of the angel descending from the heavens with the Holy Grail, paraphrasing Wagner's own lengthy description of the meaning of the music of the prelude. The mediation of the musical and dramatic depiction of religious ideas, through both the

---

[23] Sorba, 'To Please the Public', 606.
[24] The others being fatherland, love and suffering ('patria, amore, religione, dolore'), Benedetto Bermani, *Schizzi sulla vita e sulle opere di Giuseppe Verdi* (Milan: Ricordi, 1848) quoted in Smart, 'How Political Were Verdi's Operas', 199.
[25] *La Moda*, 8, 15 February 1843, quoted in ibid., 198.
[26] Quoted in Susan Rutherford, *Verdi, Opera, Women* (Cambridge: Cambridge University Press, 2013), 74.
[27] Enrico Panzacchi, *Wagner: ricordi e memorie* (Bologna: Zanicchelli, 1883), 65–6.

performative experience of contemporary theatre-going and Italians' own religious identities, became increasingly self-conscious in this period.

This was reinforced as social Catholicism strengthened.[28] One example highlights how this religious revival might have met the widening audience for opera at the turn of the twentieth century. In the wool-making business of the industrialist Alessandro Rossi in the Veneto, religious values and observation were at the heart of Rossi's model of paternalist capitalism.[29] Not only did he encourage devotional habits among his workers at Schio, near Vicenza, but the cultural amenities of the burgeoning *nuovo quartiere operaio* included the eventual construction of the Teatro Civico by his nephew, Barone Alessandro Rossi, which opened in 1909 with a production of *Mefistofele*. Boito's opera could hardly be described as innovative in 1909, and in larger theatres its revival now prompted ennui among critics. Yet its religious themes and resolution would certainly have been consistent with the Catholic outlook of Schio's patron. Margherita is redeemed for her sins, fornication and infanticide, which would have been familiar risks to the female workforce of the textile mills, as she is transported to Heaven. Faust is also redeemed, and a chorus of angels emphasises the final triumph of heavenly grace and forgiveness. The choice of opera was praised by Ricordi's periodical *Ars e Labor*, which evidently found the strong contrast between natural and supernatural scenes fitting, an allegory perhaps for the intimate relationship between the spiritual and the temporal which Rossi's model of proletarian religious enterprise represented:

the ethereal plane, where celestial choirs sing Hosannas, and the dark caves where witches cackle, the tumultuous ramparts, the silent laboratory, the squalid prison cell, the Grecian garden, all find in Schio's theatre a most worthy resonance and the most suitable setting[.][30]

The Persistence of Censorship

The absorption of foreign repertoire and stylistic innovation had to negotiate a new climate in which the provisions of the Piedmontese constitution

---

[28] Helena Dawes, 'The Catholic Church and the Woman Question: Catholic Feminism in Italy in the Early 1900s', *The Catholic Historical Review*, 97/3 (July 2011), 484–526.

[29] Alice A. Kelikian, 'The Church and Catholicism', in Adrian Lyttleton (ed.), *Liberal and Fascist Italy* (Oxford: Oxford University Press, 2002), 50–3; Raffaele Romanelli, *L'Italia liberale 1861–1900* (Bologna: Mulino, 1979), 324–38.

[30] 'Il Nuovissimo Teatro Civico di Schio', *Ars e Labor*, 1909, 15 July, 508–9.

on censorship replaced those of the pre-unification states. During the *primo ottocento*, strict pre-authorisation of libretti limited almost any direct references to Christian religion. The *grands opéras* imported from Paris, for example, were re-clothed in locales distanced from a Catholic setting and with religious scenes and text excised so that, for example, at its premiere in Florence in 1842, *Les Huguenots* became a battle between Royalists and Puritans in Civil War England as *gli Anglicani*.[31] The system was far from monolithic or consistent. The Papal States and Bourbon provinces were generally more problematic, as the various travails of mid-career Verdi attest in Rome.[32] Recent evidence suggests that the Habsburg kingdom of Lombardy-Venetia afforded more local autonomy than Risorgimentalist narratives or later musicological interpretations have claimed.[33] Regarding post-unification censorship, existing descriptions continue to be at best simplistic and sometimes misleading, giving the impression that censorship of opera was immediately swept away.[34] In fact, the law continued to prohibit 'anything which might offend the predominant religion' as well as liturgical ceremony, profanation of religious symbols, staging religious figures which might give rise to religious offence or dressing characters in costume which might reference the various ecclesiastical orders.[35] This gave considerable latitude for provincial discretion, despite the supposedly centralised system. One example is the play *Cristo alla Festa di Purim* (1894), by the republican writer and politician Giovanni Bovio, which was banned in many provinces across Italy under pressure by Francesco Crispi, but allowed in others, including Venice and Turin.[36] In

---

[31] The censored version had originally been made for Munich in 1838 as *Die Anglikaner und die Puritaner*. In parallel, another censored version circulated in Italy as *I Guelfi e i Ghibellini*. Staffieri, *Musicare la storia*, 93–8.

[32] Andreas Giger, 'Social Control and the Censorship of Giuseppe Verdi's Operas in Rome (1844–1859)', *Cambridge Opera Journal*, 11/3 (November 1999), 233–65.

[33] Axel Körner, '*Che il pubblico non venga defraudato degli spettacoli ad esso promessi*: The Venetian Premiere of *La traviata* and Austria's Imperial Administration in 1853', *Verdiperspektiven*, 3 (2018), 93–109.

[34] For example, 'censorship was not a problem for operatic composers after the unification of Italy': Gossett, 'Becoming a Citizen', 61.

[35] Irene Piazzoni, *Spettacolo, istituzioni e società nell' Italia post-unitaria 1860–1882* (Rome: Archivio Guido Izzi, 2000), 135–8.

[36] Michele Nani, 'Il Cristo di Bovio e il suo pubblico', in Carlotta Sorba (ed.), *Scene di fine Ottocento: L'Italia fin de siècle a teatro* (Rome: Carocci, 2004), 147–92. The play was set to music by Giovanni Giannetti and premiered in Turin in 1905, where the play's performance eleven years earlier in the city was recalled in the press to burnish Turin's liberal reputation. P. A. Omodei, 'Cristo alla festa di Purim', *La Stampa*, 4 December 1905; Andrew Holden, 'Opera Avanti a Dio! Opera and Religion in Liberal Italy', unpublished PhD thesis, Oxford Brookes University (2019), 87–8, 159–60.

Turin, the Piedmontese made great play of the granting of freedom of religion under the Albertine constitution, yet in the 1860s operas like Meyerbeer's *Roberto il Diavolo* and Gounod's *Faust* were performed in pre-existing censored versions with religious references or scenes excised.[37] Torinese politicians of clerical opinion were offended by the local premiere of Verdi's *La forza del destino* in February 1873. Speaking for them in Turin's *consiglio comunale*, Nicolis de Robilant expressed his sadness that:

> the city's main theatre, subsidised by the Comune, saw the sacred religious rites of the Catholic religion of the vast majority of citizens publicly prostituted on stage. In Verdi's score of *La forza del destino* . . . in the second Act right in the middle of the stage is presented an altar exactly the same as Catholics use during Divine Service on top of which is a Madonna identical to the holy image of her which the *torinesi* are used to venerating for centuries in one of our local churches . . . unfortunately the current state of our laws allows such things but the speaker didn't understand how it could be permitted by the Municipality subsidising the theatre, and how taxpayers could be expected to support the use of their taxes in such a way.[38]

What is particularly notable about this tirade is the direct association made between the religious staging and specific local religious observance and iconography, which would become a key mode for Catholics to interpret religious scenes in later works such as Puccini's *Tosca* and Wagner's *Parsifal*.

Despite the progressive direction of legal restrictions, informal censorship, particularly pressure from the clerical press and the Church, continued to police the limits of tolerance, especially where ecclesiastical dignity and images of the divine were concerned, and helped shape attitudes towards the influx of French and German opera and Italian innovations in staging religious themes. Francesco D'Arcais, in his first years in post-Papal Rome, regularly complained about the continuing censorship of prose drama and opera portraying historical religious figures, notably Cardinal Brogni in Halévy's *L'Ebrea*. Yet even he admitted that censorship might be justifiable to prevent satire of living churchmen.[39] Nearly twenty

---

[37] Archivio Storico Teatro Regio di Torino, Fondo A, Testa 490, *Faust, Dramma lirico in cinque atti Dei Signori Barbier e Carré. Traduzione italiana del signor Achille de Lauzières. Musica del Maestro C. Gounod. Da rappresentarsi al Regio Teatro di Torino, Il Carnevale 1864* (Milan: Lucca, 1864); Archivio Storico Città di Torino (ASCT), Collezione Simeom, Serie L, 314, *Roberto Il Diavolo*, opera in cinque atti, *libretto stagione carnevale 1871–1872* (Milan: Lucca, 1872).

[38] Guilio Bissaldi, 'Rassegna Musicale' *La Gazzetta Piemontese*, 12 February 1873; ASCT, *Raccolta Atti Municipali di Torino* – Annata 1873, parte I, 200–1.

[39] *L'Opinione*, 2 October 1871.

years later in 1890 he was a member of the jury that was implicated in a blatant case of religious censorship during the Sonzogno competition in which Mascagni's *Cavalleria rusticana* was triumphant, when one long-listed entry, *Il Veggente* (*The Prophet*) by Enrico Bossi, was disqualified because of its staging of Christ as a singing role. The opera was produced at Milan's Teatro dal Verme in June 1890, but clerical protests were enough to have the composer, Enrico Bossi, himself devoutly Catholic, abjectly withdraw it, publicly professing his horror at offending religious sensibility.[40] Meanwhile Enrico Gastaldon, whose own version of Verga's *Cavalleria rusticana*, *Mala Pasqua*, premiered in Rome at the same time, was also attacked by the clerical press for the opera's sacrilegious staging of a religious procession. Changes were made, excising some of the religious panoply, and the run cut short, leaving the Roman newspaper *La Voce della verità* jubilant. In contrast, Mascagni's version received no such opprobrium and its staging was warmly received by the Catholic press.[41] This confusing picture of national, regional and local restrictions on subject matter and staging suggests that the scope to explore religious themes and ideas within the vocabulary of operatic *italianità* in Liberal Italy was bounded by assumptions and restrictions not so different from earlier decades, in which *grand opéra* had been adapted for Italian stages.

The Meyerbeerian Legacy in the Supernatural

Meyerbeer's spectacular rendering of the supernatural in *Robert le Diable* became a template for the *scapigliato* generation to create an amalgam of the fantastical and supernatural, mixing Germanic influences with Italian tradition in what Adriana Guarnieri Corazzol calls 'un fantastico "mediterraneo" alternativo'.[42] Boito's *Mefistofele* was the foremost example of this. Read alongside Gounod's own interpretation of Goethe's *Faust*, Italian audiences were sometimes confused about these rival depictions of the supernatural and diabolical. In Turin, the Italian home of positivism, one can read a tension between philosophical interpretations of the duality between

---

[40] *Il Veggente, poesia di Gustavo Macchi, musica di Enrico Bossi* (Milan: Stabilmento G. Civelli, 1890); 'Dichiarazione del M. Bossi a proposito del "*Veggente*"', *La Voce della Verità*, 24/25 June 1890. *Il Veggente* was translated into German as *Der Prophet* and performed in several German cities from 1896, see Corrado Ambiveri, *Operisti minori dell'ottocento italiano* (Rome: Gremese Editore, 1998), 25–6.
[41] 'Il defecit della *Mala Pasqua!*', *La Voce della verità*, 25 April 1890.
[42] Adriana Guarnieri Corazzol, *Musica e Letteratura in Italia tra ottocento e novecento* (Milan: Sansoni, 2000), 169.

good and evil, and the popularity of the conventional Catholic musical and dramatic effects. When revived at the Regio in 1870, the critic of *La Gazzetta Piemontese*, while professing moderation between the fanatical devotees and detractors of *Faust*, focused on a negative comparison with Goethe:

> To our mind above all, the part of Mefistofele is a mistake. Of the original and new, and completely modern devil of Goethe, nothing remains in the musical character of Gounod's Mefistofele. That of the French maestro is still the traditional devil of the stage: a Bertramo [sic] transposed to another setting, ... of this subtle genius of doubt, of this incarnation of scepticism ... nothing remains in our view ... dressed like the devil of choreographed action and masked balls, red and black, two strong colours for example while the [Goethean] Mefistofeles was dressed in grey, an uncertain colour, you could even say sceptical, but still *it is not the doubt of the philosophical devil which torments the modern intelligence, rather it is the affirmation of the Catholic demon*.[43] (Emphasis added)

Boito's *Mefistofele* met with greater critical approval in Turin. The effect of the Epilogue clearly overwhelmed Ippolito Valetta, who summarised the final confrontation between good and evil for his readers thus:

> Mefistofele waits in the doorway for the soul [of Faust], summoning his sirens. Against the genius of evil Faust defends himself with his Bible: the celestial vision appears and becomes more and more breath-taking: basking in this light Faust dies while a shower of light and flowers puts Satan to flight .... The point of climax of the epilogue comes with this splendid chorus of the celestial throng ... and it is after a scene of this nature that you understand the power of art and how you bless the artist who reveals beauty with such miraculous spirit.[44]

---

[43] Cronaca Cittadina, *La Gazzetta Piemontese*, 5 January 1870. 'A nostro credere, soprattutto è sbagliata la parte del Mefistofele. Dell'originale e nuovo e tutto moderno diavolo di Goethe non rimane nulla nel carattere musicale del Mefistofele di Gounod. Quello del maestro francese è sempre il diavolo tradizionale delle scene: un Bertramo traposto in altro ambiente, ma che ubAa i lineamenti della sua fisionomia; di quel genio sottile del dubbio, di quell'incarnazione dello scetticismo argomentante che seppe esprimere il gran poeta tedesco, ci pare che non ne rimanga nulla. Gli artisti che rappresentano quella parte aiutano a questo falsamento del carattere mefistofelico: vestono come il diavolo delle azioni coreografiche e dei balli mascherati: rosso e mero, due colori positivi, per dir così mentre il Mefistofele era vestito di grigio, un colore incerto, diremo quasi scettico, ancor esso: non è più il dubbio del diavolo filosofico che tormenta l'intelligenza moderna, è l'affermazione in contrario del demonio cattolico.'

[44] Ippolito Valetta, 'Rivista Musicale', *La Gazzetta del Popolo*, 3 January 1876. 'Mefistofele attende l'anima al varco, evoca le sirene. Contro la tentazione del genio di male Faust si difende col Vangelo: la celestiale visione appare e si fa vieppiù splendida: beandosi in essa Faust muore mentre una pioggia di luce e di fiori mette in fuga Satana ... Ma il punto culminante dell'epilogo sta in quel splendido coro delle falangi celesti che abbiamo udito nell'epilogo [sic]: l'effetto cresce con l'entusiasmo di Faust e colla rabbia di Mefistofele; ed è dopo un quadro di questa natura che si comprende la potenza dell'arte, e che si benedice all'artista chi svela allo spirito meravigliato il bello come tutte le sue attrattive.'

Boito's *Mefistofele* clearly managed to animate the Turin critics artistically, intellectually and perhaps chauvinistically, in a way which Gounod's French adaptation of the revered German poet never could. Yet although *Mefistofele* would continue to be revived in Turin regularly until World War I, Gounod's version remained better box office.

Alberto Franchetti, in *Asrael* (1889), created a more eclectic variation on these themes. Ferdinando Fontana's libretto was taken directly from a contemporary version of Flemish folk stories by Samuel-Henri Berthoud.[45] More broadly the opera draws on *Mefistofele*, Goethe's *Faust* and *Lohengrin*. Giuseppe Depanis, in a detailed account in *La Gazzetta Letteraria* following the Turin premiere in December 1890, summarised its subject as 'a new variation on the theme of redemption through love, this theme for which Faust and Tannhäuser are saved'.

In the sketches for the original production in Reggio Emilia preserved in the Ricordi archive (Figures 9.1 and 9.2), Asrael is treated to a distinct costume for each act, through which one can trace the evolution of his character from Fallen Angel in Hell with Lucifer, through medieval knight in Brabant, to a transfigured angel.[46] He literally sheds, scene by scene, the scarlet hue of his devilish persona and assumes the spotless, blinding white aura of Christ himself.

Depanis, despite being closely linked to the Teatro Regio, was remarkably objective about the strengths and weaknesses of the libretto, the score and the staging. As he concluded, *Asrael*'s success turned on the ineffability of the supernatural illusions which the librettist and composer were seeking to realise. 'The struggle between the angels and demons is conceived and realised with serious intentions. But the musical beauties of this finale would be better appreciated if the demons and angels didn't appear on stage.'[47] This was unfortunate, because musically these celestial scenes were considered some of the finest in the score. Reception in other quarters was more enthusiastic. *La Gazzetta del Popolo*'s critic judged it a work that was 'organic and vital', but was also seized with doubts about the unity of musical ideas and how the Wagnerian influences were worked through

---

[45] Samuel-Henry Berthoud, *Légends et traditions surnaturelles des Flandres* (Paris: Garnier, 1862), 67–187; Emanuele D'Angelo, *Leggendo libretti: da Lucia di Lammermoor a Turandot* (Rome: Aracne, 2013), 174.

[46] The complete set of figurini can be viewed on the Ricordi archive website at www.digitalarchivioricordi.com/ (last accessed 23 October 2021).

[47] Giuseppe Depanis, 'Asrael di Franchetti', *La Gazzetta Letteraria*, 10 January 1891. 'La lotta tra gli angeli ed I demoni è concepita e svolta con grandiosità di intendimenti. Ma le bellezze musicali di questo finale sarebbero meglio apprezzate se I demoni e gli angeli non apparissero sulla scena.'

Figure 9.1 *Asrael* (1888), costume sketch (figurino), Act I/iii (Alfredo Edel) ICON010178 Archivio Storico Ricordi © Ricordi & C. S.r.l. Milano – www.archivioricordi.com

Franchetti's 'Italian brain'.[48] In a brief paragraph referencing the staging, he listed the scenes which received the warmest applause, including 'the stunning scene in paradise, that scenically is one of the finest things imaginable'.[49] In *La Gazzetta Piemontese* we find a not-dissimilar mixture of approbation for the

---

[48] 'Sacco Nero', *La Gazzetta del Popolo*, 28 December 1890.

[49] 'Sacco Nero', *La Gazzetta del Popolo*, 28 December 1890; 'i primi applausi scoppiano ... alla stupenda scena del paradiso che, scenograficamente è una delle cose più fini immaginabili'.

Figure 9.2 *Asrael* (1888), costume sketch, Act IV (Alfredo Edel) ICON010181. Archivio Storico Ricordi © Ricordi & C. S.r.l. Milano – www.archivioricordi.com

courageous ideas of a youthful work, alongside reservations about its musical structure and dramatic pacing. The critic, Ernesto Ferrettini, was complimentary about Franchetti's fusion of German style in the Wagnerian and Goldmarkian influences, with Italian taste:

The best German music today is that written in Italy, said one illustrious critic, and he wasn't wrong. Franchetti, a natural rather than vulgar artist, feels the importance of Wagnerian opera, but realises where it's incompatible with our sense of feeling, our climate, our musical education.[50]

This neatly encapsulates the permeability, even on guarded terms, of operatic *italianità* in the new Italy, while also referencing the different dimensions which needed to be considered, psychological, environmental and cultural.

A final example of how French and German models can be traced through these operatic expressions of the supernatural can be seen in *La tentazione di Gesù* (1902) by Carlo Cordara, which used a libretto from the poet Arturo Graf.[51] This was the only opera in Italy which had the audacity to break the European-wide taboo on personifications of the Deity. The poem and libretto dramatise the New Testament story of the three temptations by Satan in the wilderness, transforming them into a series of exotic visions worthy of any of the *Faust* adaptations, including a 'temptation of love' in which flower-clad maidens suggest a further point of reference in *Parsifal*.[52] Satan is characterised very much in the philosophical mould of the cynical, sarcastic Mefistofeles of Boito (when he tells Christ 'you are difficult to please'), while indulging in the exotic pleasures of Gounod's version.[53] In this innovative setting, a prelude with a 'celestial theme' is followed by a 'prologo sinfonico' depicting the desolate landscape and dark atmosphere in which Satan appears to Christ in the wilderness. This used the familiar 3/8 metre derived from Meyerbeer, which James Parakilas has termed 'the topos of the "sicilienne of diabolical temptation"'.[54] The musical expression of Jesus' invocation of God the Father is followed by an offstage divided chorus of angels singing 'Glory to God' and 'Peace on Earth to men pure and faithful', accompanied also by offstage trumpets, and emerging from the

---

[50] '*Asrael* di A Franchetti al Teatro Regio', *La Gazzetta Piemontese*, 28 December 1890. *La Gazzetta Piemontese* would become *La Stampa* in 1894.

[51] Arturo Graf, 'La tentazione di Gesú', *Nuova Antologia* 1901 April; *Poemetti drammatici* (Milan: Treves, 1905). This collection brought together a series of poems published in *Nuova Antologia* including 'Mefistofele', 'La resurrezione di Lazzaro' and 'La dannazione di Don Giovanni'. For Graf's place within Italian literature and criticism see Girolamo de Liguori, *I Baratri della Ragione: Arturo Graf e la cultura del secondo Ottocento* (Manduria: Lacaita, 1986).

[52] This vision in Graf's poem described them as 'naked or scantily-clad' dancers ('ignude e mezzo discinte'), but clearly this was either impractical on stage or judged too risqué, so they became merely 'beautiful women crowned with flowers' ('bellissime donne coronate di fiori'). Carlo Cordara, *La tentazione di Gesù: mistero lirico in un atto di Arturo Graf. Riduzione per Canto e pianoforte* (Florence: Mignani, 1903) 31-2.

[53] 'Difficile sei di contentar!' *La tentazione di Gesù: mistero lirico in un atto di Arturo Graf Musica di Carlo Cordara Teatro Vittorio Emanuele di Torino Ottobre 1902* (Milan: Ramperti), 11.

[54] Cordara, *La tentazione di Gesù*, 65-6; James Parakilas, 'Religion and Difference in Verdi's Otello', *The Musical Quarterly*, 81/3 (Autumn, 1997), 377-8.

distance, growing gradually louder, all reprising the celestial theme from the prelude. Strikingly, the cover illustration of a surviving copy of the piano/vocal score of *La tentazione di Gesú* shows a bearded Jesus in profile looking towards a dream-like vision of Jerusalem and Calvary beyond, bordered with exotic and highly suggestive flowers, reminiscent of the early designs for the Epilogue of Boito's *Mefistofele* and the angelic incarnation of Franchetti's Asrael pictured above in Figure 9.2.[55] The critic in *La Stampa* praised the young composer for his distinctive artistic fantasy, while identifying significant influences – the seriousness of the setting and characterisation, and the elevated mystical, oratorical text suggested to him Wagner's *Parsifal*, while the melodic ideas and descriptive instrumentation reminded him of *Les Béatitudes* of César Franck. He noted that the subject and its seriousness were far from the 'intrigues of love' which presumably readers expected to feature somewhere in an Italian opera.[56]

Stagings of Liturgy by the *Giovane Scuola*

Many of the most prominent examples of liturgical scenes by the *giovane scuola*, the generation of composers born in the 1850s and 1860s, continued to be in the style of what William Ashbrook described as 'historical verismo'. This sought to update the *grand opéra* model of Meyerbeer and Halévy, repurposing it for the new Italy by projecting an imagined sense of *italianità* lost since medieval and Renaissance times. On the strength of the virtues seen in *Asrael*, Franchetti was recommended for the commission to write an opera for the fifth centenary of Columbus' voyage to the Americas. Within this sub-genre, Franchetti's *Cristoforo Colombo* is often cited as a prominent failure in its presumed function as an operatic symbol of the new nation's historic intent.[57] Yet the Act II finale, when monks intoning

---

[55] This copy is in the library of the Accademia Santa Cecilia in Rome. It is also worth noting that 1902 was also the year of the Prima Esposizione internazionale d'arte moderna decorative in Turin, when art nouveau (*stile liberty* or *stile nuovo*) was first introduced to Italy on a large scale, in the city where it would have a particular impact. See Richard A. Etlin, 'The Search for a Modern Italian Architecture', *The Journal of Decorative and Propaganda Arts*, 13, Stile Floreale theme issue (Summer 1989), 94–109; *Mefistofele*, Bozzetto, Siparietto per l'Epilogo (Carlo Ferrario) Teatro alla Scala (1881). Archivio Storico Casa Ricordi, ICON004313.

[56] 'La tentazione di Gesù: mistero lirico in un atto di Arturo Graf. Musica di Carlo Cordara', *La Stampa*, 15 October 1902 (signed i. a. v.; author unidentified).

[57] For example, Körner, *Politics of Culture*, 247; Luca Zoppelli and Arthur Groos, 'The Twilight of the True Gods: "Cristoforo Colombo", "I Medici" and the Construction of Italian History', *Cambridge Opera Journal*, 8/3 (November 1996), 251–69. Verdi commented to Ricordi on the event of the premiere of Colombo: 'Ah, Franchetti loves a spectacular mise-en-scène? Different

the *Salve Regina* are cut short by a mutiny shortly before the sighting of land, was judged its most effective passage. When we examine the plainsong used, we find it is almost an exact quotation of a contemporary chant (Figure 9.3).[58]

Figure 9.3 *Cristoforo Colombo*, Act II, Scene VI. 'Salve Regina'. Luigi Illica e Alberto Franchetti, *Cristoforo Colombo, Opera completa per canto pianoforte* (Milan: Ricordi, 1893), 207–8

The *Liber Usualis* published in 1903 gives this version of the *Salve Regina* for use at Compline during the Feast of the Trinity and during Advent (Figure 9.4).

Though shorn of the melisma in the original, this quotation of a chant, which the devout among audiences for *Cristoforo Colombo* would recognise, offers an intriguing interpretation of the 'veristic' use of liturgical music and effects in opera. Rather than adapting archaic but often anachronistic tunes to connote times past, as composers such as Meyerbeer

> from me, who detests them. What is necessary, and nothing more. With the grand mise-en-scene one always ends up doing the same thing . . . bass drum and cymbals . . . masses of people . . . and farewell drama and music!! They become secondary.' As Verdi had only relatively recently finished tinkering with versions of *Don Carlos*, in which he and his librettists had enthusiastically dramatised the *auto-da-fé* scene to provide a suitable grand-opera climax to Act III, this comment seems uncharitable, if not disingenuous. Letter to Ricordi, 10 October 1892, quoted ibid., 257.

[58] Ibid., 268.

Figure 9.4 *Salve Regina* plainsong chant. *Liber Usualis* (Rome: Tornaci, 1903), 92

had done, or researching 'authentic' liturgy as Puccini did for *Tosca*, Franchetti weaves a familiar plainsong chant through the scene. The same *Salve Regina* chant was later quoted by Ildebrando Pizzetti in his incidental music for Gabriele D'Annunzio's play *La Nave*, which was premiered in Venice at Teatro La Fenice in 1907, underscoring how the same realistic liturgical music could be repurposed within very different projects promoting a new sense of *italianità*.[59]

An alternative use of ecclesiastical drama to produce a specifically Catholic reading of an opera can be seen in Puccini's *Tosca*, which is usually characterised as deeply anticlerical, echoing Puccini's assumed prejudices as well as Sardou's French source drama. Some contemporary critics and early generations of musicologists also criticised *Tosca* for lacking musical and dramatic effectiveness, or for not embodying their conception of how Puccini should have advanced his position as the inheritor of Verdi's mantle and the international representative of Italian lyric art. Many have judged the opera harshly for what they perceived as a music-less percussive sound-world, highlighting the extraneous use of bells and other acoustic effects, undermining conventional ideas of operatic *italianità*.[60] Mosco Carner suggested the premiere of *Tosca* was problematic because the opera 'threw an odd light on the Catholic Church and would probably go against the grain of many

---

[59] Ben Earle, *Luigi Dallapiccola and Musical Modernism in Fascist Italy* (Cambridge: Cambridge University Press, 2013), 48–50.

[60] Wilson, *The Puccini Problem*, 86–8. One of the few recent analyses to consider the reception of *Tosca* in its contemporary urban context is Arman Schwartz's reference to literature about the changing significance of bells in the industrialising urban centres of the late nineteenth century. Arman Schwartz, 'Rough Music: *Tosca* and Verismo Reconsidered', *19th-Century Music*, 31/3 (Spring 2008), 228–44.

spectators, to say nothing of the Vatican'.[61] Arman Schwartz concludes that 'despite, or rather because of the massive empirical effort expended on realistic scene painting, the final result is curiously unmoving, dead'.[62] Other contemporary Roman sources suggest why these interpretations of *Tosca* fail to illuminate the reaction of Catholics or the Church, or consider the broader Roman response to the religious setting. During the first run of *Tosca*, the clerical newspaper *La Voce della verità* fulminated about the iniquities of anticlerical and immoral performances in popular theatre, and promoted the indivisibility of *cattolicismo* and *romanità*.[63] So although it concurred with much of the lukewarm and negative assessment that *Tosca* was a step backwards for Puccini as a composer, among the few highlights it singled out was the *Te Deum*: 'the only point in the evening which generated real enthusiasm was the grand finale of the first act', hardly a sign that Catholic opinion found the work problematic.[64] The liberal *Il Messaggero* was most expansive about it:

> The Te Deum, which ends the first act so joyfully, is a work of genius by Puccini. The liturgical song, the powerful Christian hymn – accompanied by organ, bells and the orchestra – soars up high on wings, achieving a rare fullness, a sonority, an expansion of sound unheard of ... also admired was the staging which was truly lavish, and the religious procession in its colourful costumes ... it was received with enthusiastic acclaim by the audience who wanted an encore.[65]

By the third performance on 19 January, even *La Tribuna*, which had received the premiere sceptically, was reporting 'the success of *Tosca*'. Significantly, it said that among the encored pieces was 'the exquisite prelude to act three, which, unfairly, was received in silence

---

[61] Mosco Carner, *Giacomo Puccini: Tosca* (Cambridge: Cambridge University Press, 1985), 64. See also Michele Girardi, *Giacomo Puccini: His International Art*, trans. Laura Basini (Chicago: Chicago University Press, 2000), 167–9; David Rosen, '"Pigri ed obesi Dei": Religion in the Operas of Puccini', in Arthur Groos and Virgilio Bernardoni (eds.), *Madama Butterfly: l'orientalismo di fine secolo, l'approccio pucciniano, la ricezione, Atti del convegno internazionale di studi Lucca – Torre del Lago 28–30 maggio 2004* (Florence: Olschki, 2008), 280–3.

[62] Schwartz, 'Rough Music', 228, 237. [63] 'Romanità, *La Voce della Verità*, 6 March 1900.

[64] '... si entusiasmò veramente, l'unica volta nella serata, al grandioso finale del primo atto', *La Voce della Verità*, 16 January 1900.

[65] *Il Messaggero*, 16 January 1900. 'Il Te Deum con cui si chiude felicemente il primo atto è una genialissima trovata del Puccini. Il canto liturgico, il forte inno cristiano – con accompagnamento d'organo di campane e di orchestra – si eleva alto, alato, acquista una pienezza strana, una sonorità una estensione mai udite. ... Ammirata assai la messa in scena veramente sfarzosa ed il corteo religioso nei varipointi costumi ... accolto dalle acclamazioni entusiastiche del pubblico che ne volle la replica.'

on the opening night'.⁶⁶ This suggests a rather different perspective on the reception of the prelude depicting the Roman dawn in the fields around Castel Sant'Angelo, with the shepherd boy singing, and the bells of his flock, the dome of St Peter's clearly in view in Adolfo Hohenstein's backcloth (Figure 9.6). By 1900 this area, the Prati di Castello, was a sea of new mansion and office blocks, and the sprawling half-built Corte di Cassazione, but as late as the last years of the 1880s, it was still a semi-rural idyll, which attracted Romans for bathing and recreation amidst fields and vineyards in the shadow of the walls of the castle and St Peter's. For a portion of the Roman audience, those with nostalgic memories of pontifical Rome, or an outsider's appreciation of it, Hohenstein and Puccini's depiction referenced not only an historical anachronism of 1800, but also the lived memory of Romans and visitors to the city of only a generation before. One way to observe this perspective is through the watercolours of Ettore Roesler Franz. 'Roman by birth and tongue', Roesler Franz was a descendant of eighteenth-century Bohemian immigrants.⁶⁷ Over two decades from 1876 he documented through photography scenes of the transformation of Rome, including the destruction of bridges, villas, churches and theatres, the embanking of the Tiber and the daily life of Romans experiencing these seismic changes. Many of these vanishing scenes he translated into three series of watercolours, *Roma pittoresca*. The third series was exhibited at the Teatro Nazionale in 1897, just three years before the premiere of *Tosca*. Among the areas he documented was the Prati.

It is entirely plausible that Roesler Franz attended the opening of *Tosca* in January 1900, and 'heard' his own painting of a shepherd boy by the banks of the Tiber with his sheep (Figure 9.5). This time he is courting a young girl, and we might say he is rather older than Puccini's shepherd boy with his unbroken voice, but the parallel is nonetheless striking. In any case, the effect, for this part of the audience, was anything but 'curiously unmoving, dead'. Lost perhaps, but not dead.

---

⁶⁶ *La Tribuna*, 20 January 1900.
⁶⁷ Maria Elisa Tittoni, 'Ettore Roesler Franz: "romano per nascita e per lingua"', in Maria Elisa Tittoni, Federica Pirani and Maria Paola Fornasiero (eds.), *Paesaggi della Memoria: Gli acquerelli romani di Ettore Roesler Franz dal 1876 al 1895* (Rome: Mandragora, 2004), 11–15.

Figure 9.5 Ettore Roseler Franz, *Ai Prati di Castello – S. Carlo al fondo* (1889) © Rome – Sovrintendenza Capitolina ai Beni Culturali – Museo di Roma in Trastevere

The Italian *Parsifal*

Emma Carelli was much praised in the Roman press for bringing *Parsifal* to the Costanzi simultaneously with Bologna (minus the one-hour-later start time), and other European cities, as among the first staged productions to beat the expired ban on productions beyond Bayreuth. Its universal, ecstatic reception has no parallel among opera in this period. While this was a reaction repeated elsewhere in this European '*Parsifal* Year', its reception in Rome shows how Italian cities could reinterpret Wagner's legacy and the themes in *Parsifal* according to their specific cultural

Figure 9.6 Recreation of Hohenstein's original set and costumes of *Tosca* (Act III, prelude) at the Teatro dell'Opera di Roma, directed by Alessandro Talevi (2015). Reproduced by kind permission of Teatro dell'Opera di Roma

agendas. Catholic theological allusions within the opera were celebrated and taken as confirmation of religious truth, and of Wagner's presumed intentions. While the influence of Wagner's Lutheran heritage was referenced, any sense that the opera's symbolism, or music, might have non-Catholic qualities was largely ignored. The Catholic *Il Corriere d'Italia* was proud to report that the first extract of *Parsifal* to be performed in Italy had been the prelude, in Rome on 2 March 1883, and the first performance of the Grail scene from Act III had taken place in the Sala Costanzi in March 1884.[68] The official Vatican publication, *L'Osservatore Romano*, took Wagner's message as a demonstration both of Christian truth and the religious transfiguration of his supreme pagan hero, Siegfried.

In *Parsifal* are united all the manifestations of Christianity, the ecstatic joy of the spirit and the mystical emotions of the Catholic rites ... a divine idea soars up through great technical skill and an ideal becomes a hymn of redemption which lifts off towards the eternal sky, crowning the triumph of Siegfried turned towards God ...

Christianity proclaims the divinity of the words: *Joy is suffering because suffering is joy*, and by extolling Man, Wagner reprises this theme and writes his Christian dogma ... And Parsifal is truly the transfiguration of Siegfried.[69]

---

[68] *Il Corriere d'Italia*, 1 January 1914.
[69] *L'Osservatore Romano*, 3 January 1914. 'Nel Parsifal furono riassunte tutte le manifestazioni del cristianismo, la gioia estatica dell'anima e le sensazioni mistiche dei riti

Even liberal publications relished the humanistic messages within the opera and the indebtedness to Roman Catholicism. Alberto Gasco, in *La Tribuna*, was transported:

> Wagner, staging the mysteries of the Christian faith may have managed with his genius, with the chants and rich harmonies which convey the dramatic vision, to erase the doubt which gnaws even the spirit of the believer, and would work, by supreme virtue of his art, the unbeliever to sense the intangible feeling of the mystical dream ... The audience left full of wonder or of fear ... wanting to celebrate the mystery of Grace, of the Christian redemption extolling the belief that Christ is the Redeemer to mankind and that Parsifal, hero of Christian Love, exhibits on stage.[70]

Of course, one of the points of inspiration for *Parsifal* to which Italians were often keenest to refer, was Wagner's indebtedness to the music of Palestrina. The musicologist Sebastiano Arturo Luciani, writing towards the end of the Costanzi's epic run of twenty-two performances, concluded that:

> *Parsifal* is genuine *musica sacra*, the only such music that has appeared in Europe since Palestrina and Bach ... Wagner's nature is mystical and sensual at the same time, as it manifests itself in the marvellous, tragic and eternal struggle between spirit and flesh ... Thus our epoch, which is both sensual and spiritual, shows a bent towards devoutness, and *Parsifal* satisfies this instinct and unconscious desire in all of us ... With this [work] Wagner's dream has come to fulfilment: the public, in the broadest sense of the word, the people, receive the drama in a spirit of religious devotion, as in a ritual.[71]

---

cattolici ... Nel Parsifal si eleva un concetto divino che attraverso la più grande saggezza tecnica e ideale diviene un inno di redenzione che si slancia verso l'azzurro eterno, coronando il trionfo di Sigfrido slanciato verso il Dio ... Il Cristianesimo proclama la divinità della formula: La gioia è dolore perché il dolore è gioia, e per esultare l'Uomo Wagner riprese questa formula e scrisse il suo domma cristiano ... E Parsifal e veramente la trasfigurazione di Sigfrido.'

[70] 'Wagner, sceneggiando I misteri della fede cristiana sarebbe forse riuscito col suo genio, coi canti e le armonie fascinose disposti intorno alla visione drammatica, a sciogliere il dubbio che insidia anche l'animo del credente, e avrebbe tratto, per virtù suprema della sua arte, I miscredenti a provare la sensazione indefinita del sogno mistico ... Già il preludio, che fu definito a causa dei suoi temi melodici che le raffigurano, il poema sinfonico delle tre virtù teologali, Fede Speranza e Carità, vi immette nella disposizione di spirito adatta allo spettacolo mistico. E questo, si svolge, esteriormente, come le sacre rappresentazioni di un tempo, meravigliose allo sguardo, significative al pensiero. Gli apparecchi e le trasformazioni sceniche dei misteri cristiani, gl'incantesimi dei misteri antichi si rinnovavano. Gli spettatori ne uscivano allora pieni di meraviglia o di spavento ... Volendo celebrare il mistero della grazia, della redenzione cristiana egli esalta il sentimento che fu di Cristo Redentore fra gli uomini e che Parsifal, eroe di carità, impersona sulla scena.' *La Tribuna*, 3 January 1914.

[71] S. A. Luciani, 'Dopo l'ultima di Parsifal', *Harmonia* (Rome) 2/3 (22 March 1914), 22–3, quoted in Katherine R. Syer, 'Parsifal on Stage', in William Kindemann and Katherine Rae Syer (eds.), *A Companion to Wagner's Parsifal* (Rochester, NY: Camden House, 2005), 293.

Among those who saw the first Roman *Parsifal* was Vittorio Gui, who was to become one of the work's foremost Italian interpreters. He later amplified this connection in a specifically Roman context:

> whoever has had the good fortune to hear the music of Palestrina in the great Cathedral of Rome, cannot have missed forming the powerful analogy of feeling when they then hear, for example, the finale of the third act of *Parsifal*.[72]

The music of *Parsifal* was, in this sense, seen as not just particularly Italian, but especially Roman, yet even Gui did not feel the need to reference the Lutheran origin (the Dresden Amen) which forms the basis of the polyphony they so admired.

Religion, in all these operas, can be seen as offering a set of markers in which an evolving but unstable sense of *italianità* in the post-unification decades was tested and contested. Such markers were often inherited from *grand opéra* models directly imported or developed anew by Verdi and his successors, and native innovation was further refracted through the prism of local conditions. Religious modes were central to efforts to cultivate a new Italian operatic style in the post-Verdi era, as well as a crucial aspect of the intellectual class's demonstration of its cosmopolitanism, which could speak equally powerfully to the wider Italian public, whether observant Catholics or secular Liberals.

---

[72] Vittorio Gui, *Battute d'Aspetto: Meditazioni du un musicista militante* (Florence: Monsalvato, 1944), quoted in Vittorio Frajese, *Dal Costanzi all'Opera*, vol. 2 (Rome: Edizione Capitulum, 1977), 78–9.

10 | Arcadia Undone

Teresa Carreño's 1887 Italian Opera Company in Caracas

DITLEV RINDOM

'How sad it is to leave the shores of the homeland!' declared Venezuelan journalist-cum-travel writer Gonzalo Picón Febres in the winter of 1886, in the first of a series of articles published in *La Opinion Nacional*, the leading liberal newspaper in Venezuela.[1] Warming to his theme, Picón Febres outlined the reasons for his nostalgia since emigrating to New York:

> You miss the air that descends from the distant mountain peaks, the clearing in the jungle in whose shadow you meditate for many hours, the walk in the orchard where you go late in the afternoon to enjoy the last aroma of the flowers and the last notes of the birds . . . You miss the smoke rising from the peasant's chimney, the abandoned ruins in which the swallow sings its eternal lament. You miss the guitar strumming to the reflection of the moon, the night song the farmer sings under the eaves of his cabin . . . You miss, in the end, the splendour of your sky, the majesty of your mountains, the sounds of your river springs, the cadence of your breezes, the singing of your birds, the indescribable poetry which fierce nature contains within its fertile bosom.[2]

Picón Febres evoked an alluring vision of Venezuela, in which sights, smells and (above all) sounds combine to form a sensuous landscape: nothing less, in fact, than a tropical Arcadia. The concluding reference to 'fierce nature' glances at a more violent alternative, but otherwise nothing disturbs the musicalised idyll of the author's vision. Picón Febres' article was timely, both for its idealised portrayal of Venezuela's musicality – with a final hint of menace – and its contrast of this with the urban environment of New York.

Only a few weeks later Teresa Carreño – Venezuela's most internationally renowned musician – arrived in Caracas from New York, where she had emigrated nearly twenty years earlier as a child prodigy. This would be only her second visit to the country, following a highly acclaimed piano recital tour in 1885–6 at the government's invitation. Rather than performing in concerts, however, Carreño this time arrived as the impresario of an Italian

---

* I would like to thank Juan Francisco Sans, Cristina Schnell, Linda Gill and Dylan Joy for help in Venezuela and at the University of Texas at Austin, and above all Hugo Quintana for his indispensable archival assistance in Caracas. Thanks also to Benjamin Walton, Roger Parker and Matthew Head for their comments on earlier versions of this chapter.

[1] *La Opinion Nacional*, 28 December 1886.   [2] Ibid.

opera company organised with her New York-based husband, the Italian baritone Giovanni Tagliapietra. The troupe of around fifty-five soloists, dancers and chorus was scheduled to perform a wide range of repertory from March 1887, including the Venezuelan premieres of *Carmen*, *Les Huguenots* and *Mignon* by Ambroise Thomas, alongside works by Verdi, Donizetti and Bellini (among others). Yet barely six weeks after opening, the company folded with huge debts. Cancelled performances, dwindling audiences and even fears of a bomb made further productions impossible. Carreño never again returned to Venezuela. For her, it would seem, tropical Arcadia had instead revealed its dangerous side, Caracas's sensuous harmony apparently resistant to an imported operatic soundscape.

Operatic failures seem often to have an irresistible appeal for the historian: the extravagant ambition, the miscalculated hopes, as though the entire elaborate edifice of opera had come crashing down on contact with reality. Yet few failures can have been more poignant than Carreño's, occurring as it did during a period intended both to celebrate her multifaceted abilities and to elevate the operatic culture of Caracas – a city whose musical environment could hardly be considered equal to New York, Buenos Aires, London or Paris either in diversity or in artistic standards. It is little surprise, then, that Carreño's two visits have become a regular episode in histories of Venezuela's musical life as well as an inevitable hiccup in biographical studies of her by Marta Milinowski and Mario Milanca Guzmán.[3] These accounts have attributed the company's failure to a mixture of political and administrative problems, suggesting that Carreño's associations with the national government made her operatic endeavour an obvious target for protest during a period of rising public discontent, and that the logistics of running an opera company were a step too far for a pianist-composer. But while these circumstances undoubtedly go a significant way in explaining the company's closure, broader issues surrounding the opera company and its failure remain unexamined. Such an approach can also nuance familiar outlines of transatlantic operatic mobility, while providing a valuable corollary to recent studies of operatic failure in European environments.[4] More than three quarters of Carreño's

---

[3] Marta Milinowski, *Teresa Carreño, 'By the Grace of God'* (New Haven, CT: Yale University Press, 1940); Mario Milanca Guzmán, *Teresa Carreño: Gira Caraqueña y Evocación (1885-1887)* (Caracas: Lagoven, 1987); also Milanca Guzmán's 'Dislates en la obra Teresa Carreño, de Marta Milinowski', *Revista de música latinoamericana* 8/2 (1987), 185–215.

[4] Gundula Kreuzer, *Curtain, Gong, Steam: Wagnerian Technologies of Nineteenth-Century Opera* (Oakland: University of California Press, 2018), 215–38; and Benjamin Walton, 'Technological Phantoms of the Opéra', in David Trippett and Benjamin Walton (eds.), *Nineteenth-Century Opera and the Scientific Imagination* (Cambridge: Cambridge University Press, 2019), 199–226.

'Italian opera' troupe, for example, were recruited from New York, with only a few extras picked up by Tagliapietra in Milan in early 1887; the importation of Italian opera was, this time, carried out via the north. Such geographical mediation raises broader questions about the status of Italian repertory in Caracas, at a time when Italian opera was highly familiar and an established symbol of civilisation – at times even seen as a perfection of nature – yet the Italian immigrant population was relatively small and other repertoires were arriving in greater numbers. More generally, this attention to operatic mobility within the Americas can elucidate the cultural work performed by Italian operatic activity by the late nineteenth century, when it was increasingly marked as an Italian national product yet susceptible to new forms of cultural and technological mediation.

To some degree, the movement of Italian opera from North to South America was not entirely new. Several US opera companies – including the Strakosch and Maretzek – had taken troupes to Central America during the 1850s and 1860s (to Mexico and Havana), and indeed Tagliapietra himself appears to have participated in such a transcontinental tour; the Maurice Grau company even travelled down to the Río de la Plata in the early 1880s, offering the first South American performances of *Carmen*.[5] Yet these touring companies were, typically, brought over wholesale from Europe before travelling outside the United States, and were in any case in sharp decline by the 1880s, as Italian-language opera companies in the United States diminished (and English-language opera boomed) in response to widening class divisions. The New York locus of Carreño's company is thus significant and suggests a renewed attention to the Latin American market by North American entrepreneurs – including by Carreño herself.

Focusing on Italian opera in Venezuela can also shed further light on the broader history of the country at this time. Studies have long divided the country's history into pre- and post-petroleum eras: it turned from a minor agricultural economy to a global powerhouse almost overnight. More recently, though, historians have highlighted the continuity of political and economic structures from the late nineteenth century onwards, when Venezuela's domestic and foreign policies began to crystallise.[6] Italian

---

[5] John Rosselli outlines the main Latin American circuits for European troupes earlier in the century in 'Latin America and Italian Opera: A Process of Interaction, 1810–1930', *Revista de Musicología* 17/1 (1993), 139–45. These included one covering New York, New Orleans and Havana, and a separate Central American circuit across Mexico, Panama, Costa Rica and Guatemala that could also extend to Venezuela.

[6] John V. Lombardi, *Venezuela: The Search for Order, the Dream of Progress* (Oxford: Oxford University Press, 1982); and Judith Ewell, *Venezuela: A Century of Change* (Stanford, CA: Stanford University Press, 1984).

opera's endurance as a cultural practice throughout this period can further challenge this divide, even as the specific production model for staged opera in Caracas was undergoing its own shifts. My focus in what follows is therefore specifically on the period when Caracas's global position was incipient but not yet defined; its economic and operatic potential, like its oil, still bubbling beneath the surface.

Ariel Sings

Teresa Carreño's return to Venezuela had been long awaited. Born in Caracas in 1853 to a wealthy family closely connected to the political elite, Carreño emigrated to New York in 1862 and was soon introduced to pianist-composer Louis Moreau Gottschalk, her subsequent mentor.[7] Unsurprisingly, her Venezuelan background prompted much discussion and furthered her public image as an 'automatic genius' produced by nature itself.[8] Contrasts were regularly drawn between her onstage assurance and her childlike behaviour elsewhere, her abilities encouraging critics to reach for scientific terminology to convey a mysterious talent. For one such critic, it was as though she had been possessed by the spirit of a long-dead performer; for another, as though she were moved by the unseen magnet of the telegram.[9] Even with the United States in the grip of civil war, Venezuela's turbulent political and geological histories were also much remarked upon, in particular the ongoing Federal Wars of 1859–63 that would kill nearly a quarter of Venezuela's population. 'Few would have supposed that the most gratifying entertainment of the season – the one capable of reviving from our hearts the nightmare of pain and apprehension, and of internecine war, under which our country withers – would come to us from far-off Venezuela', commented *The Providence Daily Post* in January 1863:

Caracas – almost a synonym for civil discord, and sounding very much like those physical convulsions, by one of which, it was once destroyed – is the native place of

---

[7] On Carreño's training, see Laura Pita, 'Teresa Carreño's Early Years in Caracas: Cultural Intersections of Piano Virtuosity, Gender and Nation-Building in the Nineteenth Century', PhD dissertation, University of Kentucky (2019).
[8] On eighteenth-century ideas of genius and the mechanical, see Annette Richards, 'Automatic Genius: Mozart and the Mechanical Sublime', *Music and Letters*, 80/3 (1999), 366–89.
[9] *Boston Post*, 5 January 1863 (Teresa Carreño Papers, Special Collections Library, Vassar College, Scrapbook 1; henceforth TCSC, S1; *Providence Daily Post*, 19 January 1863 (TCSC, S1). *The Commercial Advertiser*, New York, 16 December 1862 (TCSC, S1) likewise remarked on the 'magic of genius' which transformed the 'young tropical bird' into an adult at the keyboard.

the little sylph who comes upon the stage with wings of silk and in drapery of white [. . . her father] has brought to us from the mighty Orinoco and the shadows of the mighty Andes, a spirit as fascinating and beautiful as 'Ariel' . . . Her notes are echoes of her native land. The tourist in a fine extravagance has said: – 'See Naples and then die', but *while dying* he would now pray to hear Teresa Carreño.[10]

Such extravagant rhetoric doubtless reflected an unfamiliarity with prodigies, but it also confirmed perceptions of Venezuela as a distinctly problematic emblem of the 'diapason of nature': a land at once lusciously fertile and horribly prone to catastrophe. Carreño's music making could nonetheless offer an idealised representation of this ferment, her phrases growing 'like the exuberant fruits and flowers of her native tropics – in flavour and colours, aroma and form alike delicious and symmetrical'.[11]

The association of Caracas with Naples, which closed the quotation above, also gestured towards long-standing imaginative links between Venezuela and Italy, connections that would become even more prominent in succeeding decades. Venezuela's name originally signified 'little Venice' – a reference to the coastal houses on stilts encountered in Maracaibo by early European visitors. US and British travel accounts throughout the nineteenth century had highlighted the country's tropical scenery and alluring soundscape, anticipating much of the rhetoric found in Picón Febres's articles (and typically indebted to earlier accounts by Humboldt and Darwin).[12] William Eleroy Curtis's *The Capitals of Spanish America* (1888) recorded a special affection for Caracas, which notwithstanding its history of earthquakes and its insufferable insects was still 'one of the most delightful places of residence in the world', and in a country that offered virtually every landscape known to man.[13] For visitors from New York, Curtis argued, the nine-day boat journey to Caracas was 'one of the most delightful in the world', providing access to an alternative world enjoyed by their Spanish-American neighbours.[14] The mobility of rhetoric surrounding *italianità* with regard to the Spanish Caribbean would be encapsulated by several US travel companies from the late nineteenth century onwards. The New York and Cuba Mail Steamship Company proclaimed the region 'the lands of song and

---

[10] *Providence Daily Post*, 19 January 1863.   [11] Ibid.
[12] Examples include Robert Semple, *A Sketch of the Present State of Caracas* (London, 1812) and John Hawkshaw, *Reminiscences of South America from Two and a Half Years' Residence in Venezuela* (London, 1838). Semple was born in Boston in 1766 and published travel accounts of Spain, Italy, Germany and Sweden before working as a governor under the Hudson Bay Company.
[13] William Eleroy Curtis, *The Capitals of Spanish America* (London: n.p., 1888), 265.
[14] Ibid., 257.

sunlight', the rhetoric of de Staël and Rousseau now conveniently transposed to the fringes of the southern hemisphere.[15]

For the young and privileged Carreño, such exoticism was clearly an advantage. By 1865 she had given recitals throughout the United States, and she soon headed to Cuba, Madrid, London and Paris to further her career, eventually settling in the French capital. Introductions to Rossini, Liszt and Gounod sealed her reputation as a musical wonder. Opera also played a major part in her career from her earliest performances. Thalberg's *Norma* and *Moïse* fantasias were regular warhorses, alongside potpourris inspired by *Ernani* and *Lucia di Lammermoor*. By the 1870s, opera would take on an even more explicit role for Carreño, as she reportedly stepped in as Marguerite de Valois for a performance of *Les Huguenots* in Scotland in 1872 organised by Colonel Mapelson, the impresario then running operatic seasons in London as well as managing Carreño; by the 1880s he was also working in New York and had significant relationships with transatlantic singers such as Adelina Patti and Italo Campanini. On Carreño's return to New York in the mid-1870s, she experimented further on stage, performing Zerlina in *Don Giovanni* with the Maurice Strakosch company. Although she soon returned to the piano, Strakosch remained highly significant for Carreño's career, arranging tours with a host of prominent North American singers. In line with practices of the period, Carreño regularly performed in mixed bills during the 1870s and 1880s all over the United States; occasionally she would even sing an aria herself at the end of her concerts. Several of her female collaborators – including Emma Abbott and Clara Louise Kellogg – were themselves distinguished operatic entrepreneurs and provided further professional models for Carreño, identifying opportunities for female impresarios unable to compete with men in original-language production within the United States.[16]

The invitation to return to Caracas in 1885 thus arrived at a propitious moment in Carreño's career. Established as a virtuoso of the first order, Carreño also enjoyed professional relationships with an exceptionally wide range of international musicians. By the 1860s she and Venezuela were closely linked in the US public imagination, the former mutating the latter's dangerous forms into musical manna. Her divorce from her first husband,

---

[15] New York Historical Society, Bella C. Landauer Collection, Series II, Box 121. The company operated under the abbreviation the 'Ward Line' from the 1840s until the 1930s; the clipping is undated but strongly suggests the late nineteenth century.

[16] See Katherine K. Preston, *Opera for the People: English-Language Opera and Women Managers in Late 19th-Century America* (Oxford: Oxford University Press, 2017).

violinist Émile Sauret, had created a scandal but his successor, Tagliapietra, cemented Carreño's relationship with the operatic world: born in Italy, he had emigrated to New York in the 1870s and was admired for his rich tone and sure technique. Caracas's *Diario de Avisos* reported gossip in 1881 that Carreño, who had 'conquered Europe and North America' was considering a return to Venezuela with a concert tour and an Italian opera season.[17] The postal invitation that arrived from interim President Joaquín Crespo in 1885 finally confirmed her visit: Ariel would soon return home.

Caracas Before the Blowout

Caracas was then in the midst of a promising new era. Following the victory of the Liberals in the Federal Wars, the city had enjoyed more than two decades of peace and relative prosperity shaped in large part by President Antonio Guzmán Blanco, who would rule the country for most of the 1870s and 1880s. An autocratic figure, Guzmán Blanco consolidated Caracas's economic and political power within Venezuela and became known as 'El ilustre Americano'. During three terms in office he pursued an ambitious programme of liberal economic and social reform, establishing a national currency, boosting international trade, sponsoring public education and sharply reducing the powers of the Catholic Church. Transport and communication infrastructures were also improved: the first railway line in the country opened in 1883 between Caracas and the nearby port of La Guaira, and a telegraph system with New York established. Within Caracas national progress was advertised via buildings such as the National Pantheon (1874) and the Teatro Municipal (1881), part of a significant programme of public works.[18] Guzmán Blanco remained a controversial figure, however. Despite efforts to model himself after Simón Bolívar, he earned a reputation for snobbery and corruption and spent much of his time in Europe; having served as ambassador to both Spain and France between his presidential terms, he eventually retired to Paris.

Notwithstanding these visible signs of modernisation, Venezuela remained a largely agricultural economy. Coffee, sugar, cocoa and cattle were the country's main exports and national infrastructural reforms were funded in large part by US and British investment; projects such as the

---

[17] 'Teresa Carreño', *Diario de Avisos*, 4 October 1881. Carreño's cousin Manuel lived in Caracas and facilitated discussions with the local government.

[18] Arturo Almandoz, 'The Shaping of Venezuelan Urbanism in the Hygiene Debate of Caracas, 1880–1910', *Urban Studies*, 37/11 (2000), 2073–89.

Caracas–La Guaira railway were frequently built by US companies. This dependence on US finance and technology reflected both Venezuela's modest population and the difficult terrain of parts of the interior, which had long impeded the movement of people and goods; Venezuela was the only South American country to enjoy a direct steamship service to the United States.[19] As Judith Ewell has shown, however, Venezuelan consumers tended to favour European goods over North American ones and Venezuela enjoyed a significant trade surplus with the United States, in spite of efforts by the government there to expand its economic empire in South America following the Civil War.[20] By the 1880s, asphalt offered a further link in this delicate United States–Venezuela economic partnership. The Guanoco Asphalt Lake had long been used by indigenous communities and Spanish settlers to mend shipping, but the development of asphalt-paved roads in the United States during the 1870s led to massive increases in demand. The Venezuelan government signed a concession for the exploitation of the lake in 1883 that passed to the New York & Bermúdez company two years later; controversially, the profits largely went north. Exploration of the lake – the second largest in the world – confirmed suspicions of vast oil deposits under Venezuelan soil and their economic potential, even if major explorations would not take place until the 1910s. 'Let us establish our industries', declared *La Opinion Nacional* in January 1887 regarding a further exploration site near Lake Maracaibo. 'Let us think upon the exploitation of our immense natural riches and dedicate ourselves to this work, that honours and exalts man.'[21]

Opera had long played a role in this broader narrative of social progress. The Teatro Caracas was inaugurated in October 1854 (with Verdi's *Ernani*) in response to frustration at the city's poor performance spaces for visiting troupes; the local press acknowledged it was 'not one of those magnificent [theatres] of Europe that attract the attention of travellers for their richness and elegance', but it accommodated 1,200 visitors and featured the first gas illumination system in Caracas.[22] The earlier

---

[19] Judith Ewell, *Venezuela and the United States: From Monroe's Hemisphere to Petroleum's Empire* (Athens, GA: University of Georgia Press, 1996), 71–2. The preference for the United States was motivated both by geography and by a long-running territorial dispute with Great Britain.

[20] Ewell, *Venezuela: A Century of Change*, 18. According to the 1894 *Anuario Estadístico*, Venezuela's population was 2,444,816.

[21] 'Petróleo refinado en Venezuela', *La Opinion Nacional*, 15 January 1887.

[22] 'Teatro de Caracas', *Diario de Avisos*, 24 October 1854, cited in Pita, 'Teresa Carreño's Early Years in Caracas', 468. Valuable overviews of Caracas's operatic seasons are offered by Isabel Áretz, 'Le avventure del melodramma in Venezuela (1783–1914)', in Anna Laura Bellina

Teatro Coliseo had opened in 1831, with intermittent performances including the local premiere of *Il barbiere di Siviglia* in 1836, but it soon closed and was replaced with a variety of temporary venues. The years following 1863 witnessed an increasing number of Italian companies performing works by Rossini, Donizetti, Bellini and Verdi, as well as a number of French and Spanish troupes. Operatic seasons were typically brief, yet as Isabel Áretz and José Peñin have shown, companies brought over by (typically non-Italian) impresarios such as Bernabé Díaz gave audiences access to an expanding repertory of works and a ready supply of new European performers, while encouraging the production of homegrown zarzuelas.

Operatic reviews also appeared in the major newspapers, most notably *La Opinion Nacional*, the *Diario de Avisos* and *El Granuja*. These publications represented a range of political views, but given Caracas's size there was significant crossover in personnel, with *La Opinion Nacional* closely linked with the liberal establishment. *El Zancudo* (1867–8; 1880–3) and *La Lira venezolana* (1882–3) were moreover established as the first quasi-musicological journals in Venezuela, featuring musical news from Europe and North America alongside piano transcriptions and critical studies of composers and works.[23] Italian opera was a cornerstone of both publications, with authors drawing on long-established Romantic tropes to praise the 'immortal Bellini' and Verdi.[24] *La Lira venezolana* also aimed to improve Venezuela's own 'dejected' musical culture, arguing for Venezuela's innate artistic fertility in spite of its poor musical infrastructure. A country 'prodigiously favoured by nature', Venezuela was ideally positioned to transcend its natural state and approach the ideal, transforming the 'dissonances' and 'tempests' of the human soul into spiritual harmony.[25]

(ed.), *Il Teatro dei Due Mondi: L'opera italiana nei paesi di lingua iberica* (Treviso: Diastema, 2000), 219–36; and José Peñin, 'Venezuela y la ópera: una pasión decimonónica', in Alvaro Torrente Sánchez-Guisande and Emilio Francisco Casares Rodicio (eds.), *La ópera en España e Hispanoamérica: una creación propia*: vol. 2 (Madrid: Universidad Complutense de Madrid, 2001), 237–66.

[23] Hugo Quintana offers an overview in 'Otros cincuenta años de crítica y de recepción musical en Caracas (1861–1911)', *Revista anual del instituto nacional de musicología Carlos Vega* 24 (2016), 19–50.

[24] Salvador Llamózas, 'Bellini: 1', *La Lira venezolana*, 1 February 1883.

[25] Salvados Llamózas, 'Lira venezolana', *La Lira venezolana*, 28 October 1882; this was the magazine's first issue. Ramón de la Plaza, prominent Venezuelan intellectual and contributor to *La Lira venezolana*, published a seminal volume in 1883 entitled *Ensayos sobre el arte en Venezuela*, in which he drew upon Rousseau's *Essai sur l'origine des langues* to argue for the suitability of Spanish for music drama.

By the early 1880s, opera was even more firmly linked to the state via the opening of the Teatro Municipal, an Italian-style theatre usually known as the Teatro Guzmán Blanco. The theatre enjoyed both a generous government subsidy and the regular presence of the President and his wife. The opening season featured more than ten works, while the 1883 Centenary Exposition brought another celebratory season headed by local star tenor, Fernando Michelena.[26] Significantly, however, the theatre seated no more spectators than the Teatro Caracas, reflecting the unvaryingly modest population of the city – barely 55,000 by 1881.[27] In that context, the opera house could offer not only familiar ideas of civilisation, but also the possibility of momentary respite from an isolated, tedious environment. 'Where can one find more attractions than at the opera?' asked *La Opinion Nacional* shortly after the Teatro Municipal opened:

It fills the eye and penetrates the heart with myriad profound impressions; it charms the gaze and transports the imagination to other times and places. And even putting aesthetic matters to one side, aren't the social delights offered by the theatre still more delicate and expansive after the soul has refreshed itself in this oasis of art? ... In only a few days the company will leave us, and we will return to the usual monotony and the eternal complaint that we lack amusements and spots of solace where to rest and give solace and amusement to one's spirit.[28]

In spite of such complaints, however, Caracas still offered several other diversions. Bullfighting, theatre, dances and carnivals all attracted substantial audiences, while the Unión Filharmónica presented chamber and orchestral concerts including operatic arias. For frustrated opera lovers, Plaza Bolívar also provided evening recitals and military band performances, featuring a range of operatic extracts more varied than might be enjoyed at the theatre, from Rossini to Wagner's *Lohengrin*. Listings published in local newspapers throughout the 1880s reveal the variety of operatic highlights performed in non-theatrical contexts, as well as their co-habitation with popular local dance forms. And for those who stayed at home, *La Opinion Nacional* ran updates on lyric activity elsewhere: from the global triumphs of Patti to the latest tenor rivalries at Madrid's Teatro Real. The operatic premieres of Verdi and Gounod were

---

[26] José Antonio Calcaño, *La ciudad y su Música* (Caracas: Conservatorio Teresa Carreño, 1958), 309. Michelena pursued a US career from the mid-1880s, singing regularly with the Emma Abbott company.

[27] The lighting system was imported from New York: see 'Teatro Guzmán Blanco', *La Opinion Nacional*, 4 January 1881.

[28] 'Revista Teatral', *La Opinion Nacional*, 14 March 1881. The author was responding to performances of *Il trovatore* and *Ruy Blas*.

keenly awaited news, even if the operas themselves remained unstaged in Caracas for years to come.

Operatic Hopes, Operatic Horrors; or Sylphs and Earthquakes

In this intermingled mood of aspiration and stasis, it is little surprise that Carreño's operatic season was keenly awaited. Her 1885–6 concert tour across Venezuela had witnessed an outpouring of public interest, with massed crowds greeting her arrival and sonnets published in her honour. Carreño also knew how to please her public, organising gala concerts for the young and embarking on plans to establish a national conservatory. During her recitals she treated audiences to operatic excerpts, in at least one case singing a duet from *Il trovatore* with Tagliapietra.[29] When she returned to New York in October 1886, her ambitions to visit Caracas a few months later with an opera company were welcomed: another triumph for Carreño, and for Caracas, surely beckoned.

The eventual composition of the troupe appears to have relied largely on Carreño's and Tagliapietra's extensive network of New York contacts. The two soprano prima donnas, Adela Aimery and Linda Brambilla, the two basses, Bologna and Ricci, and the prima ballerina, Maria Bonfanti, had all been recruited there by January 1887; according to *El Granuja*, twenty members of the chorus were also contracted from the Mapleson and Strakosch companies, with the orchestra and dancers likewise coming from New York, to be supplemented by a few Venezuelan and Italian musicians.[30] Tagliapietra then travelled to Milan, bringing baritone Tomaso Noto, tenors Egisto Guardenti and Alessandro Passetti, mezzo-soprano Clementina Prampolini and ballet conductor and cellist 'Señor Cazorati' directly to Caracas to round out the company.[31] Carreño's wing arrived in late February, Tagliapietra's ensemble a few days later; an early report relayed the boast that it would be 'the best and most complete that had ever come to Venezuela'.[32]

A closer look at the ensemble suggests its soloists comprised a mixture of the promising, the established and those who had seen better days (Figure 10.1). The sopranos, both young, were promoted via press clippings from Spanish and Italian newspapers. Aimery, the heavier-voiced of

---

[29] See *La Opinion Nacional*, 11 January 1886.   [30] 'Opera italiana', *El Granuja*, 5 February 1887.
[31] 'Opera italiana', *Diario de Avisos*, 1 March 1887.
[32] 'Correspondencia: De la Guaira', *Diario de Avisos*, 28 February 1887.

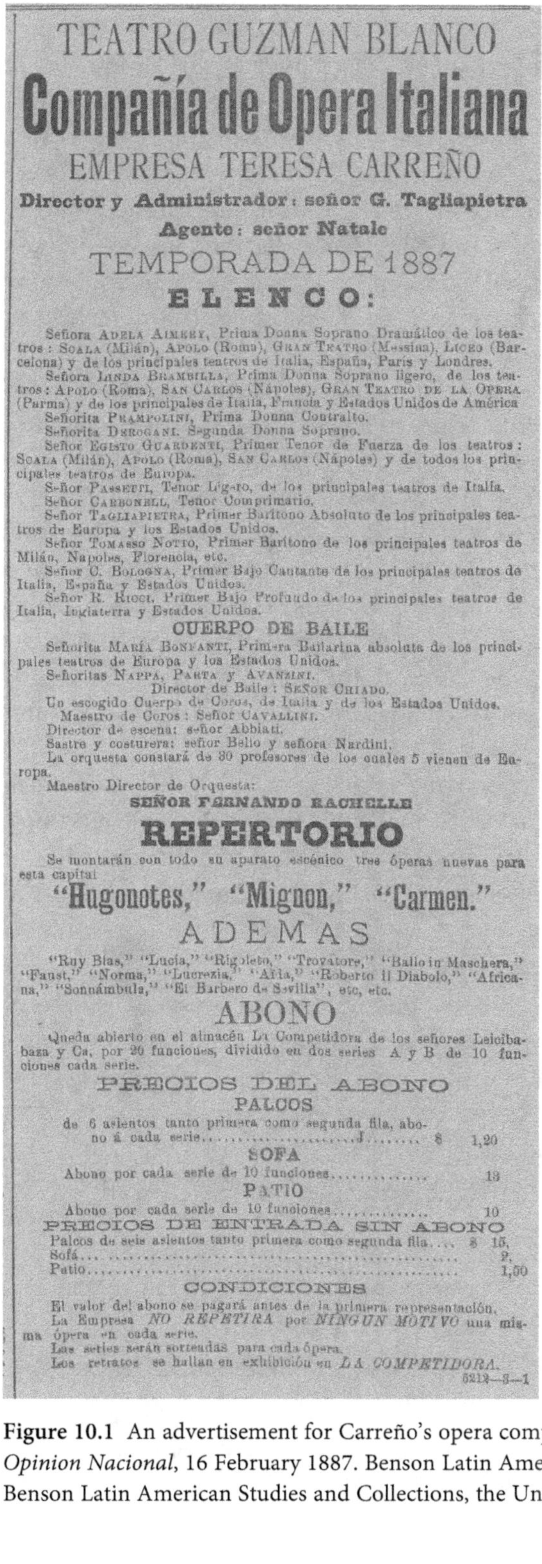

TEATRO GUZMAN BLANCO

Compañía de Opera Italiana

EMPRESA TERESA CARREÑO

Director y Administrador: señor G. Tagliapietra

Agente: señor Natale

TEMPORADA DE 1887

ELENCO:

Señora ADELA AIMERY, Prima Donna Soprano Dramático de los teatros: SCALA (Milán), APOLO (Roma), GRAN TEATRO (Messina), LICEO (Barcelona) y de los principales teatros de Italia, España, París y Londres.

Señora LINDA BRAMBILLA, Prima Donna Soprano ligero, de los teatros: APOLO (Roma), SAN CARLOS (Nápoles), GRAN TEATRO DE LA OPERA (Parma) y de los principales de Italia, Francia y Estados Unidos de América

Señorita PRAMPOLINI, Prima Donna Contralto.

Señorita DEROGANI. Segunda Donna Soprano.

Señor EGISTO GUARDENTI, Primer Tenor de Fuerza de los teatros: SCALA (Milán), APOLO (Roma), SAN CARLOS (Nápoles) y de todos los principales teatros de Europa.

Señor PASSETTI, Tenor Ligero, de los principales teatros de Italia.

Señor CARBONELL, Tenor Comprimario.

Señor TAGLIAPIETRA, Primer Barítono Absoluto de los principales teatros de Europa y los Estados Unidos.

Señor TOMASSO NOTTO, Primer Barítono de los principales teatros de Milán, Napoles, Florencia, etc.

Señor C. BOLOGNA, Primer Bajo Cantante de los principales teatros de Italia, España y Estados Unidos.

Señor R. RICCI, Primer Bajo Profundo de los principales teatros de Italia, Inglaterra y Estados Unidos.

CUERPO DE BAILE

Señorita MARÍA BONFANTI, Primera Bailarina absoluta de los principales teatros de Europa y los Estados Unidos.

Señoritas NAPPA, PARTA y AVANZINI.

Director de Baile: SEÑOR CHIADO.

Un escogido Cuerpo de Coros, de Italia y de los Estados Unidos.

Maestro de Coros: Señor CAVALLINI.

Director de escena: señor Abbiati.

Sastre y costurera: señor Bello y señora Nardini.

La orquesta constará de 30 profesores de los cuales 5 vienen de Europa.

Maestro Director de Orquesta:

SEÑOR FERNANDO RACHELLE

REPERTORIO

Se montarán con todo su aparato escénico tres óperas nuevas para esta capital

"Hugonotes," "Mignon," "Carmen."

ADEMAS

"Ruy Blas," "Lucía," "Rigoleto," "Trovatore," "Ballo in Maschera," "Faust," "Norma," "Lucrezia," "Aida," "Roberto il Diabolo," "Africana," "Sonnámbula," "El Barbero de Sevilla", etc, etc.

ABONO

Queda abierto en el almacén La Competidora de los señores Leicibabaza y Ca, por 20 funciones, dividido en dos series A y B de 10 funciones cada serie.

PRECIOS DEL ABONO

PALCOS

de 6 asientos tanto primera como segunda fila, abono á cada serie.......................... $ 1,20

SOFA

Abono por cada serie de 10 funciones.............. 13

PATIO

Abono por cada serie de 10 funciones.............. 10

PRECIOS DE ENTRADA SIN ABONO

Palcos de seis asientos tanto primera como segunda fila..... $ 15,

Sofá.. 2,

Patio.. 1,50

CONDICIONES

El valor del abono se pagará antes de la primera representación.

La Empresa *NO REPETIRA* por *NINGUN MOTIVO* una misma ópera en cada serie.

Las series serán sorteadas para cada ópera.

Los retratos se hallan en exhibición en *LA COMPETIDORA.*

5212—8—1

Figure 10.1 An advertisement for Carreño's opera company, as published in *La Opinion Nacional*, 16 February 1887. Benson Latin American Collection, LLILAS Benson Latin American Studies and Collections, the University of Texas at Austin the two, had sung in Barcelona a few years earlier in the second cast of *L'Africaine* at the Liceu, alongside appearances in Rome; Brambilla, a lyric coloratura, had made her professional debut in 1885 (in Milan) before embarking on a concert tour of the United States. Other performers were more experienced and indeed familiar in Caracas. In addition to Tagliapietra, Prampolini had sung in Venezuela and in other South American theatres on several occasions; she had been contracted by impresario Cesare Ciacchi to sing in Buenos Aires and Montevideo in 1886 and had previously ventured as far as Melbourne.[33] The male singers were in general less highly touted, but Egisto Guardenti was also a regular on the South American circuit. Then in his late thirties, he specialised in spinto roles and appears to have been highly erratic in quality; he had sung with success throughout Italy but his appearances in *Norma* in 1882 in Buenos Aires were savaged by the Spanish-language press.[34] The ballerina Maria Bonfanti was something of a coup for the company. Born and trained in Milan, she emigrated to New York and in 1885–6 acted as prima ballerina of the Metropolitan.[35] As with several of her colleagues in the troupe, she was promoted as much for her North American experience as her European credentials, and returned to New York shortly after the company folded.

The decision to open the season on 5 March 1887 with Verdi's *Un ballo in maschera* was widely praised. Verdi's French-influenced work offered ample opportunities for Aimery, Brambilla, Prampolini, Guardenti and Noto to display their abilities, as well as featuring a fine dance interlude by Bonfanti and 'Señor Chiadi'.[36] Reviews acknowledged the difficulties of assembling a first-rate ensemble at short notice as well as stressing the high standards expected by audiences in Caracas; but they were initially welcoming. *Lucia di Lammermoor* and *Il trovatore* followed, the former offering a showcase for the fresh-voiced Brambilla and lyric tenor Passetti; Brambilla was highly praised. *Faust, La traviata, Rigoletto* and *Aida* were then scheduled to fill up the rest of March, with the French premieres planned for April and May alongside *La sonnambula, Robert le diable,* Filippo Marchetti's *Ruy Blas, La*

---

[33] See *La Opinion Nacional*, 30 April 1886.

[34] *Gaceta Musical*, 30 July 1882; cited in John Rosselli, 'The Opera Business and the Italian Immigrant Community in Latin America 1820–1930: The Example of Buenos Aires', *Past and Present* 127 (1990), 155–82 (176).

[35] Maria Bonfanti's personal papers are now held at the Jerome Robbins Dance Division, New York Public Library for the Performing Arts.

[36] See *La Opinion Nacional*, 7 March 1887. *Un ballo in maschera* had also been performed in the Teatro Municipal's first season, the press emphasising its popularity in spite of Verdi's aggressive vocal writing: *La Opinion Nacional*, 11 January 1881.

favorita, *Lucrezia Borgia*, *L'Africaine* and *Norma*. For Caracas, this represented a musically ambitious programme, mixing Italian repertory staples with two lesser-known Meyerbeer works and three French novelties. The advertisement published in *La Opinion Nacional* is revealing both for the prominence given to the soloists (in comparison with the repertory), and the attention drawn to the new French works. The list of older repertory finishes inconclusively with 'etc., etc.', suggesting that despite the sale of subscriptions at local department store La Competidora, the final details of the season were probably decided during rehearsals in Caracas.

As Milinowski and Milanca Guzmán have noted, however, problems quickly began to emerge. Aimery fell ill and was replaced by Brambilla for several performances of *Faust*.[37] The musical director, local conductor Fernando Rachelle, then cancelled several performances in April and was substituted by the first violinist and then by Carreño herself, who conducted three different operas and even performed Liszt's sixth Hungarian Rhapsody as an interlude. Initial public enthusiasm for the company's singers also seems to have waned. By early April some had turned on Tagliapietra, penning letters to *La Opinion Nacional* criticising his diminished vocal estate in *Faust*. Rather than weather the storm, Tagliapietra withdrew from the rest of the season, declaring that such hostility towards a veteran singer made his position untenable; a performance of *Rigoletto* was also cancelled.[38] Guardenti and Passetti suffered from increasingly negative press, the latter being condemned as entirely inadequate. 'This artist is not fit for Caracas', lamented the *Diario de Avisos* in mid-April after *La sonnambula*. 'And if the company persists in ignoring the displays of disapproval with which the public greets him, they are conspiring against their own success even more than their worst enemies'.[39] Audiences eventually diminished, and ticket prices were reduced. By the end of April the company had closed with barely half of the scheduled operas performed and the French premieres all cancelled. Carreño's debts were finally settled by the government; the sets and costumes brought over from Europe for the new works were bought by the theatre alongside Carreño's piano.

Some of the factors that contributed to the company's failure were clearly beyond their control – illness above all. Carreño was much praised

---

[37] Milanca Guzmán also points to tensions between Aimery and Carreño later in the season, citing a letter published in *El Siglo* on 16 April 1887 announcing Aimery's departure from the troupe: *Teresa Carreño*, 55–6.

[38] *La Opinion Nacional*, 1 April 1887. The *Diario de Avisos* also defended Tagliapietra in a review of *La traviata*: 'Opera italiana', 4 April 1887.

[39] 'Opera italiana', *Diario de Avisos*, 16 April 1887.

for her contributions as a conductor and Brambilla had impressive vocal resilience; but rehearsing and performing a dozen challenging works in limited time was almost certain to lead to vocal exhaustion and cancellations, with compromises inevitable. Yet, seen differently, illness was also just the most obvious sign of the complex logistics of touring opera at this time and the challenges they posed to a rhetoric of civilisation. The operatic promise of social progress could only be achieved if everything went as planned; that is, when the labour behind this man-made 'oasis of art' was successfully concealed.[40] The weakness of some of the soloists exposed further challenges to such fantasies, highlighting the complexities of assembling a first-class ensemble to match the splendour of the Teatro Municipal. Constructing local monuments to urban progress in Caracas did not guarantee an appeal for foreign artists, nor a demand by local audiences; the architecture might endure but operatic troupes would need to be recalled each season, continually assessed against past and imagined operatic iterations, and potentially found wanting.[41]

The reference in the *Diario de Avisos* to the company's 'worst enemies' also hints at murkier reasons for its failure. Carreño's celebrity and her links to the government would have made her an obvious target for political dissent, and certainly the diminishing coverage in *La Opinion Nacional* during the final weeks suggests embarrassment that this quasi-official venture was failing.[42] Carreño's own later correspondence with Guzmán Blanco blamed local opponents for the dwindling audiences, although her need to avoid censure and cover expenses were surely a factor here.[43] By early 1887 elections were looming and Guzmán Blanco's achievements in office were being hotly debated: supporters claimed that the Liberal Party was responsible for all of the economic gains of the last two decades, yet inequality remained rife and the President's approval ratings were in decline.[44] The musical deficiencies of Carreño's troupe at Guzmán Blanco's theatre could thus serve as a metonym for wider disappointments: dreams of progress exposed as false promises, an ideal shattering as painfully as one of Passetti's top notes.

---

[40] On similar tensions earlier in the century, see Benjamin Walton, 'L'italiana in Calcutta', in Suzanne Aspden (ed.), *Operatic Geographies: The Place of Opera and the Opera House* (Chicago: University of Chicago Press, 2019), 119–32.

[41] These issues are outlined in reviews by references to previous performers such as tenor Francisco Mazzoleni.

[42] In her (highly anecdotal) biography of Carreño, Milinowski suggests Rachelle's cancellations were related to fears of a bomb in the theatre.

[43] See Jesús Eloy Gutiérrez (ed.), *Teresa Carreño: Cartas y documentos: Compilación documental (1863–1917)* (Caracas: La Campana Sumergida, 2018).

[44] Guzmán Blanco would retire in 1888, but his successor was a close associate.

Yet it is questionable whether any Italian opera company in Caracas could have fulfilled some of these elevated fantasies by the late 1880s, regardless of links with the government. Part of the difficulty was repertory. If the Carreño company could boast of offering the 'best and most complete' season Caracas had yet enjoyed, it was nevertheless one in which the majority of the Italian works were extremely familiar. Verdian warhorses had been performed across numerous seasons and the bel canto offerings were similarly hackneyed, individual arias frequently performed at the Plaza Bolívar.[45] The effects of this familiarity were unpredictable. Repeated exposure might lead to boredom and a willingness to abandon the theatre, but it could also generate a legitimate sense of connoisseurship as performances of repertory works by one troupe were assessed against the previous year. This sense of routine or even staleness was presumably intensified by details of the operatic staging, since sets for the Italian works were owned by the Teatro Municipal rather than imported from the United States or Europe with the troupe; opera here signalled not technological modernity but rather a reliance on the old. Any deficiencies in musical quality by the Carreño troupe were thus more (rather than less) likely to be noted by audiences and critics, even if they had not enjoyed first-hand exposure to operatic celebrities within Venezuela. Carreño's troupe had nowhere to hide.

The tensions surrounding Italian opera as a symbol of urban progress are suggested further by coverage of Verdi's *Otello*, premiered in Milan exactly one month before the Carreño season opened. Reported on the front page of *La Opinion Nacional* via a correspondent in Madrid, Verdi's opera was also covered through reprints from the *Revue des Deux Mondes*, drawing Venezuelan readers into an international network of music criticism. On the one hand, attention to Verdi's latest work could indicate participation in a broader cultural moment, aligning readers with elites in Milan, Paris, London and Madrid (even if *Otello* would not arrive in Venezuela for several years). In light of the modest Italian immigrant population in Venezuela – barely 3,000 by 1891 – Verdi's work could to some degree be attended to as a cosmopolitan symbol of progress, however closely linked it was to Italian culture.[46] Intermittent newspaper coverage of Italy in Venezuela at this time focused primarily on the Vatican and on Italy's colonial wars in Africa, alongside adverts for Italian food and fashion. It seems clear, then, that for

---

[45] *La Opinion Nacional* described *Il trovatore* as the opera most familiar to Caracas's audience: 'Opera italiana', 16 July 1883.

[46] On Italian immigration, see Susan Berglund, 'Italian Immigration in Venezuela: A Story Still Untold', *Center for Migration Studies* 11/3 (1994), 173–209.

Venezuelan readers Italian opera could operate as part of an international aesthetic canon largely separate from the latest Italian political developments.

At the same time, however, Italian opera was clearly bound up with local Venezuelan politics. Chosen to open key operatic seasons in 1881, 1883 and 1887, Verdi's operas functioned as part of an official soundtrack to the Guzmán Blanco era, omnipresent in elite Caracas society. To some degree this is hardly unusual, yet Verdi was in many ways an ideal musical figurehead for Guzmán Blanco's government. By the 1880s the composer was typically portrayed in the Venezuelan press as a conservative, establishment figure: a composer who may have kept abreast of international musical trends, but who was primarily associated with his operas from the 1850s as well as his supposed involvement with the Risorgimento; a political period now nearly as distant as Venezuela's own Federal Wars.[47] Rather than a symbol of revolutionary populism or of a nascent avant-garde, Verdi represented a once 'revolutionary' figure now firmly linked to the liberal state. Given Guzmán Blanco's emulation of Bolívar, Verdi was thus a perfect symbol: *Il trovatore* and *Ernani* represented not political ferment but the established political order. Seen in those terms, the Italian repertory chosen by the Carreño company was not only musically familiar (probably *too* familiar) but came freighted with years of official association: ideas even far superior artists removed from the Guzmán Blanco administration would have struggled to shake off.

It may appear, then, that Carreño's Italian opera company was doomed from the start – her singers overworked, her repertory old. Yet reports from initial performances suggest that official narratives of progress were only part of the story for Venezuelan audiences, and that Italian staples could elicit significant public approval – albeit not always in the ways demanded by critics. Alongside positive commentary, several reviews expose tensions between critical aspirations and the public's expectations, ones that complicate Italian opera's political associations. The revival of *Aida*, for example, appears to have been coolly received by audiences with the exception of the slave dances, a matter of serious consternation for the *Diario de Avisos*:

> Was it because of the faces the little black people made? We believe so and we sincerely condemn it ... The magnificent conclusion of this [second] act, this magnificent piece of contemporary art, was performed without any errors yet the public didn't offer a moment of applause to celebrate it. How do you explain such a thing? Encoring the dance of the blacks and yet not having a clap for the grand finale![48]

---

[47] The review of *Ernani* at the Teatro Municipal in *La Opinion Nacional*, 2 July 1883, is typical.
[48] 'Opera italiana', *Diario de Avisos*, 29 March 1887.

Critical ire is directed here both at insufficiently elevated audience values and at pleasure in black dancing: the public's values are seen as worryingly out of kilter. The racial politics of late nineteenth-century Venezuela are crucial in this context, since while racial democracy had been promoted by the government since the 1860s (recognising Venezuela's exceptional ethnic blend and distinguishing it from countries such as Brazil), efforts to whiten the population by European immigration (including Italian) were actively encouraged.[49] Criollo waltzes and indigenous music were likewise sanctioned; but Italian opera remained the government soundtrack. Even if Italian opera staged ethnic difference, then, it was also marked by critics as a whitened space of social progress: a 'perfection of nature' that actual operatic performances and audiences threatened to undo.[50] A subsequent revival of *La traviata* exposed similar tensions, with reviews stressing the opera's morally edifying tale of redemptive love while noting that the matadors' chorus and dancing were especially applauded.[51] In both cases, racialised ideas of progress on the part of critics could only be sustained so far; the performing body dragged fantasies of the ideal back down to earth.

In this context, it seems especially unfortunate that Carreño should have scheduled her French works – especially the Meyerbeer operas, with their rich opportunities for ballet – for the abandoned second half of the season. The decision to bring a dance ensemble to Caracas was clearly one of Carreño's wisest moves, given the popularity of dances such as the Venezuelan waltz and *joropo*: the local premiere of *L'Africaine* in 1881 even featured Andalusian songs and dances in Andalusian dress during the second interval.[52] More generally, however, it is clear that critical and public excitement were by the 1880s increasingly directed towards French and Spanish works, Meyerbeer's and Gounod's operas being acclaimed as the height of theatrical spectacle and artistic ambition. The Teatro Caracas – sidelined for elite occasions by the Teatro Municipal – was regularly used by zarzuela and *opéra bouffe* companies and attracted enthusiastic crowds; *La Opinion Nacional* also reported on Madrid's zarzuela premieres, assessing the extent to which recent works were progressive or stylistically different from opera. Such discussions both allowed for the self-consciously advanced, work-centred criticism that was increasingly hard to sustain in relation to older Italian operas, and encouraged consideration of the future of musical

---

[49] Winthrop R. Wright, *Café con leche: Race, Class, and National Image in Venezuela* (Austin: University of Texas Press, 1990).
[50] For more on these tensions elsewhere, see Naomi André, *Black Opera: History, Power, Engagement* (Urbana: University of Illinois Press, 2018).
[51] 'Opera italiana', *Diario de Avisos*, 4 April 1887.   [52] *La Opinion Nacional*, 26 March 1881.

composition in Venezuela, at a time when diplomatic relations with Spain were rekindled across South America. Progress, when desired, could thus come from many places. If Caracas did not enjoy the best performers, citizens might at least hear the latest works from Italy, Spain, France or elsewhere as 'civilisation' itself was refashioned.

Taming Arcadia

The collapse of the company was the humiliating end of Carreño's career as an impresario. 'Hissed by the Venezuelans' declared the *New York Times*, reporting that the audience had booed in 'regular earthquake fashion' from the outset.[53] Italian publications passed over the company in silence: a further reflection of the almost exclusively North American profile of the troupe. Forty-five members eventually returned to New York, with only seven going to Milan; Aimery and Brambilla stayed on in Caracas for several months, giving recitals and offering singing lessons before making their way north. The stresses of the experiment also appear to have put an insurmountable strain on Carreño's and Tagliapietra's marriage. The couple divorced soon afterwards: Carreño relocated to Berlin, Tagliapietra eventually settling in the United States to become a respected singing teacher.

Carreño's failure was far from the end of Italian opera in Caracas, even if the arrival of successful new works in the 1890s – by Mascagni, Leoncavallo and Puccini – would be delayed by the outbreak of civil war in 1892. But expectations were tempered by the company's failure, with subsequent seasons witnessing a shift towards more French and German repertory: *Carmen* premiered later in 1887. And for North American operatic entrepreneurs, Carreño's humiliation could serve as a stark reminder of the challenges of such a human enterprise, in which a reliance on repertory opera simply brought an alternative set of challenges to those associated with performing unknown newer works. If Italian opera was an emphatically international industry by the 1880s – one in which American-based performers could credibly compete with European ones – then the Italian repertory carried its own, complex, local histories, from favourite singers to political appropriations – histories that any visiting troupe would need to negotiate. Progress or civilisation were not guaranteed outcomes, nor were they even audience goals; the terms of local success were frequently unknowable in advance.

[53] 'Hissed by the Venezuelans', *The New York Times*, 3 April 1887.

The company's breakdown might be examined, then, from a variety of theoretical perspectives, each underlining in different ways the challenges the troupe faced. Carreño's ambivalent position as a female entrepreneur (albeit one enjoying significant social, economic and cultural capital) certainly echoes difficulties encountered by other female impresarios, in her case intensified by her standing both as a divorcée and a national celebrity.[54] And while her venture was widely anticipated and her contributions praised, her husband was nonetheless advertised as 'director and administrator', the established gender roles weakening when Tagliapietra withdrew. What is more, from a musical and technological viewpoint, the troupe's shortcomings also reveal tensions between Italian opera's global mobility and the changing aesthetic expectations in Venezuela, a familiar repertory clashing with heightened theatrical aspirations. Carreño's failure might even appear a significant way station on the line towards the broader decline of 'adequacy' as a meaningful artistic standard during the late nineteenth century: her celebrity was insufficient to compensate for performances failing to enchant.[55]

Above all, a postcolonial (or post-occidental) lens can help to clarify the ideological stakes surrounding Italian opera in Venezuela throughout this period. Following Walter Mignolo and others, one needs to focus on the dynamics of cultural dependency revealed by the troupe's failure, with ambitions to align Caracas's operatic culture with metropolitan examples exposing it (and Carreño) to ridicule – even as this failure also demonstrated the operatic sophistication of Caracas's audiences in ways that challenge ideas of centre and periphery.[56] The unwillingness of audiences to conform to 'modern' standards of behaviour also offers a revealing instance of 'misplaced ideas'; Italian operatic practices reconceptualised in Venezuela to critical disappointment.[57] In this context, however, it is crucial to underline the shifting status of these geographies and dynamics of dependency for Caracas: in particular with the United States now an increasingly vital economic and cultural link. From a North American perspective, too, Venezuela was both a crucial site of neocolonial expansion and a tantalising imaginative space, echoing representations within Venezuela itself: a place of natural bounty teetering between Arcadia and the apocalypse.

---

[54] See Susan Rutherford, 'The Prima Donna as Opera Impresario: Emma Carelli and the Teatro Costanzi, 1911–1926', in Hilary Poriss and Rachel Cowgill (eds.), *The Arts of the Prima Donna in the Long Nineteenth Century* (Oxford: Oxford University Press, 2012), 272–89.

[55] On the decline of 'adequacy', see Emily Dolan's review of Kreuzer's *Curtain, Gong, Steam* in *Music and Letters*, 100/3 (2019), 560–2.

[56] Walter Mignolo, *Local Designs/Global Histories* (Princeton, NJ: Princeton University Press, 2000).

[57] Roberto Schwarz, *Misplaced Ideas: Essays on Brazilian Culture*, trans. John Gledson (London: Verso, 1992), 19–32.

In this context, perhaps it is no surprise that as US and European companies moved in to exploit the oil resources of Venezuela in the 1910s and 1920s – which were made instantly famous by the blowout at Barroso 2 in Cabimas in 1922 – the US gramophone industry also started to enter the Venezuelan musical marketplace.[58] The extractive economy of Venezuelan petroleum could be coupled with the mixed model of the recording conglomerate, with Venezuelan music now recorded and resold to Caracas's elites alongside discs of Italian opera. There was, surely, no trouble in paradise when Caruso or Tetrazzini were played on the gramophone; the risks of human failure had already been expunged in recording sessions in Camden, New Jersey. Opera might now be enjoyed on the exclusive patios of Caracas, amid the cultivated tropical plants and imported French furniture. As a contemporary photograph suggests, the arcadian lushness of the local landscape could even be tamed and brought indoors: a European winter garden ready for a winter that would never arrive (Figure 10.2). And as Italian operatic voices harmonised with the 'natural' music of birds, breezes

Figure 10.2 Typical patio (inner open court) of the house of a wealthy family, four persons, Caracas, (1910). New York (State) Education Dept, Division of Visual Instruction. Instructional lantern slides, c. 1856–1939. A3045-78, 14181, New York State Archives

[58] For a recent study, see Sergio Ospina Romero, 'Recording Studios on Tour: The Expeditions of the Victor Talking Machine Company through Latin America, 1903–1926', PhD dissertation, Cornell University (2019).

and rivers in Venezuela, perhaps too – in the distance – were heard the sounds of oil extraction, the earth's riches plundered with earthquakes thoroughly man-made. Liberal progress, in the operatic sphere or elsewhere, thus carried its own complex legacy of failures, re-imagined ambitions and tales of nature vanquished; civilisation, in Caracas as elsewhere, painfully intertwined with the voices of destruction and loss.

11 | Italian Impresarios, American Minstrels and Parsi Theatre

Sonic Networks and the Negotiation of Opera in Colonial South and South East Asia

RASHNA DARIUS NICHOLSON

'Music should be taught, if possible, in every school', the Scottish missionary John Murdoch averred in his *Hints on Education in India* published in 1871.[1]

It is on the fact that it is a direct moral and religious agency that music (by which is meant mass and part singing from notation) rests its claim to rank first among the subsidiary subjects of instruction ... But Music is not only in itself a direct moral agency and a medium for direct moral teaching; it is also the best auxiliary to the other moral and religious instruction of the school, because it *repeats* what has been already conveyed in a dogmatic or illustrative form and it does so with melodious and grateful associations.[2]

By 'repeating what [had] already been conveyed' through other subjects, such as English literature, theology, geography and science but 'with melodious and grateful associations', colonial music education, according to missionaries, government officials and social reformists, 'consummated and crowned the civilizing mission of the arts'.[3] In the Asian outposts of Empire, the music that was taught and played in missionary schools, theatres, opera houses and the homes of local merchants and European administrators functioned as a tool of power consubstantial with the higher authority of civilisation, Enlightenment ideals of reason and progress and the moral economy of imperialism. Katherine Bergeron describes how music, the practising of scales 'in tune' and playing in unison, regulates

---

I would like to thank Axel Körner for his useful comments. All translations from Gujarati are my own. I have followed the ALA-LC transliteration system and have replaced Pha with Fa.

[1] John Murdoch, *Hints on Education in India; with Special Reference to Vernacular Schools* (Madras [Chennai]: Scottish Press, 1871), 111.

[2] John Murdoch, *Hints on Government Education in India; with Special Reference to School Books* (Madras [Chennai]: C. Foster and Company, 1873), 73.

[3] John Alzog, *Manual of Universal Church History*, 3 vols. (New York: Benziger Brothers, 1912), vol. 2, 1055. For a description of the civilising mission of the social reformist theatre in India see Rashna Darius Nicholson, *The Colonial Public and the Parsi Stage: The Making of the Theatre of Empire (1853–1893)* (Cham: Palgrave Macmillan, 2021).

the ear, orders the body and renders material, physical, visible and audible a collection of discrete values, facilitating forms of self-surveillance and the interiorisation of societal norms.[4] Of all musical forms, opera was the archetypal form of elite colonial culture, the sonic equivalent of Shakespeare facilitating the internalisation of a hierarchy of values, 'harmonising' social bodies and functioning as an index of supercultural control.[5] Accordingly, Michael McClellan suggests that opera in colonial Hanoi should not be viewed as mere entertainment. Instead, it served several related 'civilising functions' – the consolidation of colonial order and identity; the celebration of aesthetic refinement; the demonstration of technological superiority and cultural prowess and the defence of the imperial project.[6]

However, the reception of opera was notoriously difficult to regulate. Bad actors, public apathy or derision, unintentional parody and error could easily disrupt opera's intended dramatic effect, unwittingly exposing ambivalences and contradictions implicit in the colonial project.[7] While articulating national prestige and justifying colonial expansion, opera simultaneously evoked memories of home for the British soldier in India that 'surround[ed] like phantoms the imagination of the exile'.[8] For locals on the other hand, 'opera' signified not only the hegemony of imperial law, but also the potential for its subversion through the parallel law of the marketplace. In the colonial outposts of Bombay, Singapore, Hong Kong and Batavia, 'opera' transmuted into artistic forms markedly different from musical productions in Western Europe. By denoting a large swathe of performances, from Italian travelling companies and American blackface minstrels to Parsi theatre troupes, the term 'opera' no longer merely signified the pinnacle of the tradition of Western classical music. Instead 'opera' came to represent a composite intercultural, polyvocal dialogue, signifying different meanings for different publics. This essay demonstrates how the 'periphery' of Empire marked the 'periphery' of colonial opera as a genre. It attempts to chart the slippery semantic terrain of 'opera' as it travelled eastwards during

---

[4] Katherine Bergeron, 'Prologue: Disciplining Music', in K. Bergeron and P. V. Bohlman (eds.), *Disciplining Music: Musicology and Its Canons* (Chicago: University of Chicago Press, 1992), 1–4.
[5] See Rashna Darius Nicholson, '"A Christy Minstrel, a Harlequin, or an Ancient Persian"?: Opera, Hindustani Classical Music and the Origins of the Popular South Asian "Musical"', *Theatre Survey*, 61–3 (2020), 331–50.
[6] Michael McClellan, 'Performing Empire: Opera in Colonial Hanoi', *Journal of Musicological Research*, 22/1–2 (2003), 135–66 (141–2).
[7] Ibid.
[8] Joseph Mainzer, *Music and Education* (London: Longman, Brown, Green and Longman, 1848), 13.

the period of colonial globalisation, to demonstrate how forms of sovereignty were acoustically negotiated. The tale is a convoluted one, as colonial entrepôts experienced breakneck expansion, progressively embraced ethnically, socially, linguistically and religiously heterogeneous publics and hosted a gamut of transregional entertainments which are notoriously under-researched despite their lasting imprint on the sonic landscape of South and South East Asia. Moreover, operatic troupes travelling the subcontinent, the Malay Archipelago and Australasia between 1860 and 1890 left few traces: weekly advertisements, infrequent reviews and a rare photograph.

In this essay, I address this representational failure by charting the itinerant routes and analysing the differential impact of two obscure, yet enormously influential Italian impresarios in Asia: Augusto Cagli and Giovanni Pompei. By doing so, the essay attempts to partially answer what opera meant for audiences in South and South East Asian entrepôts: Whose values did Italian touring companies articulate? What publics did they legitimise? How was the signifier 'opera' used or misused? What place did opera have in the colonial cultural economy and how did companies respond to the complexities of the colonial entertainment marketplace? These questions implicitly allude to the larger question of legitimate cultures and alternative subcultures, or the ways in which individual and communal identities were sonically constituted. If on the one hand Italian opera, performed before governors and European civil servants, worked as a social rite that upheld a shared mythology of European civilisation and progress, American burlesque opera and Parsi 'Hindustani opera' constitute as evidence of a polycentric, radical, de-centralised and potentially anti-colonialist vision of musical meaning making. As *the* nineteenth-century art form, opera not only reinforced imperialist ideals, but also enabled their subversion among emerging proto-nationalist subgroups through sweeping sonic and semantic migration. For most of Cagli's and Pompei's patrons, opera was elitist – a mark of social distinction separating 'us' from 'them'. On the other hand, for local populations in Bombay, Singapore, Hong Kong and Batavia, Italian opera was either inaccessible, incomprehensible or, in its American and Hindustani avatars merely quotidian and comic, signifying cosmopolitanism, modern consumption and the possibility of acoustic playfulness and subversion. In brief therefore, this chapter calls for a reappraisal of 'opera', calling into question what the genre meant on the stages of the theatre of Empire. Far from the grand opera houses of Paris and London, 'opera' slid into melodramas and comic interludes, American popular tunes and Urdu *ghazals*, mirroring as much the imperial ambitions of colonial statesmen as of publics being imagined into being.

Musical Networks

Although Indian Ocean steam shipping had commenced as early as approximately 1830, the 1860s witnessed a sea change in maritime communications and transportation with the opening of the Suez Canal and the Red Sea route and the development of submarine telegraphy. In 1830 a letter from England to India took between five to eight months to reach its destination. In the 1850s this time was reduced to thirty to forty-five days.[9] To describe these technological revolutions and their impact on the development of increasingly interconnected colonial economic, political and social networks during this period is to rake over well-worked ground. However, comparatively little attention has been paid to the development of cultural, and more specifically, sonic networks bound together by emerging maritime trade routes.

As American watches, gilt frames for photographs, stereoscopic cameras and eau de cologne reached the homes of affluent Asian communities, European and American music too became a staple of a burgeoning transregional Asiatic sonic landscape. Due to Bombay's critical position as the proverbial 'gateway' to British India and South East Asia in the colonial trade, the city rapidly transformed into a regional hub for musicians who followed the commercial transhipment routes of Empire. The city thus constituted the first port of call for not only *vin crémant* or creaming champagne but also the 'Royal English Opera Bouffe Company'. In 1863 alone, musicians from Australia performed several concerts and 'Ethiopian serenading entertainments', a Miss Emma Grattan performed musical burlettas such as the *Swiss Cottage* with such songs as 'Over the Sea', 'Cigars and Cognac' and 'Shells of the Ocean', and a Herr Wehle and Herr Kletzer played Chopin and Mendelssohn, before moving further east.[10] These performances differed from the concerts that took place at the Town Hall or the homes of wealthy *seths* (Indian merchants) prior to the epoch-making fifties.[11]

---

[9] Daniel R. Headrick, *The Tools of Empire: Technology and European Imperialism in the Nineteenth Century* (Oxford: Oxford University Press, 1981), 130; Roland Wenzelhuemer, *Connecting the Nineteenth-Century World: The Telegraph and Globalization* (Cambridge: Cambridge University Press, 2012).

[10] 'Evenings at Home!', *Bombay Gazette*, December 8, 1863, 1; 'Evenings at Home!', *Bombay Gazette*, December 15, 1863, 1; 'Herr Charles Wehle and Herr Feri Kletzer's Second Concert', *Bombay Gazette*, November 23, 1863, 2; 'Herr Wehle, and Town Hall', *Bombay Gazette*, December 2, 1863, 1; 'Town Hall', *Bombay Gazette*, November 13, 1863, 1; 'Town Hall', *Bombay Gazette*, November 21, 1863, 1; 'Herr Kletzer's Farewell Concert', *Bombay Gazette*, December 10, 1863, 3.

[11] Dosabhai F. Karaka, *History of the Parsis . . .* (London: Macmillan, 1884).

During the early period of Indian social reform, music played no mean part in the agenda of the 'civilising mission' propounded by missionaries, East India Company officials and local reformists.[12] Private amateur concerts, religious hymns in missionary schools, private European tutors and regular performances by garrison bands – the acoustic equivalents of Bacon, Hobbes and Mill – sonically designated a hierarchy of cultural standards with classical music in prime place and developed 'conforming musical bodies' to strengthen systems of social control.

However, with the advancement of naval technology, capital rather than colonial policy began to shape cultural transmission and exchange. Increasingly, amateur performances by and for local British residents, that is, for 'society', gave way to concerts by travelling American and European companies for the 'public', that is, for an exceptionally heterogeneous audience comprised of a wide cross-section of the colonial population. In order to be profitable, troupes were increasingly obliged to cater to a growing indigenous middle class, thereby facilitating a 'form of audience development, aimed ... at entering them into the oldest Western theatrical contract: paying an entry fee in exchange for entertainment'.[13] In so doing, music became part of an entertainment economy predicated on the consumption of 'a market-mediated cultural commodity, an investment in global citizenship'.[14] The purchase of a plethora of products as diverse as Swiss watches, ice cream and minstrel-concert tickets that were linked to forms of cultural capital, allowed audiences in Bombay, Calcutta, Singapore and Hong Kong to express a mode of quotidian cosmopolitanism. Colonial entrepôts therefore became portals through which European and American cultural and, specifically, sonic influence penetrated the non-European world, creating new acoustic interests, lifestyle choices and forms of supraregional identification.

American Minstrels and 'Burlesque Italian Opera'

Of all music forms, opera was deemed to be at the top of the hierarchy – by the turn of the nineteenth century, it had come to be viewed as the hallmark of European national culture. However, in approximately fifty years it had reached Australia, South Africa, the Americas and, not least, South and

---

[12] Marie Korpe, *Shoot the Singer! Music Censorship Today* (London: Zed Books, 2004), vol. 1, 8.
[13] Christopher B. Balme, 'The Bandmann Circuit: Theatrical Networks in the First Age of Globalization', *Theatre Research International*, 40/1 (2015), 19–36 (28).
[14] Nicholson, 'A Christy Minstrel, a Harlequin, or an Ancient Persian', 346.

South East Asia in an astonishingly wide variety of forms, diverging from its European origins. Crucially, Edwin Pearce Christy's Minstrels, frequently referred to simply as the Christy Minstrels, and Dave Carson's San Francisco Minstrels were the first to perform such a variant under the moniker 'Burlesque Italian Opera', in Bombay between 1855 and 1863.[15] American blackface minstrel troupes performing comic opera achieved popularity in South Asia long before their 'authentic' Italian operatic counterparts, and exercised a tight hold on the imagination of Bombay's theatre-going public who had hitherto only read of 'authentic' Italian opera in books and newspapers.[16] The term 'opera' therefore first attained currency in Western India through minstrel companies that enjoyed sell out performances and immense popularity. By the mid-nineteenth century, itinerant American blackface minstrel troupes had become a staple of the transcontinental entertainment circuit by exploiting established tropes and genres such as British burlesque, performing in reputable venues, appropriating the marketing language of legitimate, bourgeois entertainments and most significantly, parodying European music with Italian opera in prime place. Commended in newspaper reviews for their close semblance to operatic originals while often exposing merely a loose link to African-American roots, these companies complicated traditional divisions between the *haut ton* and the *canaille*.[17] Renee Lapp Norris complicates the idea of blackface minstrelsy as a working-class genre by describing how minstrelsy transformed itself into a form of mainstream, global popular culture through opera parodies using show tunes of essentially European origin. Carson, for instance, was adored by colonial officers, the comprador elite and the working classes in Bombay. His knowledge of Hindustani, his farces on the Bombay police, dance girls and the Indian mercantile community and not least his memorable tunes exemplified, in the words of Bradley Shope, 'a cosmopolitanism that had meaning within a complex matrix of historical and cultural reference points that resonated on a global

---

[15] 'The German Minstrels and Madame Klippel', *Bombay Gazette*, 1 April 1862, 1; 'The Original Christy's Minstrels', *Bombay Gazette*, 30 October 1863, 1; 'The Christy Minstrels', *Bombay Gazette*, 4 November 1863, 2; 'The Christy Minstrels', *Bombay Gazette*, 12 November 1863, 2; 'Christy's Minstrels', *Bombay Gazette*, 18 November 1863, 2; 'The Christy Minstrels', *Bombay Gazette*, 23 November 1863, 2; 'The Original Christy's Minstrels', *Bombay Gazette*, November 27 1863, 1; 'The Christy's Minstrels', *Bombay Gazette*, 27 November 1863, 3; 'Theatre Royal, – Grant Road', *Bombay Gazette*, 9 October 1863, 1; and 'The San Francisco Minstrels', *Bombay Gazette*, 10 October 1863, 2.

[16] Bradley Shope, *American Popular Music in Britain's Raj* (Rochester, NY: University of Rochester Press, 2016), 35.

[17] Renee Lapp Norris, 'Opera and the Mainstreaming of Blackface Minstrelsy', *Journal of the Society for American Music*, 1/3 (2007), 341–65 (343).

scale' even as it powerfully propagated existing racial hierarchies and prejudices.[18] The repertoire of blackface minstrel companies such as Carson's therefore functioned in Bombay as an imaginary gateway to a global, consumerist entertainment culture thriving in the global metropoles of New York, London and Paris. Simultaneously, however, it drew on established colonial taxonomies of communal identity, social hierarchy and race, thereby reinforcing European and non-European material, historical, ethnic and cultural distinctions.

Increasingly, minstrels began to perform comic opera not only in public spaces for audiences of all classes, but also at intimate private gatherings, thereby fashioning themselves as respectable entertainment suitable for the local elite.[19] Therefore, although the cosmopolitan aesthetic of Carson's San Francisco Minstrels progressively appealed to a new demography of spectators who had never visited the theatre, the company was also increasingly hired by wealthy Parsi merchants to perform in their homes in lieu of the nautch, as they were considered honourable amusement.[20] In a similar vein, the Christy Minstrels, described by the local press as a 'musical treat [...which has] not been hitherto obtainable in Bombay',[21] were engaged by the Parsi opium magnate Sorabjee Jamsetjee Jeejeebhoy to give a concert for his close friends and the Parsi pupils and teachers of the Sir Jamsetjee Parsee Benevolent Institution and the Elphinstone School. 'The Minstrels', according to the press, 'did full justice to the programme, which contained a good number of selections [which were performed] to the great admiration and amusement of the juvenile audience, who at the conclusion of each piece testified their approbation with loud cheers'.[22] Newspapers increasingly posited minstrel musical pieces such as Carson's 'Parsee Girl of the Period' and 'Bengalee Babu' as morally righteous entertainment suitable for university students; as innocent entertainment safe for children and women and as harbingers of civilisation and progress, thereby positing minstrelsy as another tool in the cog of imperial power. By defining themselves as instruments of moral advancement, reinforcing sociopolitical and racial distinctions that validated colonialism's 'universal' frames of reference, occupying the

---

[18] Shope, *American Popular Music*, 4.
[19] 'Mr Sorabjee Jamsetjee Jeejeebhoy', *Bombay Gazette*, 30 November 1863, 2.
[20] "Oratnu gāeṇ-Rāṇḍonā nāc.", *Rāst Goftār*, 25 October 1863, 540–1. See Shope, *American Popular Music*, 39.
[21] 'The Original Christy's Minstrels', *Bombay Gazette*, 30 October 1863, 2.
[22] *Bombay Gazette*, 30 November 1863, 2.

bourgeois space of the playhouse and using the same production techniques and terms of reference as Italian opera, American minstrel companies rendered 'opera' a slippery, cross-referential, playful, aprescriptive yet ultimately hegemonic designation.

Augusto Cagli: Opera in the Subcontinent

The growing ambivalence of the signifier 'opera' beyond Europe was substantially compounded by the increasingly transregional peripatetic journeys of Italian companies themselves. Katherine Preston notes how the financial footings of opera in America were profoundly dissimilar to those in Europe, as opera production was not sustained in the United States by administrative, municipal or aristocratic subventions.[23] In contrast with the capitals of Europe, where a stable of artists were sustained through subsidies and where travelling opera companies were increasingly a relic of the past, opera companies touring the Americas and South and South East Asia were itinerant and therefore heavily dependent on box-office earnings and mass appeal. Opera, as Preston remarks, 'had to earn its keep'.[24] Accordingly, commercial viability dictated production decisions – where to perform, which cities were cost-effective in terms of transportation, what and where to advertise and what, above all, should be performed in order to attract the largest section of the public. Opera troupes thus increasingly resembled their burlesque counterparts, operating under comparable economic constraints, working under the management of similar impresarios and attempting to attract the same heterogenous audiences of mixed social standing in order to keep afloat.

Shortly after Carson's performances, in 1864 the Italian soprano Gemma Onorati was invited to perform concerts in Bombay by several British residents.[25] Her husband Augusto Cagli soon realised that Bombay and, by extension, South and South East Asia, were untapped markets for Italian opera. An opera committee comprising the merchant philanthropists Jagannath Shankarsheth and Jamsetjee Jeejeebhoy was established, and in November 1864, Cagli's company performed *Il trovatore*, previously performed by the Christy Minstrels, at the Grant Road Theatre. The opera was

---

[23] Katherine K. Preston, 'To the Opera House? The Trials and Tribulations of Operatic Production in Nineteenth-Century America', *The Opera Quarterly*, 23/1 (2007), 39–65, 41.
[24] Ibid.   [25] *The Times of India*, 19 March 1864, 3.

repeated several times over the course of the next two months along with *Lucrezia Borgia*, *Linda di Chamounix*, *Norma* and *Lucia di Lammermoor*.[26] The Italian company also threw in renditions of 'God Save the Queen' and a polka dedicated to Jeejeebhoy in a manner reminiscent of the burlesque opera troupe that had performed at the same venue a few months prior.[27] Consequently Cagli, following the model of American minstrel productions, attempted to produce a species of 'variety show' consisting of short excerpts of operas and popular musical interludes, in order to better cater to Bombay's mixed audience.

However, while Carson's musical performances needed little explanation in the local vernacular press, as they were performed in English and enjoyed mass cross-cultural appeal due to their use of parody and pastiche, Cagli's Italian opera had to be translated, or rendered comprehensible for the local middle classes through reformist newspapers such as the *Rāst Goftār*.[28] In an article entitled 'Operā' published on 26 February 1865, the *Rāst* described the necessity of 'utam rītnī sudhrelī gamat' ('high class, reformed entertainment') for Bombay, which was ostensibly beginning to compete with London in industrial and cultural affairs. *Gamat* (amusement) must be accompanied by *sīkhāmaṇ* (learning), the anonymous journalist said. Opera, according to the *Rāst*, was a 'gāeṇ rūpī nāṭak' (musical form of theatre) characterised by songs instead of dialogue, and as 'the best of the best European music' it constituted a cultural stamp of morality and virtue.[29] Consequently, although both Carson's burlesque opera and Cagli's Italian opera functioned as tools of colonial civilisation and progress, the Italian opera, unlike minstrel burlesque opera, had an elitist, palpably didactic function for a growing class of local reformists and British civil servants akin to the religious hymns of missionary schools and marching band tunes on the Esplanade. Cagli's company's dependence on season subscriptions managed by British residents and affluent local merchants, rather than merely ticket sales, indicates whom the Italian opera catered for and what purpose it implicitly served. As a result, even though the troupe attempted to expand its spectatorial base through an eclectic repertoire, Italian opera – like Shakespeare, ballroom dancing and forks and knives – was perceived

---

[26] Charles Pitt, 'Opera's Indian SpringI', *Opera*, 52/7 (2001), 808–14 (810–11). [27] Ibid.
[28] The *Rāst Goftār* was established in 1853 for the moral advancement of Bombay's Parsi- and Gujarati-speaking population.
[29] 'Operā', *Rāst Goftār tathā Satya Prakāś*, 26 February 1865, 131–2.

as alien and indubitably didactic and therefore was not, according to the *Rāst*, to the tastes of the growing local theatre-going public. At the end of their three-month Bombay season, Cagli's company had, nevertheless, made a notable impression on Bombay's British residents and on the city's increasingly class-conscious aristocratic-merchant population (some of whom, for instance, had begun taking music lessons from the troupe's first violinist).[30]

The troupe subsequently left for Poona and Calcutta in April 1865. As Calcutta had a larger population of British residents, the city 'enjoyed a notable advantage over Bombay' in securing successful seasons of Cagli's opera.[31] Bombay's small population of British and local elites who had begun competing with Calcutta for edifying European amusement were nevertheless loath to throw in the towel in terms of their efforts to secure an Indian base for an Italian operatic empire. Consequently, a Bombay committee was formed that created a subscription list and secured deposits in order to engage an opera company from Italy with Cagli's assistance. After several months of suspense and many misgivings in the local press as to whether the endeavour would come to fruition, on 10 November *The Times of India* announced that the forty-member company had left Italy and was due to perform *Faust* on the opening night, with Amalia Jackson as prima donna and Signor Reina as first baritone (see Figure 11.1).[32] Once again, the troupe was both sponsored and commended by the city's wealthy British residents. However, the *Rāst* was quick to declare its failure among the broader section of the theatre-going public. Despite introducing gas lighting at the Grant Road Theatre, the first in the Presidency, Bombay's local population was weary of the Italian 'novelty' characterised by an unusual trilling that was, unlike Dave Carson's repertoire, not suited to local tastes. As an anonymous critic of Cagli's Italian performances noted:

How long it will continue attractive to the Natives as a novelty, is of course a question. Novelties cannot continue to be so for ever, and to go to a crowded musical entertainment, unable to understand a word of what you hear, may please the ear, but it cannot give full satisfaction to the mind, at least to those who do not understand music. An Englishman who is a musician, though he may not understand Italian, will so enjoy the music of an Italian Opera, that the words are of little importance, and will not

---

[30] *The Times of India*, 20 December 1865, 2.   [31] *The Times of India*, 7 May 1874, 2.
[32] *The Times of India*, 14 October 1865, 2; *The Times of India*, 16 December 1865, 2; *The Times of India*, 10 November 1865, 2.

Figure 11.1 Portrait of Augusto Cagli c. 1864, Hibling & Fields, Accession Number (H29438), courtesy: Picture Collection, State Library Victoria

materially add to his enjoyment or pleasure. On the other hand, an Englishman who is not a musician nor an Italian scholar, but who is fond of music, is likely to prefer an English Opera, where he can understand the language and the sentiment as well as appreciate the music. It seems but reasonable that a Parsee understanding English would in like manner appreciate an English Opera, more than he would an Italian one, and all Natives would probably appreciate an Opera in the vernacular most of any. An Englishman may just as well go to an Hindustani Opera (if there were such a thing) as to an Italian Opera, if he is acquainted with neither of these languages ... What a *novelty* a Hindoostanee Opera would be. Here is an opportunity for 'Young Bombay' in the musical and theatrical line.[33]

Poignantly, a 'Hindoostanee Opera' was not long in coming.

[33] 'Norman', 'Out-Door Amusements: To the Editor of "The Times of India"', *The Times of India*, 15 November 1865, 2.

Giovanni Pompei: Opera in East and South East Asia

Cagli's difficulties in Bombay were significantly compounded by a crop of new Italian impresarios who increasingly encroached on his turf. While Cagli's company performed at the Grant Road Theatre, a new Italian impresario, Giovanni Pompei, conducted the local brass band at the Roman Catholic Cathedral at Kalbadevi for the benefit of an orphanage on Nesbit Road, and subsequently held a concert of several amateurs at the Town Hall. Pompei first began his Asian musical career by giving allegedly mediocre concerts comprising of airs from *Il barbiere* and *Cenerentola* for the European residents of Singapore, China and Java (Sorabaya, Pasoeroean, Probolingo and Samarang). Subsequently, he tried to set up an opera troupe in Batavia in 1862.[34] At this early stage, Pompei was already expressing a desire to bring out an Italian company of 20, due to the great demand for opera in a town of 6,000, largely wealthy, European residents.[35] However, 'Een Liefhebber' ('An Enthusiast') swiftly lambasted Pompei's proposal as too expensive and risky in light of the mediocrity of his concerts and relative anonymity.[36] Stung by the controversy, Pompei swiftly left Batavia and turned up in Bombay three years later. Pompei, following the growing network of South and South East Asian commercial shipping routes, had begun to tour and was therefore the first to take advantage of a rapidly developing Asian transportation network. In many respects, his early travels foreshadowed the development in the late nineteenth century of an established transregional entertainment circuit; this was made possible by an intricate web of shipping and railway lines, cheap transportation and the archipelagic character of South East Asia, all of which rendered short visits to port cities such as Singapore, Batavia, Surabaya and Manila cost-effective and easily manageable. As Nadi Tofighian notes, British Malaya and the Dutch East Indies were widely toured by entertainment companies due to

---

[34] 'Nederlandsch-Indie. Batavia', *Java-bode: nieuws, handels- en advertentieblad voor Nederlandsch-Indie*, 5 April 1862, 3; 'Nederlandsch-Indie. Batavia', *Java-bode: nieuws, handels-en advertentieblad voor Nederlandsch-Indie*, 26 March 26 1862, 3; 'Batavia', *Bataviaasch handelsblad*, 3 March 1862, 3; 'Advertentie', *Java-bode: nieuws, handels- en advertentieblad voor Nederlandsch-Indie*, 2 April 1862, 2.
[35] 'De Opéra te Batavia', *Bataviaasch handelsblad*, 30 April 1862, 35.
[36] Een Liefhebber, 'Ingezonden Stukken', *Java-bode: nieuws, handels- en advertentieblad voor Nederlandsch-Indie*, 3 May 1862, 4.

short distances between cities, their well-developed infrastructure, and a key location at the crossroads of India, China, Japan and Australia.[37]

Although during his first months in Bombay Pompei directed glees sung by local amateur groups, such as the Byculla Boys, and charged moderate prices of admission, he rapidly began to seriously challenge Cagli's monopoly of the burgeoning Asian operatic circuit.[38] On 8 January 1867, Pompei absconded from Bombay on the China Mail with Cagli's star singer Madame Bouché (originally from La Scala) and Signor Reina in tow. Due to Pompei's hasty flight, two dancers, five ballet girls and several men were abandoned in Bombay without the means to cover their living expenses or return home to Ancona.[39] A few months later in April 1867, the *Hong Kong Daily Press* began to provide coverage of Madame Bouché, Madame Veralli, Signor Reina and Signor Piccioli's performances in *Il trovatore*, an opera which, though 'commonplace and hackneyed' in England, was an absolute novelty in China.[40] The impresario thus not only brought Italian opera to the then-sleepy backwater of the Pearl of the Orient, but also predated the veritable flood of European and American artists in colonial port cities. At this early stage, Hong Kong was a place where the 'monotony of life [was] varied with the malady alternating with boils or dysentery'.[41] Consequently, despite the lack of a chorus, the omission of several arias and the insufficient number of artists, Pompei's company enjoyed 'great success before the most crowded house which [had] yet to be seen' in Hong Kong.[42] Thereafter, the company's performance of *Il barbiere di Siviglia* was given 'with as much success as attended either of the previous representations'. The newspaper showered praises on Signor Reina's 'admirable acting' and Madame Veralli's 'finished singing and sweet, rich voice' and appearance, all of which elicited 'furious applause' – largely because such entertainments were unknown to the British residents of the region.[43] It also compared the performers to the stars of London and Paris, noting that, by doing so, it was 'placing them on a level with the artists to be

---

[37] Nadi Tofighian, 'Mapping 'the Whirligig of Amusements' in Colonial Southeast Asia', *Journal of Southeast Asian Studies*, 49/2 (2018), 277–96 (284).

[38] *The Times of India*, 18 November 1865, 2; *The Times of India*, 13 December 1865, 2; *The Times of India*, 19 December 1865, 2.

[39] 'Hundred Years Ago: From the Times of India April 23, 1867', *The Times of India*, 23 April 1967, 7; Pitt, 'Opera's Indian SpringI', 812.

[40] 'THE ITALIAN OPERA', *Hong Kong Daily Press*, 5 April 1867, 2; 'The Italian Opera', *Hong Kong Daily Press*, 8 April 1867, 2.

[41] Laurence Oliphant, *Narrative of the Earl of Elgin's Mission to China and Japan, in the Years 1857, '58, '59* (New York: Harper & Brothers, 1860), 57.

[42] 'The Italian Opera', *Hong Kong Daily Press*, 6 April 1867, 2.

[43] 'The Italian Opera', *Hong Kong Daily Press*, 4 April 1867, 2.

heard in European capitals, and judging them by an appeal to that standard'.[44] Subsequently, after a performance of *Don Pasquale* the newspaper went a step further, proclaiming that 'it would have been difficult for any operatic company in Europe to have furnished better representatives for Don Pasquale and Norina'.[45]

The company had therefore taken Hong Kong by storm, and proceeded to Manila with high hopes and full pockets. Manila, unlike Hong Kong and Singapore, had a relatively long acquaintance with European music. Pompei's company, presumably finding a secure base of European patrons, spent several months there before returning to Hong Kong in March 1868. Now 'old Hong Kong favourite[s]', they performed *Lucia di Lammermoor* at the Lusitano Theatre. Thereafter they set off for Singapore, a strategically located and rapidly growing port that controlled trade routes to the East Indies, China and Japan.[46] On reaching Singapore in May 1869 under the new name 'The Royal Batavia Opera Company', they began performances of *La traviata*, *Lucrezia Borgia* and *Norma* with a new cast from Italy and Calcutta.[47] As 'the visit of an operatic company in Singapore [was] so rare', *The Straits Times* noted its citizens were 'quite prepared to be satisfied with the best efforts of any fairly qualified Company in the East'.[48] It was therefore, the 'novelty' of Italian opera along with its symbolic capital that contributed in no mean measure to Pompei's unbroken string of successes without subscription seasons. As in Hong Kong, after its first performances the company was described as 'fully equal to most of the provincial Opera Companies in Europe'. Singapore's British residents, acutely aware of the emblematic value of opera, wholeheartedly embraced the Italian troupe, sending them off Singapore's 'stage with the applause that they so well deserve[d]'.[49] However, Singapore for Pompei was merely a stepping stone to the more lucrative market of the Dutch Indies.

As early as October 1868, the *Bataviaasch Handelsblad* carried advertisements from the Board of the Bataviasche Schouwburg (Batavia

---

[44] 'The Italian Opera', *Hong Kong Daily Press*, 10 April 1867, 2.
[45] 'The Italian Opera', *Hong Kong Daily Press*, 13 April 1867, 2.
[46] 'The Italian Opera', *Hong Kong Daily Press*, 14 March 1868, 2.
[47] 'Koncert- en Opera-nieuws', *Java-bode: nieuws, handels- en advertentieblad voor Nederlandsch-Indie*, 10 March 1869, 5; 'Afloop der Uitbesteding door het Departement van Burgerlijk Openbare Werken van Vijf Bruggen op 13 February 1869', *De locomotief: Samarangsch handels- en advertentie-blad*, 22 February 1869, 1; 'Bataviasche Schouburg', *Java-bode: nieuws, handels- en advertentieblad voor Nederlandsch-Indie*, 27 March 1869, 3.
[48] 'THE ROYAL BATAVIA OPERA COMPANY', *The Straits Times*, 8 May 1869, 2.
[49] 'The Royal Batavia Opera Company', *The Straits Times*, 15 May 1869, 1; 'The Royal Batavia Opera Company', *Straits Times Overland Journal*, 20 May 1869, 3.

Theatre) announcing subscriptions to raise 4,000 gulden for the passage and payment of the Italian company of twenty-two.[50] On arriving in Batavia from Singapore, the troupe presented *Lucrezia Borgia*, *Trovatore* and *Rigoletto* on 7, 11 and 14 June respectively to great acclaim.[51] On 14 and 16 June, the company performed concerts comprising of arias and even dances, reflecting the mixed character of Pompei's operatic repertoire.[52] Pompei spent many fruitful months in Batavia; the number of performances, new rounds of monthly subscriptions and increasingly positive reviews indicate that his company was loved by Batavia's and eventually Samarang's publics.[53] However, as in Calcutta, it was the seasonal subscriptions organised by the cities' Dutch residents that enabled Pompei to sustain his large troupe.

Having tasted success in the Dutch Indies, an emboldened Pompei returned to India by way of Singapore and Manila in 1871 and subsequently set up a partnership with his erstwhile nemesis Cagli.[54] The impresarios had unquestionably realised that Italian opera was more likely to make a headway in the region through their combined efforts, and they thus buried their previous rivalry under the hatchet. The Cagli–Pompei syndicate under the management of William Saurin Lyster, comprising five prima donnas, three first tenors, two baritones, three basses, numerous choir members, ballet dancers, and orchestra players capable of performing forty-four different operas, then embarked for Melbourne. Simultaneously, Cagli and Pompei set up a second company for Calcutta's 1871–2 season that was managed from afar.[55] After disembarking in Melbourne on 16 February 1872, the new company, with its star singers Margherita Zenoni and Leandro Coy, proved a great success.[56] Its performances at the Princess Theatre were described as 'uncomfortably crowded' (see Figure 11.2).[57]

---

[50] Hoogeven, 'Voorstellingen', *Bataviaasch handelsblad*, 31 October 1868, 3; 'ITALIAANSCHE OPERA', *Bataviaasch handelsblad*, 21 October 1868, 4; 'Eene Italiaansche Opera te Batavia', *Java-bode: nieuws, handels- en advertentieblad voor Nederlandsch-Indie*, 28 November 1868, 5.

[51] 'Italiaansche Opera', *Java-bode: nieuws, handels- en advertentieblad voor Nederlandsch-Indie*, 2 June 1869, 2; 'DE OPERA', *Java-bode: nieuws, handels- en advertentieblad voor Nederlandsch-Indie*, 9 June 1869, 4.

[52] 'Théâtre de Batavia', *Bataviaasch handelsblad*, 12 June 1869, 3.

[53] 'Théâtre de Batavia', *Bataviaasch handelsblad*, 7 July 1869, 3; 'Opera', *Java-bode: nieuws, handels- en advertentieblad voor Nederlandsch-Indie*, 7 July 1869, 5.

[54] 'News of the Week', *The Straits Times*, 23 April 1870, 2; 'News of the Week: TUESDAY, 19th APRIL', *The Straits Times*, April 23, 1870, 3.

[55] 'Opera', *Java-bode: nieuws, handels- en advertentieblad voor Nederlandsch-Indie*, 6 March 1871, 5.

[56] 'Shipping Intelligence', *The Argus*, 17 February 1872, 4.

[57] 'The Opera', *The Age*, 9 August 1872, 3.

Figure 11.2 The Italian Opera Company, 1871, Hibling & Fields, Accession Number (H96.160/1642, H96.160/1643), courtesy: Picture Collection, State Library Victoria

Parsi Opera

However, India – the first port of call for European and American musicians – was a different story, which indicated that change was on the horizon. Faced with the non-appearance of the star singers and a distinctly inferior company, Bombay's and Calcutta's audiences frowned upon Cagli's and Pompei's new season.[58] 'Night after night' the singers appeared 'before half empty houses'. 'The public', an anonymous writer declaimed, 'are not drawn to the Opera House, and if the public will not pay the expenses, there will probably be an inconveniently heavy bill at the close of the season for the committee to settle as they best can'.[59] As these criticisms indicate, subscriptions were no longer able to secure the company's success. The novelty of Italian opera had completely worn. Instead, Calcutta and Bombay paid tribute to 'Dave Carson's "gooks"',[60] the French opera of Monsieur and Madame Berger DePlace and Alice May, the Anglo-Italian opera of Mademoiselle Thalberg and more significantly, a then little-known genre called Parsi or 'Hindoostanee' opera.

---

[58] See Esmeralda Monique Antonia Rocha, 'Imperial Opera: The Nexus between Opera and Imperialism in Victorian Calcutta and Melbourne, 1833–1901', PhD thesis, University of Western Australia (2012), 115, for a description of the reception of Cagli's performances in Calcutta.

[59] *The Times of India*, 24 January 1872, 4.   [60] Editorial, *The Englishman*, 31 October 1872, 2.

The Parsi theatre, established in 1853 by a group of reformists for the moral benefit of the Parsi community, grew in two decades into South and South East Asia's largest and most influential theatrical phenomenon. In the first two decades of its existence, the theatre's adaptations of the *Shahnama*, and subsequently Shakespeare, increasingly incorporated music during the *entr'actes*. Taking inspiration from European troupes, these interludes were included to divert audience attention during scene changes. However, shortly after Cagli's and Pompei's performances in Bombay, on 5 November 1870, Bombay's first full-length 'opera', *Rūstam tathā Śohrāb*, was performed at the Grant Road Theatre.[61] Impressed by 'Italian opera troupes', the Parsi journalist Nasarvānjī Āpakhatyār produced this first Parsi performance, set to European and local melodies and played by an 'efficient [European] band'.[62] Intriguingly however, the opera consisted of several Gujarati songs and burlesques comprised of 'an Ethiopian ballet'. Evidently Āpakhatyār, despite professing to be inspired by the Italian model, had in actuality developed this first Parsi opera in the image of the problematic blackface minstrel musical productions that enjoyed popularity across class, caste, ethnic and religious groups in Bombay during the 1860s. As one 'PMM' in the *Bombay Gazette* disparagingly remarked, 'here were these fellows with, as we afterwards found, Mr Apakhtyar between them, dressed once for all to represent a Christy minstrel, a harlequin, or an ancient Persian as occasion may require, with no voices to speak of, singing away the most indifferent songs'.[63] The peculiar taxonomy – Christy minstrel/ harlequin/ancient Persian – indicates the ghosting of blackface minstrelsy in what would become a pan-Asian popular theatrical phenomenon. Melodrama, comic-opera tunes, harlequinade, *ghazals* and blackface itself would become staples of the repertoire of 'Hindustani opera' that began to circulate across the subcontinent in 1873. Increasingly, troupes such as the Victoria, Elphinstone and Alfred Theatrical Companies from Bombay performing 'Hindustani' or 'Parsi operas' competed with the Italians and Americans for the same venues and audiences. However, while the Italians were reliant on subscriptions and catered to British residents and the indigenous elite and reformist classes, Parsi troupes, following the lead of the American minstrel

---

[61] *Rāst Goftār tathā Satya Prakāś*, 23 October 1870, 701; *Rāst Goftār tathā Satya Prakāś*, 30 October 1870, 717; *Rāst Goftār tathā Satya Prakāś*, 6 November 1870, 733.
[62] Dhanjībhāi N. Paṭel, *Pārsī Nāṭak Takhtānī Tavārīkh* (Bombay: 'Kaysare-Hind' Paper Printing Press, 1931), 59; 'Parsee Opera, Concert, &c', *Bombay Gazette*, 3 December 1870, 2.
[63] PMM, 'The Parsee "Opera"', *Bombay Gazette*, 16 December 1870, 3.

companies, made opera droll, accessible and quotidian, and relied primarily on ticket sales, that is, public patronage.

As the anonymous critic of Cagli's opera had foretold, 'all Natives would probably appreciate an Opera in the vernacular most of any'.[64] Parsi companies enjoyed the best of both worlds: the symbolic capital of the term 'opera' that signified cosmopolitanism and mediated access to the finest of European culture, and a form of reportorial playfulness unconstrained by the limits of cultural authenticity and accuracy. By 1875 therefore, the denomination 'opera' in South Asia had become charged with several disparate connotations: the refined, sterilised culture of the subcontinent's British residents, the popular tunes of the Americans that appealed to both British and local communities and finally the Parsi or Hindustani form that functioned as a mode of sonic escapism for the urban middle and working classes. The success of the Parsis was considerably aided by the industrialisation of Asian entrepôts and the rapid influx of impoverished immigrant populations from the hinterland. These changes in demography had a significant impact on the sonic landscape of these colonial outposts as penniless workers began to throng the theatre after the drudgery of the working day. Parsi operas such as *Benajhīr ane Badremunīrno Opera*, which consisted of '80–100 songs', toured Bombay, Bhavnagar, Poona and beyond, dictating the repertoires of theatres, monopolising venues, establishing new forms of theatrical management, cultivating the musical tastes of the public and making commercial viability an imperative in an increasingly cut-throat transregional entertainment market.

During this time, Cagli left Australia for South Africa and became, in 1875, the first manager to bring Italian opera to Cape Town. However, by the time he returned to the East in 1878, Bombay, Calcutta, Singapore and Hong Kong were overcrowded with English, French, American and not least Indian competitors. American minstrel, *opera buffa* and Parsi theatre troupes had taken over the musical touring route in South and South East Asia that had been used by Pompei two decades prior. By 1875, Dave Carson's Minstrels, who had hitherto been a mainstay of India's colonial cultural landscape, played their repertoire of 'beautiful songs ... and charming French ballads' with '*la prima donna d'Afrique* J. C. Talbot' at the Theatre Royal, Town Hall, Singapore. The company's first performance before 'a very large audience' was described by *The Straits Times* as 'enough to make a Diogenes almost split his sides with laughing'.[65] Subsequently,

---

[64] Norman, 'Out-Door Amusements', 2.
[65] 'Monday, 2nd August', *The Strait Times,* 7 August 1875, 5.

performances of 'a grand burlesque operatic scena', the humorous sketch of 'an operatic rehearsal' and the 'comic opera, entitled "Forty Winks"' acquainted Singaporean audiences for the first time with burlesque opera.[66] Thereafter, Carson's minstrels left for British India, and subsequently Batavia, Shanghai and Hong Kong.[67] The company was replaced by Alice May, who had brought her thirty-six-member Royal English Opera and Opera Bouffe Company from Bombay and Calcutta to Singapore on her way to Hong Kong and Shanghai.[68] In Hong Kong, 'Elicia' May's company was preceded by an ensemble performing Offenbach's *Le Violoneux* at the Theatre Royal.[69] May visited Hong Kong several times with her troupe, which produced Charles Lecocq's *La Fille de Madame Angot*, Jacques Offenbach's *The Grand-Duchess of Gerolstein* and Michael Balfe's *Satanella or the Power of Love*.[70] Thereafter, in 1881, the Parsi Victoria Theatrical Company arrived in Singapore and was immediately a wild success there. News rapidly spread of the Parsi repertoire of flying demons set to American popular tunes and Hindustani *ghazals*, and the company was soon invited to perform for King Thibaw Min in Burma (see Figure 11.3).

Subsequently the Parsis followed the itinerary of the Italians, stopping multiple times in Batavia, Hong Kong and Singapore before returning to India in 1885. They were followed by other companies such as the Elphinstone Club, which performed *Indar Sabha*, *Shirin Farhadno Gayanrupi Opera*, *Goolay Bakavali*, *Saṅgīt Rustam-Sohrab* and *Janealam and Anjoomanara* at Jalan Besar in Singapore. These productions, described in advertisements, posters and newspaper articles as 'native operas', 'fairy operas' or 'talismanic operas', indicate how the term 'opera' came to designate a fluid repertoire of Hindustani musical performances. Like American minstrel companies, Parsi theatre troupes touring East and South East Asia used the word 'opera' to denote musical plays that comprised references to local politics and topical issues, European and Indian melodies, Indo-Persian tales and musical genres and even the use of white- and blackface through the use of face paint and *habsī* or 'Ethiopian characters'. In this regard, Parsi

---

[66] Advertisement of Dave Carson's Minstrels at Theatre Royal, Town Hall, Singapore, *Straits Observer*, 13 August 1875, 2; a reminder of Dave Carson's programme on the same night with brief review, *The Straits Times*, 3 August 1878, 4.

[67] 'Passengers', *Straits Time Overland Journal*, 24 February 1876, 1.

[68] 'Monday, 1st November', *The Straits Times*, 6 November 1875, 4; 'Miss Elicia May's Opera Company at the Theatre Royal', *Hong Kong Daily Press*, 31 July 1876, 2.

[69] 'The French Opera Comique Troupe', *Hong Kong Daily Press*, 21 February 1876, 2.

[70] 'Local and General', *The China Mail*, 3 September 1878, 2; 'Local and General', *The China Mail*, 23 August 1878, 3.

Figure 11.3 Bālīvālā, a famous singer-actor, and his Victoria Theatrical Company, which extensively toured South and South East Asia at the turn of the century. *Baliwalla, the Parsee Actor, Known as the Irving of India, and Part of His Troupe, Bombay, India, 1902.* Photograph. www.loc.gov/item/2020681371/

companies both reinforced as well as subverted the racialised logic of American minstrel repertoire, tapping into audiences' desires for cosmopolitan citizenship by replicating and lampooning existing forms of cultural consumerism. Parsi troupes, not reliant on aristocratic patronage, subscriptions and subventions, not only served to visually and acoustically connect the British Empire's disparate linguistic and territorial constituencies, but also provided a sonic experience of the 'modern' through the signifier 'opera'.[71] 'Opera' connoted European high civilisation even if Parsi spectacles of flying demons and twirling fairies, and malapropism and topical parody signified a distortion of the signification of the expression, verging more often than not on caricature. As a jumble of French *opéra bouffe*, *opéra comique* and English burlesque opera, the Parsi opera that took over the South and East Asian market rendered traditional differences between the classical and popular confused beyond measure. Consequently, 'opera' came to possess a high degree of ambiguity for South and South East Asia's many publics, who lapped up these new forms of opera even as Italian opera troupes struggled to find venues and attract audiences. For instance, in the 1876–7 season in Bombay, *opera bouffe* through May's *La Sonnambula*, *La Fille de Madame Angot* and *The Grand-Duchess of Gerolstein* and Madame Carlotta Tasca's *Satanella* and *Genevieve de Brabant* played to full houses while the new Italian company of Signor Giacinto Inzoli was placed in 'an

---

[71] Nicholson, 'A Christy Minstrel, a Harlequin, or an Ancient Persian?'

awkward and humiliating position', performing 'before empty benches' and thereby incurring 'heavy liabilities'.[72]

Cagli, now a French Chevalier d'Honneur, therefore returned to an overhauled and saturated musical landscape in Asia in 1878. His performances of *La Sonnambula, Don Pasquale, Un Ballo in Maschera* and *Il Trovatore* under the patronage of the Governor, though commended by the local press, were performed to a 'moderately filled house'.[73] In January 1879, Cagli's company, now down from eighteen to ten including Giovanni Guarnieri as Maestro Direttore, Rosa Genolini and Tamburini Coy as Prime Donne Assolute and Leandro Coy as Primo Tenore Assoluto, left for Allahabad and Calcutta and subsequently moved onto Batavia[74] and Singapore.[75] In Singapore, although *The Straits Times* praised the artists, the newspaper declaimed, 'in any other part of the world all the leading members of society would have taken a pleasure in supporting such a troupe by taking tickets for all the nights that the performances were advertised for, but, in Singapore, alas! the elite appear to have buttoned their pockets with a vengeance'.[76] Singapore's audiences, now exposed to a mindboggling variety of opera, had wearied of the Italians. The company moved on to Shanghai, making the 'first complete attempt to represent Italian opera' there, and then Saigon, where the government offered Cagli 'a large subsidy'.[77] A year later the troupe returned to Shanghai, where an anonymous reviewer cuttingly noted that their production of *Lucrezia Borgia* was given 'to the smallest audience that has been seen at the Lyceum for many a long day, there being only one box occupied, not a soul in the balcony, and only about fifty people in the pit', resulting in 'a total failure from a financial point of view'.[78] 'Signor Cagli may well despair for the

---

[72] 'Miss Alicia May's Opera Company', *The Times of India*, 2 February 1876, 2; *The Times of India*, 26 February 1877, 1; *The Times of India*, 29 January 1874, 1; G. Inzoli, 'The Italian Opera Troupe: To the Editor of the Times of India''', *The Times of India*, 22 January 1874, 3.

[73] 'The Italian Opera Troupe: To the Editor of the Times of India', *The Times of India)*, 30 April 1878, 3.

[74] 'The Italian Opera Company', *The Times of India*, 6 January 1879, 3; 'Théâtre de Batavia', *Bataviaasch handelsblad*, 3 May 1879, 2; 'Théâtre de Batavia', *Java-bode: nieuws, handels- en advertentieblad voor Nederlandsch-Indie*, 7 February 1879, 2; 'Théâtre de Batavia', *Java-bode: nieuws, handels- en advertentieblad voor Nederlandsch-Indie*, 7 April 1879, 2.

[75] 'Passengers', *Straits Times Overland Journal*, 8 November 1879, 1; 'Monday, 9th August', *The Straits Times*, 14 August 1880, 5; 'Thursday, 5th August', *The Straits Times*, 7 August 1880, 6.

[76] 'Wednesday, 4th August', *The Straits Times*, 7 August 1880, 6.

[77] 'Editorial Selections: The Municipality and the Theatre', *The North-China Herald and Supreme Court & Consular Gazette*, 13 January 1881, 26 and 'Clippings', *The North-China Herald and Supreme Court & Consular Gazette*, 24 August 1880, 200.

[78] 'Amusements: Italian Opera Company "La Sonnambula" "La Favorita" "Crispino e la Comare" "Lucrezia Borgia"', *The North-China Herald and Supreme Court & Consular Gazette (1870–1941)*, 27 January 1881, 72.

success of his second series of operatic representations', another writer argued, 'when an absolute novelty in Shanghai, like Monday's performance, fails to draw even a moderately filled house'.[79] Crucially, a critic while reviewing Cagli's performances highlighted how

> the Chinese regular drama is all opera. … The almost exclusive employment of the falsetto is somewhat wearying to Western ears, and the scenery and stage management leave much to be desired to our ideas; but it is opera nevertheless and we think the native theatres would be treated with more respect by foreigners if this fact were generally recognised.[80]

As with Parsi opera, the symbolic value of the Italians would propel discursive shifts in local performance forms – for instance, from *huju* to 'Shanghai opera' – in order for these to 'be treated with more respect'. These terminological changes indicate the long-term influence that the Italians effected on a grammar of performative concepts and their narratological functions within a regulated hierarchy of symbolic cultural value.

After their stay in Shanghai, the company journeyed to Hong Kong, where Cagli attempted to unsuccessfully drum up support to form a bigger company through the Italian consul Chevalier Musso.[81] Eventually, it made its way to Australia through Batavia and stayed there until the company broke up in 1883.[82] Although Cagli attempted to continue his operatic ventures in Batavia, in 1887 he was compelled to flee the city after a particularly poorly received concert, and in 1888 the *Java-bode* published news of his death in Manila and the takeover of his company by Signor Balzofiore.[83] While Balzofiore's successful performances in Batavia and Surabaya served to perpetuate Cagli's operatic legacy, in Singapore *The Straits Times* noted that troupes from Italy had ceased their visits, as the financial results of a season of performances given by several companies which had latterly played there were very discouraging. 'There is much less attraction in these operas when performed in the East, without an effective

---

[79] 'The Italian Opera Company: "Martha." "Il Trovatore"', *The North-China Herald and Supreme Court & Consular Gazette*, 1 February 1881, 99.

[80] 'Editorial Selections: The Municipality and the Theatre', *The North-China Herald and Supreme Court & Consular Gazette*, 13 January 1881, 26.

[81] 'Siam News', *The Straits Times*, 29 September 1881, 14.

[82] 'Figaro', *The Lorgnette*, 14 January 1882, 2; 'De Opéra', *Soerabaijasch handelsblad*, 27 April 1882, 2.

[83] 'Slamat Taoon Baroe', *De locomotief: Samarangsch handels- en advertentie-blad*, 3 January 1888, 2; 'INGEZONDEN STUKKEN. De Italiaansche Opera. Mijnheer de Redacteur', *Bataviaasch handelsblad*, 28 July 1887, 3; 'Nederlandsch-Indië. Batavia, 15 Juni', *Java-bode: nieuws, handels- en advertentieblad voor Nederlandsch-Indie*, 15 June 1888, 4.

orchestra or a full chorus and in a miniature theatre', the newspaper declared.[84]

Pompei, who had entered into a partnership with the singer Carlotta Patti, was allegedly also 'making desperate efforts to raise a subscription... to bring out an opera troupe' to India, even as people doubted its likely success. 'Business', an anonymous writer declared, 'was too bad for people to throw away money on opera boxes and stalls'.[85] In 1880 Pompei took a company to Shanghai, Yokohama and subsequently Java and Australia, where the troupe subsequently broke up. Similarly, in March 1884, *The Times of India* remarked on the 'very straitened circumstances' of an unnamed Italian opera company who had left India for Italy with 'empty purses'.[86] As people patronised 'English *opera bouffe*, French *opera bouffe*, and light burlesque plays, to the exclusion of more elevated entertainments', the demand for Italian opera in Asian colonial entrepôts had all but ended. Australia too, with the death of Lyster, witnessed *opera bouffe* 'rapidly gaining ground' and by 1881, the *Sydney Mail* declared it as having 'the upper hand'.[87] Simultaneously, Parsi and Chinese opera enthralled local populations who had no desire for 'high class, reformed' music that repeated the 'moral and religious instruction of the school... with melodious and grateful associations'.[88] Moreover, the enormous expenses of travel, the risk of maintaining 'employees and supernumeraries and artists of every grade' and the cosmopolitan tastes of the ticket-paying public contributed further to bringing the curtain down on the Italian opera's first brief sojourn in the colonial East.[89] Unable to compete for the same artists, advertisements and places to perform as its alleged imitators, Italian opera, despite or perhaps due to its reputation as elevated entertainment, had been pushed out of the cut-throat South and South East Asian acoustic marketplace. The metaphor of the Italians' expulsion from this new competitive, capitalist Asian sonic world was realised in Hong Kong when Mr Willard of Willard's Musical Comedy and Opera Company, which toured Bombay, Calcutta, Singapore, Batavia, Surabaya, Hong Kong, Yokohama and Penang, purposefully blocked an Italian operatic troupe from performing.

[84] 'Italian Opera', *Straits Times Weekly Issue*, 14 January 1890, 1.
[85] Newspaper's own correspondent, *The Times of India*, 29 September 1881; 'Amusements in India', *The Lorgnette*, 1 March 1881, 2.
[86] 'Italian Opera', *The Times of India*, 11 March 1884, 3.
[87] 'Music and Drama', *The Sydney Mail and New South Wales Advertiser*, 12 March 1887, 533.
[88] Murdoch, *Hints on Government Education*, 73.
[89] 'Madame Nilsson on the Future of the Opera', *The Times of India*, 9 June 1884, 6.

When Mr Willard's company was performing here a couple of months ago there was a troupe of high class and most accomplished Italian artistes in the Philippine Islands. The Italians intended to perform for a season in Hong Kong ... Hearing this, Mr Willard who is one of the cleverest and most energetic managers we have ever come across in a somewhat lengthy and varied career among the profession, checkmated the Italian Company by booking the City Hall Theatre for the month of October. This was an ordinary trick of the trade and no doubt Mr Willard was perfectly justified in using all the legitimate means available in preventing an opposition from spoiling his prospects by fattening on the fleshpots of Hong Kong. He succeeded to the letter; the Italian company, unable to perform here ... had to break up, and the members are now on their way home.[90]

Opera and Aural Modernities

Although Cagli's and Pompei's lengthy peripatetic journeys across South, East and South East Asia were described by their contemporaries writing in colonial newspapers as enormously influential, their long-term impact on Asian morphologies of sound has suffered a surprising lack of scholarly notice.[91] The largely forgotten Italians, who were among the first of many opera impresarios that sought to find new sources of sustenance in Asia against the backdrop of the precipitous decline in aristocratic patronage of European music; the new ways of listening that had been borne in with the Industrial Revolution; and the concomitant increased traffic of capital, people and artistic forms, embody the lyricism of marginality in this first phase of cultural globalisation. At the height of its performances in the 1860s and '70s, Italian opera made a mark among colonial officers and local reformists in Bombay, Calcutta, Singapore and Hong Kong as an imperial supraculture – the best of European art. Simultaneously, however, touring minstrel and Parsi companies increasingly drew on the high-culture connotations of Italian opera to market their own musical wares, which enjoyed far wider and greater appeal. Even as artistic networks, forms of patronage and institutional forms radically metamorphosed, the connotation of opera shifted in Asia –from a myth of moral advancement, civilisation and progress, to cosmopolitan consumption linked to the market-mediated hawking of hybrid cultural wares. The term 'opera' as used in Hindustani and Chinese performance forms in the nineteenth, twentieth and twenty-first centuries is

---

[90] 'Hong Kong Friday, September 28, 1888', *The Hong Kong Telegraph*, 28 September 1888, 2.
[91] See Shope, American Popular Music.

thus inextricably entwined with the spectral presence of Augusto Cagli's and Giovanni Pompei's landmark tours, reflecting the remediation of music by the forces of capitalism in the age of Empire. Although the Italians were subsequently ignored and eventually forgotten in colonial and postcolonial Asian cultural histories, they inadvertently animated conceptualisations of sonic desirability and auditory worth. Through the interpellation of musical communities that were coming into being between Bombay and Batavia, opera facilitated the acoustic negotiation of sovereignty, ushering in an aural grammar of modernity along with its visual counterpart.

12 | *German National Identity and Operatic* Italianità

Franchetti's and Leoncavallo's Operas on German Myths

RICHARD ERKENS

In 1870 Antônio Carlos Gomes confronted the Milan audience of the Teatro alla Scala with the Brazilian jungle (*Il Guarany*). The following year Giuseppe Verdi produced his famous depiction of Egypt at the time of the pharaohs (*Aida*). A generation later, in 1898, Pietro Mascagni was the first Italian composer to evoke Japanese culture on stage (*Iris*), till then almost unknown to Italian audiences.[1] These examples serve to demonstrate how, over the course of the nineteenth century, Italian opera increasingly embraced non-traditional subjects and especially representations of the exotic. The changing historical and geographical contexts of these plots provoke questions over the impact of this kind of exoticism on these works' reception, particularly among those audiences that identified with the foreign cultures represented on stage.[2] The semantics of operatic *italianità* abroad were closely connected to questions of identity and otherness, experienced and reflected through the means of a specific Italian art form, where the audiences' own identity is viewed through the particular prism of operatic *italianità*. Where the work itself took part in the construction of myths regarding the nation portrayed on stage, its reception could have had an alienating effect on audiences, especially towards the end of the long nineteenth century when the process of nation-building in Italy and Germany was at its peak and debates about national identity incited heated debates.[3]

---

[1] Cf. Michele Girardi, 'Un'immagine musicale del Giappone nell'opera italiana *fin-de-siècle*', in Paolo Amalfitano and Loretta Innocenti (eds.), *L'Oriente. Storia di una figura nelle arti occidentali (1700–2000)* (Rome: Bulzoni, 2007), 583–93; Alan Mallach, *Pietro Mascagni and His Operas* (Boston, MA: Northeastern University Press, 2002), 105–28; and in a broader context cf. Ian Littlewood, *The Idea of Japan: Western Images, Western Myths* (London: Secker & Warburg, 1996).

[2] A well-known case is the first Japanese reception of Giacomo Puccini's *Madama Butterfly* in 1914, cf. Arthur Groos, 'Return of the Native: Japan in *Madama Butterfly/Madama Butterfly* in Japan', *Cambridge Opera Journal* 1/2 (July 1989), 167–94.

[3] Regarding the recently well-researched reception of Verdi in Germany in this context, cf. Gundula Kreuzer, *Verdi and the Germans. From Unification to the Third Reich* (Cambridge: Cambridge University Press, 2010); for a focus on the academic discipline that claimed musical superiority cf. Mauro Fosco Bertola, 'Beyond Germanness? Music's History as "Entangled History" in German Musicology from the End of the Nineteenth Century to the Second World

The two operas discussed in this chapter were produced within the specific cultural atmosphere of debates on national identity in Italy and Germany, two countries that are often described as 'late nation states'. Meanwhile, both works have quite different backgrounds, despite being composed at almost the same time. Alberto Franchetti's *Germania* (Milan, 1902) was written primarily for the Italian opera market, with its plot exemplifying the birth of a foreign nation and its 'baptism in blood' during the so-called 'Battle of Nations' that took place near Leipzig in October 1813, a key event of the later Napoleonic Wars.[4] Depicting an episode of the modern history of Italy's northern neighbour was of considerable political significance. At the time of the opera's premiere, Germany's economy was growing fast, and its new armament programme was considered a genuine threat to the international order. At a time when the peninsula was suffering an ongoing domestic crisis associated with its still-incomplete process of inner nation-building and with the authoritarian policies of Prime Minister Francesco Crispi, who considered Bismarck a model of modern statesmanship, Germany's development during those years served, for many Italians, as a blueprint for Italy's own modernisation.[5] Franchetti's new opera could be read as a reflection upon these debates.

Leoncavallo's *Der Roland von Berlin* was commissioned by the German Emperor Wilhelm II as a celebration of the Hohenzollern dynasty, to be premiered at the court theatre in Berlin. The premiere was postponed to December 1904, due to problems regarding the libretto and Leoncavallo's persistent delays during a composition process which took over a whole decade.[6] The reception of both operas was conditioned by the fact that their origin, plot and production oscillated between these two national contexts. Studying their German reception serves as an example of how ideas of *italianità* were debated from two different perspectives: on the one hand, this

War', in Fernando Clara and Cláudia Ninhos (eds.), *Nazi Germany and Southern Europe, 1933–45: Science, Culture and Politics* (Basingstoke: Palgrave Macmillan, 2016) 25–37.

[4] Cf. Richard Erkens, 'Die Nation als dramatis persona: Zur dramaturgischen Konzeption von Luigi Illicas und Alberto Franchettis Deutschland-Oper *Germania*', in Richard Erkens and Paolo Giorgi (eds.), *Alberto Franchetti: L'uomo, il compositore, l'artista* (Lucca: Libreria Musicale Italiana, 2015), 187–219.

[5] Christopher Duggan, 'Politics in the Era of Depretis and Crispi, 1870–1896', in John A. Davis (ed.), *Italy in the Nineteenth Century*, Short Oxford History of Italy (Oxford: Oxford University Press, 2000), 171, 177.

[6] Cf. Konrad Dryden, *Leoncavallo: Life and Works* (Lanham, MD: Scarecrow Press, 2007), 55–56, 88–93.

regards the works themselves, and the question of how their German plots relate to the opera's musical material; on the other hand, public debate over these productions in Germany reveals how operatic *italianità* was perceived as a threat to Germans' own understanding of their national identity.

A review in the *Berliner Börsen-Zeitung*, published the day after the premiere of Leoncavallo's *Roland*, illustrates the complexity of these works' reception, the hostility behind it, and the role of national ideology within these debates:

> And now the music! First, the national moment comes into question. Mr Leoncavallo tried to protect himself against not deserving the right, as an Italian, to compose such a completely German and more specifically *brandenburgish* subject. He called upon Rossini's *Tell* and Gounod's *Margarethe* as testimony for his 'just cause'. Well, how are the Swiss freedom heroes doing in this Italian light? Do they have even the faintest resemblance to the magnificent, earthy figures in the drama by our Schiller? And what has Gounod made of Goethe's comely Gretchen? A sentimentally inspired Parisian *grisette* that is absolutely out of the reach of Germanic sensibility! No, it remains, music is only in a certain sense an international art. In its basic elements, it is bound to nationality and will always bear the colour of the soil from which it stems, like literature, painting, sculpture – in short, like all art.[7]

The critic describes a composer working within a foreign national context, and who finds himself on the defensive, hard-pressed by his need to acquire an understanding of national art that is unachievable by foreigners. The example suggests that, at least in Germany, Italian operas on German national myths were regarded as a challenge to domestic claims of Germany's alleged operatic supremacy. The idea of an Italian opera, 'exoticised' thanks to the integration of aspects of German culture, was met with suspicion in Germany; seen as non-authentic, and therefore constituting a threat to German composers. According to the critics, it would have been better to have these topics treated by German composers. In short, the premiere of Leoncavallo's *Roland* provoked an unprecedentedly harsh reaction, coming as it did at the time of the Wilhelminian age, which would leave a profound impact on Germany's operatic life and related public opinion. At the same time, however, this burgeoning cultural climate also worked as an incentive for Italian composers to obtain access to the opera market north of the Alps.

---

[7] *II. Beilage der Berliner Börsen-Zeitung*, 14 December 1904 (no. 585), 8.

On the Emperor's Command: Leoncavallo's Homage to the Hohenzollern Family

Leoncavallo's *Der Roland von Berlin* represents a rare (and at the time antiquated) example of an opera commissioned specifically to celebrate a sovereign's dynasty. This context is key to understanding its origin: the pompous court of Wilhelm II, described by historian John C. G. Röhl as a 'late blossom of court culture', and one of the 'most characteristic features of the Wilhelminian Empire'.[8] In direct reaction to the successful productions of *Pagliacci* and *I Medici* at the Berlin court opera, the thirty-five-year-old monarch himself selected the composer in February 1894, at a time when his so-called 'new course'[9] in politics, following Bismarck's dismissal, had already been consolidated. The fresh musical agility and sense of glorification of the patriotic past embodied by Leoncavallo's works, as well as in the emperor's personal taste, may have compelled this offer. Following a suggestion by the opera director and composer Count Bolko von Hochberg,[10] *Der Roland von Berlin* was to be based on a novel of the same name written in 1848 by Willibald Alexis, which thus demonstrates how this commission was embedded in the court's current cultural policy, aimed at increasing 'the monarchy's charisma'.[11] The intended result of this endeavour was, above all, the commemoration of the famous rulers of the Hohenzollern family through the production of an opera that was more dynastic than national.[12] Defining how the emperor was meant to be represented on stage, Michael A. Förster describes the intended role of the monarch as 'a guarantor of peace, justice and the people's welfare',[13] which would be best exemplified by a scene representing the pacification of an uprising and the subsequent pardoning of the respective ringleaders. As possible examples for a plot, Alexis considered several of the emperor's ancestors and related material for a historical drama to be located in the capital of Berlin. Frederick II (1413–71), Prince-Elector of the Margraviate of

---

[8] Cf. John C. G. Röhl, *Kaiser, Hof und Staat: Wilhelm II. und die deutsche Politik* (Nördlingen: C. H. Beck, 22007), 78.

[9] Cfr. John C. G. Röhl, *Wilhelm II. (vol. 2) Der Aufbau der Persönlichen Monarchie 1888–1900* (Munich: C. H. Beck, 2001), 350–80.

[10] Dryden, *Leoncavallo*, 61, note 53.   [11] Röhl, *Kaiser, Hof und Staat*, 112.

[12] Cf. Michael A. Förster, *Kulturpolitik im Dienst der Legitimation: Oper, Theater und Volkslied als Mittel der Politik Kaiser Wilhelms II* (Oxford: Peter Lang, 2009), 78–85. See also Manfred Haedler, 'Das zeitgenössische Werk im Spielplan der Lindenoper während der wilhelminischen Ära und der Weimarer Republik', in *Studien zur Berliner Musikgeschichte: Vom 18. Jahrhundert bis zur Gegenwart* (Berlin: Henschel, 1989), 175–83.

[13] Förster, *Kulturpolitik*, 62.

Brandenburg from 1440, was one of the emperor's favourite ancestors and seemed an ideal embodiment of these ideas. Nicknamed Irontooth, the margrave was remembered for subduing the quarrelling medieval twin cities of Berlin and Cölln, by dismantling the so-called Roland status in which their privileges were enshrined.[14] It was for these reasons that he was deemed an appropriate figure with which to draw historical connections to Wilhelm II's own idea of inspiring a new imperial myth according to which the Hohenzollern dynasty appeared as the saviours of the German nation.[15] Unsurprisingly, the emperor insisted that throughout the libretto the margrave would be referred to by his highest rank, namely as Elector.[16]

The court's programme of cultural policy, namely the fusion of the nation's history with that of the ruling dynasty, also included an urban project in the capital city, which seemed equally inimitable and gigantic. One year after Wilhelm II commissioned Leoncavallo's opera, he also contracted (and paid for) the building of a broad new boulevard in Berlin (in the Tiergarten district, close to the Brandenburg Gate), the so-called Siegesallee, which featured thirty-two marble statues representing Hohenzollern sovereigns, from the first margraves of Brandenburg up to the Prussian kings. This included a marble statue of the opera's protagonist Elector Frederick II, as well as a monumental fountain with a 'restored' and thus 'domesticated' statue of Roland, which concluded the southern end of the boulevard (the Rolandsbrunnen at Kemperplatz). This demonstration of imperial power reached its peak in 1901 on the occasion of the bicentenary of the Kingdom of Prussia, when the new avenue was officially inaugurated. However, the official celebrations did not include the premiere of *Der Roland von Berlin*, as had been planned, as Leoncavallo had failed again to finish the score on time. It was only three years later, in 1904, that Leoncavallo travelled to Berlin to present his opera to the emperor. He was photographed on the occasion in front of the Rolandsbrunnen (see Figure 12.1), an image which was then used for the official press release announcing the opera's upcoming premiere. The delay of the premiere and the wider context of the court's imperial politics of culture, as well as the idea that an Italian composer might write an opera on a 'German myth' – all this became a template for negative responses to the work, which had begun from the moment the opera was commissioned ten years earlier. The

---

[14] A detailed summary of the plot in English can be found in Dryden, *Leoncavallo*, 258–71.
[15] Förster, *Kulturpolitik*, 92.
[16] Ibid. The libretto's denomination is 'Kurfürst Friedrich, Markgraf von Brandenburg'.

Figure 12.1 *Leoncavallo and the Rolandsbrunnen*, newspaper picture by Emilio Rendich: *Berliner Tageblatt* (*Der Welt-Spiegel*), 11 December 1904, (99/1904), 4
Source: Staatsbibliothek zu Berlin–Preußischer Kulturbesitz

category of national identity ultimately became a projection screen for all kinds of imaginations and political intentions.

Wilhelm II himself seemed unconcerned that the choice of an Italian composer might be perceived as problematic. In fact, with no knowledge of German, Leoncavallo was unable to read the novel by Willibald Alexis on which the opera was supposed to be based. Its translation took two years, and only then was Leoncavallo able to begin his work on the libretto, which was then to be retranslated back into German.¹⁷ In addition to questioning Leoncavallo's familiarity with the work's necessary *couleur locale* and the *couleur historique* of medieval Brandenburg, the German newspapers openly queried why no German composer had been found to compose an opera of such national significance.¹⁸ Therefore from the very beginning of the process Leoncavallo seemed to be in a losing position. Whatever aesthetic decisions he took were doomed to be questioned by public opinion, since the substantive assessment of the opera itself was too closely entangled with political views on the emperor's own policies. Criticising Leoncavallo became an opportunity to voice criticism of the emperor per se. As a consequence, when the work's premiere was first reviewed, the newspapers were well aware of the event's prestige within the context of the nation's dynastic policies. According to one newspaper, the event was foremost a 'théâtre pare',¹⁹ a performance in the presence of the ruling dynasty, staged for the court and the capital's high society. In order to assess the event's full meaning, it must be remembered that the Berlin court opera was one of the few royal theatres in Europe that directly formed part of the imperial court, which also secured its finances.²⁰ Due to this position, the premiere's finale was met with the expected (and indeed nearly guaranteed) applause, owing in part to the starring cast of Emmy Destinn, Baptist Hoffmann and Geraldine Farrar, whose participation contributed considerably to the evening's success. However, the critics reacted harshly towards the opera itself, which they interpreted as the direct result of the emperor's cultural policies. As Adolf Weissmann wrote in the *Berliner Volks-Zeitung* the following day, 'Hohenzollern-Weather! It speaks for the Empress' sense of music that she did not even appear.'²¹

A Model of Inner Nation-Building: Franchetti's Battle of the Nations

By representing the Elector of Brandenburg storming the city walls of Cölln and Berlin in order to settle the disputes between his citizens and establish

---

¹⁷ Cf. Luisa Longobucco, *'Il Rolando di Berlino' di Leoncavallo: documenti per la sua storia* (Bisignano: Apollo Edizioni, 2019).
¹⁸ Cf. Josef-Horst Lederer, '"Er scheiterte an einem Beginnen, das sein Ehrgeiz ihn nicht hatte ausschlagen lassen ... " – Zur Zeitkritik an R. Leoncavallos historischem Drama *Der Roland von Berlin*', in Lorenza Guiot and Jürgen Maehder (eds.), *Nazionalismo e cosmopolitismo nell'opera fra '800 e '900, Atti del 3° Convegno internazionale 'Ruggero Leoncavallo nel suo tempo'* (Milan: Sonzogno, 1998), 181–91.
¹⁹ *Berliner Tageblatt*, 14 December 1904 (no. 635), 2.   ²⁰ Röhl, *Kaiser, Hof und Staat*, 89f.
²¹ *Berliner Volks-Zeitung*, 14 December 1904 (no. 585), 3.

himself as their new protector, Leoncavallo's *Roland* primarily glorified the dynasty's past. Arguably, the opera also claimed political legitimisation for the ruling family's hegemony over its subjects and lauded it for uniting the nation in the face of regional conflicts. Contrary to Leoncavallo's opera, Luigi Illica's historical drama *Germania* did not focus on a ruling dynasty, but on the German people themselves. It showed the birth of an imagined 'inner nation', exemplified by the liberation from Napoleonic occupation and culminating in the so-called Battle of the Nations of 1813. Thus it depicted a patriotic struggle, which for an Italian audience, according to Davide Ceriani, 'closely paralleled the Risorgimento experience of fighting the Austrians'.[22] From a German perspective, however, it was more difficult to decode the work's aesthetic language. For a German audience, the exoticism that Illica and Franchetti used to depict the German context remained largely impenetrable, as Germans were unable to see themselves as 'others'. Meanwhile, it was this 'otherness' that was needed to make the work meaningful, if viewed through an Italian lens.

The fictional narrative of the opera's three main protagonists is set against the historical background that commenced with the Battle of Jena and Auerstedt in 1806, and is subsequently enriched with a number of historical episodes from the German resistance to Napoleon, including the arrest of the publisher Johann Philipp Palm in Nuremberg, the execution of Napoleon's would-be assassin Friedrich Stapß in Schönbrunn and events around the 'Luisenbund' and the 'Tugendbund' in the struggle for liberation. Around fifty famous historical characters were depicted or mentioned in the libretto, although the plot's protagonists were characterised as common people, including students, publishers and young women, who see their futures foiled as a result of the French occupation.[23] As a consequence of the political events around them, they become beggars, adulterers, traitors or even just soldiers, simply because a 'normal life' no longer seems possible under the conditions of the occupation. Only after overcoming their inner conflicts do these people find the determination to unite their forces against Napoleon, with the volunteer corps under General Lützow and the charismatic figure of the Prussian Queen Luise playing leading roles in forging the people together. The opera's final act shows the countless dead soldiers on the final day of the battle. Among them is one of the plot's protagonists, the wounded Federico Loewe who, while dying, enthusiastically enounces the nation's liberation: 'O libera Germania'.

---

[22] Cf. Davide Ceriani, 'Romantic Nostalgia and Wagnerismo during the Age of Verismo: The Case of Alberto Franchetti', *Nineteenth-Century Music Review*, 14 (2017), 11–42.
[23] Cf. Erkens, 'Die Nation', 187–219.

Franchetti's *Germania* stands for a nation's 'baptism in blood' and ends with the apotheosis of its victory over the enemy, its actual message reduced to the causes of this triumph. According to the opera's ideas, victory was entirely due to the patriotism of the people's martyrs, whose sacrifice was subsequently instilled with religious meaning: they had died on the 'altar of fatherland'.

Germania was the product of the famous publisher Ricordi, whose intentions were mainly commercial and which operated largely independently of political considerations. The work's premiere at the Teatro alla Scala in Milan in 1902 was a great success. Directed by Arturo Toscanini, its cast included Enrico Caruso, Mario Sammarco and Amelia Pinto. The opera instantly became the composer's most popular work in Italy and abroad, albeit with the exception of Germany, where only two performances, one in Karlsruhe (1908) and the other in Hamburg (1913), took place before the outbreak of World War I. The composer, whose mother was German,[24] hoped in vain for a positive reception of the opera in Germany. In order to promote the work, a symphonic poem entitled *Nella foresta nera*, which was based on music for the opera's Black Forest Act and played on elements of nostalgia, had been performed in 1900 in Milan and Bologna, directed by Arturo Toscanini. The question might be asked as to whether Franchetti also hoped for the support of Wilhelm II, perhaps with the idea of producing his work before the long-delayed opera by Leoncavallo appeared. It is possible that the work's nationalist content was boosted for commercial reasons to increase its likelihood of being promoted abroad. Hints pointing in this direction might be identified in the correspondence that took place between Franchetti and Illica when the composer first suggested the subject in 1898. At the time, they commented on a related note in a French newspaper:

> Did you read the article in the *Figaro* from the 16th of this month? It says nothing more than that the Emperor of Germany is interested in our opera – if it was not the *Figaro* that carried this information, you could almost believe it!![25]

Indeed, a few days earlier *Le Figaro* had reported from Milan that

> Mr Illica, author of the libretto of *La Bohème* by Mr Puccini, is currently working on a libretto entitled *Germania* for which Baron Franchetti is writing the music. The subject of the work is drawn from the German wars of liberation and puts on

---

[24] His mother was Sara Luisa Rothschild, a daughter of the famous banking family in Vienna; for biographical notes cf. Roberto Marcuccio, 'Alberto Franchetti (1860–1942): una biografia essenziale', in Erkens and Giorgio (eds.), *Alberto Franchetti*, 349–52.

[25] Unpublished letter from Alberto Franchetti to Luigi Illica, Treviso, 24 July 1898 (Piacenza, Biblioteca Passerini Landi, Fondo Illica).

stage Stein, Gneisenau, Blücher, Körner, Humboldt etc. It is said that the Emperor of Germany is very interested in this new work by the Italian composer.[26]

Even if this information was incorrect (since no other European newspaper reported the news of the emperor's interest in the work), it agitated Franchetti and Illica. Ultimately the event gave birth to the idea of presenting the libretto to the German emperor, knowing that his commission from Leoncavallo was still unfinished: 'In a few days, Ricordi will arrive and maybe also Illica, intending to travel to Berlin in order to present the libretto of *Germania* to the Emperor',[27] Franchetti wrote to his father. Several days later he informed him that Illica was still considering writing to the emperor, even if by then the newspaper hoax seemed obvious: 'One sees that he [Illica] takes the canard of the *Figaro* seriously.'[28] Unlike in Leoncavallo's case,[29] a dedication of the work to the German emperor would not have been appropriate, but the opera's eventual dedicatee, the Countess Annina Morosini Rombo, was considered to be an acquaintance of the emperor. Known at the time as the most beautiful woman of Venice, the countess had first met the German emperor in 1894; from then on the emperor ostensibly never missed an opportunity to visit her elegant salon when staying on his yacht *Hohenzollern* in Venice. However, even these personal ties did not ultimately lead to support for the opera's staging in Germany. Germany eventually saw two productions of the work, thanks to the efforts of Georg Göhler, a passionate conductor and music director in Karlsruhe and Hamburg, but these did not count among Germany's most prominent theatres.[30] To the composer's satisfaction, however, at least the Hamburg production of 1913 took place during the centenary of the Battle of the Nations.

German Folk Song and Wagnerism versus *Italianità*

Leoncavallo and Franchetti were faced with the same fundamental problem when it came to the musical dramaturgy of their operas: how to produce

---

[26] *Le Figaro*, 16 July 1898 (no. 187), 4.
[27] Unpublished letter from Alberto Franchetti to his father Raimondo, Baden-Baden, 3 August 1898 (Venice, Archivio privato Franchetti).
[28] Unpublished letter from Alberto Franchetti to his father Raimondo, Baden-Baden, 8 August 1898 (ibid.).
[29] Such a dedication would not have seemed advisable given the anti-Semitic disposition of Wilhelm II (cf. Röhl, *Kaiser, Hof und Staat*, 203–22), which the well-informed Franchetti family, who were Jewish, must have been conscious of.
[30] Cf. Erkens, 'Die Nation', 214.

a 'German soundscape'. In the case of Leoncavallo's *Roland*, the issue was exacerbated by an even greater historical distance to the events, compared to Franchetti's *Germania*. In order to find an authentic musical language for the German context, both composers turned to an idea of musical exoticism largely derived from the experience of French *grand opéra*. The use of folk songs, especially for incidental music, was by then a well-established practice in Italian opera, but the more common compositional technique of exoticism, which Carl Dahlhaus has defined as the 'principle of integrable anomaly' and which was to be embedded into the European tonal system,[31] did not serve for these works. For the plot of *Madama Butterfly*, Puccini was able to find an appropriate musical language by using Japanese percussion instruments and East Asian melody, even if some of the material he used turned out to be of Chinese rather than Japanese origin.[32] However, in the case of Leoncavallo's and Franchetti's operas, the geographical proximity and close cultural ties between Italy and Germany made these kind of inaccuracies more problematic. Furthermore, the potential to relate musical exoticism to German folklore and national identity was certainly more limited.

These limitations notwithstanding, both operas employed 'authentic' musical sources. In Leoncavallo's case, the German critic and musicologist Wilhelm Tappert selected sixteenth- and seventeenth-century music, which the composer incorporated into the score and also published separately as an appendix to the piano reduction (Example 12.1). Leoncavallo used this musical material almost exclusively for the work's incidental music.[33] Meant to be understood as examples of ancient folk music, the music is played by an orchestra on stage (Tempo di Gavotta III, 18 or Rigaudon III, 39), including the dances of the third act, which feature Eva's engagement to Melchiore, prior to their marriage. Likewise, the musical motive of the Elector is derived from a Renaissance dance from 1577, in this case an Allemande, as pointed out in the appendix to the piano reduction. Understandably, the Allemande is not the only motive chosen to characterise the opera's principal character.

In Franchetti's *Germania*, the use of pre-existing musical material is more complex because quotations are not limited to incidental music but appear consistently throughout the musical texture. Whether these are direct quotations (like Carl Maria von Weber's famous male chorus *Lützows wilde Jagd*

---

[31] 'Prinzip der integrierbaren Regelwidrigkeit', cf. Carl Dahlhaus, *Die Musik der 19. Jahrhunderts*, in Dahlhaus, *Gesammelte Schriften*, vol. 5, ed. Hermann Danuser (Laaber: Laaber, 2003), 299.
[32] Cf. W. Anthony Sheppard, 'Puccini and the Music Boxes', *Journal of the Royal Musical Association*; 140/1 (2015), 41–92.
[33] Cf. Hans-Joachim Wagner, *Fremde Welten: Die Oper des italienischen Verismo* (Stuttgart and Weimar: Metzler, 1999), 188–95.

Example 12.1 Leoncavallo, *Der Roland von Berlin*, vocal score, appendix, 515

ANHANG:

Bearbeitete altdeutsche Themen zum Vergleiche wie sie im Original klangen.

No.1 Allemande (1577). Thema des Kurfürsten

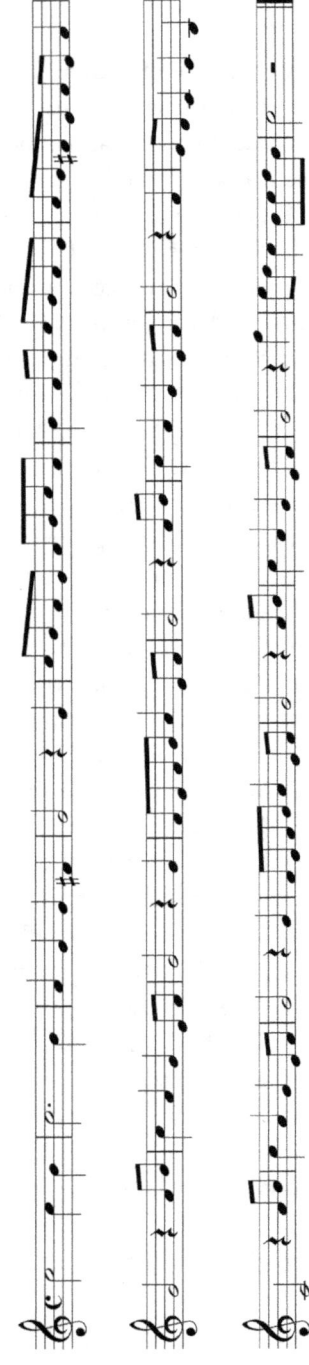

in the Prologue (rehearsal number 38)) or allusions to well-known tunes (such as in Federico's arioso 'Studenti! Udite, o voi', right before the Weber example), in Franchetti's case these form a complex network of motives that shape the musical dramaturgy, evoking an almost continuous 'German soundscape'. Moreover, the original quotations were not indicated by Franchetti, although he seems to have used a famous collection of German students' songs, the *Allgemeines Deutsches Kommersbuch*.[34] The start of the opera's Prologue provides a striking example of how the idea of 'exoticism', achieved by means of 'authentic' music, infiltrates the score and as a consequence impacts on the work's *italianità*. Almost the entire instrumental prelude is conceived as a medley of three students' songs, immediately followed by a German folk song which is used as diegetic music after the rising of the curtain (Example 12.2). Within this scene, the old beggar Lene Armuth teaches her grandson Jebbel the song she sings to receive compassion from passers-by. German audiences, however, might have been more likely to recognise the tune as the melody of the well-known love song 'Der Sehnsucht Treue', which was later also used as the tune for an even more famous lullaby ('Weißt Du wieviel Sternlein stehen').[35] As the following example shows, the orchestral part likewise is written as diegetic music, using the reduced woodwind textures of a bourdon bass together with the clattering figures of the clarinet part to imitate a barrel organ.

Another problem of musical dramaturgy that the two composers faced, and one which was even more complex, was the challenge of Wagnerism. Both Franchetti and Leoncavallo belonged to a generation of Italian composers that had been profoundly influenced by Wagner.[36] It is therefore not surprising that also in their 'German operas' we find allusions to Wagnerian music, which seriously undermined their works' aesthetic

---

[34] A detailed analysis of the score from this perspective is in Richard Erkens, *Alberto Franchetti – Werkstudien zur italienischen Oper der langen Jahrhundertwende*, Perspektiven der Opernforschung vol. 19 (Oxford: Peter Lang, 2011), 229–78.

[35] Ibid., 241f.

[36] Cf. Jay Nicolaisen, *Italian Opera in Transition, 1871–1893* (Ann Arbor: University of Michigan Press, 1980); Julian Budden, 'Wagnerian Tendencies in Italian Opera', in Nigel Fortune (ed.), *Music and Theater: Essays in Honour of Winton Dean* (Cambridge: Cambridge University Press, 1987), 299–332; Jürgen Maehder, 'Formen des Wagnerismus in der italienischen Oper des Fin de siècle', in Annegret Fauser and Manuela Schwarz (eds.), *Von Wagner zum Wagnérisme: Musik-Literatur-Kunst-Politik* (Leipzig: Leipziger Universitätsverlag, 1999), 449–85; Richard Erkens, 'Sinfonismo und Wagnerismo: Imitationen der Musiksprache Wagners in Italien', in Arne Stollberg, Ivana Rentsch and Anselm Gerhard (eds.), *Gefühlskraftwerke für Patrioten? Wagner und das Musiktheater zwischen Nationalismus und Globalisierung*, Thurnauer Schriften zum Musiktheater vol. 26 (Würzburg: Königshausen & Neumann, 2017), 431–73.

Example 12.2 Franchetti, *Germania*, beginning of the Prologue, full score, rehearsal number 2 ('canzone popolare dell'epoca')

message for two different reasons. The use of Wagnerian elements could not be explained as examples of musical exoticism, intended to add a certain *couleur historique,* because both works were set in periods predating Wagner, even if the German composer was born just a few months before the 'Battle of the Nations' that figured so prominently in Franchetti's opera. Nevertheless, for the first time in the history of Italian opera, Franchetti employed Wagner tubas, used here to depict the battleground during the *intermezzo sinfonico,* undoubtedly to great musical effect.[37] Nevertheless, even if this final scene of *Germania* is certainly one of the most impressive pieces Franchetti ever wrote, for a German audience the use of Wagner tubas – so closely associated with the imagery of the *Ring des Nibelungen* – could hardly have been convincing as a feature illustrating the soundscape of the Napoleonic Wars.

Further problems arose when taking account of stylistic attributes related to issues of national identity. If Wagnerism failed as a means of adding *couleur historique* to the plot, it almost goes without saying that it did not work as a feature of operatic *italianità* – the aesthetic framework in which these supposedly exotic elements were meant to be embedded. Furthermore, Wagnerism had no constitutive function within the drama's overall conception. As allusions to Wagner served no dramatic purpose, they had to be viewed as a rather vague reference to an imaginary 'German soundscape', which meant that German audiences must have responded to them with a certain suspicion. How one read these allusions was conditioned by one's national background. An Italian or a non-German audience could read any allusions to Wagner as indicators of an aesthetic modernity. German listeners or audiences more closely familiar with Wagner's work, however, tended to see such references as generally unproblematic. The problem arose from the fact that both operas, especially in Germany, were received mainly as Italian operas, which meant that any references to Wagner tended to undermine aesthetic expectations arising from the works' supposed *italianità*. They did not even correspond to expectations associated with the operas by Verdi, Mascagni and Puccini that had been staged, with great success, in Germany.[38] Finally, neither

---

[37] Cf. Jürgen Maehder, '"La giusta prospettiva dell'orchestra": Handwerkliche und ästhetische Grundlagen der Orchesterbehandlung bei den Komponisten der "giovane scuola"', *Studi pucciniani,* 3 (2004), 123.

[38] For a statistical approach to analysis of the reception of Italian opera in Germany from 1900 onwards (mainly a comparison between performances of Wagner and Verdi), cf. Matthias Brzoska, 'Verdi und Wagner in Deutschland. Zur Aufführungsstatistik 1900–2010', in Norbert Abels (ed.), *Verdi & Wagner: Folkwang Symposium 2013* (Frankfurt am Main: Frankfurt Academic Press, 2014), 53–70; cf. also Josef-Horst Lederer, *Verismo auf der*

Leoncavallo's nor Franchetti's works could be compared to what Germans knew as *Nationalopern*; this described works like Carl Maria von Weber's *Der Freischütz*, although the term itself was considered problematic even at the time.[39] Instead, for German audiences these works seemed to lack any authentic elements of national identity, leaving an impression akin to having the nation's heroes speaking 'broken German' on stage.

A final musical example serves to illustrate this point. Compared to Franchetti, Leoncavallo was even more explicit in imitating Wagner's style, directly echoing phrases of the German's works at almost every musical climax. These thinly veiled allusions to Wagner took the shape of particular melodic lines or of examples of instrumentation.[40] For instance, in the first act of his *Roland*, when the opera's hero Henning Mollner opens the city gates for the arrival of the Elector, Leoncavallo directly combines Wagner's leitmotiv of the sword *Nothung* with that of the *Feuerzauber* from *Die Walküre* (Example 12.3):

Employed to underline the hero's decisiveness, the passage recalls the mythical figure of Siegfried, ready to destroy Wotan's spear. These examples inevitably raise the question of whether Leoncavallo was simply imitating a semantically charged musical style or whether these examples were intended as conscious references to Wagner. Whatever his reasoning, the reactions show that German audiences had difficulties accepting these aesthetic decisions as means of depicting their national character. A brief overview of the main arguments employed by the German critics will illustrate the reasons why both operas failed across the Alps. Their perceived hybrid character, wavering between two national identities, was at the core of the critics' arguments.

---

deutschsprachigen Opernbühne 1891–1926: Eine Untersuchung seiner Rezeption durch die zeitgenössische musikalische Fachpresse, Wiener musikwissenschaftliche Beiträge vol. 19 (Vienna, Cologne and Weimar: Böhlau, 1992).

[39] For a recent discussion of this term cf. Michael Walter, 'Die "Nationaloper"', in Jörg Zedler (ed.), '*Was die Welt im Innersten zusammenhält*': *Gesellschaftlich-staatliche Kohäsionskräfte im 19. und 20. Jahrhundert* (Munich: Herbert Utz, 2014), 13–57. See also Natalia Nicklas, *Nationalisierung der deutschen Oper im späten Vormärz 1840–1848*, Beihefte zum Archiv für Musikwissenschaft vol. 79 (Stuttgart: Franz Steiner Verlag, 2017).

[40] The representativeness of the selection of scores with which Jean-Jacques Velly compares the orchestration of Leoncavallo has to be questioned because of their blatantly obvious Wagnerian tendencies; cf. Jean-Jacques Velly, 'Quelques aspects du traitement orchestral dans "Le Roland de Berlin"', in Lorenza Guiot and Jürgen Maehder (eds.), *Letteratura, musica e teatro al tempo di Ruggero Leoncavallo: Atti del 2°Convegno internazionale di studi su Ruggero Leoncavallo* (Milan: Sonzogno, 1995), 167–74. Leoncavallo also used similar references to Wagner in other works. See Jürgen Maehder, 'Timbri poetici e tecniche d'orchestrazione – influssi formativi sull'orchestrazione del primo Leoncavallo', in ibid., 141–65.

Example 12.3 Leoncavallo, *Der Roland von Berlin*, Act I, vocal score, rehearsal number 36, 69f

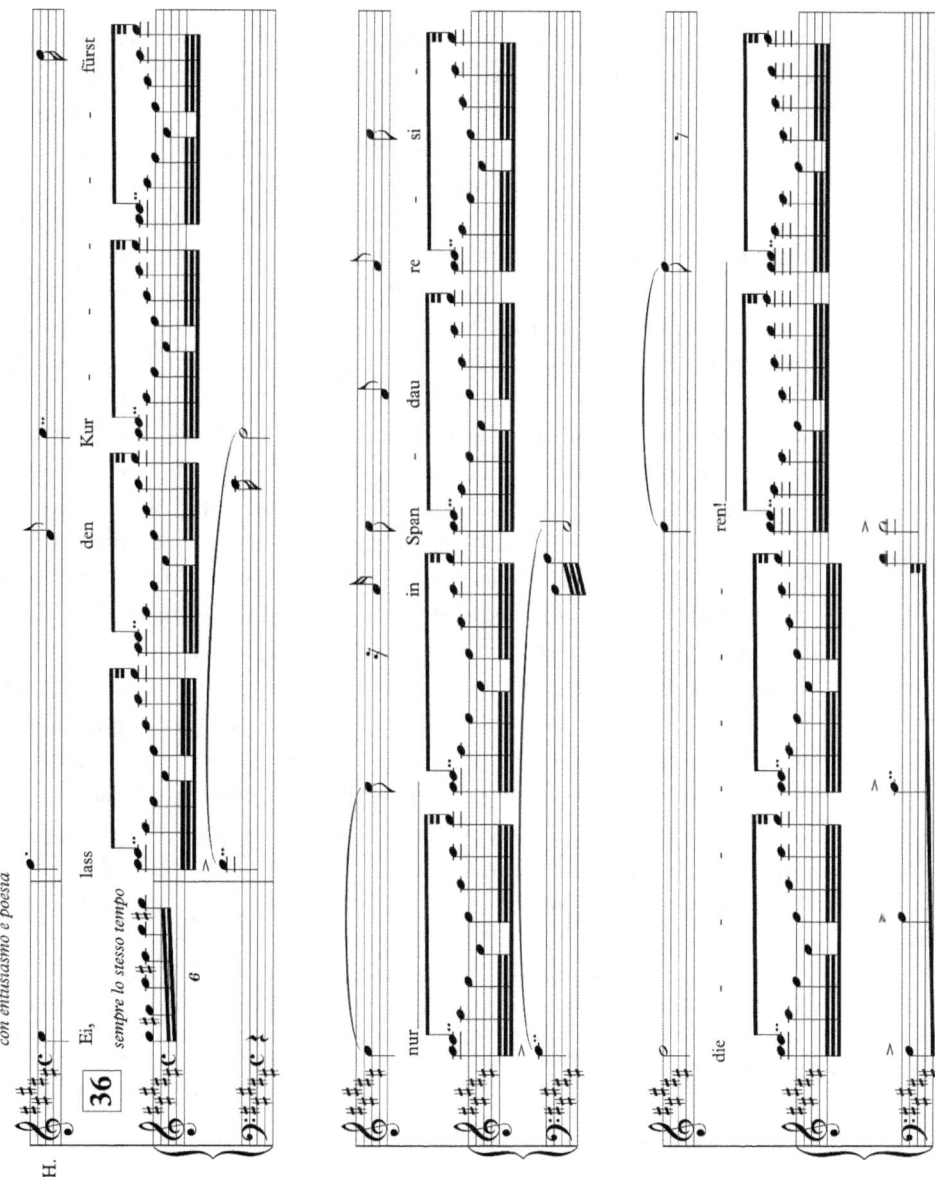

Italianità without Homeland

Compared to the reception of Leoncavallo's *Roland*, the German press discussed Franchetti's *Germania* in slightly more neutral terms, as the debate did not have to respond to the backdrop of the court's questionable cultural policy, which had been so evident in Leoncavallo's work. This was true at least of the opera's production in Hamburg in 1913; responses to *Germania*'s earlier production in Karlsruhe had been largely in line with the scathing reviews of *Roland*.[41] What the reviews of both works shared was an almost oppressive use of national categories as a way of confronting the tension arising from an Italian opera written on a German topic.

Illica's libretto was generally thought to be unbalanced, with the opera's heroic and patriotic topic disappearing behind a chain of relatively simple episodes in a love story.[42] There were a number of historical inaccuracies of which the Italian librettist could not have been aware, but which were noted by the German audiences. Likewise, the press commented on a few unintended comical effects. A much more serious issue, however, seemed to be the opera's main protagonists and the way they were portrayed in the work. According to its critics, the opera did not appropriately show their idealism and the 'great deeds' which had made up the essence of their struggle for liberation.[43] In the words of the critics they were 'wimps', '*Heuler*', rather than real 'men'.[44] Furthermore, Franchetti was accused of having composed using a patchwork of musical styles, echoing the sounds of Verdi and Wagner, and of playing a 'game with the wrong cards'.[45] According to a newspaper from Baden, the melodic lines seemed fragmented, while an exaggerated use of brass covered up the voices. The score mostly contained 'atmospheric painting',[46] but to no dramatic effect, because the music lacked any 'character' or 'backbone'.[47] Directly pointing to the hybridity of the

---

[41] The reception of *Germania* at the Metropolitan Opera House in New York in 1910 was influenced by other factors, as Davide Ceriani has shown: while a more heterogeneous audience guaranteed a good run, the mostly anti-Italian and pro-German (and pro-Wagner) critics invoked similar arguments against the opera; cf. Davide Ceriani, 'The Reception of Alberto Franchetti's Works in the United States', in Erkens and Giorgi (eds.), *Alberto Franchetti*, 271–99.

[42] Interestingly, this is in line with one of the most comprehensive and critical analyses of *Germania* in Italy, published by Luigi Torchi in *Rivista musicale italiana*, 9 (1902), 377–421.

[43] *Badische Presse*, 11 November 1908 (no. 525, morning edition).

[44] Von Stecken, *Badischer Beobachter*, 12 November 1908 (no. 260, first edition).

[45] *Badische Presse*, 11 November 1908.

[46] *Badischer Beobachter*, 11 November 1908 (no. 259, first edition).

[47] *Badischer Beobachter*, 12 November 1908.

German–Italian soundscape, Franchetti had tried to appear scholarly while abandoning his own 'nature'.[48] The press approved of the German singers, the conductor and the staging, praising the cast's hospitability towards the Italian composer, but remarked that the audience of the premiere would have noticed their lack of 'patriotic feelings',[49] a failure to express anything that could have been understood as 'essentially German'.[50] As it remained in essence an 'Italian' opera, efforts to make the work more German were deemed superficial. In the words of *Der Volksfreund*, they only gave it a 'hybrid status', turning it into a work without a homeland. Ultimately, an Italian opera was considered incompatible with a libretto that had the search for German national identity at its core. Only a 'good modern German opera' produced by a German theatre was considered capable of treating such topics.[51] As a final point, *Der Volksfreund* described Franchetti as a 'patron of the arts' rather than as a composer in his own right, which could easily be read as a reference to widespread anti-Semitic stereotypes that denied that any Jewish composer had the ability to produce true art, ideas that were propagated in particular by the second edition of Wagner's *Das Judenthum in der Musik* of 1869.[52]

While the few German productions of *Germania* generated only regional press coverage, the premiere of *Der Roland von Berlin* evoked a much greater response, in particular in the German-language press.[53] Initially about forty performances of the work took place,[54] suggesting that the work was not considered a straightforward failure, but perhaps a modest success. Nevertheless, the press condemned almost every aspect of the work. The libretto, written by the composer himself, was considered superficial, not sufficiently respectful of the novel on which it was based. The *Berliner Börsen-Zeitung* considered its main characters to be rather 'boring', sentimental and pathetic.[55] The *Augsburger Allgemeine* described them as 'lifeless creatures' with no 'psychological motivation'.[56] The plot

---

[48] *Der Volksfreund*, 11 November 1908 (no. 265), 4.   [49] *Badische Presse*, 11 November 1908.
[50] *Badischer Beobachter*, 12 November 1908.   [51] *Der Volksfreund*, 11 November 1908.
[52] *Der Volksfreund*, 11 November 1908. See also Jens Malte Fischer (ed.), *Richard Wagners "Das Judenthum in der Musik": eine kritische Dokumentation als Beitrag zur Geschichte des Antisemitismus* (Frankfurt am Main: Insel, 2000).
[53] As Lederer pointed out, the voices of discord were already beginning to be heard when the news of the imperial commission started to spread in 1894; cf. Lederer, '"Er scheiterte an einem Beginnen', 183f.
[54] Cfr. Alan Mallach, *The Autumn of Italian Opera: From Verismo to Modernism, 1890–1915* (Boston, MA: Northeastern University Press, 2007), 252.
[55] *II. Beilage der Berliner Börsen Zeitung*, 14 December 1904.
[56] *Augsburger Allgemeine*, 16 December 1904 (no. 574, early evening edition), 1.

was seen as stringing together dramatic effects without any proper 'organic development';[57] these were cluttered together with a profusion of visual effects, which made it difficult to appreciate the music.[58] The tragic ending, Henning's death, was severely criticised as a 'deep tragic failure'.[59] This point in particular could be read as a criticism of Leoncavallo's failure to respond to the emperor's aim of producing an opera without a tragic ending.[60] Finally, the critics raised issues of style, questioning the way in which an ordinary love story between simple citizens was turned into heroism, and thus demonstrating the extent to which issues of class and social difference still marked the political and cultural debates of the late *Kaiserreich*. Like Franchetti, Leoncavallo was accused of having presented his audiences with a rather formulaic patchwork of musical styles.[61] His tendency to imitate Wagner was one point of contention; passages that were apparently reminiscent of *Pagliacci* were another. Some critics perceived the entire development of the score, which ultimately seemed to lack any dramatic sensitivity, as too demanding and difficult for the listener. It was considered trivial and devoid of any real inspiration, producing an effect of 'empty pathos'.[62] While in the case of Franchetti the critics questioned his status as a composer, the *Berliner Volks-Zeitung* rated Leoncavallo as a 'composer of Cabaret', whose work could easily have been accepted as a 'tragicomedy'.[63]

Perhaps unsurprisingly, the harshest criticisms of Leoncavallo referred to the circumstances of the opera's origin as a work directly commissioned by the emperor without consideration of the language barriers which would make the arrangement of the libretto, with its multiple translations and retranslations sent back and forth, so complicated. Some voices commented ironically that this commission was the 'triumph of the postal system'.[64] Others claimed that they felt sorry for the composer, arguing that for political reasons he should have never accepted a task they considered aesthetically too challenging for an Italian composer. Despite the poor response to the premiere, Leoncavallo was congratulated by the emperor, which prompted the reviewers to emphasise their moral obligation 'to tell the truth', and to direct their criticisms directly at the court's cultural politics. In their view, a German composer should have been commissioned to write this work. Leoncavallo did not even speak

[57] *Augsburger Allgemeine*, 16 December 1904. [58] *Berliner Volks-Zeitung*, 14 December 1904.
[59] *Neue Freie Presse*, Vienna, 16 December 1904 (no. 14481, morning edition), 1.
[60] Cf. Förster, *Kulturpolitik*, 104. [61] *Neue Freie Presse*, 16 December 1904.
[62] *II. Beilage der Berliner Börsen Zeitung*, 14 December 1904.
[63] *Berliner Volks-Zeitung*, 14 December 1904. [64] *Neue Freie Presse*, 16 December 1904.

German; however, even a foreigner that spoke German would not have been capable of handling this patriotic topic, nor would he have had the necessary empathy for German culture. Any such opera produced by a foreigner would necessarily fall short of having a 'German heartbeat'.[65] According to the critics, if anything the work's production, although not the work itself, had been a success, due to its sumptuous staging and an excellent cast. The singers and the conductor Karl Muck had 'saved' the poor score from total failure; but they were all considered 'victims of a regrettable mistake'.[66] As in the case of Karlsruhe's production of *Germania*, the applause for Leoncavallo was merely owed 'to a sense of duty towards hospitality';[67] but even here racist remarks were at hand: some of the most hostile critics referred to anti-Semitic stereotypes to describe Leoncavallo as an 'Italian Jew', which he was not, and as a 'neurasthenic composer', whose 'clumsy fingers' had offended German literature.[68] In the words of Josef-Horst Lederer, Leoncavallo (even more so than Franchetti) became a 'victim of the critics', one who paid the price for a mistaken cultural policy and for public resentment against the perceived dominance of operatic *italianità* on the German stage.[69]

The arguments employed by the German critics demonstrate how operatic *italianità* was increasingly met with hostility. Both operas discussed here seemingly crossed the boundary of what was considered legitimate in matters of musical identity. Their plots were considered too far removed from the emotional ideals that the audiences generally associated with German myths when they were represented on stage. The scores were read as an unauthentic patchwork of different musical styles. The 'national' forces that were employed to perform these foreign works would have been put to better use if they had produced an opera by a 'national' composer. Instead, Leoncavallo and Franchetti had produced a variety of operatic *italianità* for the German stage that simply did not appeal to local audiences. The example reveals a simple reasoning that characterises any cultural encounters as clashes of cultures, where any other is almost automatically considered a threat to one's own identity. In turn, claims of cultural and/or political hegemony over the other become a frequent reaction to such encounters, which the media then happily exploit, if only for the sake of a good story. The example of the German reception of these two operas therefore sheds new light on the subtle and complex mechanisms

---

[65] *Augsburger Allgemeine*, 16 December 1904.   [66] *Berliner Volks-Zeitung*, 14 December 1904.
[67] *Berliner Tageblatt*, 14 December 1904 (no. 635, morning edition).
[68] *Deutsches Volksblatt*, Vienna, 17 December 1904 (no. 5732, morning edition).
[69] Lederer, 'Er scheiterte an einem Beginnen', 188.

behind the geopolitical confrontations over national interests that were able to explore patriotic feelings on the eve of World War I. How, exactly, those national resentments that were projected onto opera (or on art in general) worked always depended on the specific contexts in which those works were produced.

Under different circumstances, the meaning and evaluation of the same works could be quite different, or even the opposite of their previous reception. During the July Crisis of 1914 and at the outbreak of World War I, the movie *Germania*, produced in Italy and based on Franchetti's music, was premiered in New York. In its review dated 11 July 1914, the magazine *Movie Picture World* revealed the film's intention 'to stir the hearts of all Teutonic people, and all liberty-loving folk, to patriotic fervour' and recommended its screening for 'special occasions such as Teutonic festivals and the like'.[70] In hindsight this suggestion seems fatally prophetic. During the autumn the film was released as an item of war propaganda in several German cities.[71] Under its new title *Das Volk steht auf* (a direct quote from a famous poem by the patriotic poet Theodor Körner), the plot, which in its operatic format had been torn to pieces by the German critics a few years before, was suddenly perceived as a 'magnificent patriotic movie', presented to German audiences alongside the 'latest images from the theatre of war'.[72]

---

[70] *Moving Picture World*, 11 July 1914, 275.

[71] Cf. Erkens, 'Die Nation', 210–14; regarding the orchestral score of the film music see also Olivier Huck, *Das musikalische Drama im 'Stummfilm': Oper, Tonbild und Musik im Film d'Art* (Hildesheim, Zurich and New York: Olms, 2012), 152–66.

[72] Cinema advertising in *Rosenheimer Anzeiger-Rosenheimer Tagblatt*, 29 November, 60/277 (1914).

13 | (Opera) Fever in Belle Époque Manaus

Italianità at the Teatro Amazonas, 1897–1907

ROSIE MCMAHON

The subject of Italian opera in the Amazon calls to mind Werner Herzog's 1982 film *Fitzcarraldo*, in which it is rendered as the crazed dream of the eponymous protagonist.[1] Early on in the film, raving atop a church tower while frenziedly ringing its bell, Fitzcarraldo repeatedly cries, 'I want my opera house! I want my opera house! I want my opera house!' But opera houses had spread to the Amazon long before the early twentieth century, the period in which the film is set. The city of Belém do Pará, located at the mouth of the Amazon River, already had one in the eighteenth century, and its current edifice was inaugurated in 1876. Macapá and São Luís, both also coastal Amazonian cities, had opera houses in 1775 and 1817, respectively, long before the arrival of the Portuguese court in Brazil, described in Chapter 1 of this book.[2]

One Amazonian city, admittedly, lagged behind. Founded as a military outpost in 1669, the town of Manaus had remained little more than a geopolitical marker throughout Brazil's colonial period and after independence in 1822. In 1850, it was made the capital city of the newly created province of Amazonas, and when Brazil transitioned from a monarchy to

---

[1] *Fitzcarraldo*, directed by Werner Herzog (Werner Herzog Filmproduktion, 1982). Scholarly examinations of music and the representation of opera in *Fitzcarraldo* include Ronald Dolkart, 'Civilization's Aria: Film as Lore and Opera as Metaphor in Werner Herzog's *Fitzcarraldo*', *Journal of Latin American Lore*, 11/2 (1985), 125–41; Jacob-Ivan Eidt, 'Aesthetics, Opera, and Alterity in Herzog's Work', *CLCWeb: Comparative Literature and Culture*, 14/1 (2012); Roger Hillman, *Unsettling Scores: German Film, Music, and Ideology* (Bloomington: Indiana University Press, 2005), 140–6; Paulo Kühl, 'Visões cinematográficas da ópera nos trópicos', *Art Research Journal*, 4/1 (2017), 57–75; Richard Leppert, 'Opera, Aesthetic Violence, and the Imposition of Modernity: Fitzcarraldo', in Daniel Goldmark, Lawrence Kramer and Richard Leppert (eds.), *Beyond the Soundtrack* (Berkeley: University of California Press, 2007); Holly Rogers, 'Fitzcarraldo's Search for Aguirre: Music and Text in the Amazonian Films of Werner Herzog', *Journal of the Royal Musical Association*, 129/1 (2004), 77–99. See also John Rosselli, 'The Opera Business and the Italian Immigrant Community in Latin America 1820–1930: The Example of Buenos Aires', *Past and Present*, 127 (1990), 155–82 (156).

[2] Eighteenth-century Brazilian *casas de ópera* did not necessarily host Italian opera, which only became widespread with the arrival of the Portuguese court in Rio de Janeiro in 1808. Nevertheless, they were indoor venues that hosted music-theatre productions and had boxes, stage backdrops and lighting. Rogério Budasz, *Opera in the Tropics: Music and Theater in Early Modern Brazil* (New York: Oxford University Press, 2019), 157–61.

a republic in 1889, all the provinces became states and gained substantial power over their own finances. In the Amazon, these events coincided with an unprecedented boom in exports of natural rubber, which precipitated a substantial increase in the region's wealth. Owing to its central Amazonian location, Manaus became a vital hub for the rubber trade, attracting economic migrants both from other parts of Brazil and from Western Europe.[3] This wave of immigration was accompanied by a new urbanisation project inspired by European ideals of modernity, chiefly Baron Haussmann's Paris. It aimed to modernise and beautify Manaus in order to encourage more immigration, capital and consumption.

Following these developments, Manaus opened a new opera house, the Teatro Amazonas, on 31 December 1896. Architecturally, the Teatro differed significantly from its predecessor venues: whereas earlier theatres in Manaus were usually made of wood and palm leaves from the surrounding rainforest, the Teatro was built of stone and steel, with many of its materials and furnishings imported from Europe.[4] A week after its inauguration, the opera house's auditorium was filled with the sounds of Amilcare Ponchielli's *La Gioconda*, transported across the Atlantic to Manaus by the Brazilian impresario Joaquim Franco's Italian Opera Company.

Setting the Scene

At the turn of the twentieth century, Manaus's population comprised Brazilians of mixed European and indigenous heritage, foreign immigrants, Brazilian immigrants and a small number of Afro-Brazilians.[5]

---

[3] The city's population grew from 8,500 in 1852 to over 50,000 by the 1890s. Edinea Dias, *A Ilusão do Fausto: Manaus – 1890–1920* (Manaus: Valer Editora, 1999), 38; Barbara Weinstein, *The Amazon Rubber Boom, 1850–1920* (Stanford, CA: Stanford University Press, 1983), 57.

[4] Otoni Moreira de Mesquita, *Manaus: História e Arquitetura (1852–1910)* (Manaus: Valer Editora, 2006), 205–28; see also *Diário Oficial*, 12 March 1895. Several Italian artists contributed to the interior design, including Domenico de Angelis (1853–1900), who had previously worked on the Theatro da Paz, the opera house at Belém. Mário Ypiranga Monteiro, *Teatro Amazonas* (Manaus: Valer Editora, 2003), 174–6, 190–4; Rose Silveira, *Histórias Invisíveis do Teatro da Paz* (Belém: Editora Paka-Tatu, 2010), 226–36. For more information on Manaus' early performance venues, see Simone Villanova, 'Sociabilidade e Cultura: a história dos "pequenos teatros" na cidade de Manaus (1859–1900)', unpublished master's dissertation, Universidade Federal do Amazonas (2008).

[5] Dias, *A Ilusão do Fausto*, 36–7. In having a small Afro-Brazilian population, Amazonia contrasted with Brazil's north-east and south-east, both of which had large African populations until slavery was abolished in 1888. The Amazon was distant from the main slave trade routes throughout the colonial period. Moreover, although the Brazilian government omitted to enforce the ban on the trade in 1831, persistent transatlantic smuggling was still prevented from

There are no extant official figures regarding the city's foreign contingent, but it seems to have been substantial: a Portuguese encyclopedia published in 1901, for example, asserted that foreigners counted for two-fifths of the population.[6] In contrast with South American operatic centres such as Buenos Aires, though, the largest foreign group in Manaus was not the Italians, but the Portuguese, who were heavily involved in overseeing the rubber trade alongside British, French, German and North American migrants. Some Italians undertook smaller business ventures in the city alongside Spaniards, Syrians and Lebanese, but there was no 'ready-made diasporic Italian context', as Benjamin Walton puts it.[7]

An institution for the elite, like most nineteenth-century opera houses, the Teatro's 700 seats accommodated only a small proportion of this diverse population on any one night. Moreover, although Manaus' elite comprised two strata – an established political group made up of Brazilians educated abroad, and the largely foreign *nouveau riche* of the rubber trade – the local press rarely mentioned any foreign names in relation to the Teatro.[8] Foreigners and rubber barons may have attended events, but the venue was primarily depicted (at least journalistically) as a place for cementing the social ties of the resident political class.

The impresario behind any given season was, more often than not, either the Brazilian Joaquim Franco (c. 1858–1927) or the Portuguese José Fernandes ('Juca') de Carvalho (1865–1948). Between them, these two entrepreneurs maintained extensive transatlantic networks that allowed them to source musicians in Europe (and occasionally North America) for seasons in Manaus.[9] The amount of opera they brought was relatively small, with only four Italian companies (in 1897, 1901, 1902 and 1906) and two French companies (in 1906 and 1907) appearing during this period. Their seasons were interspersed with revues, *zarzuelas*, variety shows and

---

reaching the north of Brazil by British naval ships stationed in the Caribbean. Weinstein, *The Amazon Rubber Boom*, 11, 44.

[6] Mesquita, *Manaus: História e Arquitetura*, 147.

[7] Benjamin Walton, 'Italian Operatic Fantasies in Latin America', *Journal of Modern Italian Studies*, 16/4 (2012), 460–71 (463). Weinstein, *The Amazon Rubber Boom*, 50–8.

[8] Ana Maria Daou, *A cidade, o teatro e o 'paiz das seringueiras': práticas e representações da sociedade amazonense na passagem do século XIX–XX* (Rio de Janeiro: Rio Books, 2014), 207–16.

[9] Biographical information on these impresarios is scarce, but some further details about their lives and musical activities can be found in Monteiro, *Teatro Amazonas*, 287–323; Márcio Páscoa, *A vida musical em Manaus na Época da Borracha (1850–1910)* (Manaus: Imprensa Oficial do Amazonas/Funarte, 1997), 93–100; Márcio Páscoa, *Ópera em Manaus* (Manaus: Valer Editora, 2009), 29, 45–50; Vicente Salles, *A Música e o Tempo no Grão-Pará* (Belém: Conselho Estadual de Cultura, 1980), 351.

dramatic works, performed by Brazilian, Portuguese, Spanish, Japanese and North American companies.[10]

Verdi was the composer most featured in the Italian opera seasons, his contribution mainly topped up with other international standards such as Mascagni's *Cavalleria rusticana*, Leoncavallo's *Pagliacci* and Puccini's *La bohème*. More old-fashioned bel canto operas were also performed, including Donizetti's *Lucrezia Borgia* and *Lucia di Lammermoor*, and Bellini's *La sonnambula*. The two French seasons then introduced French *grand opéra* (alongside a selection of operettas), featuring works such as Meyerbeer's *L'Africaine* and Gounod's *Faust*. The most distinguishing feature of these programmes, however, was the frequent inclusion of *Il Guarany*, the most famous opera by the Brazilian composer Antônio Carlos Gomes (1836–96).[11]

Despite the small size of Manaus' Italian population, the arrival of opera there is unsurprising: besides opera's long-standing presence in other parts of Brazil, the country as a whole saw high levels of Italian immigration around the turn of the twentieth century. Aided by subsidies from the Brazilian and Italian governments, most of these migrants travelled to Brazil to work on coffee plantations.[12] French culture also had a strong presence in Brazil throughout the nineteenth century, particularly influencing fashion, theatre, architecture, literature and the visual arts. The French language was taught in schools in Manaus from as early as 1848, and the city even nicknamed itself the 'Paris of the tropics'.[13]

---

[10] For a more complete chronology of opera and other performances at the Teatro during these years, see Monteiro, *Teatro Amazonas*; Márcio Páscoa, *Cronologia Lírica de Manaus* (Manaus: Valer Editora, 2000).

[11] English-language scholarship on Carlos Gomes remains scarce, but for a brief introduction to the composer and his operas, see Gerard Béhague, 'Gomes, (Antônio) Carlos', *Grove Music Online* (Oxford University Press, 2001), last accessed 15 January 2020: www.oxfordmusiconline.com/grovemusic/view/10.1093/gmo/9781561592630.001.0001/omo-9781561592630-e-0000011423?rskey=epTzmE. For an insightful reception history of *Il Guarany*, see Cristina Magaldi, 'Two Musical Representations of Brazil: Carlos Gomes and Villa-Lobos', in Carmen Nava and Ludwig Lauerhass (eds.), *Brazil in the Making: Facets of National Identity* (Oxford: Rowman and Littlefield, 2006), 205–28. For a comparison of the *Il Guarany* libretto with its original literary source (José de Alencar's 1857 novel *O Guarani*), see Maria Alice Volpe, 'Remaking the Brazilian Myth of National Foundation: "Il Guarany"', *Latin American Music Review*, 23/2 (2002), 179–94 (180–7).

[12] While Brazil needed to replenish a workforce depleted by the abolition of slavery in 1888, Italy was plagued by an economic crisis during this period. Warren Dean, 'Economy', in Leslie Bethell (ed.), *Brazil: Empire and Republic, 1822–1930* (Cambridge: Cambridge University Press, 1989), 236–40; Boris Fausto, 'Society and Politics', in Bethell (ed.), *Brazil: Empire and Republic*, 260–1.

[13] Augusto César Lopes Gonçalves, *O Amazonas: esboço histórico, chorographico e estatistico até o ano de 1903* (New York: Hugo J. Hanf, 1904), 92–3; Páscoa, *Ópera em Manaus*, 188–9.

Notable in its complete absence throughout the Amazon, however, was German opera: only one (failed) attempt was made to stage a Wagner opera during this period, when *Lohengrin* was advertised on the 1900 programme at Belém's opera house, the Theatro da Paz. Yet, although the Belém performance never took place, a latent enthusiasm for Wagner undoubtedly simmered among the *amazonense* press.[14] Two of Manaus' music critics adopted the pseudonyms 'Wagner' and 'Lohengrin', and the pseudonymous 'binocolini' (a columnist for the local newspaper *Amazonas* from 1890 to 1893) had called for Wagner operas to be performed in Manaus before the Teatro was even built.[15]

A move from Italian or French works to Wagner would have mirrored the operatic sequence that took place in imperial Rio de Janeiro, which, in its turn, imitated European tastes. Although Wagner's initial reception in Rio (in 1883) was a cold one, his operas became increasingly popular once European music criticism began to proliferate in the city, at which point homegrown critics transferred their allegiance and began to predict the downfall of Italian repertory.[16] The Italian (or French) to German sequence was so fully recognised, in fact, that it was much later parodied by the Colombian novelist Gabriel Garcia Márquez in his famous magical realism novel *Love in the Time of Cholera*. On Juvenal Urbino's introduction of opera to the novel's unnamed Colombian town, the narrator wryly comments, 'it never reached the extremes Dr Urbino had hoped for, which was to see Italianizers and Wagnerians confronting each other with sticks and canes during the intermissions'.[17]

The *opéras comiques* and operettas performed at the Teatro (usually in Italian translation) included internationally popular works by Robert Planquette, Franz von Suppé, Daniel Auber and Jacques Offenbach. Occasional zarzuela companies from Spain performed such works as *La Gran Via*, by Federico Chueca and Joaquín Valverde, and *La Tempestad*, by Ruperto Chapí. Portuguese and Brazilian companies also provided operettas and revues in the Portuguese language. The Silva Pinto Company, for example, travelled to Manaus from Rio in 1898, 1903 and 1906, performing classic Portuguese revues such as *Tim-tim por tim-tim*, by Antônio de Souza Bastos and Plácido Sticchini. The company also performed

---

[14] The term *amazonense* refers to somebody or something from the Brazilian state of Amazonas.
[15] Páscoa, *Ópera em Manaus*, 187–8.
[16] Cristina Magaldi, *Music in Imperial Rio de Janeiro* (Lanham, MD and Oxford: Scarecrow Press, 2004), 48–50.
[17] Gabriel Garcia Márquez, *Love in the Time of Cholera* (New York: Penguin Modern Classics, 2007), 52.

Brazilian revues that were popular in Rio at the time, including *Capital Federal*, by the renowned Brazilian playwright Artur Azevedo (1855–1908).[18]

On occasion, the Teatro's audiences also listened to Shakespeare, admired acrobatic feats or watched a 'pygmy company' of talented diminutive siblings performing ventriloquist acts.[19] Several of the Brazilian and Portuguese companies also put on new revues, written by residents of Manaus, which dealt with Amazonian themes. They included *O Senhor Especial* (performed in 1899), *O Regedor* (in 1901), *Acre* (in 1903), *Chico Francisco* (in 1903) and *Manaus em revista* (in 1906). Even though they were few in number, the incorporation of these revues into the Teatro's repertory shows that the local population did not exclusively consider it a venue to be passed through by foreign works and companies: efforts at locally grounding activities took place, albeit on a small scale.

Fantasies of Global Civilisation

The impresario Franco's name first began to appear in the Amazonian newspapers in the mid-1880s, when he was praised for his conducting skills: 'The *maestro*, Senhor Joaquim Franco, is indefatigable; a highly distinguished teacher, he works miracles with the small forces at his disposal. It is impossible to demand more from such a microscopic orchestra!'[20] When he later drew on his transatlantic networks to bring Italian opera companies to Manaus' Éden theatre (a predecessor of the Teatro Amazonas), it proved essential for him to undertake the required journeys in person. On one occasion, he was unable to do so, and instead telegraphed instructions to the Vittorio Delliliers theatrical agency in Milan regarding the kinds of performers he wanted.[21] His instructions were not followed accurately, however, and his irate comments on the resulting confusion appeared in *Amazonas*:

It is easy to assess how much this deplorable abuse by the agency in Milan frustrated the programme I had planned for this season. Deprived of a dramatic soprano as well as a dramatic tenor with the ability to sing dramatic operas, it was therefore impossible for the company to stage *Norma*, *[La] forza del destino*, *[Il] trovatore*, *Ruy Blas*, *[Un] ballo in maschera*, *Poliuto*, *[La] Gioconda*, *Jone*, *[I due]*

---

[18] Páscoa, *A vida musical em Manaus*, 134.   [19] Monteiro, *Teatro Amazonas*, 210, 270, 327–9.
[20] *Diário de Belém*, 11 July 1884.   [21] Páscoa, *Ópera em Manaus*, 53.

Foscari, the two last ones not yet heard, and for all of which that same agency sent me costumes, scenery and sheet music, as I can prove.[22]

This misfortune was just the beginning of a string of difficulties that Franco faced. The opera company that he sourced in 1896 had originally been due to inaugurate the Teatro on 5 September that year (the date commemorating Amazonas' designation as a province), but its debut was postponed by several months owing to delays in the major building works on the opera house. Being already en route to Amazonia, the company managed to arrange an extra stop in Belém, where it put on some performances at the Theatro da Paz in the meantime.[23] Based on local press reports, however, the company's season there was not entirely successful. One newspaper commented, 'Franco's company was infelicitous in its farewell ... staging a performance of *Un ballo in maschera* in which only Senhores [Vincenzo] Maina, [Francesco] Bonini, [Maria] Peri and [Ettore] Conti saved themselves. Everything else was a shipwreck, including the rather depleted orchestra.'[24]

From that point on, Franco's difficulties only increased. Two days after his company's 1897 debut in Manaus, the Amazonas government decided to lower the ticket prices for the remainder of the season;[25] the decision suggests that the opening night was not well attended. In fact, the whole season may have been badly attended, judging by the complaints made by Franco about his financial straits in the following months.[26] There were also issues with performances finishing late at night, frequent repetition of repertory, last-minute changes of programme and performers being paid late.[27] It may have been this glut of impresarial ineptitude that prompted the governor of Amazonas, Fileto Pires Ferreira (1866–1917, governor 1896–8), to refuse to offer financial support to the next Italian opera company due to perform at the Teatro, the Raphael Tomba Company. The decision would subsequently be reversed, but, at the time, Fileto Pires declared that the local government would no longer subsidise opera companies, instead allocating funds only to groups performing operettas or drama.[28] Italian opera had, if temporarily, fallen out of favour in Manaus.

---

[22] *Amazonas*, 10 March 1893, in Páscoa, *Cronologia Lírica de Manaus*, 94–5.
[23] *Folha do Norte*, 4 October 1896; 27 October 1896; Páscoa, *Ópera em Manaus*, 61.
[24] *Folha do Norte*, 28 December 1896.   [25] *Diário Oficial*, 9 January 1897.
[26] *Diário Oficial*, 13 November 1897. It is impossible to know for certain, however, as records of attendance were only kept between 1898 and 1899; furthermore, opera was relatively often a loss-making business for nineteenth-century impresarios. See John Rosselli, *The Opera Industry in Italy from Cimarosa to Verdi* (Cambridge: Cambridge University Press, 1984), 13–15.
[27] Monteiro, *Teatro Amazonas*, 171–87.   [28] Monteiro, *Teatro Amazonas*, 173–80.

The references in the Amazonian press to 'shipwrecks' of performances and 'depleted' or 'microscopic' orchestras imply that there was some tension between the grandiose, Italianate Teatro and the resources with which it was filled. The operatic ideal perhaps did not quite fit with the reality. This circumstance was far from unique to Manaus, of course: there are many similarly deflating reports from travellers (usually European) observing opera around the globe during the nineteenth century. The Frenchman Victor Jacquemont (1801–32), for example, wrote of the 'detestable company' and 'still more execrable orchestra' at the Rio opera in 1828; in 1836, the English novelist Emily Eden (1797–1869) complained that a contralto in Calcutta was 'immensely fat, with a cracked voice'; and a visitor to Buenos Aires in the 1850s commented that the opera house 'might be put on a footing with one of the most inferior establishments of London', denouncing its performers as 'perhaps a trifle above mediocrity'.[29] Nevertheless, neither disparagement from visiting Europeans nor any of the deficiencies perceived by local critics significantly eroded the local confidence in opera's civilising qualities.

On 9 April 1907, the pseudonymous columnist 'Nano', writing in the Manaus music magazine *A Platea*, referred to opera in terms of the 'spiritual education of a people'; later in the same column, he mentioned his admiration for Franco's 'enviable tenacity in the pursuit of the civilising work he began many years ago'.[30] A columnist in the following week's edition referred to the Teatro as 'a worthy monument to the other factors of civilisation in this auspicious land'.[31] Such rhetoric hints at the extent to which opera was conflated with civilisation in the Amazon, no matter how inadequately it was performed.[32] Of course, part of the job of the *A Platea* columnists was to dictate taste for their readership, a readership that primarily comprised the Teatro's regular attendees. As one of its editions humorously stated, '*A Platea* is the most widely circulated newspaper ... inside the Teatro Amazonas'.[33] It is therefore unsurprising that its writers wholeheartedly promoted the familiar image of opera as a civilising force.

---

[29] L. Hugh De Bonelli, *Travels in Bolivia, With a Tour across the Pampas to Buenos Ayres, etc.* (London: Hurst and Blackett, 1854), vol. 2, 312, in Walton, 'Italian Operatic Fantasies in Latin America', 464; Victor Jacquemont, *Letters from India* (London: Edward Churton, 1835), vol. 1, 70, in Walton, 'Italian Operatic Fantasies in Latin America', 464; Emily Eden, *Letters from India* (London: Richard Bentley, 1872), vol. 1, 107, in Benjamin Walton, '*L'italiana* in Calcutta', in Suzanne Aspden (ed.), *Operatic Geographies: The Place of Opera and the Opera House* (Chicago; London: University of Chicago Press, 2019), 124. Compare similar examples in the introduction to this volume.

[30] *A Platea*, 9 April 1907.   [31] *A Platea*, 16 April 1907.

[32] See Walton, '*L'italiana* in Calcutta', 124–5.   [33] *A Platea*, 20 April 1907.

Opera in the Time of Yellow Fever

Following his initial 1897 season, Franco did not bring another opera company to the Teatro until 1906, instead remaining in Manaus to work as a music teacher at the Academia das Belas Artes.[34] In the interim years, space opened up at the opera house for touring companies of various musical styles and genres. The remainder of 1897 saw the arrival of Tomba's Italian company (which put on a season despite the state governor's short-lived misgivings), as well as performances by a variety company from North America and a dramatic season put on by the Brazilian Dias Braga Company.[35] The last of these groups prompted a mournful response from the Amazonian poet Thaumaturgo Vaz (1869–1921), writing under the pseudonym 'Júlio Clemente'. In a poem published in the local newspaper *O Rio Negro* on 20 August 1897, Vaz commented on a production of Louis Péricaud's and Gaston Marot's 1889 stage play *Jack the Ripper*:

Mr Dias Braga, what are you doing
With your company . . .
Why do you bring us
Weeping instead of joy?

Are these sorrows not enough
That we have offstage?
Wars, intrigues, villainy
And deaths that cause suffering?

. . . And excuse my urge
To ask you favours . . .
But I cried the whole night long
I need now to laugh.[36]

It is unclear whether the poet's call for more cheerful productions was motivated by specific melancholies, but there was certainly reason for sorrow 'offstage' that year: a smallpox epidemic affecting Amazonas and various other parts of Brazil. Boats arriving in Manaus were quarantined and disinfected before disembarkation, and disinfectant was also applied to the opera house in an attempt to combat the disease.[37] It is understandable that local residents, including the poet Vaz, might have wanted the Teatro

---

[34] Páscoa, *Ópera em Manaus*, 68.   [35] Monteiro, *Teatro Amazonas*, 207–13.
[36] *O Rio Negro*, 20 September 1897, in Monteiro, *Teatro Amazonas*, 213.
[37] *Diário Oficial*, 7 August 1897.

to serve as an avenue for escapism during this time, rather than as a reminder of the mounting death toll.

Tomba's season that year was a success. Besides receiving praise in the *amazonense* press, the company's conductor waxed lyrical in the Milanese magazine *Le Quinte* on his return home, writing, 'The evening in Pernambuco was exciting, that of Pará magnificent, that of Manaus delirious'.[38] The following year, on 8 October, the Manaus newspaper *A Federação* published the upcoming programme for the company's imminent return visit. Several weeks later, however, Tomba's secretary attended the newspaper's offices to explain why the company had failed to arrive for the advertised season: on receiving a warning by telegram from a contact in Belém, the performers had become alarmed by the risks they ran travelling to a region so ravaged by disease and had elected to travel to Rio instead.[39]

Three years later, an Italian operetta company was disastrously afflicted by another disease during its season at the Teatro, one of the most feared ailments in South America at that time: yellow fever. The Calil and Aprea Italian Operetta Company suffered fourteen deaths from the virus while in Manaus, including the loss of its conductor, and the remaining performers cut their season short to return to Italy in light of the tragedy.[40] The incident was soon reported on (and sensationalised) by the musical press back in Europe, with the Parisian *Le Monde Artiste* taking care to emphasise the 'dramatic side of the situation'. After pointing out that the fever's 'ravages' had begun following a masked ball, its column recounted members of the company being 'suddenly seized with fear' and reported that a feverish prima donna had died from haemorrhaging after biting her tongue in a fit of hysteria.[41]

These two examples are just a small selection of the many instances of Italian companies cancelling performances in Manaus in response to reports of epidemics. It is, moreover, impossible to know how many more companies may have been put off arranging to travel to the city in the first place. It is indisputable, of course, that there were deaths from various diseases during this period; however, this state of affairs was not restricted to the Amazon. Yellow fever, for example, was widespread throughout Brazil, including in Rio.[42] Although disease caused real concerns, then, it is worth questioning why companies were more willing to perform in Rio than in Manaus even though yellow fever was prevalent in both cities.

---

[38] *Le Quinte* 1897, in Monteiro, *Teatro Amazonas*, 242.
[39] Monteiro, *Teatro Amazonas*, 242–5.   [40] Ibid., 295–7.   [41] *Le Monde Artiste*, 20 May 1900.
[42] Monteiro, *Teatro Amazonas*, 242–5, 335; Jeffrey Needell, *A Tropical Belle Époque* (Cambridge: Cambridge University Press, 1987), 251.

The explanation (at least, one explanation) is that several European publications during this period contended that the Amazonian climate was inherently unhealthy.[43] In 1901, for example, the Italian Gemma Ferruggia (1867–1930) had her Amazonian travelogue published in Milan. In it, she reports her encounters with yellow fever in Manaus in vivid terms, describing the chilling screams of a compatriot struck by the disease in the Italian-owned Hotel Cassiano. Filled with 'terror', 'nervousness' and 'anguish', she is then relieved to behold an Italian steamship, the Re Umberto, arriving at the docks ready to take her home: 'Incapable of joy, and incapable of tears, I remained for a long time, motionless: I stared at our flag, and I do not know what beneficent wave of tears came to me from the sight of those blessed colours unfurling in the wind – greeting and salvation.'[44]

The powerful Amazonian intellectual Frederico José de Santa-Anna Nery (1848–1901) sought to counteract the negative images that Ferruggia and others cultivated of the Amazonian climate. In 1899, he had his book *Le Pays des Amazones* published in France; it was also published in Italian (in 1900) and English (in 1901).[45] In it, he complains that, 'Emigrants from Europe have avoided Amazonia because of the generally spread prejudice on this side of the Ocean which regards these beautiful lands as uninhabitable, or, at least, very dangerous to foreigners. Ignorance has attributed to them an unbearable temperature, and an atmosphere laden with pestilent miasma.'[46] In an attempt to assuage this 'prejudice', he declares that Europeans too often view all hot countries in the same light and have probably confused the Brazilian Amazon with its neighbour French Guiana (which, he muses, probably deserves its 'evil reputation'). He then proceeds to explain away the high mortality rates in Manaus during 1897:

The year 1897 was one of exceptional mortality for Manáos, for that town was struck at the same time by an epidemic of small-pox, imported by a steamer, and by an outbreak of malaria, principally due to the removal of earth occasioned by the great public works then being undertaken. Notwithstanding that, the report presented by Dr Gouveia, the Director of Hygiene, is still reassuring. The number of deaths during that year (1897) rose to 1,323 in a population which is no less than 45,000. The death-rate was therefore 29.4 per 1000, but if from this number we

---

[43] See Mesquita, *Manaus: História e Arquitetura*, 184–5.
[44] Gemma Ferruggia, *Nostra Signora del mar dolce: Missioni e paesaggi di Amazzonia* (Milan: L. F. Cogliati, 1901), 397–8.
[45] *L'Amazzonia*, 15 January 1900. The first French edition of the book was published in 1884, but the 1899 edition was substantially rewritten. Frederico José de Santa-Anna Nery, *The Land of the Amazons*, trans. G. Humphery (London: Sands and Company, 1901), ix.
[46] Nery, *The Land of the Amazons*, 53.

deduct 232 deaths from small-pox, there remains only a death-rate of 24.25, which may be regarded as the annual average death-rate of [Rio].[47]

Nery's efforts to promote the Amazon, however, were not especially successful. For one thing, mortality rates rose significantly shortly after 1897, with yellow fever proving particularly destructive in 1900, the year in which the Italian operetta company was so disastrously afflicted.[48] Even seven years later, during Manaus' 1907 opera season, several columns in *A Platea* emphasised the continuing difficulties involved in securing European companies to perform at the Teatro: 'The struggle that must be waged in Europe to organise a company bound for the extreme north of Brazil is incalculable. Unfortunately it is still believed there that the foreigner comes to these shores only to die.'[49] Throughout its initial decade, then, the Teatro faced a constant obstacle in its efforts to attract touring companies to a region consistently viewed as disease-ridden.

The musical and theatrical companies' reaction to yellow fever and other diseases in Manaus can be read on two levels. On one level, the threat to life was real; on another, the depiction of a city plagued by epidemics plays into larger tropes regarding disease in the tropics.[50] As Jessica Howell has shown, by the end of the nineteenth century, many European travellers had honed the technique of blaming disease contracted in tropical regions on climate. Although this technique was invoked for a wide range of reasons (sometimes to encourage imperial expansion, sometimes to discourage it, sometimes to emphasise the heroism of the individual writer's endeavours, and so on) it was nevertheless invoked persistently, even after scientific experiments had begun to show that many 'tropical diseases' were *not* directly contracted from the surrounding environment.[51] Although Manaus' elite considered their city and its opera house to be participants in a global civilisation, Italian (and French) musicians and journalists regarded and portrayed it as a dangerous place. Local narratives of progress that adopted opera (perhaps Italy's most famous cultural export) as their pennant were undermined from overseas by inhabitants of the very nation that furnished this imposing icon of civilisation.

---

[47] Ibid., 55–6.   [48] Gonçalves, *O Amazonas*, 69.
[49] *A Platea*, 13 April 1907; see also 9 April 1907.
[50] See Martin Mahony and Georgina Endfield, 'Climate and Colonialism', *Wiley Interdisciplinary Reviews: Climate Change*, 9/2 (2018); Pablo Mukherjee, 'Cholera, Kipling, and Tropical India', in Greg Garrard (ed.), *The Oxford Handbook of Ecocriticism* (Oxford: Oxford University Press, 2014).
[51] Jessica Howell, *Exploring Victorian Travel Literature: Disease, Race and Climate* (Edinburgh: Edinburgh University Press, 2014), 1–23.

Sifting the Local, the National and the International

When the impresario Franco reemerged on the Manaus opera scene in 1906, he did so by way of Paris, where he had managed to source his first French opera company. Prior to its arrival, the company's upcoming season was enthusiastically publicised in *Amazonas*:

> We will very shortly have a splendid theatrical season. Maestro Franco, who, as we know, left for Europe to organise a French company of opera and operetta, was able to gather in Paris elements of the first order ... The artists have an established reputation and many of them have already worked at the Opéra and the *opéra comique* of Paris, the two best opera houses in France.[52]

While neither the means by which Franco managed to secure this company in Paris nor his motivations for switching from Italian to French performers and repertory are entirely clear, he certainly had a network of personal contacts that reached as far as Paris. The French conductor Edouard Boni (dates unknown), for example, had conducted Franco's 1897 Italian company, having previously worked with numerous French orchestras from Cherbourg to Marseilles.[53] Franco furthermore organised several concerts in both Manaus and Belém with the Brazilian violinist and composer Elpídio Pereira (1872–1961), who studied at the Paris Conservatoire in 1890–2 and 1898–1903.[54] This link with the Parisian institution had another significant outcome: the second and last of Franco's French opera companies, which put on a season from 30 March to 29 May 1907, performed Carlos Gomes' *Il Guarany* in a new French translation that had been made by Jules Algier, reportedly a professor of voice at the Conservatoire.[55] This 1907 performance was the first time that the opera had ever been put on in French, a feat that *A Platea* described as 'a victory for Maestro Franco and for his company'.[56]

The most famous of Carlos Gomes' operas (he wrote eight), and the only one to have retained a foothold in the international repertory until the present day, *Il Guarany* was also the only one of his works performed at the Teatro in its early years. This was the case despite the personal connections

---

[52] *Amazonas*, 27 May 1906, in Monteiro, *Teatro Amazonas*, 370.   [53] *A Platea*, 9 April 1907.
[54] Páscoa, *Ópera em Manaus*, 145–54; Elpídio de Britto Pereira, *A música, o consulado e eu: memórias de Elpídio Pereira* (Rio de Janeiro: n.p., 1957).
[55] Although Algier (18??–1933) certainly gave singing lessons in Paris, the Conservatoire has no records of him in its archive (*L'Œuvre*, 12 December 1933; *Le Petit Journal*, 12 December 1933). It is possible that the Amazonian press claimed he had taught there in order to imbue him with higher status.
[56] *A Platea*, 7 May 1907.

the composer had with the Amazon, having lived his last years in Belém, where he died in 1896. That city's Theatro da Paz did not programme many more of his works, adding only productions of *Salvator Rosa* (in 1882) and *Fosca* (in 1895).[57] Franco's opera companies therefore (if perhaps unconsciously) treated Carlos Gomes' works as though their value lay solely in *Il Guarany*, the only one to premiere at Milan's Teatro alla Scala (in 1870) and to achieve renown in Europe.

Adapted from José de Alencar's 1857 novel *O Guaraní*, the opera is set in sixteenth-century colonial Brazil and tells the story of the love of Peri (chief of the indigenous Guaraní tribe) for Ceci (the daughter of a Portuguese nobleman, Don Antonio). Their romance is overlaid onto an ongoing conflict between the Portuguese and the local Aimoré tribe, which is complicated by the treachery of a group of Spaniards residing in Don Antonio's house. The opera ends with a dramatic explosion, as Don Antonio blows up his own home, killing himself and taking the enemy Aimorés and the duplicitous Spaniards with him. Moments before carrying out his suicide mission, Don Antonio allows Peri, who has at this point converted to Christianity, to flee the castle with Ceci in his charge.[58]

The world premiere of the new translation took place at the Teatro on 13 May 1907, on which day a special extended edition of *A Platea* was circulated in homage to Carlos Gomes. Two weeks earlier, the magazine had already been stoking the enthusiasm of the Manaus audiences, commenting, 'If things go well and no unexpected difficulties hinder the good will of Maestro Franco, the performance of *[Le] Guarany* will be, without doubt, the centrepiece of this opera season'. The article went on:

> Manaus must pride itself on this privilege – the masterpiece of our ever mourned Carlos Gomes, for the first time sung in the language of Victor Hugo, in this beautiful theatre, thanks to the State Government, the only one in Brazil today that aspires to educate public taste through the most beautiful of the Fine Arts, and to our tireless *maestro* Joaquim Franco . . . who spared neither efforts nor sacrifices to

---

[57] Márcio Páscoa, *Cronologia Lírica de Belém* (Belém: AATP, 2006), 62, 124.

[58] For a more detailed plot summary, see Gerard Béhague, 'Guarany, Il', *Grove Music Online* (Oxford University Press, 2002), last accessed 15 January 2020, www.oxfordmusiconline.com/grovemusic/view/10.1093/gmo/9781561592630.001.0001/omo-9781561592630-e-5000009516?rskey=JW72G4&result=1. Peri's escape with Ceci is visually depicted in a painting hung in the Teatro's Salão Nobre, a lavishly decorated room kept for social activities. It is the only one of the opera house's decorative features that depicts an indigenous Amazonian, such that the one nod to indigeneity actually alludes to Christianity prevailing over indigenous beliefs. For more information on the paintings in the Salão Nobre, see Ana Maria Daou, 'Natureza e civilização: os painéis decorativos do Salão Nobre do Teatro Amazonas', *História, Ciências, Saúde – Manguinhos*, 14 (2007), 51–71.

fulfil his promise – to bring, among the repertory of the company he was organising, *Le Guarany*, sung by French artists in their own language.[59]

It is worth considering the 'tireless *maestro*'s' motivations for commissioning this translation of the opera from its original Italian into French. His French company might naturally be expected to sing in French much better than in Italian, but he could have left this work for Italian companies to perform or commissioned a Portuguese-language edition. As with the change from Italian to French companies, it is impossible to know what was in Franco's mind when he made this decision. It is possible, however, to glean something from the reactions to it displayed in the local musical press. A further extract from *A Platea* aptly demonstrates the peculiar sense of patriotism associated with this performance of *Le Guarany*:

All those who had the unforgettable pleasure of watching the elegant *soirée* on Monday – the most brilliant artistic event Amazonas has had – observed the beauty of the work of J. Algier, who knew how to sift the verse with perfection ... The house was full. There vibrated Art and Patriotism. *Guarany* is very national: its music has ferocious roars and subtleties of feeling ... And, to finish this article, we will make on behalf of the *amazonense* audience a request that we consider fair. It desires, it wants, it asks through us, that the next performance of *Guarany* be conducted by Maestro Joaquim Franco. Nothing more reasonable. And Maestro [Edouard] Boni ... cannot be offended, for we have not spared him applause. It is a question of patriotism; the people wish that, for just one night, *Guarany*, [composed] by a Brazilian *maestro*, should also be conducted by a Brazilian *maestro*.[60]

This strident assertion of the opera's national character must be unpacked: it was, of course, written by a Brazilian composer, but a Brazilian composer who spent most of his professional life in Milan. It was furthermore composed to premiere at the Teatro alla Scala, to an Italian libretto and in a Verdian musical style adorned by Donizettian flourishes in the part of Ceci. The opera's plot, admittedly, tells of Brazil, and Maria Alice Volpe has gone so far as to argue that it symbolises the origins of Brazilian history through its depiction of miscegenation.[61] Beyond that, though, the extent to which it could be described as Brazilian remains a complex question.[62]

---

[59] *A Platea*, 30 April 1907.   [60] *A Platea*, 18 May 1907.
[61] Volpe, 'Remaking the Brazilian Myth of National Foundation', 180–7.
[62] Questions about what constitutes *brasilidade* (Brazilianness) circulate prolifically in scholarship on Brazil. For a concise review of the literature on varying manifestations of *brasilidade* in the early twentieth century, see Barbara Weinstein, 'Postcolonial Brazil', in José C. Moya (ed.), *The Oxford Handbook of Latin American History* (Oxford: Oxford University Press, 2011), 222–3.

There is, then, a strategic handling of local, national and international interests underlying the *A Platea* extract: this 1907 performance of *Le Guarany* was an instance of the Teatro attempting to promote its local artistic credentials by channelling the successes of a national musical hero through the measuring system of European standards. Furthermore, its supposed educational function was espoused by another columnist of *A Platea*, who humorously construed the new translation as a necessary relief from the deluge of Italian opera with which Manaus had been assaulted up to that point (albeit a 'deluge' of only six seasons, including those that took place before the Teatro was built). He wrote, 'And Maestro Franco, perceiving the symptoms of this aural gastralgia, undertook to cure it by way of periodic applications of French remedies.' He then proceeded on a more serious note, though, to clarify his opinion: that one could not *really* ever get bored of Italian opera, as Verdi alone provided enough variety to satisfy even those with the most eclectic tastes. Even so, he was adamant that 'the spiritual education of a people cannot be established with [exposure to] only one school, only one style'.[63] Admittedly, this is the opinion of only one journalist, but it perhaps gives us licence to interpret the shift from Italian to French opera as a striving for the variety desired by an urban elite concerned with their city's improvement and aiming to compete with the cultural centres of Europe. Seen in this way, the *Le Guarany* premiere provided a means for the Teatro to sift and combine two foreign operatic influences in pursuit of local aggrandisement. The Italian and the French were not interchangeable – it was not the case that either would do as a representation of Europeanness – but they were valuable cumulatively.

***

In line with historical precedent, the personal transatlantic networks established by a Brazilian and a Portuguese impresario encouraged the Amazon's adoption of Italian (and briefly French) opera at the turn of the twentieth century. The political elite for which the Teatro functioned was so eager to engage in their idea of global civilisation that, no matter what went wrong in practice (from 'shipwrecks' of performances to 'microscopic' orchestras) the rhetoric of opera's civilising qualities largely held strong. Portrayals of the Teatro in Italy and France, however, were another matter, and the spate of local epidemics comprised a major obstacle to attracting performers. Although the threat to life was real, texts published

---

[63] *A Platea*, 9 April 1907.

in these two countries also dramatised the situation, demonising the tropics such that local narratives of civilisation were undermined from abroad. Even so, the 1907 premiere of *Le Guarany* provided a means for Manaus to interweave two foreign operatic influences with strands of patriotism for the sake of local prestige. Shortly after the *Le Guarany* performance, though, the local economy crashed when the region lost its monopoly on the global rubber trade, taking with it the resources to sustain any more opera of any national background for the next ninety years.

14 | Between 'Sung Theatre' and Asakusa Opera

In Search of *Italianità* in Early Japanese Opera History

MICHAEL FACIUS

In his seminal study on the early history of opera in Japan, Masui Keiji divides his narrative into five stages.[1] The first one is a prologue of isolated encounters with Western sung theatre in the confined space of Dejima, an artificial island in the bay of Nagasaki where the Dutch were permitted to trade between the seventeenth and nineteenth centuries. The second stage, which Masui dubs a prehistory, is one of an increased Western presence in Japan after the formal opening of diplomatic and trade relations with Europe and the United States in the 1850s. It allowed sung theatre to thrive in the foreign quarters of the port cities, albeit almost exclusively performed by Euro-American troupes for Euro-American audiences.

Masui's next turning point is the first Japanese-led attempt to perform a European opera, a version of Gluck's *Orfeo ed Euridice*, at the Tokyo Music School in 1903 and its wider context of intensifying conceptual and practical engagement with European performing arts. The fourth and fifth stages, finally, are marked by a gradual emergence of local institutions and traditions of operatic performance epitomised by the establishment of the privately run Imperial Theatre in 1911, and their vernacularisation leading up to the Great Kanto Earthquake of 1923 in the form of vaudeville and cabaret-like genres in the popular Tokyo entertainment district of Asakusa.

To mark these developments as 'early history' implies, of course, another juncture and underlying value system: the beginning of a substantial 'unadulterated' performance history of the Western operatic canon. Masui states this

---

* In accordance with Japanese usage, Japanese names are given in the main text with the family name first; footnotes follow the Western order. I would like to thank Axel Körner for his invitation to contribute to this volume, editorial patience and valuable comments. *Grazie mille* to Luca Artuso for pointing me towards additional resources on Italian artists in Meiji Japan. Many thanks also to Hoang Nguyen for discussing and enjoying opera with me while I prepared the first drafts. Research for this article was funded by a British Academy Newton International Fellowship.

[1] Keiji Masui, *Nihon no opera: Meiji kara Taishō e* (Tokyo: Min'on ongaku shiryōkan, 1984). Other significant Japanese-language works on the early history of Japanese opera are; Keiji Masui, *Nihon opera shi*, 2 vols. (Tokyo: Suiyōsha, 2003); Shin kokuritsu gekijō (ed.), *Nihon no opera: Kaigai kara no juyō to nihon opera no shinka* (Tokyo: Shin kokuritsu gekijō un'ei zaidan, 2012); and Yoshio Sagawa, *Nihon opera no kiseki: Ayumi, sakuhin, hito* (Tokyo: Geijutsu gendaisha, 2006).

more directly in his comprehensive two-volume history, which brings the narrative up to the present, by describing the years after 1923 as a 'warm-up time' for the period when 'opera finally began'.[2] This 'true' beginning is ushered in by none other than a performance of Giacomo Puccini's *La Bohème* at the Public Hall in Tokyo's Hibiya Park in June 1934 under the aegis of the Japanese tenor Fujiwara Yoshie (1898–1976).

Fujiwara's *Bohème* is a fitting starting point for a reflection on the significance of *italianità* – a coherent image and recognition of Italy and its cultural power in the field of opera – in Japanese opera history. The 1934 performance was indeed the first one in Japan to include all four acts of the opera and to be given completely in Italian (apart from Satō Yoshiko's Musetta, who sang in French due to an emergency swap of singers).[3] This late first for Italian opera in Japan begs the question as to what role Italy and a sense of Italianness had played in the six preceding decades. There were, in fact, all sorts of Italian influences right from the 1870s, but for reasons to be explored below, they failed to add up to a notion of *italianità* or a heightened relevance of Italian models for opera in Japan.

It is useful to briefly dwell on the historiographical meaning of the caesura of 1934. Despite the immense efforts Masui undertook to give early opera history its due recognition at a time where most scholars believed it to be 'of little importance from a contemporary perspective', it is still underwritten to some extent by a Eurocentric chronology that measures Japanese sung theatre against the yardstick of the European, and here implicitly Italian, operatic tradition.[4] Even Jürgen Osterhammel's magisterial global history of the nineteenth century perpetuates this perspective by highlighting not the first composition of an opera in Japanese, but the 'opening of the first large Western-style theatre' in 1911 in his short sketch of the history of the genre in Japan.[5]

More than anything, the case of Japan seems to circumscribe the limits of the spread of Western art forms, especially when considered in the framework of the 'long nineteenth century' as in Osterhammel's *Global History* or, indeed, in this volume. It is, however, not the aim of this chapter to reclaim early opera history from a Eurocentric narrative. Scholars in global cultural and intellectual history have rigorously questioned and dismantled both overt and implicit Eurocentric assumptions of value and artistic development for the last two

---

[2] Masui, *Nihon opera shi*, vol. 1, 194 and 222.   [3] Masui, *Nihon opera shi*, vol. 1, 222.
[4] Masui, *Nihon no opera*, vi.
[5] Jürgen Osterhammel, *The Transformation of the World: A Global History of the Nineteenth Century* (Princeton, NJ: Princeton University Press, 2014), 5–7.

decades.⁶ For opera history, Michael McClellan's article on opera in colonial Hanoi or Rashna Nicholson's chapter on South East Asia in this volume are two important contributions that argue for the centrality of local modes of adaption.⁷ More generally, scholars have been critiquing the limiting preoccupation with fidelity and *Werktreue* that often informs opera studies independently of transcultural connections, to point out that opera is in fact the adaptive art form par excellence.⁸

For Japanese opera, Ōnishi Yuki has recently offered a substantial book-length revision of previous accounts of early opera history that investigates the subtly shifting processes of cultural translation in librettos, music and performance praxis.⁹ Attending to one specific episode, Matsumoto Naomi has made the point that the Italian choreographer Vittorio Rosi's short-lived efforts to stage opera at the Imperial Theatre after 1912 were not a 'failure', but a noteworthy form of 'syncultural construction'.¹⁰

Building on these insights, this chapter approaches opera history as a process of cultural translation and transculturation and examines presences and absences of Italian influence to reflect on the meaning of *italianità* in Japan. To do so, it begins with a recapitulation of the setting in which Western opera was first introduced. It then discusses, in turn, several factors that shaped the Japanese engagement with this cultural form: the state and cultural policy, cultural and linguistic translation, aesthetic theories and vernacularisation. All of these, as the chapter shows, intertwined in a way that precluded a heightened relevance for Italian opera qua Italian opera until the late 1930s.

---

⁶ Madeleine Herren, Martin Rüesch, and Christiane Sibille, *Transcultural History: Theories, Methods, Sources* (Berlin: Springer, 2012); Samuel Moyn and Andrew Sartori, *Global Intellectual History* (New York: Columbia University Press, 2013). David Hebert, 'Cultural Translation and Music: A Theoretical Model and Examples from Japan', in Noriko Takei-Thunman and Nanyan Guo (eds.), *Cultural Translations: Proceedings of the Workshop/Symposium in Varberg and Kyoto* (Gothenburg: Göteborgs Universitet, 2011), 20–40; Yayoi Uno Everett and Frederick Lau (eds.), *Locating East Asia in Western Art Music* (Middletown, CT: Wesleyan University Press, 2004).

⁷ Michael McClellan, 'Performing Empire: Opera in Colonial Hanoi', *Journal of Musicological Research* 22/1–2 (2003), 135–66; Rashna Darius Nicholson, 'Italian Impresarios, American Minstrels and Parsi Theatre: Sonic Networks and the Negotiation of Opera in Colonial South and South East Asia' in this volume (Chapter 11).

⁸ Linda Hutcheon and Michael Hutcheon, 'Adaption and Opera', in Thomas Leitch (ed.), *The Oxford Handbook of Adaption Studies* (Oxford: Oxford University Press, 2017), 305–23.

⁹ Yuki Ōnishi, *Nihongo opera no tanjō: Ōgai, Shōyō kara Asakusa opera made* (Tokyo: Shinwasha, 2018). For another recent case study in Japanese music history, see Margaret Mehl, *Not by Love Alone: The Violin in Japan, 1850–2010* (Copenhagen: The Sound Book Press, 2014).

¹⁰ Naomi Matsumoto, 'Giovanni Vittorio Rosi's Musical Theatre: Opera, Operetta, and the Westernization of Modern Japan', in Michela Niccolai and Clair Rowden (eds.), *Musical Theatre in Europe 1830–1945* (Turnhout: Brepols, 2017), 351–86.

Early Intersections between Japan and Western Opera

The earliest encounters with European musical theatre took place in a very circumscribed setting: the small man-made island of Dejima in the harbour of Nagasaki, to which the Dutch trading outpost was confined throughout the Tokugawa period (1600–1868).[11] A limited number of Japanese literati and scholars had permission to visit, and they were entertained in the quarters of the *opperhoofd* with music and theatrical performances by the Dutch residents. We know, for example, of a performance of an opera-like piece called *The Two Hunters and the Dairy-Maid* in 1820, because the famous writer Ōta Nanpo (1749–1823) recorded it in a collection of miscellanea, casually labelling it a 'Dutch impromptu comedic play' (*oranda niwaka shibai kyōgen*) and thus highlighting its commensurability with Japanese theatrical tradition.[12]

These rare and rather inconsequential events aside, a substantial presence of opera made itself felt only after the opening of diplomatic and trade relations with the United States and the major European countries in the later 1850s.[13] From then on, foreigners were permitted to take up residence in designated neighbourhoods in port cities such as Yokohama and Kōbe. The well-known *Yokohama-e* woodblock prints created by Japanese artists around 1860, mentioned in the introduction to this volume, afford us a glimpse into the vibrant bustle of the European and American neighbourhood in Yokohama and the exotic appearance and customs of its residents. One of these prints also depicted a grand marching band with trumpeters and drummers, illustrating both the novel presence of Western music in Japan and its perceived strangeness.[14]

Soon, the Western residents began performing operas and operettas. Given the dominance of the anglophone presence and the amateur character of these performances, staged works leaned towards lighter English-language comedic operas such as Arthur Sullivan's *Cox and Box*. When the

---

[11] Grant K. Goodman, *Japan: The Dutch Experience* (London: The Athlone Press, 1986).

[12] Masui, *Nihon no opera*, 2f; see also Yuichi Takeuchi, 'Dejima no ongaku fūkei: "Nagasaki Oranda shōkan nikki" ni miru ongaku kiji (1801–1822)', *Kokuritsu ongaku daigaku kenkyū kiyō*, 34 (1999), 328–36.

[13] For a general background of the geopolitical situation in Japan in the 1850s, see L. M. Cullen, *A History of Japan, 1582–1941: Internal and External Worlds* (Cambridge: Cambridge University Press, 2003), 175–204 and Andrew Gordon, *A Modern History of Japan: From Tokugawa Times to the Present* (Oxford: Oxford University Press, 2020), 47–59.

[14] Simon James Bytheway, 'The Arrival of the "Modern" West in Yokohama: Images of the Japanese Experience, 1859–1899', in Donna Brunero and Stephanie Villalta Puig (eds.), *Life in Treaty Port China and Japan* (Basingstoke: Palgrave Macmillan, 2018), 247–68.

Gaiety Theatre on Yokohama's Honchō-doori opened its doors in December 1870, it became the go-to venue for Western performing arts, and soon enough not just amateur groups, but also professional opera troupes from all over Europe made a stop there during their world tours.[15] It was mostly foreigners performing for foreigners, and the shows were dominated by English, American, French and Russian troupes and an eclectic mix of excerpts and individual arias from operas by most of the major composers.

One of the rare records of Italian singers visiting in this period is of Maria Palmieri, prima donna at La Scala, and her sister Alice Persiani.[16] They gave what was advertised as a 'grand costume concert' at the Gaiety in September 1875 and were even invited to perform at the Imperial Palace. The satirical magazine *Japan Punch*, published by the English cartoonist Charles Wirgman, featured a caricature commemorating the event that depicted empty seats, dancing rats in the aisle and an Italian caption chaffing: 'His Majesty, preferring his concubine, was conspicuous by his absence. General cheerfulness among the rats, the impresario embarrassed.'[17]

As this shows, Western commentators were quite conscious of the cultural gap between European opera and its Japanese audiences. While the above cartoon was no more than an expression of Wirgman's personal assumptions, the first Japanese reactions to the foreign cultural form were indeed not overly enthusiastic. Early Japanese observers of the productions in Yokohama commented on the strangeness of European-style vocal expression. Adventurous producers in the world of Japanese *kabuki* theatre who attempted contemporary plays that incorporated Western settings and singing styles were met with similar reactions. When the Shintomi-za theatre in Tokyo staged Kawatake Mokuami's *The Strange Tale of the Castaways: A Western Kabuki*, whose grand finale was set outside the Paris Opéra and contained a real operatic scene performed by the Royal English Opera Company, which was visiting Japan at the time, the audience was 'seized with a wild fit of hilarity at the high notes of the prima donna, who really was not at all bad. The people laughed at the absurdities of European singing', as the British Japanologist Basil Hall Chamberlain related in his *Things Japanese*.[18]

---

[15] Sagawa, *Nihon opera no kiseki*, 13.

[16] For another example see Rashna Darius Nicholson's chapter in this volume, which mentions the Italian impresario Pompei visiting Yokohama with his company in 1880 (Chapter 11).

[17] Masui, *Nihon no opera*, 18f.

[18] Siyuan Liu, 'Paris and the Quest for a National Stage in Meiji Japan and Late-Qing China', *Asian Theatre Journal*, 26/1 (2009), 54–77, at 63.

While the Japanese grappled with what they came to describe as Western civilisation, European artists and audiences likewise became infatuated with imagining life and culture in Japan.[19] It became a recurring trope in European opera, most famously in Gilbert and Sullivan's Savoy opera *The Mikado* and Giacomo Puccini's *Madama Butterfly*. The composers of both operas made contact with Japanese in England and Italy respectively to add a degree of realism to their works: Gilbert and Sullivan visited the Japanese Village, an exhibition of Japanese culture in the Knightsbridge area of London, and hired residents to instruct their cast in Japanese manners.[20] Puccini corresponded with Ōyama Hisako, the wife of the Japanese ambassador in Italy, about Japanese music.[21] Yet, Japanese 'local flavour' in these works mainly served as a foil to negotiate European self-images and did not stray beyond the realm of exoticism and orientalism.[22]

Still, both works are an integral part of early Japanese opera history, as they were also watched, commented upon and later performed by Japanese, thus acting as a site of two-way cultural translation. Western companies had also made a first unsuccessful attempt to stage *The Mikado* in Kōbe as early as November 1885, mere months after its premiere in London. Two years later, in 1887, Salinger's Opera Bouffe Company finally performed the operetta at the Gaiety, but censored and under the new title of *Three Little Maids from School*, to avoid irritating Japanese sensibilities and charges of lese-majesty.[23] When *Madama Butterfly* made its way to Japan, it was cut into pieces and embedded in other art forms. At the first performance in January 1914 at the Imperial Theatre, an excerpt from the second act was performed in Italian, followed by Japanese songs and the national anthem 'Kimigayo', which reportedly received the strongest applause. Even in 1914, there was still little incentive for Japanese producers and audiences to appreciate its composer as a famed Italian maestro. Without even

---

[19] Grace E. Lavery, *Quaint, Exquisite: Victorian Aesthetics and the Idea of Japan* (Princeton, NJ: Princeton University Press, 2019).

[20] Hugh Cortazzi, *Japan in Late Victorian London: The Japanese Native Village in Knightsbridge and The Mikado, 1885* (Norwich: Sainsbury Institute for the Study of Japanese Arts and Cultures, 2009).

[21] Arthur Groos, 'Return of the Native: Japan in Madama Butterfly/Madama Butterfly in Japan', *Cambridge Opera Journal*, 1/2 (1989), 167–94; at 169f.

[22] Josephine Lee, *The Japan of Pure Invention: Gilbert and Sullivan's The Mikado* (Minneapolis: University of Minnesota Press, 2010); Arthur Groos, 'Madama Butterfly between East and West', in Arman Schwartz and Emanuele Senici (eds.), *Giacomo Puccini and His World* (Princeton, NJ: Princeton University Press, 2016), 49–84; W. Anthony Sheppard, 'Puccini und der Exotismus', in Richard Erkens (ed.), *Puccini-Handbuch* (Stuttgart: J. B. Metzler, 2017), 144–57.

[23] Lee, *Japan of Pure Invention*, 192.

mentioning Puccini, a review of the evening instead celebrated David Belasco, who had written the play which became Puccini's inspiration, for introducing Japanese customs to Western audiences. More fundamentally, roles were reversed from performances in Europe: the Japanese songs that had served as an exotic backdrop for Puccini became the main attraction, while the excerpt from *Madama Butterfly* turned into the exotic ingredient of the programme.[24]

The Meiji Government, Nation-Building and Western Music

The immediate dynamics behind the early intersections between opera and Japan largely emerged from Western audiences, troupes and composers who extended their imagination and activities to a Japanese setting. For the time being, the globalisation of opera met its limits in the indifference of Japanese audiences. Neither was the Japanese government especially proactive in taking up opera. The new government of Emperor Meiji, which came to power in 1868, embarked on an extensive reform programme with the purpose of strengthening the Japanese state vis-à-vis the Western imperial powers. This programme of self-strengthening rested upon the investigation and adaption of Western customs and institutions in pursuit of the construction of an imagined Japanese national community.[25] Early treatises in the 1860s such as *Conditions in the West*, compiled by the influential intellectual Fukuzawa Yukichi (1835–1901), described social and cultural institutions and forms across European countries and the United States as variations of one overarching civilisation.[26] While aware of national differences, Japanese thinkers eclectically took up what they found relevant and useful. Cultural aspects associated with the level of civilisation to which intellectuals and the government now aspired played a major role here, as the government strove to define a canon of national art and exhibit it in newly founded national museums.[27]

---

[24] Groos, 'Return of the Native', 178f.
[25] Carol Gluck, *Japan's Modern Myths: Ideology in the Late Meiji Period* (Princeton, NJ: Princeton University Press, 1985); Kevin Doak, *A History of Nationalism in Modern Japan: Placing the People* (Leiden: Brill, 2007).
[26] Carmen Blacker, *The Japanese Enlightenment: A Study of the Writings of Fukuzawa Yukichi* (Cambridge: Cambridge University Press, 1964).
[27] Dōshin Satō, *Modern Japanese Art and the Meiji State: The Politics of Beauty*, trans. Hiroshi Nara (Los Angeles: Getty Research Institute, 2011); Alice Y. Tseng, *The Imperial Museums of Meiji Japan: Architecture and the Art of the Nation* (Seattle: University of Washington Press, 2008).

Officials came to seek out the perceived excellence of individual countries in particular fields and hired experts from these countries to teach in Japan. Here, the government recognised Italy's leadership in the arts: it hired three Italian artists in the 1870s to teach at the Technical Art School in the subjects of painting, sculpture and architecture, respectively.[28] A complementary measure of Meiji cultural policy was to send Japanese students abroad to study the languages, cultures and academic disciplines of Western countries. Two representative cases in the fine arts were the painter Kawamura Kiyoo (1852–1934) and the sculptor Naganuma Moriyoshi (1857–1942), who studied at the Accademia di Belle Arti in Venice.[29] Taki Rentarō (1879–1903), mentioned in the introduction of this book, went to study music in Leipzig.

Shortly after its rise to power in 1868, the government sent an embassy of high-ranking officials, the so-called Iwakura mission, on an eighteen-month-long trip across Europe and the United States to penetrate the inner workings of Western societies.[30] The mission took note of every detail and reported it back to the government at home. Its members first encountered European opera at performances of Wagner's *Tannhäuser* in Brussels and of *Lohengrin* in Berlin. Apart from the performance on stage, they were also attentively following the performance of national prestige communicated through the architecture of the opera house, its social rituals and the attendance of high-ranking government officials.[31] Despite opera's role as a 'pre-eminent contributor to nationalism' in Europe, however, it never became a major ingredient of Meiji period (1868–1912) nation-building policies.[32]

One apparent reason for this was surely the complexity of opera as a composite art form. Attempts to inject operatic elements into second mention, decursivize theatre, such as Kawatake's *Western Kabuki*, were unsuccessful due to long-standing institutional and generic

---

[28] Emiko Yamanashi, 'Western-Style Painting: Four Stages of Acceptance', in J. Thomas Rimer and Toshiko McCallum (eds.), *Since Meiji: Perspectives on the Japanese Visual Arts, 1868–2000* (Honolulu: University of Hawai'i Press, 2012), 19–33, at 19; see also Teresa Ciapparoni La Rocca, Pierfrancesco Fedi and Maria Teresa Lucidi (eds.), *Italiani nel Giappone Meiji (1868–1912): Atti del convegno internazionale bilaterale* (Rome: Università degli studi di Roma La Sapienza, 2007).

[29] Motoaki Ishii, *Meijiki no Itaria ryūgaku: Bunka juyō to gogaku tokushū* (Tokyo: Yoshikawa kōbunkan, 2017).

[30] Kunitake Kume, *Japan Rising: The Iwakura Embassy to the USA and Europe*, ed. Chushichi Tsuzuki and R. Jules Young (Cambridge: Cambridge University Press, 2009).

[31] Liu, 'Quest for a National Stage', 59.

[32] Suzanne Aspden, 'Opera and National Identity', in Nicholas Till (ed.), *The Cambridge Companion to Opera Studies* (Cambridge: Cambridge University Press, 2012), 276–98, at 276.

traditions that proved resistant to this kind of innovation.[33] Recreating a full-blown Western-style opera from scratch, on the other hand, required familiarity with the underlying traditions of singing, dancing, acting and orchestral music. Choreography, tonality and instruments all differed starkly from their Japanese counterparts, as did librettos and other staples of Western composition.

Among these elements, the government showed the greatest interest in music. As with other cultural forms, it assessed the value of music for its programme of state-building and modernisation and picked out what it deemed useful. Historian Ury Eppstein thus spoke of the state's functionalist attitude towards Western music.[34] The first site of adaption was the military, where Western march music was introduced to reform military training as early as from the 1850s. With a new education system set up in 1872, singing and music also entered the school curriculum, even though the lack of teachers, instruments and familiarity with Western music meant that implementation was slow and gradual. In 1879, the Ministry of Education set up a Music Research Institute to investigate both Western and Japanese music, train educators and musicians and publish text- and songbooks.[35] In 1887, this institute became the Tokyo Music School; with the invitation of Western musicians, more systematic training began.

It is here that a Japanese group of musicians and performers made the first attempt to produce an opera. In July 1903, graduates of the school staged Christoph Willibald Gluck's *Orfeo ed Euridice*. The performance, which was directed by the French Noël Peri and accompanied at the piano by the Russian-German Raphael von Koeber, both professors at the school, included background paintings, costumes and lighting and was, despite being invitation-only, reported widely and favourably in the press. According to Masui Keiji, the school's *Orfeo* was a 'ground-breaking event and the genuine beginning of the history of opera in Japan'.[36] Yet, rather than a state-funded or -backed undertaking, the school's *Orfeo* was a singular experiment based on the initiative of its students. The

---

[33] On kabuki theatre, see Samuel L. Leiter (ed.), *A Kabuki Reader* (Armonk, NY: M. E. Sharpe, 2002) and Kevin J. Wetmore, Jr, Siyuan Liu and Erin B. Mee, *Modern Asian Theatre and Performance 1900–2000* (London: Bloomsbury, 2014), 17–44.

[34] Ury Eppstein, 'Musical Instruction in Meiji Education: A Study of Adaption and Assimilation', *Monumenta Nipponica*, 40/1 (1985), 1–37, at 2. See also Ury Eppstein, *The Beginnings of Western Music in Meiji Japan* (Lewiston, NY: The Edwin Mellen Press, 1994); Bonnie C. Wade, *Music in Japan* (Oxford: Oxford University Press, 2005); and Judith Ann Herd, 'Western-Influenced "Classical" Music in Japan', in Alison McQueen Tokita and David W. Hughes (eds.), *The Ashgate Research Companion to Japanese Music* (London: Routledge, 2008), 363–82.

[35] Eppstein, *Beginnings of Western Music*, 48f.   [36] Masui, *Nihon opera shi*, vol. 1, 37.

government's reaction was harsh. Male and female actors practising and performing together was seen as morally dubious in a country where female roles were traditionally played by male actors, a tradition known as *onnagata*.[37] The Ministry pronounced a ban on operatic production at the school, which would not be lifted until after World War II.[38]

Meiji Japan as a Transcultural Space

As neither the term opera nor the art form it designated were part of the Japanese cultural tradition before the latter half of the nineteenth century, adaption necessarily entailed an intense effort of linguistic and cultural translation. The 1903 production of *Orfeo* at the Tokyo Music School is a case in point. As the transliteration of the title in the libretto, *Orufoisu*, hints at, the group of translators led by Ishikura Shōsaburō (1881–1965) had based their performance on a German edition, in which the diphthong in the titular hero's name would be pronounced closer to 'oi'. The edition, a translation by Alfred Dörffel and Otto Singer published by Peters in Leipzig, fused both the French and Italian versions of the opera.[39] When the producers translated the libretto into Japanese, they used a classical diction to approach the elevation of the original; Euridice, in a clever nod to the Italian name, became the equally elegant Yurihime (Lily Princess).[40]

The published version of the Japanese libretto touched on language differences in some detail. Admitting that their translation attempt was 'immensely difficult, if not to say impossible', the translators, switching to a register of academic linguistics, discussed the morphological distance between Japanese and European languages and its effects on the libretto and the match of music and vocal enunciation. Under these circumstances, they concluded that even to 'transmit only one fifth of the meaning of the original' presented high hurdles. However, to 'forcibly carry out this impossible work without dwelling on its failures seems the only path present musical conditions allow for'.[41]

This rather downbeat assessment reflected a new aspiration to 'get it right' that had not been in evidence to the same extent in earlier years. The

---

[37] See Katherine Mezur, *Beautiful Boys/Outlaw Bodies: Devising Kabuki-Female Likeness* (New York: Palgrave Macmillan, 2005), esp. ch. 5, 115–36.
[38] Masui, *Nihon opera shi*, vol. 1, 46f.
[39] Juri Giannini, *Interpretation zwischen Praxis und Ästhetik: Hans Swarowsky als Übersetzer von Opernlibretti* (Vienna: Hollitzer, 2019), 231. Libretto: Christian Willibald Gluck, *Orpheus*, adapted by Alfred Dörffel and Otto Singer (Frankfurt: Peters, 1904).
[40] Masui, *Nihon no opera*, 107f.
[41] Kageki kenkyūkai, *Gurukku saku kageki Orufoisu* (Tokyo: Tōbunkan, 1903), 3f.

later nineteenth century was marked by a relaxed transculturalism enabled by an unspoken convergence between the rambunctious performance tradition of Japanese popular theatre and the type of Western opera performances commonly encountered in Japan: rather than valuing the integrity of a composition or 'work', both amateur and professional troupes often presented just one act, abridged versions, arias from several works, and other patterns of mixing, adapting and excerpting.[42]

A decade before *Orfeo*, in November 1894, a charity concert for the Japanese Red Cross, sung by amateurs, was held at Tokyo Music School. The first act of Charles Gounod's *Faust*, 'Faust's Cabinet', was followed by 'Wotan's Farewell' from Wagner's *Die Walküre*. A Mr Braccialini employed at the Italian embassy sang Faust in Italian, while a Mr Gutenhoff of the Austrian embassy gave Mephistopheles in German, accompanied by Tokyo Music School Professor Franz Eckert and a choir of students. The audience was pleased, and the English-language newspaper *Japan Weekly Mail*, while pointing out the difficulties of preparing the performance, praised the concert:

> No expert is ignorant of the difficulties connected with the *mise en scène* and instrumentation of an opera like *Faust*, difficulties formidable in any country and almost deterrent in Japan, where such an undertaking is unprecedented. With regard to the music, however, a *deus ex machina* has been found in the person of Professor Eckert .... As for the orchestra under his guidance, well instructed and well led, it will certainly awaken memories of opera in the West.[43]

What had changed in the decade between the two performances at the school were expectations of how an emerging Japanese opera should deal with its transcultural character and relation to Western opera. Similar discussions were taking place in kabuki circles, where three positions emerged: *shin-kabuki*, which incorporated Western elements to modernise and innovate kabuki, *shinpa*, which aimed at making 'Western drama Japanese', and *shingeki*, which made 'Japanese theatre Western'.[44] Clearly, Ishikura and his collaborators were leaning towards an ideal of authentic reproduction, in their case conceived primarily in textual terms, of Western opera. The question was threefold: to what extent should Western elements be taken up and integrated into a Japanese tradition?

---

[42] On the kabuki performance tradition, in which audiences would spend all day at the theatre, but also eat, drink, chat and leave from time to time, see Yuichiro Takahashi, 'Kabuki Goes Official: The 1878 Opening of the Shintomi-za', *The Drama Review*, 39/3 (1995), 131–50.

[43] Quoted in Shin kokuritsu gekijō, *Nihon no opera*, 35.

[44] Wetmore, Liu and Mee, *Modern Asian Theatre*, 18.

Should new transcultural forms wear their hybrid character on their sleeve? And against which standard should achievement be measured?

Since opera was a new cultural form, positions and institutional allegiances were not as clear-cut as in the kabuki world. It is still instructive to give an example here of composers who chose to go the opposite route of incorporating Western elements into traditional genres. Almost simultaneously to the Music School's production of *Orfeo*, Kitamura Sueharu (1872–1931), another graduate of the school, composed a piece called *Dream at the Encampment* about a soldier dreaming of a reunion with his mother back in his home country, only to wake up to an enemy attack. The work was given as a middle act at the Kabuki-za in Tokyo in 1905.[45] The press praised it as the first Japanese-language opera, but in Kitamura's mind, the piece was instead closer to a *katarimono*, a spoken narrative accompanied by music, infused with the style of a Western ballad.[46] In kabuki, sung passages exist, but mostly in a recitative fashion, to create atmosphere or to accompany dance scenes; even then, they are mostly performed not by the actors, but by on- or offstage music ensembles.[47] The piece, fusing a recitative choir with an onstage soldier and an offstage mother expressing their emotions directly in song, can thus be interpreted both as a step towards Western operatic forms and as an innovation in traditional drama.

Even as the first Japanese-language operas were written and performed, voices longing for the performance of pure Western opera grew louder. In 1911, a commentary in the popular magazine *Taiyō* lamented the difficulties of creating an environment where opera could thrive. The occasion was the establishment of an opera department at the Imperial Theatre earlier that year. The author distinguishes between *kageki*, a Sinitic loan translation literally meaning 'sung drama' or 'sung theatre', as a generic term, and *opera*, a direct loan from European languages, which he used to designate the Western tradition:

As of yet, there is no such thing as 'opera' (*opera*) in our country. This is quite unsatisfactory. If possible, I wish for the Imperial Theatre to hire Western musicians and actors who perform opera . . . . Presently, when everything is imitation and direct translation from the West, it is not particularly surprising that we are

---

[45] J. title: *Roei no yume*. Sagawa, *Nihon opera no kiseki*, 15f.
[46] Yuki Itō, 'Opera to kabuki to "joji shōka" no kyori: Kitamura Sueharu "Roei no yume"', *Chōiki bunka kagaku kiyō*, 19 (2014), 41–58, at 46.
[47] Alison McQueen Tokita, 'Music in Kabuki: More than Meets the Eye', in Tokita and Hughes (eds.), *Companion to Japanese Music*, 229–60; William P. Malm, *Nagauta: The Heart of Kabuki Music* (Rutland, VT: Charles E. Tuttle, 1963), esp. 34–6 and 49–55.

just aping Western opera. . . . But is it even possible for Japanese people to stage a performance of authentic Western opera? This is where we are doubtful. As long as it is just the melodies that are in a Western style while the words are Japanese, half of the charm of the music will be spoilt. As a result, will our countrymen not inevitably misunderstand the true meaning of opera? . . . We must not forget that, until a proper Japanese opera emerges, all attempts will, in short, just be a poor imitation of the West.[48]

For this author, translation and overtly hybrid forms are inferior to both a 'proper' Japanese and an authentic Western opera. But even while these new notions of authenticity and *Werktreue* crystallised, actual performance continued to be marked by translation for the next decades. Following the example of Ishikura, proper names of the characters of Western works were mostly rendered as a traditional Japanese equivalent: as with Giuseppe Verdi's *La traviata*, which in a production at the Royal Theatre in Akasaka in 1919 became the *Camelia Princess* (*tsubaki hime*), perhaps tying in with a previous familiarity of the novel by Dumas that was the basis for Verdi's opera, and that had been translated into Japanese twice under the same title.[49]

Late Meiji Intellectuals, Wagner and Aesthetic Theory

As these calls for 'proper' and 'authentic' opera demonstrate, discourse about opera gained traction around the turn of the century. Beginning from the 1890s, Western philosophical notions of art and aesthetics were discussed on a larger scale, which gave artists and intellectuals a new conceptual framework independent of the 'functionalist' state perspective that had evaluated Western music mainly by what it could do for Japan's modernisation.[50] In one early publication in the vein of the mid-century surveys of Western civilisation, the author, discussing various facets of European culture in a question-and-answer style, also touches on opera. He defines it in opposition to theatre, mostly in terms of social status, comparing the audience of 'royalty and noblemen' of the opera with the Japanese

---

[48] 'Teikoku gekijō no kageki', *Taiyō* 17/13, 1 October 1911, 24.
[49] Masaaki Nakano, 'Honkoku Rōshī opera kageki "Tsubaki hime"', *Bungei kenkyū*, 121 (2013), 19–50. The two translations of Dumas' novel are: Alexandre Dumas fils, *Tsubaki hime*, trans. Shūtō Nagata (Tokyo: Waseda daigaku shuppanbu, 1903); Alexandre Dumas fils, *Tsubaki hime*, trans. Banka Fukunaga (Tokyo: San'yōdō, 1916). For the context of literary adaption, see J. Scott Miller, *Adaptions of Western Literature in Meiji Japan* (Basingstoke: Palgrave Macmillan, 2001).
[50] Michael F. Marra, 'The Creation of the Vocabulary of Aesthetics in Meiji Japan', in Rimer and McCallum (eds.), *Since Meiji*, 193–211.

Noh theatre, which had historically been associated with the imperial court and *shogunal* government.[51] Later opera-themed publications also compared Western opera with kabuki.[52] The point here is less whether such comparisons are accurate, but more that Japanese authors were increasingly discussing the characteristics of opera and its connections to indigenous art.

This same period also saw the first opera histories and guides, such as Andō Hiroshi's *Synopsis of Opera*, which took its inspiration from Charles Annesley's popular *The Standard Operaglass*.[53] Among the twenty operas introduced in Andō's *Synopsis*, only two were written by Italian composers: Verdi's *Rigoletto* and Mascagni's *Cavalleria rusticana*. Similarly, while most opera histories discussed Italian opera, and Italy was duly paid homage to as the historical origin and centre of opera, it was rarely presented as a decisive force in the present.[54] Instead, for most Japanese intellectuals and artists, German opera, and specifically Wagner, took pride of place. In the substantial *Western Music History* published in 1916 by Tomiogi Tomoyoshi, professor at the Tokyo Music School, the influence of Wagner had become so entrenched that he was presented as the decisive turning point in the history of opera, as the chapter title 'Opera before Wagner' illustrates.[55]

The interest in German and Wagnerian opera arose in the wider cultural context of the 1880s and 1890s, when Germany and the German-language cultural sphere came to be seen as a model in a range of fields, from law, the military and medicine to art music. At the Tokyo Music School, it was Rudolf Dittrich (1861–1919), an Austrian organist, who established a German-centred outlook on musical culture.[56] Kōda Nobu (1870–1946), who is now known as the first composer of violin music in Japan, studied in Vienna and began teaching at the Tokyo Music School shortly

---

[51] Nishi Kosei, *Seiyō fūzokuki* (Osaka: Shinshindō, 1887), 14f.
[52] For example Umeno Kaoru, *Opera rōmansu* (Tokyo: Baikōsha, 1919).
[53] Hiroshi Andō, *Kageki kōgai* (Tokyo: Shūbunkan, 1906). Charles Annesley, *The Standard Operaglass: Detailed Plots of The Celebrated Operas* (New York: Brentano's, 1899).
[54] For example Iwatarō (Gakusai) Fujinami, *Kageki to kageki haiyū* (Tokyo: Bunseisha, 1919).
[55] Tomoyoshi Tomiogi, *Seiyō ongaku shikō* (Tokyo: Kyōeki shōsha, 1916), 431.
[56] Bernd Martin, *Japan and Germany in the Modern World* (New York: Berghahn, 1995); Christian W. Spang and Rolf-Harald Wippich (eds.), *Japanese-German Relations, 1895–1945: War, Diplomacy and Public Opinion* (Abingdon: Routledge, 2006). For a revisionist perspective on German influence in the mid-Meiji years, see Toru Takenaka, 'The Myth of "Familiar Germany": German–Japanese Relationships in the Meiji Period Reexamined', in Joanne Miyang Cho, Lee Roberts and Christian W. Spang (eds.), *Transnational Encounters between Germany and Japan: Perceptions of Partnership in the Nineteenth and Twentieth Centuries* (Basingstoke: Palgrave Macmillan, 2016), 19–34.

after her return. She and other instructors at the school praised Wagner publicly and instigated an interest among the younger generation. Many exchange students had come into contact with Wagner during their time in Europe as well. Shortly, professors and students at several elite universities, such as Tokyo Imperial University and Keiō University, founded Wagner societies to study his work and thought and apply his insights to Japanese art.[57]

Influential literary figures such as Tsubouchi Shōyō (1859–1935) also chimed in. Tsubouchi had studied Western literature and published a seminal text on the essence of the novel in 1885–6. He became interested in opera shortly after, and wrote a treatise called *A New Theory of Musical Theatre* in which he reflected on the foundations of opera.[58] In the same year, he translated his theoretical insights into practice by writing a script that transposed a traditional Japanese tale of the boy Urashima Tarō, who leaves his home to live under the sea, into an opera formally patterned after Wagner's *Tannhäuser*, replacing Japanese music with that of Western opera.[59]

Some of the people involved in the *Orfeo* production, such as Ishikura Shōsaburō, were also members in Wagner societies, and it appears that they had originally planned to stage *Tannhäuser*, had it not been for Professor Peri's counsel to go with a less challenging piece. Gluck, as a great reformer of German opera, seems to have been the next best option.[60] In a textbook he penned not long after the *Orfeo* performance, Ishikura singled out Gluck as a central figure in the history of opera, whose work stands as a direct contrast to Italian opera: 'Italian-style opera was completely destroyed by the lion's roar of Gluck'.[61] The 'duty' of German opera was to take over the civilisational development of music from Italy, leading it to new heights. Needless to say, this mode of narrating the history of opera as a teleological progression of stylistic development conceived along national lines was in tune with and probably inspired by contemporary German accounts.[62] It was also amenable to Japanese thought at the time, which was preoccupied with a global hierarchy of civilisation and Japan's place in it.

---

[57] Masui, *Nihon opera shi*, vol. 1, 38.
[58] Shōyō Tsubouchi, *Shin gakugeki ron* (Tokyo: Waseda daigaku shuppanbu, 1904).
[59] Daniel John Gallimore, *Tsubouchi Shōyō's Shinkoku Urashima and the Wagnerian Moment in Meiji Japan* (New York: The Edwin Mellen Press, 2016).
[60] Masui, *Nihon no opera*, 103f.
[61] Shōsaburo Ishikura, *Seiyō ongaku shi* (Tokyo: Hakubunkan, 1905), 196.
[62] Nicholas Till, 'Introduction: Opera Studies Today', in Till (ed.), *Companion to Opera Studies*, 14f.

Fascinatingly, Wagner's appeal was entirely theoretical. It peaked at a point when only a handful of Japanese had ever seen or heard one of his operas: the first sheet music of his works became available only in 1918, while the first complete staging of one of his operas had to wait until the 1940s.[63] What attracted the younger generation of intellectuals was what they read as Wagner's 'philosophy', his critique of German society that seemed just as applicable to Japan, his insistence on opera as a national *Gesamtkunstwerk* and his fascination with ancient indigenous materials.[64] This was indeed his most lasting impact on Japanese opera practice. Next to Tsubouchi and his *Urashima*, many other Japanese composers of the early twentieth century turned to ancient myth for inspiration.[65]

Italian Artists in the Vernacularisation of Opera

Contrasting with the rarefied discourse and experiments in the circles surrounding the state-run Tokyo Music School, an entirely different dynamic occurred in the commercial realm. In March 1911, the Imperial Theatre – despite its name a privately run enterprise – opened its doors.[66] As its Western architecture attested, its mission was to become a site of cultural exchange that could introduce Japanese performing arts to international audiences while simultaneously appropriating Western forms to invigorate Japanese theatre. This ambitious plan included the training of orchestral musicians, actors – and for the first time, actresses – and a department for 'sung drama', that is, opera.[67] It was here that opera truly took root and reached mass audiences for the first time.

It was also here that two Italians left their mark on early opera history: Adolfo Sarcoli (1867–1936), a tenor singer from Siena who had originally been on his way to perform in Shanghai, but escaped to Japan due to the

---

[63] Brooke McCorkle, 'Was ist Japanisch? Wagnerism and Dreams of Nationhood in Modern Japan', in Neil Gregor and Thomas Irvine, *Dreams of Germany: Musical Imaginaries from the Concert Hall to the Dancefloor* (New York: Berghahn Books, 2019), 169–93, at 170; on Wagner reception in the subsequent decades, see Brooke McCorkle, 'Twilight of an Empire: Staging Wagner in Wartime Tokyo', in Anno Mungen, Nicholas Vazsonyi, Julie Hubert, Ivana Rentsch and Arne Stollberg (eds.), *Music Theater as Global Culture: Wagner's Legacy Today* (Würzburg: Königshausen und Neumann, 2017), 51–64.

[64] Toru Takenaka, 'Wagner-Boom in Meiji-Japan', *Archiv für Musikwissenschaft*, 62/1 (2005), 13–31.

[65] For example Masui, *Nihon opera shi*, vol. 1, 42–6.

[66] Takashi Mine, *Teikoku gekijō kaimaku: 'Kyō wa Teigeki ashita wa Mitsukoshi'* (Tokyo: Chūkō shinsho, 1996).

[67] Masui, *Nihon opera shi*, vol. 1, 58f.

upheaval of the Chinese revolution and began working at the Theatre. Also in 1911, he arranged a Japanese performance of an excerpt of an Italian opera: together with the Japanese soprano Miura Tamaki, he performed Santuzza and Turiddu's duet in Mascagni's *Cavalleria rusticana*.[68] Sarcoli was affectionately called the 'father of bel canto' in Japan in his later years because he instructed a whole generation of Japanese singers in Italian singing technique.[69] Apparently, his original inclination was to find a position at the Tokyo Music School, but, as he later recollected, he was shocked to learn that Japanese appreciation was directed overwhelmingly at 'Northern European music, and there was no study of Italian music, which is closest to my own emotional life'; so he turned to private engagements like the one at the Theatre and gave lessons from his own home.[70]

The Theatre also invited another Italian, Giovanni Vittorio Rosi (1867–?), to join its ranks. Rosi was not specifically hired by the Theatre because of his Italian nationality or expertise in Italian opera, but rather because of his international work experience. After training in ballet at La Scala, he participated in a world tour as a dancer as early as 1884, gathered experience in Buenos Aires and worked as a ballet choreographer at the Alhambra music hall in London and in New York before coming to Japan. During his time at the Imperial Theatre, Rosi was involved in over forty productions. In part due to his personal taste, in part due to the lack of familiarity with Western dance and opera of his Japanese actors, the works leaned towards the lighter genres of dance revues and operettas, mostly abridged and translated into Japanese. The performances failed to find favour with their intended audience, however, forcing the Theatre to disband the opera department and end the contract with Rosi in 1916.[71] He went on to open his own opera house, the Royal Theatre, in the Akasaka district of Tokyo, which was the first such theatre in Japan to operate on the principle of showing only one work per evening instead of a variety of excerpts.[72] Rosi had his biggest success with the first full performance of the

---

[68] Masui, *Nihon opera shi*, vol. 1, 61f.
[69] Naoe Manami has been researching Sarcoli extensively, but so far there has been no English publication on his life or work in Japan. See for example, Manami Naoe, 'Nihon ni okeru beru kanto no chichi, Adorufo Sarukori no shōgai', *Kanazawa seiryō daigaku ningen kagaku kenkyū*, 4/2 (2011), 41–4 and Manami Naoe, 'Adorufo Sarukori no ongaku katsudō ni kansuru kenkyū (1): 1911 nen, 1912 nen no Sarukori kanren no shiryō o chūshin ni', *Kanazawa seiryō daigaku ningen kagaku kenkyū*, 10/1 (2016), 23–30.
[70] Quoted in Tōru Mitsui and Manami Naoe, 'Seiyō ongaku kyōiku dōnyūki ni "min" ga hatashita yakuwari: Kanritsu kankeisha to Adorufo Sarukori', *Kanazawa daigaku kyōiku gakubu kiyō jinbungaku shakaigaku hen*, 53 (2004), 1–14, at 5.
[71] Matsumoto, 'Rosi's Musical Theatre', 370–9.   [72] Masui, *Nihon no opera*, 306.

Cavalleria rusticana in Italian in 1917. A review noted the strong Japanese accents of the performers, but welcomed the decision to perform the work in Italian nonetheless, as it meant that there were for once no problems with a poorly translated libretto.[73] Due to financial difficulties and growing animosity between Rosi and his employees, Rosi had to shut down the theatre and, frustrated, left Japan for good the following year.

Even so, the popularisation of 'sung theatre' continued. For the industrialist Kobayashi Ichizō (1873–1957), founder of Hankyū Railway, a performance at the Imperial Theatre was the impetus to dream up a new 'people's drama' or *kokumingeki*: 'What is more important than our achieving the same level as Western opera, and in fact what is most important, is that Japan has its own "*kokumingeki*", and that we create a new *kokumingeki* as an essential art of the common people to please them.'[74] To realise this aspiration, he started a girls' troupe under the name Takarazuka Opera Company in the small spa town of Takarazuka, located midway between Ōsaka and Kōbe, which he was developing with his railway line. Its first, half-accidental performance in 1914 was advertised as 'the first girls' opera in Japan'.[75] The company, which later also produced an all-female musical version of Puccini's *Madama Butterfly* in 1931, continues to be widely popular today.[76]

Some of Rosi's students also continued their activities elsewhere. Around 1916, numerous music, dance and opera halls opened in Tokyo's entertainment district of Asakusa that freely fused the art forms of operettas, musicals, vaudeville theatre and cabaret. The newly emerging genre of 'Asakusa opera', as it came to be called, represented an eclectic mix between Japanese and Western forms, performed in Japanese for a mostly lower-class audience. It was immensely popular and successful until 1923, when the Great Kanto Earthquake destroyed large swathes of the city, among them the entertainment facilities in Asakusa. Despite its relatively short life span, Asakusa opera was highly significant for Japanese opera history and beyond and is evaluated as having made a key contribution to the 'formation of modern popular culture in Japan'.[77] More germane to the

---

[73] Masui, *Nihon no opera*, 323.
[74] Quoted in Makiko Yamanashi, *A History of the Takarazuka Revue since 1914: Modernity, Girl's Culture, Japan Pop* (Leiden: Brill, 2012), 10.
[75] Yamanashi, *Takarazuka Revue*, 7.
[76] Shikō Tsubouchi, 'The Takarazuka Concise Madame Butterfly', trans. Kyoko Selden and Lily Selden, intr. by Arthur Groos, *The Asia-Pacific Journal: Japan Focus*, 14/14, no. 7 (2016), https://apjjf.org/2016/14/Selden-4.html.
[77] Charles Exley, 'Popular Musical Star Tokuko Takagi and Vaudeville Modernism in the Taishō Asakusa Opera', *Japanese Language and Literature*, 51/1 (2017), 63–90, at 64. See also

topic under discussion, the popular musical theatre given at the Imperial Theatre, the Takarazuka Revue and Asakusa opera disseminated first-hand experience of and enthusiasm for sung theatre to wider audiences.

For Masui Keiji, the success of Asakusa-style musical theatre was only circumstantially related to what was performed: 'This seems to me the least relevant reason [for its popularity], but the interest of the works itself cannot be denied entirely, as this was a period where opportunities for amusement were scarce.'[78] Similarly, Rosi's efforts have been described as a 'failure', which is perhaps fair if measured against the standard of an idealised European operatic tradition.[79] In the perspective of global cultural history, however, Rosi's activities and the success of popular musical theatre should be read as a route of amalgamation and naturalisation that was very common elsewhere in the world and even in Italy, as discussed in the introduction to this book.[80] Ironically, the two Italians, while aiming to bring Italian music and opera to Japan, spurred along a development that left it hardly recognisable as Italian from a European perspective, or, for that matter, to later generations of Japanese historians.

Conclusion

As this chapter has shown, people, plays and expertise from Italy did have a significant impact on early Japanese opera history. Yet, there was no foundation on which a strong notion of operatic *italianità* could emerge in Japan's opera world. On the one hand, the German-centrism of elite musical and intellectual circles at the turn of the century barred a systematic engagement with Italian opera as a national tradition. On the other hand, the conditions of Meiji linguistic and cultural translation and the subsequent vernacularisation of opera entailed that appreciation of some type of Italian canon was not much of a priority for either performers or audiences. On the continuum between naturalisation and authenticity, early opera history was clearly leaning towards the former.

Yūki Kobari, *Aa Asakusa opera: Shashin de tadoru miwaku no 'inchiki' kageki* (Tokyo: Enishi shobō, 2016); Chizuru Sugiyama and Masaaki Nakano, *Asakusa opera: Butai geijutsu to goraku no kindai* (Tokyo: Rinwasha, 2017); Donald Richie, 'Foreword', in Yasunari Kawabata, *The Scarlet Gang of Asakusa*, trans. Alisa Freedman (Berkeley: University of California Press, 2005), ix–xxxii.

[78] Masui, *Nihon opera shi*, vol. 1, 146.   [79] Matsumoto, 'Rosi's Musical Theatre', 353.

[80] For example, Alexandra Wilson, *Opera in the Jazz Age: Cultural Politics in 1920s Britain* (Oxford: Oxford University Press, 2019). See also Nicholson, 'Italian Impresarios, American Minstrels and Parsi Theatre'.

This changed in the course of the following decade. Partly this was a natural outcome of the now much greater familiarity of Japanese performers and audiences with Western music and opera. What was more decisive in the context of a discussion of *italianità*, however, was that both dynamics for the transculturalisation of opera – an injection of operatic elements into traditional Japanese theatre, and the openly hybrid 'lowbrow' Asakusa opera – had largely come to a halt in 1923, so that the meaning of *opera*, both as a term and as a genre, became identified with Western opera. It is a telling coincidence that the Japanese tenor Hirama Fumihisa (1900–89) began to study music in Italy that very same year, and founded a company called Opera Verdiana upon his return.[81]

It only makes sense, then, that, when Fujiwara Yoshie performed *La bohème* in 1934, one review applauded it for being so 'true to tradition'.[82] While the sporadic call for a recreation of 'proper' Western opera on Japanese soil could already be heard at the turn of the century, it was only in the 1930s that such an endeavour became a real option; from then on Italian opera rose to a much more prominent status. From a perspective of transnational opera history, it is in this sense, rather than the evaluative sense of a 'true' beginning of opera, that Masui's periodisation is still meaningful.

[81] Masui, *Nihon opera shi*, vol. 1, 208. [82] Masui, *Nihon opera shi*, vol. 1, 224.

15 | Epilogue

BENJAMIN WALTON

In the opening paragraph of his monumental 600-page *Italian Opera*, David Kimbell takes issue with his own title. The book does not tell 'the story of Italian opera' – which would have taken still more pages, he suggests, and gone beyond his own range of expertise – but rather 'the story of opera in Italy'.[1] Yet having made the distinction, Kimbell observes that the boundaries between the two remain 'shadowy and ill-defined, to say the least'.

So shadowy, in fact, as to be invisible in most standard anglophone operatic histories, where chapters on 'Italian Opera of the *primo ottocento*',[2] rub up against 'The Nineteenth Century: Italy' and 'Opera in Nineteenth-Century Italy',[3] or else take refuge behind the unimpeachably national (yet notably international) figures of Rossini and Verdi.[4] In all these cases, the geography of Italian opera seems at first sight clear-cut, only to become increasingly blurred on closer inspection. Canonic eighteenth-century italianate compositions by non-Italians (Handel, Mozart) lead the way to canonic nineteenth-century premieres of Italian opera beyond Italy (*I puritani*, *Aida*), yet all framed by the concept of the nation. As a result, the *idea* of Italian opera – its identity, its characteristics, its *italianità* – ends up entangled within national boundaries too. No surprise, then, that the most comprehensive discussion of Italian opera to be found across the four volumes of the *New Grove Dictionary of Opera* comes in the form of an entry entitled simply 'Italy'.[5]

More recently, various authors have started to position themselves to one side or the other of Kimbell's boundary. Tim Carter's *Understanding*

---

[1] David Kimbell, *Italian Opera* (Cambridge: Cambridge University Press, 1991), xiii.
[2] Donald Jay Grout and Hermine Weigel Williams, *A Short History of Opera* (New York: Columbia University Press, 2003).
[3] Roger Parker (ed.), *The Oxford Illustrated History of Opera* (Oxford: Oxford University Press, 2001); Robert Cannon, *Cambridge Introductions to Music: Opera* (Cambridge: Cambridge University Press, 2012).
[4] Roger Parker and Carolyn Abbate, *A History of Opera: The Last 400 Years* (London: Allen Lane, 2012).
[5] Lorenzo Bianconi, 'Italy', in *New Grove Dictionary of Opera* (London and New York: Macmillan, 1997), vol. 3: 837–60.

Italian Opera, for instance, insists in its preface on language rather than nation as the common thread binding Monteverdi to Puccini, before alluding to 'other values' that help to secure the connection, but that remain unelaborated.[6] Two specialist nineteenth-century histories, by contrast, join Kimbell on the Italian side (while insisting on the regional differences, local dialects and urban rivalries that challenge any stable idea of Italy from within). Emanuele Senici proposes that the initial success of Rossini's operas in the 1810s and 1820s can best be understood through their connections with Italian society of the time, regardless of resonances with enthusiasm for the composer elsewhere in Europe.[7] Similarly, Mary Ann Smart frames Italian opera – and Italian writings about opera and many other subjects – as a way to think about 'the process of "making Italy"' in the decades leading up to unification.[8]

The present book would seem to belong on Carter's side, in arguing for Italian opera as an 'international art form', in Kimbell's phrase, not only in terms of composition or performance but also in relation to how and where the idea (and ideology) of Italian opera functioned at different times. Yet in fact the chapters collected together here compellingly converge with Senici and Smart in helping to redefine the boundaries between Italian opera and opera in Italy as less geographical than conceptual. Such convergence is perhaps clearest through a shared breadth of definition across all three books: no longer a series of works, neatly divisible into score, production (almost always defined as the work's premiere) and critical reception, Italian opera instead becomes an interlocking nexus of performances in opera houses, salons and streets, realised by performers ranging from the best-paid celebrity to the most tentative amateur, all shaped by (while also helping to shape) a wider operatic discourse within Italy and without. Smart, for instance, insists on the cross-pollination of operatic discourses between Italian and non-Italian writings, shedding light on the networks of Italian political exiles in Paris during the 1830s and 1840s while showing how opera became a way of 'projecting Italian character into the world'.[9] Senici similarly argues not only that Rossini's musical dramaturgy served distinctly non-Italian philosophers such as Hegel and Schopenhauer in

---

[6] Tim Carter, *Understanding Italian Opera* (New York: Oxford University Press, 2015), x. Carter's first chapter proper then cuts the national adjective altogether, opting for the more general question of 'What Is Opera?'

[7] Emanuele Senici, *Music in the Present Tense: Rossini's Italian Operas in Their Time* (Chicago: University of Chicago Press, 2019), 14–15.

[8] Mary Ann Smart, *Looking for Verdi: Italian Opera and Political Opinion* (Berkeley and Los Angeles: University of California Press, 2018), 4.

[9] Smart, *Looking for Verdi*, 4.

their wider argument for music as 'an art of freedom and movement', but also that French views of Italian theatricality, formed in the wake of the Napoleonic invasions, helped to alter Italians' own self-perception, refracted through the French gaze.[10]

Not that such readings bring us closer to a more stable definition of Italian opera; rather, they only confirm how historically and geographically contingent any answer must be. Yet brought together, three interconnected proposals start to coalesce in place of anything more fixed: first, that the story of Italian opera – as repertory, fantasy, ideology, commodity – has always been as much about its mentalities as its sonic and material realities; second, that the supposedly more limited story of opera *in* Italy was never only *about* Italy; and third, that the shadowy boundaries between this story and the larger story of Italian opera remain largely uncharted territory.

***

How, then, do the authors in this book frame such a multifaceted idea of Italian opera? Above all, perhaps, they show that viewed through the prism of *italianità* it frequently takes the form of a nostalgic fantasy for something already lost, or something imagined elsewhere. Such an elsewhere might be Italy itself, idealised as pastoral idyll (Jacobshagen, Chapter 8) or land of song (Krahn, Chapter 3). Just as often, though, it is conceived more broadly, mediated via local traditions or conditions (Milella, Chapter 4, and Rindom, Chapter 10) or via another place, whether Paris (Berçot, Chapter 2, and McMahon, Chapter 13) or Cuba (Bentley, Chapter 6). Alternatively, it can be dispersed more widely still, across the expanding global network of opera houses performing Italian opera at the time: in the words of the Ecuadorian critic quoted by Izquierdo König in Chapter 7, 'we can feel, for a night, as if we were in Lima, or Janeiro, or Paris, London, Madrid or Milan'.

As to how such a transnational experience was defined at the time, it could be through codes of etiquette, scenery or the spectacle of a finely dressed audience. Most often, though, it came through the sound of the operatic voice, and the access it offered to what Josh Kun describes as 'audiotopias': the 'almost-places of cultural encounter' opened up by the performance of song.[11] In the case of opera, voice and song often become

---

[10] Senici, *Music in the Present Tense*, 236.
[11] Josh Kun, *Audiotopia: Music, Race, and America* (Berkeley and Los Angeles: University of California Press, 2005), 2.

inseparable in the formation of such an encounter, sustained by a fantasy of Italy which can be reinvented from one group of listeners to the next.

The idea of *italianità* thereby becomes at once stable yet infinitely malleable. Stable because the potential for this kind of imaginative encounter remained present, shaped by discourse and mediated by local conditions, wherever Italian opera was performed. Yet each such encounter not only varied according to the experience of the person listening, watching or imagining Italian opera, but also according to the nature of the Italian-ness perceived and desired; a nature itself conditioned not just by operatic criticism, but by travel literature, foreign news coverage and any number of other factors that could contribute to populating the elastic adjective 'Italian'.

At stake here is not simply an expanded geography, but an expanded understanding of opera's diffusion across the world during the nineteenth century that goes far beyond lists of performance statistics or accounts of touring troupes, and overwrites earlier histories built around a small handful of major Italian cities and their links to an even smaller handful of European capitals. The sort of new understanding developed in the course of this book, however, also raises new challenges. On the one hand, the more extensive the Italian operatic world, the thornier the task of finding commonalities between, say, notions of *italianità* in Vienna in the 1830s (Vellutini, Chapter 5) and in Caracas in the 1880s (Rindom, Chapter 10); or else the greater the temptation to fall into the assumption of unchanging national identity regardless of local conditions, characteristic of some wide-ranging global history; as Jean-Paul Ghobrial puts it: the '"Armenian merchant" in Livorno is perceived to share a common identity with an "Armenian merchant" in the Philippines, despite the great distance that separates them in both geographical and conceptual terms'.[12] What goes for Armenian merchants applies equally to Italian opera singers. Yet on the other, that same *italianità* risks becoming no more than a vessel with which to channel the grand European neocolonial project, enabling operatic audiences the world over to display their musical enthusiasms as a demonstration of a sense of superiority through taste, class, race or a mix of all three. The performance of Italian opera, then, signifies membership of a network that, in the famous words of Stendhal at the start of his *Vie de Rossini*, 'knows no other boundaries than those of civilisation'.

---

[12] Jean-Paul Ghobrial, 'Moving Stories and What They Tell Us: Early Modern Mobility Between Microhistory and Global History', *Past & Present*, Supplement 14 (2019), 243–80; here 247–8.

Against this background, the twenty-first-century celebration of nineteenth-century operatic globalisation, mobility and free circulation can, on occasion, inadvertently echo some of the triumphalist and colonialist imaginings from two centuries back, when Rossini's melodies, for instance, were pictured floating over the oceans and conquering every land that they reached through their beauty, or when Verdi proposed in 1862 that 'in the heart of Africa or in the Indies, you will always hear *Il trovatore*'.[13] Less ambitious but perhaps more typical itineraries get overlooked, meanwhile, as do the practical difficulties of boundary crossing and of staging performances in unfamiliar locations. As Nancy L. Green has suggested, enthusiasm for the transnational can rely on an 'overly optimistic vision of migrant agency', which downplays the difficulties of trying to stage opera in a way that could come close to the expectations created by its civilisational cheerleaders.[14]

As a result, the interpretative usefulness of *italianità* might seem uncertain: redefined in every place Italian opera was performed, or else complicit in a celebratory narrative of operatic expansion. Yet as many of the chapters here show, its power as an idea resides precisely in the friction generated by bringing these two sides into contact, as what Ghobrial would term 'global microhistories'. In this way, the free-flowing fantasy of *italianità* can be punctured, subverted or reconfigured in the face of an often-disillusioning reality. The potential inadequacy of the term stands revealed, yet the local histories (including the local histories within Italy) nevertheless connect through a shared belief in its power to invest any performance with transnational resonance. *Italianità* thereby becomes inseparable from the story of how Italian opera became global, but only usefully so once grounded (tempered, undermined) by being integrated within individual case studies.

And what of the chronology? Is this truly one more story of the 'long nineteenth century', as the book title suggests? On the surface, the time span might seem the most straightforward element of the title, yet placed in the context of understanding *italianità* globally it opens up some of the most interesting questions, as the chapters by Michael Facius (Chapter 14) and others indicate. For one thing, as the waves of mass emigration from Italy took off around 1880, the idea of *italianità* transformed, going from something multifaceted to becoming straightforwardly national; in the

---

[13] Letter from Giuseppe Verdi to Count Opprandino Arrivabene (5 May 1862), quoted in: Franco Abbiati, *Giuseppe Verdi* (Milan: Ricordi, 1959), vol. 1: 643.
[14] Nancy L. Green, *The Limits of Transnationalism* (Chicago: University of Chicago Press, 2019), 53.

words of one recent writer: '*Italianità* is the essence of being Italian. It is living the Italian spirit; the language, the food, the music, the art ... All those things make Italians Italian.'[15] It also took on a life of its own: in Italian printed texts the use of the word '*italianità*' only emerged around 1880, soaring during World War I, and reaching a peak around 1920 that is matched in anglophone sources, followed by subsequent decline (at least until recent academic rediscovery).[16] This no doubt suggests a variety of interpretations, but national and diasporic anxieties would surely feature among them, driven by the millions leaving (mainly southern) Italy to set up home over the Atlantic.

Might this transformation of the idea of *italianità*, then, and of the attendant changes in the culture of Italian opera after 1880, suggest instead a 'short' nineteenth century followed by a long twentieth? How does the mass transatlantic emigration intersect with concurrent developments in the performance of Italian opera around 1900?[17] How does the fugitive concept of *italianità* outlined in these chapters – as stereotype, or civilisational token, or vocal encounter – connect with the diasporic experience that underpins the *italianità* found, say, within the alternative literature of Italian-American studies? Do the histories told by scholars such as John Gennari, of Caruso's influence on Louis Armstrong, or of Frank Sinatra as the inheritor of the bel canto tradition, connect usefully with the very different types of experiences described in the present book, in cities with tiny Italian communities, such as Rio, Lima, Bombay or Tokyo?[18] And, finally, does the change in the idea of *italianità* have an impact on the early twentieth-century industry of global Italian opera, newly mediated through sound recording and film? The chapters in this book provide some answers but – happily – still more questions; and the more we find out, the more liberatingly ill-defined and productively shadowy the boundaries between Italian opera and opera in Italy may turn out to be.

---

[15] William Giovinazzo, *Italianità: The Essence of Being Italian and Italian-American* (Oakamoor: Dark River, 2018), 12.

[16] See https://books.google.com/ngrams (last accessed 15 June 2020).

[17] For a recent attempt to address this question see Ditlev Rindom, 'Bygone Modernity: Re-imagining Italian Opera in Milan, New York and Buenos Aires, 1887–1914', PhD dissertation, University of Cambridge (2019).

[18] See John Gennari, *Flavor and Soul: Italian America at Its African American Edge* (Chicago: University of Chicago Press, 2017), 31 and 36.

Index

1830 Revolution, 111
1848 Revolution, 97, 111

Abbott, Emma, 197
adaptations (of operas), 28, 46, 47, 56, 80, 89, 90–4, 95, 179, 197, 215–38, 260, 283
Adelman, Jeremy, 81
Aeschylus, 4
aesthetics, xvi, 5, 7, 16, 24, 27, 29, 32, 33, 34, 36, 37, 55, 60, 61, 67, 157, 211, 214, 215, 220, 245, 246, 253, 254, 280, 290
Africa, xvi, 39, 207, 302
Afro-Americans, 219
Afro-Brazilians, 4, 54, 262
Agricola, Johann Friedrich, 65
Aimery, Adela, 202, 204, 205, 210
Alencar, José de, 274
Alessandri, Pietro, 133
Alexis, Willibald, 242, 244
Algier, Jules, 273, 275
Allahabad, 234
Almeida, Fernando José de, 41, 44, 56
Alps, the, 11, 18, 22, 26, 30, 38, 107
Ambros, August Wilhelm, 161
America. *See* Americas, the
Americanisation, 217
Americas, the, 9, 37, 41, 49, 81, 83
  discovery of, 183
  Italian opera in, 5, 30, 38, 77, 128
  musical life, 218
  opera companies, 194, 221
  opera production, 8
  as uncivilised, 29
Ancona, 226
Andalusia, 78, 86, 87, 209
Andes (region), 133, 136, 137, 138, 139–46, 196
André Grétry
  Sylvain, 114
Annesley, Charles, 291
Anselmi, Carlotta, 43
Anselmi, Giulietta, 43
anti-Semitism, 161, 257, 259
Antognini, Cirillo. *See* Antonini, Cirillo

Antonicek, Theophil, 99
Antonini, Cirillo, 122
Āpakhatyār, Nasarvānjī
  Rūstam tathā Śohrāb, 230
Arago, Jacques, 1, 2, 4
Arequipa, 138
Áretz, Isabel, 200
Argentina, 27
aristocracy, 29, 34, 59, 108, 109, 167, 170, 172, 221, 233, 290
Armenia, 301
Armstrong, Louis, 303
Arrivabene, Count Opprandino, 167
art, 14, 33, 54, 187, 264, 281, 285
  Italian, 167
Arteaga, Stefano, 11
Ashbrook, William, 97, 183
Asia, xvi, 5, 8, 39, 249
  East Asia, 9, 37
  South East Asia, 9, 214–38
Aspden, Suzanne, 16, 17, 80
Atlantic, 31, 38, 41, 80, 82–3, 134
Auber, Daniel, 114, 159, 265
audiences, 5, 7, 218, 301
  behaviour, 300
  Bombay, 222, 230
    expectations, 222
    reception, 223
  Brazil, 38, 49, 50, 52, 54, 55, 263, 266, 267
    behaviour, 45, 52
    expectations, 46, 57, 266
    reception, 47, 51, 54, 274
  Europe, 48
  expectations, 18, 28
  Germany
    expectations, 239, 253, 254
    reception, 239, 240, 247, 254, 256–60
  India, 216
  Italy, 169, 171
    behaviour, 24
    expectations, 171, 187
    reception, 171–4, 177, 184
  Japan, 278, 282, 293, 295, 296

304

expectations, 294
  reception, 282, 284, 296
 Lima, 144
  reception, 144, 145
 Mexico, 78
  behaviour, 85
  expectations, 77, 78, 89, 90, 91
  reception, 77, 89, 94
 New Orleans
  expectations, 114, 116, 122, 123
  reception, 120, 129
 New York, 84, 126
 Singapore, 227, 234
 South Asia, 215, 220, 231
  reception, 215, 225, 228, 229
 Venezuela
  behaviour, 211
  expectations, 208
  reception, 14, 15, 19, 23, 25, 193, 200, 202, 208, 209, 210
 Vienna, 103, 105
Augsburg, 155
Augusta Victoria (German Empress), 245
aural culture, 39
Australasia, 216
Australia, xvi, 39, 217, 218, 226, 231, 235, 236
Austria. *See* Habsburg Empire
Azevedo, Artur
 Capital Federal (play), 266

Bach, Johann Christian, 17
Bach, Johann Sebastian, 156
Bacon, Francis, 218
Baden, 256
Balfe, Michael
 Satanella or the Power of Love, 232
ballet, 5, 17, 22, 26, 41, 42, 43, 45, 48, 49, 50, 51, 52, 54, 105, 108, 193, 202, 204, 209, 226, 294
Balocchino, Carlo, 96, 97, 100, 101, 102, 103, 104, 108, 110, 111, 112
Balzofiore (Signor), 235
Barbaja, Domenico, 23, 89, 99, 106, 107, 108, 109, 112
Barbieri, Elisa, 47, 48, 51
Barcelona, 204
 Gran Teatre del Liceu, 204
barrel organs, 15
Barthes, Roland, 17
Bastoggis (family), 142
Batavia, 215, 216, 225, 228, 232, 234, 235, 236
 Bataviasche Schouwburg, 227
Bavaria, 96

Bayreuth, 188
Bazzani, Luigi, 137
Beethoven, Ludwig van, 62, 64, 98, 99, 159
bel canto, 87, 168, 169, 207, 264, 294
Belasco, David, 284
Belém do Pará, 261, 270, 273, 274
 Theatro da Paz, 265, 267, 274
Bellini, Vincenzo, 102, 121, 132, 134, 193, 200
 Beatrice di Tenda, 119
 I Capuleti e i Montecchi, 118
 Il Pirata, 107, 118
 I Puritani, 121, 298
 La Sonnambula, 119, 204, 205, 233, 234, 264
 La Straniera, 118
 Norma, 118, 197, 204, 205, 227, 266
Bénard, Robert, 1
Bergamo, 43, 96
Berger DePlace (family), 229
Bergeron, Katherine, 214
Berlin, 210, 240–60, 285
 Hofoper, 242, 245
Bermani, Benedetto, 173
Bernhard, Christoph, 5
Berthoud, Samuel-Henri, 179
Berton, Henri-Montan, 90
Bettali, Gioachino, 47, 53, 57
Bhavnagar, 231
Bishop, Henry, 115
Bismarck, Otto von, 240, 242
Bizet, Georges
 Carmen, 193, 194
blackface, 124, 215, 219, 220, 230, 232
Blaze, Ange-Henri, 155
Blondeau, Auguste-Louis, 21
Blücher von Wallstatt, Gebhardt Leberecht Fürst, 248
Bohemia, 16, 109, 187. *See also* Habsburg Empire. Czech music. Prague
Boieldieu, François-Adrien, 90, 114
Boito, Arrigo, 19
 Mefistofele, 19, 167, 168, 174, 177, 178, 179, 182, 183
Bolívar, Simón, 198, 208
Bolivia, 27, 38, 135, 137
Bologna, 11, 163, 173, 189
 Teatro Comunale, 170
Bologna (Signor), 202
Bombay, 39, 215, 216, 217, 218, 219, 220, 221, 223, 225, 226, 229, 230, 232, 236, 303
 Esplanade, 222
 Grant Road Theatre, 221, 223, 225
 Roman Catholic Cathedral, 225
 Town Hall, 217, 225

Bonfanti, Maria, 202
Boni, Edouard, 273, 275
Bonini, Francesco, 267
Bordeaux, 136
Bossi, Enrico
    Veggente, Il, 177
Böttiger, Karl August, 35
Bouché (Madame), 226
Bourbons (Naples), 175
Bourbons (Spain), 77, 78, 81, 83, 85, 88
Bovio, Giovanni, 175
Brabant, 179
Braccialini (Signor), 288
Brambilla, Linda, 202, 204, 205, 206, 210
brass bands, 15, 225, 281. *See also* military bands
Braudel, Fernand, 7
Braun, Juliane, 115
Brazil, 1, 4, 8, 11, 27, 37, 39, 41–58, 239, 261–77
    agriculture, 264
    Aimoré tribe, 274
    Amazonas (province), 261–77
    Banco do Brasil, 56
    climate, 70, 271
    Guaraní tribe, 274
    landscape, 3, 4, 196
    national identity, 53
    nature, 4, 70, 239
    pardos, 54
    politics, 56, 57, 262, 263
    soundscapes, 196
Brendel, Franz, 164
Brichta, Francesco, 117, 118, 120, 126
Britain, 25, 34, 60, 62, 175, 271, 283
    as model, 82, 94
    British Empire, 214–38
    expats, 221, 223, 281
    musical life, 68, 226
    national character, 34, 35, 37, 223
    politics, 32, 33, 82
    Scotland, 197, 214
    trade, 198
    travellers, 88, 196
Brno/Brünn, 30
Brown, Matthew, 82
Brussels, 285
Bückeburg, 59
Budapest, 28
Budden, Julian, 18
Buenos Aires, 43, 50, 56, 57, 193, 204, 263, 268, 294
Bukovina, 28
Bullock, William, 88

Burma, 232
Byron, George Gordon, 24, 31

cabaret, 295
Caccini, Giulio, 5
Cádiz, 11, 90
Cagli, Augusto, 216, 221, 222, 223, 225, 226, 228, 229, 231, 234, 235, 237
Calcutta, 57, 60, 80, 218, 223, 227, 228, 229, 231, 232, 234, 236, 268
Caldwell, James, 113, 114, 116, 117, 120, 121
California, 137
Calil and Aprea Italian Operetta Company, The, 270
Camden (New Jersey), 212
Campanini, Italo, 197
canciones, 87
Candi, Pietro, 118
canon, operatic, 147, 165, 166, 208, 278, 296, 298
Canova, Antonio, 31
Cape Town, 231
capitalism, 174, 238. *See also* trade
Caracas, 39, 192–213, 301
    La Competidora, 205
    National Pantheon, 198
    Plaza Bolívar, 201, 207
    Teatro Caracas, 201, 209
    Teatro Coliseo, 200
    Teatro Guzmán Blanco, 201
    Teatro Municipal, 198, 201, 206, 207, 209. *See also* Caracas: Teatro Guzmán Blanco
    Unión Filharmónica, 201
Carafa, Michele, 86, 107
Caravaglia, Margherita, 47, 53, 57
Carelli, Emma, 188
Caribbean, 123, 196
Carner, Mosco, 185
Carreño, Teresa, 39, 192–213
Carson, Dave, 219, 220, 221, 222, 223, 229, 231
Carter, Tim, 298, 299
Caruso, Enrico, 247, 303
Carvalho, José Fernandes ('Juca') de, 263
Castil-Blaze, François-Henri-Joseph, 122
castrati, 23, 43, 47, 50, 58, 67
Castrejón, Luis, 85, 86, 87
Catalani, Angelica, 67
Catholicism, 138, 141, 174, 186, 189, 191
Cavour, Count Camillo, 168
Cazorati (Señor), 202
Cecconi, Alessandro, 119
censorship, 135, 173

Italy, 174–7
Ceresini, Paolo, 118
Ceriani, Davide, 246
Cervantes, Miguel de, 31
Chapí, Ruperto
   Tempestad, La, 265
charity concerts, 288
Cherbourg, 273
Chiadi (Señor), 204
Chile, 27, 38, 82, 133, 136, 137, 139, 140, 142, 146
China, 28, 39, 68, 225, 226, 227, 235, 249
   Revolution, 294
Chopin, Frédéric, 217
chorus, 3, 22, 159, 182, 193, 202
Christy, Edwin Pearce, 219, 220, 221, 230
Chueca, Federico
   La Gran Via, 265
Church, 31, 69, 138, 198, 207
church music, 21, 27, 43, 44, 69, 103, 171, 185
Ciacchi, Cesare, 204
Ciarlantini, Paola, 139
Cicero, 70
Cimarosa, Domenico, 26, 82, 84, 158
cinema. *See* film
citizenship, 233
Civil War
   American, 127, 195, 199
   English, 175
   Venezuela, 210
civilisation, 2, 4, 10, 25, 26, 27, 29, 35, 38, 39, 49, 57, 81, 82, 88, 125, 128, 132, 194, 206, 210, 213, 214, 216, 218, 220, 222, 233, 237, 266–8, 276, 283, 284, 290, 292, 301
civilisation, concept of. *See* civilisation
Clarette, Charles, 150
class, 21, 34, 61, 63, 70, 76, 78, 79, 83, 88, 89, 126, 140, 172, 174, 191, 194, 212, 216, 218, 219, 220, 221, 222, 230, 231, 263, 301
classicism, 31, 32, 33, 157
Clemente, Júlio. *See* Vaz, Thaumaturgo
Coccia, Carlo, 95
Colombia, 135
colonisation, 78, 81, 94, 136, 211, 301
   Britain, 39, 214–38
   France, 114, 123
   Italian, 207
   Portugal, 48, 261, 274
   Spain, 81, 83, 88, 92, 123, 130
Columbus, Christopher, 183
commedia dell'arte, 124

composers, 5, 11, 14, 15, 17, 19, 24, 38, 44, 52, 54, 70, 78, 82, 96, 114, 121, 282
   contracts, 101, 102
   Italian, 169
conductors, 21, 133, 137, 173, 202, 206, 257, 270
Congress of Vienna, 81, 99, 100, 104, 111
conservatism, 208. *See also* political thought
Constant, Benjamin, 32
consumerism, cultural, 233
Conti, Ettore, 267
Copenhagen, 11
Copiapó, 142
Coppola, Pietro Antonio, 103
   Enrichetta di Baienfeld, 103
   La Pazza per amore, 103
Cordara, Carlo
   La Tentazione di Gesù, 182, 183
Corrado Pantanelli, Clorinda, 118, 120, 133, 139–46
cosmopolitanism, 16, 17, 30, 38, 49, 111, 124, 131, 134, 135, 171, 172, 191, 207, 216, 218, 219, 220, 231, 233
Coy, Leandro, 228, 234
Coya, Francisco, 143
creoles, 78, 83, 91, 94
Crespi, Giovanni, 47
Crespin, Joaquin, 198
Crispi, Francesco, 175, 240
criticism, 295
cross-disciplinarity, 14
cross-dressing, 28
Cuba, 38, 83, 90, 117, 128–32, 137, 138, 139, 197, 300
   climate, 129
   national identity, 129
   nature, 129
cultural hybridity, 94
cultural politics, 99, 104, 105, 108, 112, 243, 256, 258, 284
cultural studies, 14
Curtis, William Eleroy, 196
Czech music, 12
Czernowitz, 28

D'Alembert, Jean le Rond, 6, 16
D'Annunzio, Gabriele, 185
D'Aubigny von Engelbrunner, Nina, 38, 59–76
D'Azeglio, Massimo, 170
Dahlhaus, Carl, 98, 99, 249
Dalayrac, Nicholas, 90
dance, 94, 209, 219, 222, 249, 289, 294. *See also* ballet

D'Arcais, Francesco, 176
Darwin, Charles, 196
David, Giovanni, 23
Davis, John, 114
Davison, James William, 148
Deasy, Martin, 124
Debret, Jean-Baptiste, 1
Dejima, 278, 281
Delacroix, Eugène, 6, 157
Delliliers, Vittorio, 266
Demaria, Cristina, 17
Denmark, 31
Depanis, Giuseppe, 179
Destinn, Emmy, 245
Dias Braga Company, 269
Díaz, Bernabé, 200
Dickens, Charles, 21, 22, 24, 25
Diderot, Denis, 6
diplomacy, 18, 198, 210, 240, 278, 283
disease, 70, 269–72. *See also* singers: medical conditions
Dittersdorf, Carl Ditters von, 17
Dittrich, Rudolf, 291
domesticity, 61, 63, 70, 71, 76
Donizetti, Gaetano, 38, 44, 96–112, 121, 123, 132, 134, 193, 200, 275
  Belisario, 119, 121
  Dom Sébastien, 111
  Don Pasquale, 111, 227, 234
  Francesca di Foix, 100, 101, 102
  Il Furioso all'isola di San Domingo, 119, 123
  La Favorita, 205
  L'elisir d'amore, 103
  L'ajo nell'imbarazzo, 50
  Linda di Chamounix, 96, 97, 111, 222
  Lucia di Lammermoor, 119, 197, 204, 222, 227, 264
  Lucrezia Borgia, 136, 205, 222, 227, 228, 234, 264
  Maria di Rohan, 111, 145
  Marino Faliero, 119
  Parisina, 118
  Poliuto, 266
  Ugo, conte di Parigi, 139
Dörffel, Alfred, 287
drama, 22, 24, 33, 42, 48, 105, 113, 114, 176, 264, 267, 269
Dresden, 17
Dumas, Alexandre (fils), 290
Duport, Louis, 108, 109
Duprez, Gilbert [also Gilbert-Louis], 122
Dutch. *See* Netherlands, the
Dutch East Indies, 225. *See also* Netherlands, the
Dvořák, Antonín, 33

East India Company, 218
Eckert, Franz, 288
Ecuador, 38, 135, 137, 138, 300
Eden, Emily, 268
education, 214, 285, 286. *See also* music education
Egypt, 239
Eichner, Barbara, 74
eighteenth century, 5, 6, 7, 11, 16, 19, 21, 27, 91, 187
elites. *See* class
Elphinstone Club, 232
Elsberger, Manfred, 60
emancipation, of women. *See* gender
emigration. *See* migration
emotions, 33, 34, 35, 37, 153, 154, 172, 193, 200, 269, 270, 294
Empire, 8, 10, 12, 33, 43, 44, 82, 99, 104, 110, 111, 136, 214, 215, 220
Empire, concepts of. *See* Empire
Ender, Thomas, 1
Endler, Franz, 99
England. *See* Britain
Enlightenment, 29, 49, 53, 214
Eppstein, Ury, 286
España, María, 137, 138, 139
Ethiopia, 217, 232
ethnicity, 16, 209, 216, 220, 230
Étienne, Charles-Guillaume, 90
Euripides, 4
Eurocentrism, 279
Europe, xvi, 5, 8, 9, 37, 54, 62, 78, 80, 81, 84, 88, 212, 281
  as model, 8, 48, 55, 56, 57, 82, 88, 134, 167, 204
  capital cities, 301
  Central, 9, 12, 13, 30
  concepts of, 26, 31, 38, 49, 53, 221
  cultural heritage, 29, 80, 218, 219, 290
  Eastern, 26, 28
  identity of, 32, 34
  Italian opera in, 11, 30
  musical life, 9, 24, 44, 50, 73, 82, 83, 84, 85, 87, 94, 188, 221, 276
Europeanisation, 2, 4, 94. *See also* Europe
everyday life, 61
exhibitions, 88
exile, 215

exoticism, 39, 88, 123, 129, 171, 182, 197, 211, 239, 241, 249, 251, 253, 281, 283, 284

Farinelli [Carlo Maria Michelangelo Nicola Broschi], 67
Farrar, Geraldine, 245
Fasciotti, Giovanni Francesco, 43, 44, 47, 50
Fasciotti, Maria Teresa, 45, 47, 48
Feind, Barthold, 5
Ferdinand I (Austria), 38, 100, 110, 111, 112
Fernandez, Dominique, 36
Ferrara, 139
Ferretti, Jacopo, 123
Ferretti, Paolo, 137, 138
Ferrettini, Ernesto, 181
Fétis, François-Joseph, 65
Figes, Orlando, 31, 83
Filangieri, Gaetano, 32
film, 14, 39, 260, 261, 303
Fiori, Gaetano, 133
Fiot, Louis, 132
Flanders, 5
Florence, 5, 7, 22, 85, 136, 159, 175
   Teatro della Pergola, 22
flute, 73
Fodor-Mainvielle, Joséphine, 23
Fogliardi, Jean Baptiste, 127
folk music, 248, 249, 251
folklore, 209, 249
Fontana, Ferdinando, 179
Foresti, Luigi, 50
Forsonari (Signor), 118
Förster, Michael A., 242
France, 32, 33, 34, 54, 82, 111, 114, 115, 116, 198, 234, 264, 271
   aesthetics, 17
   literature, 35
   as model, 94
   music, 6, 16, 68, 74, 128, 178, 210
   musical life, 66
   musicians, 23, 54
   national character, 16, 17, 35, 37, 127
   politics, 32, 33, 81
   travellers, 1, 20-1, 88
Franchetti, Alberto, 39, 180, 181, 247
   Asrael, 179, 183
   Cristoforo Colombo, 183, 184
   Germania, 39, 240-60
   Nella foresta nera (symphonic poem), 247
Franck, César
   Les Béatitudes, 183
Franco, Joaquim, 262, 263, 266, 267, 268, 269, 273, 274, 275, 276

Frankfurt (am Main), 161
Franz I (Austria), 104, 105, 110
Franzos, Karl Emil, 28
Frederick II (Prince Elector of Brandenburg), 242, 243, 245
Freemasonry, 86
French Guiana, 271
Freycinet, Louis de, 1, 2
Fumihisa, Hirama, 297

Gabici, Ludovico, 120
Gabici, Luigi, 118
Galicia (Austria), 28
Gallenberg, Robert Wenzel von, 108, 109
Galli, Filippo, 79, 95
García, Manuel, 28, 38, 77-95
   L'Abufar, ossia la famiglia araba, 86, 87, 90, 91
   Semiramis, 87
   Spanish operas, 87
   Un'ora di matrimonio, 87, 89, 90, 91, 94
García, Manuel Patricio, 84
García, Maria Felicia Anna. *See* Malibran, Maria
García, Paulina. *See* Viardot, Pauline
Garcia Márquez, Gabriel
   Love in the Time of Cholera, 265
Garibaldi, Giuseppe, 141, 146
Gasco, Alberto, 190
Gastaldon, Enrico
   Mala Pasqua, 177
gender, 14, 28, 31, 33, 34, 36, 43, 52, 53, 54, 59-76, 143, 197, 211, 287, 295
Generali, Pietro, 44, 87
   Adelina, 47
Gennari, John, 303
Genoa, 4, 21, 22, 25, 152
   Teatro Carlo Felice, 22, 24
Genolini, Rosa, 234
geography, xvi, 127, 214, 249, 300, 301
   Venezuela, 196
German Empire. *See* Germany
German lands. *See* Germany
Germany, 32, 39, 59-76, 240-60, 292, 296
   court culture, 242
   economic development, 240
   music, 7, 11, 12, 16, 17, 72, 91, 168, 177
   musical life, 9, 22, 30, 36, 66
   national character, 5, 37, 127
   national identity, 240-60
   politics, 242, 245, 258
ghazals, 232
Ghobrial, Jean-Paul, 301, 302

Giamboni (Signor), 120
Gilbert, William Schwenck, 283
Giordani, Camillo, 90
Giorgi, Raffaelle, 134
giovine scuola, 183
global south. *See* southernness
globalisation (operatic), xvi, 4, 8, 9, 13, 14, 20, 37, 40, 80, 89, 94, 122, 135, 165, 195, 200, 210, 211, 214–38, 268, 276, 284, 301, 302
Gluck, Christoph Willibald, 6, 19, 157, 292
  Orfeo ed Euridice, 39, 278, 286, 287
Gneisenau, August Graf Neidhardt von, 248
Goethe, August von, 23, 26
Goethe, Johann Wolfgang von, 23, 76
  Faust, 178, 179
  Wilhelm Meister, 26, 27
Göhler, Georg, 248
Goldmark, Karl, 181
Goldoni, Carlo, 29
Gomes, Antônio Carlos, 273, 274, 275
  Fosca, 274
  Il Guarany, 239, 264, 273–7
  Salvator Rosa, 274
Gonzaga (family), 30
Gottschalk, Louis Moreau, 195
Gounod, Charles, 197, 201, 209
  Faust, 171, 176, 177, 179, 204, 223, 241, 264, 288
Graf, Arturo, 182
grand opéra, 12, 13, 24, 29, 38, 83, 116, 169, 170, 175, 177, 183, 191, 249, 264
grand tour. *See* travel
Grattan, Emma, 217
Grau, Maurice, 194
Graun, Carl Heinrich, 70
Graz, 60
Greece (Ancient), 6, 30, 35
Green, Nancy L., 302
Grétry, André, 114
Grillparzer, Franz, 22–3, 24, 25–7, 31
Grimm, Thomas, 150
Grisi, Giulia, 139
Grossi, Tommaso, 170
Guardenti, Egisto, 202, 204, 205
Guarnieri, Giovanni, 234
Guarnieri Corazzol, Adriana, 19, 177
Guayaquil, 135, 137
Guglielmi, Alessandro
  La Quakera spiritosa, 29
Gui, Vittorio, 191
guitar, 77, 192
Gusejnova, Dina, 30

Gutenhoff (Herr), 288
Guzmán Blanco, Antonio, 198, 206, 208

Habsburg Empire, 12, 23, 26, 30, 96–112, 246
  court, 99, 100, 107, 108, 109, 111, 112
  cultural policies, 28, 97
  Küstenland, 26
  multinationalism, 9, 12, 105
Habsburg monarchy. *See* Habsburg Empire
Halévy, Fromental, 150, 161, 183
  L'Ebrea, 176
Hall Chamberlain, Basil, 282
Hamburg, 247, 248, 256
Handel, George Frideric, 298
Hanoi, 215, 280
Hanslick, Eduard, 18, 19, 150, 156, 157, 159
Haussmann, Baron Georges-Eugène, 262
Havana, 117, 120, 121, 129, 133, 135, 140, 194
  Teatro Tacón, 117, 121, 129, 130
Haydn, Joseph, 17, 36, 70, 159
  Mondo della luna, Il, 29
Hegel, Georg Wilhelm Friedrich, 299
hegemony, 80
Heidelberg, 155
Heine, Heinrich, 157, 161
Hensel, Fanny, 64
Herder, Johann Gottfried, 16
Hérold, Ferdinand, 114
Herzog, Werner
  Fitzcarraldo, 261
Heugel, Jacques-Léopold, 150, 161
Hiller, Johann Adam, 65
Hiroshi, Andō, 291
Hisako, Ōyama, 283
historiography, 6, 7, 13–15, 20, 25, 26, 31, 36, 60, 61, 62, 63, 66, 75, 76, 79, 80, 97, 111, 115, 135, 136, 147, 157, 175, 280, 298–300
Hobbes, Thomas, 218
Hochberg, Count Bolko von, 242
Hoffmann, Baptist, 245
Hohenstein, Adolfo, 187
Hohenzollern dynasty, 240, 242, 243, 245, 246
Holy Roman Empire, 110
Hong Kong, 215, 216, 218, 226, 227, 231, 232, 235, 236
  Lusitano Theatre, 227
  Theatre Royal, 232
Hugo, Victor, 274
humanism, 30, 190
Humboldt, Alexander von, 196
Humboldt, Wilhelm von, 248
Hungary, 23

Ica (Peru), 138
Ichizō, Kobayashi, 295
idealism, 15, 33
Illica, Luigi, 246, 247, 248, 256
immigration. *See* migration
imperialism, 214, 284. *See also* Empire
impresari, 5, 12, 14, 15, 37, 50, 51, 52, 53, 56, 85, 96–112, 113, 117, 133, 136, 137, 143, 144, 192–213, 214–38
incidental music, 249
India, 39, 214, 219, 228, 229, 232, 236, 302
    caste, 230
    Hindustan, 216, 219
    Hindustani music, 39, 232
    seṭhs (merchants), 217
indigenous communities, 274
indigenous populations, 49, 199, 223, 230, 262, 274
    music, 209
industrialisation, 110, 174, 194, 199, 212, 222, 262
Inzoli, Giacinto, 233
Isotta, Vittorio, 47, 54
Isouard, Nicolò, 90
italianità
    concept of, 5, 6, 8, 11, 17, 18, 20, 27, 29, 97, 99, 112, 129, 151, 183
    in Asia, 39
    in Brazil, 39
    and Empire, 9
    in France, 33
    in Germany, 9, 39, 240
    in Habsburg Empire, 9, 13
    in Italy, 191
    in Japan, 39, 280
    and religion, 185
    transnational, 196
    transnational concepts of, 33, 38
italianità (operatic), xvi, 5, 7, 8, 9, 11, 18, 19, 20, 23, 24, 27, 30, 31, 36, 37, 40, 103, 122, 132, 194, 239, 253, 298, 301
    in Brazil, 41, 49, 55
    defined by Rossini, 149, 166
    in Germany, 241, 259
    in Habsburg Empire, 97
    in Italy, 168, 171, 172, 177, 182
    in Japan, 279, 296
    in Latin America, 146
    in United States of America, 117, 131
    transnational, 20, 78, 84, 89, 95, 169, 301
Italo-Americans, 127, 139
Italy, 11, 167–91
    aesthetics, 17

backwardness, 129
Catholicism, 167
Church, 167, 172, 185
citizenship, concept of, 167
climate, 69
cultural heritage, 10, 33, 135, 168, 285
democracy, 170
demography, 167
industrialisation, 167, 174
landscape, 26–7, 31, 152
liberal period, 167–91, 239
liberalism, 172, 186, 208
literature, 167
Lombardy, 5, 96
medical conditions, 70
migration, 302
    as model, 94
modernisation, 167, 240
musical life, 7, 21, 22, 23, 24, 25, 27, 31, 36, 61, 66, 67, 68, 71, 74, 76, 106, 108, 130, 146, 151, 298–300
nation-building, 299
national character, 18, 25, 31, 34, 35, 36, 69, 76
national identity, 127, 168, 194, 240
nationalism, 10, 15, 298
nature, 152
North, 167
operas set in, 20
operatic tradition, 19, 23, 27, 28, 100, 128, 279, 291, 298–300
origins of opera, 7, 30
Papal States, 175, 187
Piedmont, 25, 176
political institutions, 32
politics, 32, 167, 168, 170, 171, 172, 174, 175, 176, 191
religion, 167
Risorgimento, 15, 141, 167, 168, 169, 171, 172, 175, 208, 246, 299
theatres, 18, 25, 139
under Napoleon, 35
Unification of, 146, 167, 168, 175
universities, 27
Izquierdo König, José Manuel, 130

Jackson, Amalia, 223
Jacquemont, Victor, 268
Japan, 9, 39, 226, 227, 239, 249, 264, 278–97
    Asakusa opera, 295, 296, 297
    Great Kanto Earthquake, 278, 295
    Iwakura mission, 285
    kabuki theatre, 282, 285, 288, 289

Japan (cont.)
  kokumingeki theatre, 295
  Meiji period, 285, 296
  music, 283
  Noh theatre, 291
  politics, 284, 287
  popular theatre, 288
  shogunat, 291
  Tokugawa period, 281
Java, 225, 236
Jeejeebhoy, Jamsetjee, 220, 221
Jesuits, 5. *See also* missionaries
John VI (Portugal), 54
Johnson, Julian, 136
Jommelli, Niccolò, 159
joropo, 209
Joseph II (Holy Roman Emperor), 29
Judaism, 28, 161
Judson, Pieter, 111

Kanne, Friedrich August, 24
Kant, Immanuel, 24
Karlsruhe, 247, 248, 256, 259
Kassel, 59
Kauer, Ferdinand
  Saalnixe, Die, 33
Keiji, Masui, 278, 286, 296, 297
Kellogg, Clara Louise, 197
Kiesewetter, Raphael Georg, 158
Kimbell, David, 298, 299
Kiyoo, Kawamura, 285
Kletzer (Herr), 217
Kmen, Henry, 115
Kōbe, 281, 283, 295
Koeber, Raphael von, 286
Kolisch, Sigmund, 153
Kolowrat, Count Franz Anton von, 110, 111
Körner, Theodor, 248, 260
Kun, Josh, 300

La Grange, Henri-Louis de, 98
La Guaira, 198
La Paz, 137
Lablache, Luigi, 23
Lambayeque, 138
Lanari, Alessandro, 136
language, 73, 77, 113, 114, 115, 116, 120, 127, 128, 130, 132, 142, 235, 258, 264, 265, 275, 279, 299. *See also* translation
Lapp Norris, Renee, 219
Latin America, xvi, 8, 13
  idea of, 80
  musical life, 27, 194

national identity, 138
nationalism, 82
opera companies, 57
Le Cerf de la Viéville, Jean-Laurent, 6
Le Havre, 44
Lecocq, Charles
  La Fille de Madame Angot, 232, 233
Lederer, Josef-Horst, 259
Leerssen, Joep, 75
Leipzig, 9, 38, 240, 285, 287
Leoncavallo, Ruggero, 39, 210
  I Medici, 242
  Pagliacci, 242, 258, 264
  Der Roland von Berlin, 39, 240–60
Leopardi, Giacomo, 172, 173
Leopoldina (Empress, Brazil), 43, 44
Liberali, Giovanni, 52
liberalism, 38, 78, 134, 191, 192, 200, 206. *See also* political thought
libretti, 11, 55, 123, 132, 242, 244, 286
Lima, 80, 133, 135, 138, 140, 142, 143, 144, 145, 300, 303
Linguet, Simon-Nicholas Henri, 70
Lisbon, 1
  São Carlos Theatre, 1
  Theatro São Carlos, 44
Liszt, Franz/Ferenc, 197, 205
literacy, 62
literary theory, 14, 147
literature, 20–8, 31–7, 38, 168, 214, 244, 264
Livorno, 301
Ljubljana/Laibach, 30
Lockroy, Edouard, 154
Lombardy-Venetia, 175. *See also* Habsburg Empire
London, 22, 23, 36, 60, 84, 85, 88, 91, 135, 193, 197, 207, 216, 220, 222, 226, 283, 300
  Alhambra music hall, 294
  Japanese Village, 283
  King's Theatre, 24, 84, 87
  Piccadilly, 88
Louisiana, 114
Louisville, Kentucky, 117
Luciani, Sebastiano Arturo, 190
Luise (Queen of Prussia), 246
Lully, Jean-Baptiste, 16, 17, 157
Lützow, Ludwig Adolf Wilhelm Freiherr von, 246
Lynch, Dominick, 84
Lyster, William Saurin, 228, 236

Macao, 57
Macapá, 261

Madrid, 83, 90, 135, 197, 207, 209, 300
  Teatro Real, 201
Mahler-Werfel, Alma, 64
Maina, Vincenzo, 267
Majocchi (Signora), 120
Majoranini, Nicola, 44, 47, 50
Malay, 216
Malaya, 225
Malibran, Eugène, 84
Malibran, Maria, 84, 85
Manaus, 39, 261–77
  Academia das Belas Artes, 269
  Éden theatre, 266
  Hotel Cassiano, 271
  Teatro Amazonas, 39, 261–77
Manfredini, Vincenzo, 7
Manfroce, Nicola, 87
Manila, 225, 227, 228, 235
Mann, Thomas, 19
Manzoni, Alessandro, 170
Mapelson, Colonel, 197
Mapleson (company), 202
Maracaibo, 196
Marchesi, Luigi, 68, 72
Marchetti, Filippo
  Ruy Blas, 204, 266
Marciali, Angelo, 47
Marconi, Giuseppe, 144
Mariani, Angelo, 173
Marot, Gaston
  Jack the Ripper, 269
Marozzi (Signora), 118
Marseilles, 273
Martí y Torrens, Francisco, 117, 119, 121, 122, 129, 130
Martini, Giambattista, 11
Mascagni, Pietro, 210, 253
  Cavalleria rusticana, 177, 264, 291, 294, 295
  Iris, 239
Maugars, Antoine, 5
May, Alice, 229, 232, 233
Mayr, Giovanni Simone. *See* Mayr, Johann Simon
Mayr, Johann Simon, 96
Mazza, Francisco Xavier, 44
Mazzini, Giuseppe, 168, 170, 173
  Filosofia della Musica, 170
McClellan, Michael, 215, 280
Medici (family), 30
medieval revival, 243, 245
Mediterranean, 25, 26, 33, 151, 177
Méhul, Étienne, 90, 114
Meiji (Emperor of Japan), 284

Melbourne, 204, 228
  Princess Theatre, 228
melodrama, 86, 123, 168, 172, 216, 230
Mendelssohn, Felix, 155, 158, 217
Menestrier, Claude-François, 5
Mercadante, Saverio, 44, 95, 107, 121
  Caritea, regna di Spagna, 118
  Normanni a Parigi, I, 121
Merelli, Bartolomeo, 38, 96–112
Metastasio, Pietro, 11, 55
Metternich, Prince Clemens von, 23, 110, 111
Mexico, 28, 38, 77–95, 194
  nationalism, 78
  politics, 86, 90
Mexico City, 38, 77–95
  Compañía de Ópera Italiana, 77
  Teatro de los Gallos, 77, 78, 85, 89, 90, 94
  Teatro Principal, 82, 85
Meyerbeer, Giacomo, 17, 19, 95, 150, 155, 159, 161, 164, 170, 182, 183, 184, 209
  Il Crociato in Egitto, 24
  L'Africaine, 204, 205, 209, 264
  Les Huguenots, 175, 193, 197
  Robert le diable, 116, 120, 122, 176, 177, 204
Micciarelli, Lucrezia, 142, 143, 144, 145, 146
Michelena, Fernando, 201
Mignolo, Walter, 94, 211
Mignotti, Angelo and Pietro, 30
migration, 18, 46, 54, 57, 192, 262, 303
  Bohemia, 187
  British, 263
  Europeans, 262
  French, 54, 263
  Germans, 263
  Italians, 127, 137, 138, 139, 142, 146, 194, 209, 264
  Latin Americans, 195
  North Americans, 263
Milan, 23, 24, 25, 28, 79, 106, 135, 137, 139, 143, 194, 202, 204, 207, 210, 240, 247, 266, 270, 275, 300
  Lazzaretto hospital, 170
  Teatro alla Scala, 100, 106, 139, 146, 171, 226, 239, 247, 274, 275, 282, 294
  Teatro dal Verme, 177
  Teatro della Canobiana, 26
Milanca Guzmán, Mario, 193, 205
Milinowski, Marta, 193, 205
military, 25, 54, 215, 240, 261, 286
military bands, 201, 218. *See also* brass bands
Mill, John Stuart, 218
minstrels (American), 215, 218–21
missionaries, 214, 218, 222. *See also* Jesuits

Mobile (city), 113
modernisation, 198, 286, 290
modernity, 10, 14, 81, 82, 111, 134, 151, 154, 207, 216, 233, 253, 262
Mokuami, Kawatake
 Strange Tale of the Castaways: A Western Kabuki, The, 282, 285
Mombelli, Ester, 22
monodies, 5
Monteverdi, Claudio, 158, 299
Montevideo, 204
Montresor, Giacomo, 117
Montresor, Giovanni, 117, 118, 120, 121, 126
moral education, 70, 105, 164, 186, 209, 214, 220, 230, 236, 237
Moriyoshi, Naganuma, 285
Morlacchi, Francesco, 103
Mozart, Wolfgang Amadeus, 17, 36, 70, 82, 84, 152, 156, 157, 158, 159, 298
 Don Giovanni, 51, 87, 158, 197
 Requiem, 159
Muck, Karl, 259
Murdoch, John, 214
music criticism, 6, 9, 18, 22, 23, 28, 37, 44, 45, 53, 55, 70, 104, 116, 148–66, 173, 179, 204, 207, 208, 209, 226, 241, 245, 254, 256–60, 265
 French, 5, 6, 300
music education, 7, 36, 38, 52, 54, 59–76, 120, 133, 137, 138, 182, 202, 210, 214, 269, 286, 294, 297
music, instrumental, 36, 72
musical authenticity, 18, 25, 91, 122, 185, 219, 231, 241, 249, 251, 253, 259, 288, 290, 296, 297
musical commodities, 56
musicology. *See* historiography
Musso, Chevalier, 235
mysticism, 168

Nagasaki, 278, 281
Nanpo, Ōta, 281
Naomi, Matsumoto, 280
Naples, 4, 5, 21, 83, 90, 91, 104, 107, 124, 127, 152, 196
 San Gennaro, 31
 Teatro San Carlo, 21, 26, 84, 106, 107, 108
Napoleon Bonaparte, 18, 32, 34, 99, 104
Napoleonic Wars, 1, 18, 21, 30, 31–6, 37, 104, 110, 240, 246, 256, 300
Nashville, 114
national character. *See* national identity. countries

national identity, 4–11, 13, 15, 16, 17, 22, 31–7, 38, 49, 60, 67, 68–76, 80, 81, 82, 124, 125–8, 132, 148, 239–60. *See also* countries
national independence
 Brazil, 41, 43, 44, 48, 50, 53, 57, 261
 Latin America, 8, 81, 82, 134
 Mexico, 77, 78, 79, 83, 86, 88, 89, 92, 94, 95
national movements. *See* nationalism
national myths, 239, 241, 243, 259, 275, 293
nationalism, 11–13, 74, 81, 115. *See also* countries
nation-building. *See* nationalism
Netherlands, the, 23, 278, 281
Neukomm, Sigismund, 54
Neumane, Antonio, 137, 139, 142, 143, 144
Neumane, Rosa, 137
New Orleans, 29, 38, 80, 85, 113–32, 133, 140
 Camp Street Theatre, 113, 114, 116
 climate, 129
 St Charles Theatre, 113, 117, 118, 120, 121
 Théâtre d'Orléans, 113, 114, 116, 118, 120, 121, 122, 124, 127, 128, 132
 Verandah Hotel (concert venue), 121
New World, 2, 4, 11, 28, 29, 49, 134
New York, 28, 83, 84, 85, 117, 126, 133, 192, 193, 194, 196, 197, 198, 202, 204, 210, 220, 294
 Italian Opera House, 126
 Metropolitan Opera, 204
newspapers. *See* press
Nobu, Kōda, 291
North America, 28, 84, 194, 197, 204, 210, 264
nostalgia, 192, 247, 300
Noto, Tomaso, 202, 204
Novara, 103
Nuremberg, 246

Offenbach, Jacques, 161, 265
 Genevieve de Brabant, 233
 Grand-Duchess of Gerolstein, The, 232, 233
 Le Violoneux, 232
Olavarría y Ferrari, Enrique, 79
Old World, 11, 29, 46, 49, 56, 57. *See also* Europe
opera
 American burlesque, 216
 Chinese, 236
 English, 114, 224
 English, burlesque, 233
 French, 13, 74, 107, 113, 114, 121–4, 128, 169, 205, 209, 210, 229, 265, 273, 275, 276

German, 22, 106, 107, 108, 110, 169, 181, 210, 265, 291
Hindustani, 216, 224, 230
Italian, burlesque, 219
Parsi, 39, 229–37
Spanish, 209
opéra bouffe, 209, 233, 236
Opera Bouffe Company, 232
opéra comique, 90, 114, 124, 233, 265, 273
opera companies, 83, 100. *See* theatre: companies
opera parodies, 219
Opera Verdiana (company), 297
operetas (Spanish), 82, 87
operetta, 232, 264, 265, 267, 270, 281, 283, 294, 295
Optschina, 26
orchestras, 3, 5, 15, 16, 21, 22, 52, 76, 91, 117, 145, 201, 228, 236, 249, 267, 268, 273, 276, 293
orientalism, 25–6, 68, 283
Orlandi, M., 118
Ōsaka, 295
Osterhammel, Jürgen, 279
otherness, 129, 131, 239, 246. *See also* orientalism

Paccini, Giovanni, 22
Pachta, Count Johann Joseph, 109
Pacini, Giovanni, 95, 103, 107
 Saffo, 136
Padua, 27
Paër, Ferdinando, 87
 Agnese, 55
Paisiello, Giovanni, 84
Palestrina, Giovanni Pierluigi da, 156, 190
Pállfy, Count Ferdinand, 109
Palm, Johann Philipp, 246
Palmieri, Maria, 282
Pantanelli, Alaide, 139
Pantanelli, Clorinda. *See* Corrado Pantanelli, Clorinda
Pantanelli (family), 133, 140, 142, 146
Pantanelli, Raffaele, 133, 134, 136, 143, 145
Panzacchi, Enrico, 173
Papanti (Signora), 118
Paquette, Gabriel, 82
Pará, 270
Parakilas, James, 182
Paris, 22, 23, 83, 86, 88, 91, 111, 114, 134, 135, 148, 151, 153, 160, 175, 193, 197, 198, 207, 216, 220, 226, 262, 264, 273, 299, 300

Champs Elysées, 156
Conservatoire, 89, 273
La Madeleine, 155
La Trinité, 159
Opéra, 273, 282
Théâtre de l'Opéra-Comique, 90
Théâtre italien, 84, 87
Parma, 17, 25
Passetti, Alessandro, 202, 204, 205, 206
passions. *See* emotions
Pasta, Giuditta, 84, 85, 139
patriotism, 74, 247, 257, 260, 275, 277. *See also* countries
Patti, Adelina, 197, 201
Patti, Carlotta, 236
Pedro I (Brazil), 42, 44, 51, 52, 54, 56, 57
Pedro II (Brazil), 57
Pedroni, Giacomo, 101
Pedrotti, Adolaide, 118
Penang, 236
Peñin, José, 200
Pereira, Elpídio, 273
Pérez Vejo, Tomás, 81
Pergolesi, Giovanni Battista, 70, 159
Peri, Maria, 267
Peri, Noël, 286, 292
Péricaud, Louis
 Jack the Ripper, 269
periphery, concepts of, 26, 211, 215
Pernambuco, 270
Perozzi, Luigi, 119
Perry, Matthew, 9
Persia (Ancient), 230
Persiani, Alice, 282
Peru, 27, 38, 133, 137, 138, 139, 142
Pesaro, 153, 155, 156, 158
Peters (publisher), 287
Petrella, Errico
 Jone, 266
Philadelphia, 84, 126
Philippines, 237, 301
Piacentini, Elisa, 47
Piacentini, Fabrizio, 43, 47, 50, 53
Piacentini, Giustina, 43, 47, 53
piano, 36, 63, 77, 192, 200, 205
 piano reductions, 15, 56, 249
Piccinni, Niccolò, 6, 19, 67, 157
Piccioli (Signor), 226
Picón Febres, Gonzalo, 192, 196
Pinto, Amelia, 247
Pires Ferreira, Fileto, 267
Pius IX, 138, 172
Pizzetti, Ildebrando, 185

Pizzoni, Domenico, 57
Plancher, Pierre (publisher), 45, 55
Planquette, Robert, 265
Plato, 70
Playford, John, 5
Poland, 12
political thought, 7, 32, 33, 38, 54
Pompei, Giovanni, 216, 225–8, 229, 236, 237
Ponchielli, Amilcare
　Gioconda, La, 262, 266
Ponte, Lorenzo da, 28, 84
Poona, 223, 231
popular culture, 295
popular song, 209
Porpora, Nicola, 65
port cities, 35, 198, 225, 226, 281
Portugal, 1, 2, 8, 11, 41–58, 263
　Royal Court, 1, 2, 11, 27, 37, 43, 44, 46, 49, 50, 51, 56
Portugal, Marcos, 54
Portuguese Empire. *See* Portugal
positivism, 177
postcolonialism, 8, 27, 38, 56, 78, 79, 80, 81, 82, 83, 86, 88, 94, 95, 115, 123, 134, 211, 214–38
Praetorius, Michael, 5
Prague, 30. *See also* Habsburg Empire; Bohemia; Czech music
Prampolini, Clementina, 202, 204
press, 148–66. *See also* press (musical)
　A Aurora Fluminense, 48
　A Federação, 270
　Allgemeine Zeitung, 155
　Amazonas, 266
　Ars e Labor, 174
　Astrea, 48
　Athenæum, The, 149
　Augsburger Allgemeine, 257
　Bataviasch Handelsblad, 227
　Berliner Börsen-Zeitung, 241, 257
　Berliner Volks-Zeitung, 245, 258
　Bombay Gazette, 230
　Daily Picayune, 113, 120, 125, 128, 130, 131
　Daily Telegraph, 154
　Der Wanderer, 100
　Diable à quatre, Le, 154
　Diario de Avisos, 198, 200, 205, 206, 208
　Didaskalia, 155
　Die Debatte, 151, 152
　East London Observer, 149
　El Comercio, 142
　El Granuja, 200, 202
　El Sol (Mexico), 77
　Gazeta do Brasil, 45, 48, 52
　Globe, The, 149, 151
　Hong Kong Daily Press, 226
　Il Corriere d'Italia, 189
　Il Messaggero, 186
　Illustrated Times, The, 149, 164
　in Asia, 237
　in Austria, 148
　in Brazil, 45, 47, 52, 53, 54, 55, 57, 266
　in Britain, 148
　in France, 53, 148
　in Germany, 148, 245, 256–60
　in India, 219, 220, 223, 234
　in Italy, 133, 137
　in Japan, 286
　in Latin America, 135
　in Mexico, 82, 83
　in New Orleans, 113, 115, 116, 120, 121–4, 125, 129, 130, 131
　in Peru, 138, 144
　in Switzerland, 148
　in Venezuela, 199, 200
　Japan Punch, 282
　Japan Weekly Mail, 288
　Java-bode, 235
　Jornal do Commercio, 53
　L'Écho de l'Amérique du Sud, 45, 47, 49, 51
　Le Constitutionnel, 158
　L'Illustration, 150
　L'Indépendant (Brazil), 45, 52, 53
　La Gazzetta del Popolo, 179
　La Gazzetta Letteraria, 179
　La Gazzetta Piemontese, 178, 180
　La Lorgnette, 122, 123, 129
　La Moda, 173
　La Opinion Nacional, 192, 199, 200, 201, 205, 207, 209
　La Stampa, 183
　La Tribuna, 186, 190
　La Voce della verità, 177, 186
　Le Figaro, 155, 247, 248
　Le Journal des Débats, 88
　Le Lapin indépendant, 155
　Le Mémorial diplomatique, 150
　Le Ménestrel, 150, 161, 166
　Le Monde Artiste, 270
　London Daily News, 154
　London Evening Standard, 154
　L'Osservatore Romano, 189
　Manchester Courier and Lancashire General Advertiser, 154
　Mexico, 94
　Morgen-Post, 160

Morning Advertiser, 162
Morning Post, 149
Movie Picture World, 260
Neue Bibliothek für Pädagogik und Schulwesen, 65
New York Times, 210
O espelho diamantino, 51, 53
O Rio Negro, 269
O Spectador Brasileiro, 45, 52
Penny Illustrated Paper, 149
Providence Daily Post, The, 195
Rāst Goftār, 222, 223
Revue des Deux Mondes, 207
Revue pour tous, 150
Saunders's News-Letter, 159
Straits Times, The, 227, 231, 234, 235
Sun, The, 149
Sydney Mail, 236
Taiyō, 289
Times of India, The, 223, 236
Venezuela, 201
Volksfreund, 257
Wiener Presse, 159
Zeitung für die elegante Welt, 65
press (musical), 7, 37, 47, 270
   A Platea, 268, 273, 274, 275, 276
   Allgemeine Musikalische Zeitung, 24
   Allgemeine musikalische Zeitung (Leipzig), 65, 70, 164, 166
   Gazzetta musicale di Milano, 15
   L'Arpa, 173
   La Lira Venezolana, 200
   Le Moniteur des pianistes, 153, 155
   Le Quinte, 270
   Musical World, The, 148, 149, 152, 160, 164
   Neue Berliner Musikzeitung, 150, 151
   Neue Zeitschrift für Musik, 164
   Neues Wiener Tagblatt, 153
   Orchestra, The, 156
   Teatri, arti e letteratura, 133
   Zancudo, El, 200
Preston, Katherine, 126, 221
programme booklets, 55
progress, 207, 208, 210, 214, 216, 220
Prussia, 24, 62, 243. *See also* Germany
public sphere, 52
Puccini, Giacomo, 19, 20, 186, 210, 253, 283, 299
   Gianni Schicchi, 20
   La bohème, 247, 264, 279, 297
   Madama Butterfly, 249, 283, 295
   Tosca, 20, 176, 185, 185, 186, 187
   Turandot, 19

Pucitta, Vincenzo, 44
Pustkow, Friedrich, 1

Quantz, Johann Joachim, 73
Querelle des bouffons, 6, 17, 37
Quito, 138

race. *See* ethnicity
Rachelle, Fernando, 205
Racine, Jean, 35, 157
Radomski, James, 79
Raguenet, François, 6
railways, 31, 199, 295
Rameau, Jean-Philippe, 157
Raphael Tomba Company, 267, 269
Ravafinoli, Vincenzo, 126
Ravaglia (Signora), 118
realism, 283
reception, 14, 80, 299. *See* audiences: reception, criticism
recording industry, 212, 303
Red Sea, 217
Reggio Emilia, 179
Reina (Signor), 223, 226
religion, 34, 38, 42, 69, 138, 140, 144, 151, 156, 167–91, 214, 216, 218, 230, 247, 274
Renaissance, 30, 183, 249
repertoire, concepts of, 12, 15, 19, 20, 23, 28, 43, 44, 70, 83, 84, 114, 122, 168, 174, 194, 200, 228, 231. *See also* canon, operatic
Restoration. *See* Congress of Vienna
Ricci, Amato, 137, 202
Ricci, Luigi, 121
   Chiara di Rosemberg, 118, 119
Ricordi (company), 137, 168, 174, 179, 247
Ricordi, Giovanni, 96
Ricordi, Giulio, 248
Rio de Janeiro, 1, 2, 3, 4, 37, 41–58, 135, 265, 266, 268, 270, 300, 303
   Capela Real, 43, 52
   Guanabara Bay, 46
   Theatrinho, 49
   Theatro Real, 41
   Theatro São João, 1, 2, 41, 43, 44
   Theatro São Pedro de Alcântara, 1, 41, 43, 44, 46, 48, 49, 52, 54, 56
River Plate, 57
Robilant, Nicolis de, 176
Roesler Franz, Ettore, 187
Romani, Felice, 86
romanticism, 33, 87, 157, 172, 200
Rombo, Annina Morosini Contessa, 248

Rome, 5, 22, 31, 32, 83, 90, 103, 171, 175, 176, 177, 186, 187, 204
   Castel Sant'Angelo, 187
   Sistine Chapel, 27
   St Peter's Basilica, 31, 187
   Teatro Apollo, 22
   Teatro Argentina, 77
   Teatro Costanzi, 188, 190
   Teatro Nazionale, 187
   Teatro Tordinona. *See* Rome, Teatro Apollo
Rome (Ancient), 69, 162
Roqueplan, Nestor, 158
Rosa, Antonio de, 117, 118
Rosi, Giovanni Vittorio, 39, 280, 294–6
Rosselli, John, 109
Rossi (Mme), 119
Rossi, Alessandro, 174
Rossi, Gaetano
   Teobaldo e Isolina, 139
Rossi, Luigi, 121
Rossi, Teresa, 118, 139–46
Rossini, Gioachino, 11, 13, 19, 20, 22, 23, 26, 31, 36, 38, 44, 49, 77, 82, 83, 84, 87, 95, 97, 98, 99, 103, 106, 115, 121, 132, 134, 147–66, 197, 200, 201, 298, 299, 302
   Aureliano in Palmira, 26, 44, 47
   Elisabetta, regina d'Inghilterra, 42, 84
   Guillaume Tell, 150, 152, 155, 158, 241
   Il barbiere di Siviglia, 23, 43, 44, 45, 47, 53, 77, 78, 84, 86, 87, 89, 90, 91, 118, 200, 225, 226
   La Cenerentola, 22, 87, 118, 225
   La Gazza ladra, 56
   L'inganno felice, 47, 118
   L'italiana in Algeri, 43, 44
   Matilde di Shabran, 56
   Moïse et Pharaon, 197
   operas in Spanish, 83
   Otello, 87, 118
   Semiramide, 118
   Tancredi, 43, 51, 118, 140
   Il Turco in Italia, 118
   Il Viaggio à Reims, 17
   Zelmira, 88, 104, 107, 118
Rothschild, James, 160
Rousseau, Jean-Jacques, 6, 7, 16, 17, 37, 62, 70, 125, 127, 130, 197
Royal English Opera Company, 217, 282
Rubini, Giovanni Battista, 122
Rugendas, Moritz, 140, 142, 143
Russia, 7, 23, 31, 62
Rutherford, Susan, 15, 37

Sacchini, Antonio, 67
Sadahide, Utagawa, *10*
Said, Edward, 26
Saigon, 234
sainetes, 82
Saint-Domingue, 123
Saint-Evremond, Charles de, 5
Sales, Pompeo, 59
Salinger's Opera Bouffe Company, 283
Salvatori, Celestin, 119
Salvatori, Salvatore, 44, 47
Salzburg, 30
Samarang, 228
Sammarco, Mario, 247
Sanctis, Francesco de, 168, 170
San Francisco, 219, 220
Santa-Anna Nery, Frederico José de, 271
Santiago (Chile), 140, 142
Santo Domingo. *See* Saint-Domingue
São Luís, 261
Sarcoli, Adolfo, 293
Sardou, Victorien, 185
Sassatelli, Roberta, 17
Sauret, Émile, 198
scapigliatura, 169
Schelle, Eduard, 159, 160
Schieroni, Teresa, 57
Schiller, Friedrich, 28, 32
Schio, 174
   Teatro Civico, 174
Schopenhauer, Arthur, 299
Schubert, Franz, 98, 99
Schumann, Robert, 155
Schütz, Heinrich, 5
Schwartz, Arman, 186
Scott, Walter, 115
   Guy Mannering, 115
   Lady of the Lake, The, 115
Sedlnitzky, Count Joseph von, 108
Senici, Emanuele, 20, 30, 299
seventeenth century, 5, 16, 30, 278
Seville, 90
sexuality. *See* gender
Seyfried, Ferdinand von, 23, 109
Shahnama, 230
Shakespeare, William, 28, 31, 35, 70, 114, 157, 215, 222, 230, 266
Shanghai, 232, 234, 235, 236, 293
Shankarsheth, Jagannath, 221
sheet music, 121, 267, 293
Sheffield, 154
Shelley (family), 34
Shope, Bradley, 219

Shōsaburō, Ishikura, 287, 288, 290, 292
Shōyō, Tsubouchi, 292, 293
Sicily, 127
Siemann, Wolfram, 111
Siena, 293
Silva Pinto Company, 265
Sinatra, Frank, 303
Singapore, 215, 216, 218, 225, 227, 228, 231, 232, 234, 235, 236
  Theatre Royal, 231
Singer, Otto, 287
singers, 11, 14, 18, 21, 22, 23, 24, 26, 47, 71, 73, 87, 88, 117, 120, 121, 128, 141, 197, 204, 257, 259
  acting, 144
  benefit performances, 50, 51, 52, 143
  casting, 23, 28, 43, 47, 266
  contracts, 44, 46, 47, 51, 53, 109, 137, 143, 144
  finances, 43, 46, 50, 51, 52, 57, 143, 205, 211
  French, 51
  illness, 208
  Italian, 24, 44, 141, 146
  Japanese, 294
  medical conditions, 70, 84, 205
  migration, 9, 16, 38, 41, 43, 44, 46, 48, 50, 56, 57, 77, 82, 133–46, 301
  self-perception of, 24, 52, 53
  slaves, 3
  stardom, 24, 202
singing, style, 5, 6, 7, 71
Singspiel, 28, 33, 38. *See also* opera: German
Sinigaglia, 138
Sitchez Briones, Joaquina, 84
sixteenth century, 7
slavery, 1, 2, 3, 4, 50, 54, 58, 123
Slovenia, 26
Smart, Mary Ann, 172, 299
social progress, 199, 206
soldiers. *See* military
Sonzogno (company), 168, 177
Sophocles, 4
Sorba, Carlotta, 172
soundscapes, 193, 249, 251, 253, 257
South Africa, 218, 231
South America, 41, 50, 57, 133–46, 204, 210. *See* Latin America
southernness, 26, 29, 36, 41, 69, 126–32, 197
Souza Bastos, Antônio de, 265
Spain, 8, 77, 86, 123, 198, 264
  as model, 82
  hispanophobia, 86
  music, 82

musical life, 8, 77, 83, 91, 130
musicians, 11, 38
national character, 5, 88, 127
politics, 81, 82, 210
Spanish Empire. *See* Spain
Spanish-America, 196
Spezia, La, 152
St Louis, 113
Stadion, Johann Philip Count of, 105, 106
Staël-Holstein, Germaine de, 21, 22, 31–7, 197
  Corinne, 21, 22, 31–6
  De l'Allemagne, 32
Staffieri, Gloria, 169
Stapß, Friedrich, 246
steamships, 120, 137, 196, 199, 217, 218, 225, 271
Stein, Heinrich Friedrich vom und zum, 248
Stendhal [Beyle, Marie-Henri], 19, 31, 36, 157, 158, 301
Sticchini, Plácido
  Tim-tim por tim-tim, 265
Stradina, Gustave, 150
Strakosch (company), 202
Strakosch, Maurice, 197
Styria, 26
Sueharu, Kitamura, 289
Suez Canal, 217
Sullivan, Arthur
  Cox and Box, 281
  Mikado, The, 283
supernaturalism, 177, 179
Suppé, Franz von, 265
supranationalism, 218
  Habsburg Empire, 30, 99, 100
  of Italian opera, 9
Surabaya, 225, 235, 236

Tagliapietra, Giovanni, 193, 194, 198, 202, 204, 205, 210, 211
Taine, Hippolyte, 21
Takarazuka, 295
Takarazuka Opera Company, 295
Taki, Rentarō, 9, 285
Talbot, J. C., 231
Tamaki, Miura, 294
Tamburini Coy (Signora), 234
Tani, Maria, 47
Tappert, Wilhelm, 249
Tasso, Torquato, 31
Teixeira de Seixas, Pedro, 52
telegraph, 198, 217, 266
Tenca, Carlo, 173
Thalberg (family), 229

Thalberg, Sigismund, 197
theatre
  architecture, 1–2, 15, 22, 25, 43, 54, 84, 86, 136, 262, 285, 293
  companies, 7, 41, 48, 49, 51, 52, 113, 117, 120, 128, 133, 192–213, 215–38
    American, 282
    Brazil, 41
    British, 282
    Cuban, 140
    European, 77, 84, 114, 194
    French, 200, 263, 282
    Italian, 46, 47, 49, 53, 57, 114, 115, 116, 121–4, 125, 128, 132, 137, 200, 235
    Latin American, 27
    Portuguese, 264, 265
    Russian, 282
    Spanish, 200
  contracts, 108
  costumes, 22, 41, 121, 136, 205, 286. *See* theatre: sets
  court theatres, 168. *See also* individual entries for countries and cities
  entertainments, 113, 218, 266
  finances, 44, 46, 49, 50, 52, 56, 85, 86, 100, 104, 105, 108, 109, 112, 114, 120, 130, 134, 193, 221, 227, 231, 236, 245, 267, 278, 293
  fires, 121
  gambling, 41, 109
  gas lighting, 116, 199, 223
  Parsi, 215, 216
  police, 108. *See also* censorship
  private boxes, 58, 77
  sets, 22, 26, 41, 135, 136, 142, 179, 187, 205, 257, 267, 286
  subscriptions, 57, 222, 233
Theremin, Karl Wilhelm von, 1
Thibaw Min (King of Burma), 232
Thomas, Ambroise, 150
  Mignon, 193
Thorvaldsen, Bertel, 31
time, concepts of historical, xvi, 5, 18, 80
Tofighian, Nadi, 225
Tokyo, 39, 303
  Akasaka, 294
  Asakusa, 278, 295
  Asakusa opera, 39
  Hibiya Park, Public Hall, 279
  Imperial Palace, 282
  Imperial Theatre, 39, 278, 280, 283, 289, 293, 294, 295
  Kabuki-za Theatre, 289
  Keiō University, 292
  Royal Theatre, 290, 294
  Shintomi-za theatre, 282
  Tokyo Imperial University, 292
  Tokyo Music School, 278, 286, 288, 291, 293, 294
Tomba, Raphael, 270. *See also* Raphael Tomba Company
Tomoyoshi, Tomiogi, 291
tonadillas, 82, 83, 87, 92
Torgau, 30
Tornel y Mendívil, José María de, 86
Torri, Alberto, 143
Toscanini, Arturo, 247
Tosi, Pier Francesco, 65
trade, 121, 217, 263, 277, 278
  Brazil, 262
  Lebanon, 263
  Spain, 263
  Syria, 263
  United States of America, 198
trade, international, 82, 129, 130, 131, 134, 198, 199
transatlantic networks, 84, 88, 193, 197, 263, 266, 276, 303
transcriptions, 200. *See* adaptations (of operas)
transculturalisation, 9, 280, 288, 297
translation, 55, 78, 132. *See also* language
  cultural, 280, 283, 287, 289, 296
  libretti, 18, 86, 90, 94, 111, 115, 122, 132, 245, 258, 275, 287, 294, 295
transnationalism, 4, 5, 7, 8, 10–15, 18, 19, 20, 25, 31, 33, 34, 35, 38, 39, 60, 61, 74, 75, 78, 79, 80, 111, 115, 136, 148, 167, 297, 302
travel, 18, 20–37, 142. *See also* migration; singers: migration
  to Asia, 225
  to Brazil, 2, 4, 268, 272
  to Europe, 285
  to France, 60
  to Germany, 5
  to Italy, 5, 18, 21, 24, 25, 26, 31, 33, 34, 60, 76
  to Mexico, 88
  to the Netherlands, 60
  to Venezuela, 196
Trieste, 26
Turin, 171, 175, 176, 177, 179
  local administration, 176
  Teatro Regio, 178, 179
Turri, Idalide, 137, 139
Tuscany, 25, 127

Ubaldi (family), 142
Ukraine, 11
United States of America, 29, 113–32, 195, 197, 204, 207, 210, 211, 221, 281, 285
universalism, 16, 188, 220
Urdu *ghazals*, 216
Uruguay, 27
USA. *See* United States of America

Vaccaj, Nicola, 84
Valetta, Ippolito, 178
Valparaíso, 133, 135, 136, 142
    Teatro Victoria, 133, 134
Valverde Durán, Joaquín
    Gran Via, La, 265
variety shows, 222, 263
Vattellina (Signor), 120
vaudeville, 278, 295
Vaz, Thaumaturgo, 269
Velluti, Giovanni Battista, 23, 24
Venetian Republic. *See* Venice
Veneto. *See* Venice
Venezuela, 39, 192–213
    Centenary Exposition, 201
    Federal Wars, 195, 198, 208. *See also* Civil War: Venezuela
    Guanoco Asphalt Lake, 199
    Lake Maracaibo, 199
    landscape, 196, 212
    nature, 192, 195, 209, 213
    politics, 194, 195, 198, 206, 207, 208
Venice, 4, 22, 23, 25, 26, 27, 29, 69, 106, 127, 139, 174, 175, 196, 248, 285
    Teatro La Fenice, 106, 185
    Teatro S. Simone, 23
Venitia. *See* Venice
Veracruz, 86, 88
    Teatro Provisional, 86
Veralli (Madame), 226
Verdi, Giuseppe, 15, 19, 20, 37, 132, 136, 159, 167, 169, 171, 175, 185, 193, 200, 201, 207, 208, 253, 256, 264, 275, 276, 298
    Aida, 19, 204, 208, 239, 298
    Alzira, 138
    Ernani, 136, 145, 197, 199, 208
    I due foscari, 145, 267
    I Lombardi, 173
    Il trovatore, 21, 202, 204, 208, 221, 226, 228, 234, 266, 302
    La forza del destino, 176, 266
    La traviata, 37, 204, 209, 227, 290
    Macbeth, 37, 136

Nabucco, 37, 173
Otello, 207
Rigoletto, 204, 228, 291
Un ballo in maschera, 204, 234, 266, 267
Verga, Giuseppe, 177
verismo, 183
Viardot, Pauline, 83, 84
Vicenza, 174
Vico, Giambattista, 32
Victoria Theatrical Company, 232
Vienna, 18, 19, 22, 23, 24, 28, 29, 30, 38, 60, 96–112, 145, 151, 152, 291, 301
    Hofoper, 29
    Kärntnertortheater, 86, 96, 97, 99, 100, 102, 103, 104, 105, 106, 107, 108, 109, 110, 111, 112
    Schönbrunn, 246
    Theater an der Wien, 109
Vignaud, Henri, 150
violoncello, 202
visual arts, 1, 4
Vitali, Raffaele, 173
Volpe, Maria Alice, 275
Voltaire [Arouet, François-Marie], 35, 70
Vormärz, 96–112

Wagner, Richard, 156, 165, 171, 181, 188–91, 256, 265, 291, 292
    Das Judenthum in der Musik, 257
    Der Ring des Nibelungen, 253, 254, 288
    Lohengrin, 170, 173, 179, 201, 265, 285
    Parsifal, 176, 182, 183, 187–91
    Tannhäuser, 170, 179, 285, 292
Wagnerism, 12, 19, 38, 39, 171, 248, 251, 253, 254, 258, 265, 291, 292, 293. *See also* Wagner, Richard
Walton, Benjamin, 13, 94, 103, 157, 263
Weber, Carl Maria von, 17, 106
    Der Freischütz, 254
    Lützows wilde Jagd, 249
Wehle (Herr), 217
Weimar, 33, 34
Weissmann, Adolf, 245
Werfel, Franz, 19
West, the, 26
Western hemisphere. *See* Americas, the; West
Westernisation, 134, 284
Wilhelm II (German Emperor), 240–60
Willard's Musical Comedy and Opera Company, 236

Wirgman, Charles, 282
Witt, Heinrich, 144
World War I, 38, 173, 179, 247, 260, 303

Yokohama, 9, 236, 281, 282
   Gaiety Theatre, 282, 283
   Honchō-doori, 282
Yoshie, Fujiwara, 279, 297
Yoshiko, Satō, 279

Yuki, Ōnishi, 280
Yukichi, Fukuzawa, 284

Zanetti, Maria, 47, 48, 54
Zapucci, Vincenzo, 133
zarzuela, 200, 209, 263, 265
Zegers, Isidora, 140, 141, 145, 146
Zenoni, Margherita, 228
Zingarelli, Niccolò Antonio, 84

For EU product safety concerns, contact us at Calle de José Abascal, 56–1°, 28003 Madrid, Spain or eugpsr@cambridge.org.

www.ingramcontent.com/pod-product-compliance
Lightning Source LLC
LaVergne TN
LVHW080304260326
834688LV00039B/1135